THE ROSE OF THE WORLD

THE ROSE OF THE WORLD

Hot Spring (Goriachy Kluitch) in the northern Caucasus
Mountains, where the manuscript of *The Rose of the World*
was buried, October 1958. (*Photo by Alla Andreeva*)

The Rose of the World

Daniel Andreev

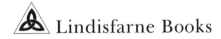 Lindisfarne Books

Translated by Jordan Roberts from the Russian *Roza Mira,*
published by Urania, Moscow, 1996.

Russian edition copyright © Daniel Andreev Charity Foundation, 1990.
English translation copyright © Daniel Andreev Charity Foundation,
1997.

Published by Lindisfarne Books
3390 Route 9, Hudson, NY 12534 USA

Library of Congress Cataloging-in-Publication Data

Andreev, Daniil Leonidovich, 1906–1959.
    [Roza mira. English]
    The rose of the world / Daniel Andreev
        p. cm
    Includes index.
    ISBN 0-940262-83-5 (pbk.)
    1. History—Philosophy. 2. Russia (Federation)—History-
Philosophy.
    I. Title.
    D16.8.A635613 1997   97-27907
    901—dc21   CIP

10 9 8 7 6 5 4 3 2 1

Printed in the United States of America

CONTENTS

BOOK I
The Rose of the World and Its Place in History

BOOK II
On the Metahistorical and Transphysical Methods of Knowledge

TRANSLATOR'S INTRODUCTION

JORDAN ROBERTS

IN PICKING UP THIS BOOK, you are about to embark on a fascinating journey. It is a journey to places where, according to the author, many of us have already been but about which we have forgotten. It is also a journey within, into that psychological space where our ideas and beliefs about God, spirituality, and religion reside. During both journeys we are likely to encounter wonder and recognition, skepticism and acceptance, rejection and admiration, confusion and long-sought understanding. For some this journey will be the start of a much longer one; for some it is but one more leg of a journey undertaken earlier; in any case, "The Rose of the World" is not a final destination.

Your guide on this journey will be Daniel Andreev, a twentieth-century Russian poet and writer. Since so much of what you are about to read requires trust in the author's testimony and trust in his voice, a biographical sketch seems in order.

Daniel Andreev was born on November 2, 1906, in Berlin. His father was the famous Russian writer Leonid Andreev. His mother, Alexandra Veligorsky, died during childbirth. Daniel's father, overcome with grief, gave the baby to Alexandra's sister, Elizabeth Dobrov, to raise in Moscow. It was a critical event in Daniel Andreev's life, for in contrast to many of the families belonging to the Russian intelligentsia at that time, the Dobrov family had kept to its Russian Orthodox faith. Daniel's childhood was marked by a deep-felt religiosity, a loving and lively home environment, contact with some of the greatest Russian minds of that time [his godfather was Maxim Gorky], and a passionate love for old Moscow. He also began to write prose and poetry.

The revolution of 1917 saw many lives changed, including Daniel's. After graduating from a Soviet high school, he found that university was closed to the son of a "nonproletarian" writer. He took continuing education courses in literature instead, and continued to write. Realizing that his gifts were incompatible with Soviet reality, he became a graphic artist and worked evenings on poetry and a novel, *Wanderers in the Night*.

He was conscripted as a noncombatant in the Soviet Army in 1942, and he participated in bringing supplies across the frozen ice of Lake Ladoga to besieged Leningrad.

After the war he returned to writing his novel and poetry, but was arrested in April 1947, along with his wife and many of his relatives and friends. He was sentenced to twenty-five years of prison (by some chance the death sentence had been temporarily suspended in the Soviet Union around the same time) and his wife was given twenty-five years of labor camp. All of his writing done previous to his arrest was destroyed.

The death of Stalin and the rise of Khrushchev eventually resulted in the review of prisoners' cases; on reviewing Daniel Andreev's case, the commission shortened his sentence to ten years. He was released to his already waiting wife in April 1957 with his health ruined, having suffered a heart attack in prison in 1954.

It was while in prison that Daniel Andreev wrote the first drafts of *The Rose of the World*, as well as *Russian Gods*—a collection of poetry—and *The Iron Mystery*—a verse play. Surely it was a daily miracle that none of these works was confiscated by the Stalinist prison regime. It was an even greater miracle that his wife was able to get the manuscripts out of the prison upon his release.

Daniel Andreev spent the last two years of his life finishing his work on the three books mentioned above. He died on March 30, 1959, entrusting the manuscripts to his wife, Alla.

Alla Andreeva, knowing the negative reception the books would get from the Soviet authorities, hid them until the mid-seventies when, through *samizdat*, a number of people were finally able to read them. But it wasn't until Gorbachev and glasnost that she could even consider publishing them. In 1989 excerpts of *The Rose of the World* were published in the magazine *Novy Mir*, followed by publication of the full text in 1991. The first edition of 100,000 copies quickly sold out, and a Russian publishing phenomenon was born. Since then several editions have been similarly sold out, including a few pirated versions.

The Rose of the World and Andreev's other works have had a tremendous impact on contemporary Russian society, with its thirst for a spiritual approach to life. The Daniel Andreev Foundation was founded in 1992, and numerous small groups and societies have formed in connection with his works.

The Rose of the World has been translated into Spanish and Czech, and now for the first time it is available to readers of English.

The English edition is not a full text version of the original book. It comprises the first six sections, approximately three-fifths of the whole. In consultation with Alla Andreeva, the author's widow, it was decided to publish the remaining sections of the book separately. Those sections take the principles elucidated in *The Rose of the World* and apply them to the history of Russia and to the future. It was felt that those chapters would appeal to a narrower group of readers, as a certain familiarity with Russian history and culture is assumed by the author. Hopefully, with the success of this edition, the remaining sections will be published in the near future. Therefore, the reader will occasionally come across references made by Andreev to later sections that are not to be found in this English edition.

In *The Rose of the World*, Daniel Andreev introduces many new terms or invests some familiar terms with a new meaning. A glossary of selected words has therefore been provided at the end of the book.

In going through *The Rose of the World*, the reader should bear in mind a few things.

It is important to remember that Andreev wrote this book in the fifties, and completed it in 1958. While the reader will no doubt be surprised by the relevance to our times of much of what Andreev writes, there also are parts that might strike the reader as outdated, erroneous, or even offensive. Every person is, to a certain extent, a product of their time and society, and Daniel Andreev is no exception. That a person's generation and society will not inform that person's works is hardly to be expected.

In connection with that, the reader should be careful to sift what Andreev calls his "experience," or revelation, from his personal opinions, ideas, or extrapolations. In relation to his opinions, one can choose to respect them or not, but the revelation given to him deserves a much more serious approach.

As Alla Andreeva writes, "Are distortions possible in communicating through human language otherworldly images and unfamiliar concepts? I think they are not only possible, but inevitable. The human mind cannot help but interpolate more customary concepts, logical conclusions, or even personal preferences and antipathies. But it seems to me that in reading Andreev, you will gain a conviction in his sincere efforts to be, as much as his gifts allow, a simple relayer of what he saw and heard." Daniel Andreev himself refers more than once in *The Rose of the World* to the danger of the personal muddying the purity of heaven-sent insight.

Thus, readers should try to avoid automatic acceptance or rejection of Andreev's revelation and give it time to resonate or not within their souls. In my judgment, a great deal will resonate within readers, for Andreev speaks of much that touches our deepest selves.

FOREWORD

ALLA ANDREEVA

EVERY BOOK, no matter what its subject matter, is written by a specific person, living in a given era, at a given time. This book is no exception. It bears the stamp of the time in which it was written and the stamp also of the author's personality against the background of his life and fate.

What traits, then, created the special blend of character possessed by the author of *The Rose of the World* and many works of poetry, which together with *The Rose*, form a single, integral, and altogether unprecedented phenomenon in the history of culture?

First, since early childhood, he manifested a pronounced creative impulse—more precisely, a poetic impulse—together with a heightened sensitivity to the sound of words. Writing became the meaning and driving force of Andreev's life, the performance of a duty laid upon him from above.

Second, he was given a passionate love of history—especially Russian history—as a living current in which all our lives flow in what is by no means a passive relation.

Above all, his was one of those natures that is filled with an innate, organic religiosity, a religious faith that was an integral part of his being, the very foundation of his self. For such people, the world is never completely closed off. "Another" world is always showing through "this" world. In *The Rose of the World*, Andreev calls the works of those who are open in this way "transparent realism."

Finally, he was an artist. There are devotees of art as there are devotees of faith. Daniel Andreev was such a person. He wrote the first draft of *The Rose of the World* in his cell in Vladimir prison and completed it in the twenty-three months of homeless wandering that remained to him before his death.

Humanity's long history knows the type of creative personality we may call "the spiritual visionary." The most famous people of such a creative type in the West are Dante and Swedenborg. Daniel Andreev was likewise such an artist. He was not a member of any "school." The states of special vision that had been conferred upon him since his early teens and that grew in prison into the sustained and brilliant light of transphysical knowledge were a gift of the Forces of Light. This is a rare gift, it is true, yet it is one that is occasionally encountered.

Prayer—and, before his arrest, church—was the only thing that helped the author attain the states that formed the foundation for writing *The Rose of the World*. At the beginning of the book, he recounts that one of the first times he awoke to a living consciousness of the world of Light was in a church, during the acathistus[1] of St. Seraphim of Sarov, whom he held in particular reverence all his life.

He called the kind of knowledge of the world practiced by spiritual visionaries "transphysical knowledge." His personal spiritual experience helped him form a comprehensive picture of the universe. That experience informed his work. While in prison, Andreev wrote drafts for his three main books: *The Rose of the World, The Iron Mystery,* and *Russian Gods*.

In *The Rose of the World,* Andreev states his main ideas in detail in prose. *The Iron Mystery* and *Russian Gods* express the same ideas in poetry.

For Andreev, the universe is many layered. The plane inhabited by humanity, *Enrof,* in Andreev's terms, is the middle plane. Above stretch the shining Worlds of Enlightenment, while the dark Worlds of Retribution oppose them from below. All religious cosmologies contain a structure of the universe of this kind: for instance, the Vale of Life, Hell, and Paradise in Christianity; Midgard, Niffleheim, and Asgard of Scandinavian mythology; and the Seven Heavens of Islam. Andreev's Worlds of Enlightenment and Retribution develop the same structure.

---

1. A lengthy Lenten hymn of the Eastern Orthodox Church, sung with the people standing.

Each of the worlds described by Andreev has its own name and purpose. For example, one of the worlds of Light, *Iroln*, is the abode of the immortal monads of humanity. Monads are made by the Creator, and the evil of the world does not touch them. The entire system of the planes comprising the many-layered world of each planet is called a *Bramfatura*. The *Bramfatura* of the Earth is called *Shadanakar*.

Every nation creates its own culture, which is different from other cultures. Here Andreev analyzes two notions that are closely connected with each other: the *supranation* and the *meta-culture*. The latter at once embraces the culture created by the nation on Earth, touches upon the lower planes connected with the demons of state systems, and blossoms in the Heavenly Countries or *Zatomis* that shine over each nation. These Heavenly Countries are free from evil and they never perish, even when the mundane reflection of the Zatomis that we experience as the culture of a particular nation dies on the Earth.

Thus, there is a shining Heavenly country being built over Russia—Heavenly Russia, Holy Russia. After physical death, the righteous—saints, heroes, and completely unknown people—ascend there in order to continue their labors for the glory of God.

The life of the Universe is the continuing struggle of the Powers of Light with the Powers of Evil and Darkness, who are allied with the being who was once the First Angel and rebelled against God and is now building his dark Universe. Evil is a phenomenon that has no roots in the Creator and is doomed. This is the cardinal difference between Andreev's concept and Manichaeism. This struggle between light and dark is now the very essence of life. Consciously or unconsciously, in all our deeds, thought, and actions, we all participate in this opposition of Good and Evil.

For Andreev, creativity, too, acquires a special meaning. There are people in the world of art whom Andreev calls "heralds"—they are artists in the broadest meaning of the word who have the gift and the duty to link Enrof and the Powers of Light. In this way, human creativity takes on special responsibility, since the artist on earth gives a form of life to something that cannot otherwise manifest in our world. This goes for images of both Light and Darkness. Many works of art created by poets, musicians, architects, and painters are rooted in worlds parallel to ours. Having acquired form on Earth, these works in turn come to life in one of the parallel worlds and are able to influence us from there. The abodes of Christ and the Mother of God, together with the vision of the Holy Cosmos, appear in unattainable heights. The anticosmos opposes them from below.

Andreev sees nature as living Essences who surround us and interact with us. He calls them Elementals.

This many-layered structure of the Universe and the ongoing struggle of Light and Darkness led Andreev to the vision of the Rose of the World. An epoch will come on Earth when the life of a united humanity will be governed by a single moral authority. Then Christian churches will unite and form a free union with all religions of Light. This epoch Andreev calls "the Rose of the World."

Here, especially, one must bear in mind the nature of the times in which Andreev lived. One must try to picture its concrete spiritual conditions.

Nowadays, the countless human abuses and acts of cruelty of those times, not to mention the pervasive denigration of the human individual, are well known. But no statistics can convey what was most important: the atmosphere of rampant anti-spirituality, the palpable daily penetration and intertwining of one's whole life by forces of Darkness—demonic forces. Anything connected with religion was considered a crime. Atheism was not merely the state religion, it was an aggressive program invested with unlimited powers to destroy everything we call "spiritual." Such a time gave rise to a vital sense of adversaries in active opposition: God and the Devil. From this point of view, anyone who served God within his or her confession or was quietly groping for a way in that direction was an ally.

In Andreev's novel, which perished at Lubyanka Prison, there was a scene that gives a key to understanding what he called open and harmonious relationship with other great world religions—*The Rose of the World.* The hero, Glinsky, a scholar of Indian culture and the leader of an underground group of idealists in Moscow that is engaged in erecting an invisible edifice in spiritual opposition to the era, is arrested. The scene is a cell crowded with people of different classes and backgrounds in the Lubyanka Prison in 1937. There are interrogations. Everyone is faced with the same hopeless future. Sharing a cell with Glinsky are a Russian Orthodox priest and a Mullah. Without a word to each other, these three all take turns saying prayers for everyone else. Silently, whenever one of those praying is taken away to be interrogated or has no strength left, he passes on his prayer vigil with a look to one of the remaining two.... Scarcely any priest would condemn such people, no matter how impermissible their spiritual practice may be from a canonical standpoint.

This is not a desire to luxuriate simultaneously in several warm pools of different religions and spiritual teachings but a desperate alignment of the spiritual community of those who are with God, in God's name—whatever different paths they may follow—against those who oppose God. Such is the tragic "ecumenicism" that was born in the prisons and camps of those godless times. The character of Daniel Andreev will always bear the stamp of an era that has already become a legend for younger generations.

Daniel Andreev is a child of Russian culture, where boundaries are always slightly blurred. This means that he solves problems that border on philosophy and sometimes theology *on a poetic level*. Poetry is a special vision of the world. One can understand this phenomenon only by going back to ancient times when there were no "poets" in the modern meaning of the word, but religious, philosophical images were expressed by human beings through the Word. It is in this sense that Andreev should be called a poet.

Such is Daniel Andreev's personality. A man of the tragic twentieth century, his work deals with the most important and most painful problems of our lives.

Moscow, November 1996

Daniel Andreev at the time when *The Rose of the World* was near
completion, October 1958, in Goriachy Kluitch (Hot Spring).
Photo by Alla Andreeva

Leonid Andreev and
Alexandra Andreeva,
Berlin, 1906

Alexandra Andreeva,
Fall 1906

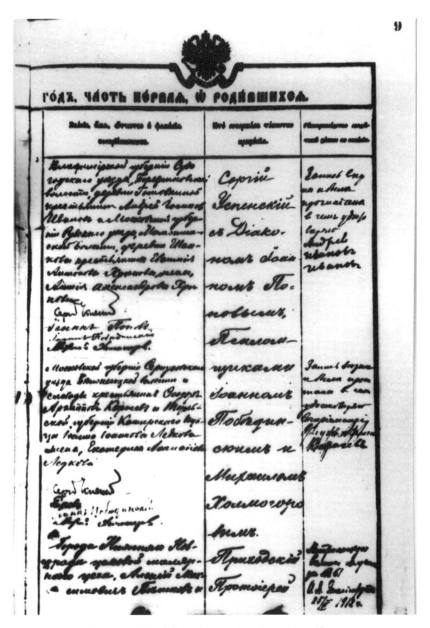

Detail of Daniel Andreev's baptismal certificate,
showing Maxim Gorky as godfather.

Daniel Andreev, 1935
Photo by E. Belousov

At the Leningrad front,
1943.

осужден *Особым Совещанием при МГБ СССР*

30/X 48² ст.ст. УК *19-58-8, 58-10ч.II, 58-11*

5. лет *тюр.зак. имущество конфисковать*

указать полностью дополнительные меры

Начало срока исчислять с *23/IV 47*

Конец срока *23/IV 57*

Был 24 XI 48 г. из *Лефортовской тюрьмы МГБ СССР Москва*

этаплов.Центр.Комиссии № 8/1-56 выписки из протокола № 4

19-58-8 переквалиф. на ч.I-58-8, наказание нов.94, 17-58-6, 58-10, ч.I 58-11 образ.

мк на чет.мер 25 л. т/з

23/VII-56 Комиссией Пре. Верхов. Совета СССР к прот. №121

Считать несовершенно. осужден. по ст 19-58-8; 58-11.

Снизить меру наказания до 10 л. т/з по Ст. 58-10 ч.II.

17/XI-56 Опред. Верх.Суда СССР постанов. особ 30/X-48 г. отменить

и направить на дорасследов.

16/XII.56 6²

Изг

Daniel Andreev's prison file.

Список вещей
Андреева Даниила Леонидовича,
передаваемых
его жене.
Андреевой Алле Александровне:

1. Книги.

1. Хинди-русский словарь. Москва 1953 г.
2. Чаттерджи и Датта. Древняя индийская философия. — М. 1...
3. Синха и Банерджи. — История Индии. — М. 1954.
4. Джавахарлал Неру. — Открытие Индии. — М. 1955.
5. Михаев И.П. Давление путешествие в Индию и Бирму. — М. 195...
6. Новиков И. Пушкин в изгнании. — М. Л. — 1947.
7. Мопассан. Рассказы и стихи — М. 1953.
8. Тагор Р. — Рассказы. — М. 1955.
9. Японская поэзия (антология). М. 1954.
10. Бальзак. — Шагрень и Саломе. — М. 1953.

2. Альбомы и тетради

1. Альбом с открытками и фото.
2. Альбомчик с барельефами и конвертов.
3-9. Семь тетрадей в ... листа темно-синих обложках, с пронумерованием по перам от N1 до N7.
10-12. Три общих тетради (одна из них — дело ... ...
13. Тетрадь за N.11.
14. 25 папок с письмами.
15. Альбомчик с видами Москвы.
16. Альбомчик открытом "По Индии"
17. Папка фото с видами. Моск. Кремль.

3. Одежда

1. Куртка синяя бумажная о/у. — 1.
2. Полотенце мохнатое — 1
3. Бумага нитяные ... — 1
4. Простыня маленькая — 1
5. Трусики — 2

Д. Андреев

List of Daniel Andreev's possessions, including the manuscript of
The Rose of the World, released by prison authorities to Alla Andreeva.

Alla Andreeva,
Mordovia Labor Camp,
1955

First photograph of
Daniel Andreev after
his release from prison,
April 1957.

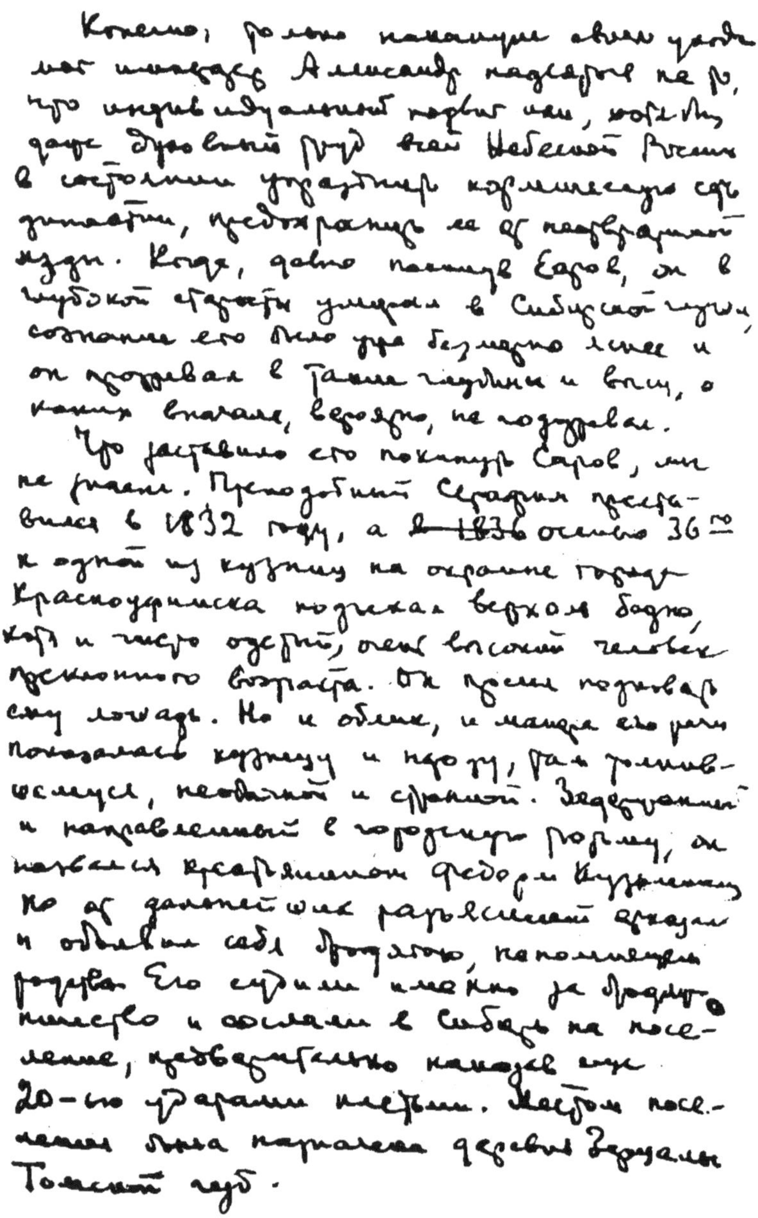

Конечно, только накануне своего ухода император Александр надеялся не на то, что индивидуальный подвиг его, хотя бы даже духовный труд всей Небесной России в состоянии удержать кармическую судьбу династии, предохранить её от надвигающейся мзды. Когда, давно покинув Саров, он в глубокой старости умирал в Сибирской глуши, сознание его было уже безмерно яснее и он прозревал в такие глубины и выси, о каких вначале, вероятно, не подозревал.

Что заставило его покинуть Саров, мы не знаем. Преподобный Серафим преставился в 1832 году, а ~~в 1836~~ осенью 36-го к одной из кузниц на окраине города Красноуфимска подъехал верхом бедно, хотя и чисто одетый, очень высокий человек преклонного возраста. Он просил подковать ему лошадь. Но и облик, и манера его речи показались кузнецу и народу, там толпившемуся, необычной и странной. Задержанный и направленный в городскую тюрьму, он назвался крестьянином Федором Кузьмичом, но от дальнейших расспросов отказался и объявил себя бродягою, не помнящим родства. Его судили именно за бродяжничество и сослали в Сибирь на поселение, предварительно наказав ещё 20-ю ударами плетьми. Местом поселения была назначена деревня Зерцалы Томской губ.

A page from the manuscript of *The Rose of the World*.

Daniel and Alla Andreeva, February 1959. *Photo by B. Chukov*

Daniel Andreev, February 24, 1959

Daniel Andreev's grave,
Novodevichy Cemetery, Moscow.

BOOK I

The Rose of the World and Its Place in History

1 The Rose of the World and Its Foremost Tasks

THIS BOOK WAS BEGUN at a time when the threat of an unparalleled disaster hung over the heads of humanity—when a generation only just recuperating from the trauma of the Second World War discovered to its horror that a strange darkness, the portent of a war even more catastrophic and devastating than the last, was already gathering and thickening on the horizon. I began this book in the darkest years of a dictatorship that tyrannized two hundred million people. I began writing it in a prison designated as a "political isolation ward." I wrote it in secret. I hid the manuscript, and the forces of good—humans and otherwise—concealed it for me during searches. Yet every day I expected the manuscript to be confiscated and destroyed, just as my previous work—work to which I had given ten years of my life and for which I had been consigned to the political isolation ward—had been destroyed.

I am finishing *The Rose of the World* a few years later. The threat of a third world war no longer looms like dark clouds on the horizon, but, having fanned out over our heads and blocked the sun, it has quickly dispersed in all directions back beyond the horizon.

Perhaps the worst will never come to pass. Every heart nurses such a hope, and without it life would be unbearable. Some try to bolster it with logical arguments and active protest. Some succeed in convincing themselves that the danger is exaggerated. Others try not to think about it at all and, having decided once and for all that what happens, happens, immerse themselves in the daily affairs of their own little worlds. There are also people in whose hearts hope smoulders like a dying fire, and who go on living, moving, and working merely out of inertia.

I am completing *The Rose of the World* out of prison, in a park turned golden with autumn. The one under whose yoke the country was driven to near exhaustion has long been reaping in other worlds what he sowed in this one. Yet I am still hiding the last pages of the manuscript as I hid the first ones. I dare not acquaint a single living soul with its contents, for, just as before, I cannot be certain that this book will not be destroyed, that the spiritual knowledge it contains will be transmitted to someone, anyone.

But perhaps the worst will never come to pass, and tyranny on such a scale will never recur. Perhaps humanity will forevermore retain the memory of Russia's terrible historical experience. Every heart nurses that hope, and without it life would be unbearable.

But I number among those who have been fatally wounded by two great calamities: world war and dictatorship. Such people do not believe that the roots of war and tyranny within humanity have been eradicated or that they will be in the near future. Perhaps the danger of one tyranny or war will recede, but after a time the threat of the next tyranny or war will arise. For me and others like me, both those calamities were a kind of apocalypse— revelations of the power of planetary Evil and of its age-old struggle with the forces of Light. Those living in different times would probably not understand us. Our anxiety would seem to them an overreaction; our view of the world would seem poisoned. But a conception of the logical consistency of historical events branded in the human mind by a half century of observing and participating in events and processes of unprecedented magnitude cannot be called an overreaction. And a conclusion that forms in the human heart through the efforts of the brightest and deepest sides of its nature cannot be poisoned.

I am seriously ill—my days are numbered. If this manuscript is destroyed or lost, I will not be able to rewrite it in time. But if, sometime in the future, it reaches only a few persons whose spiritual thirst drives them to surmount all its difficulties and read it through to the end, then the ideas planted within cannot help but become seeds that will sprout in their hearts. Whether that occurs before a third world war or after it, and even if no third war is unleashed in the near future, this book will not die if but one pair of friendly eyes passes, chapter by chapter, over its pages. For the questions it attempts to answer will continue to trouble people far into the future.

Those questions are not confined to the realms of war and politics. But nothing can shake my conviction that the most formidable dangers that threaten humanity, both now and for centuries to come, are a great suicidal war and an absolute global dictatorship. Perhaps, in our century, humanity will avert a third world war or, at the very least, survive it, as it survived the First and Second World Wars. Perhaps it will outlive, somehow or other, a dictatorship even more enveloping and merciless than the one we in Russia outlived. It may even be that in two or three hundred years new dangers for the people of Earth will appear, dangers different but no less dire than a dictatorship or a great war. It is possible, even probable. But no effort of the mind, no imagination or intuition, is capable of conjecturing a future danger that would not be connected, somehow or other, with one of these two principal dangers: the physical destruction of humanity through a war, and the spiritual death of humanity through an absolute global dictatorship.

This book is directed, first and foremost, against the two basic, supreme evils of war and dictatorship. It is directed against them not as a simple warning, nor as a satire that unmasks their true nature, nor as a sermon. The most biting satire and the most fiery sermon are useless if they only rail against evil and prove that good is good and bad is bad. They are useless if they are not based on a worldview, global teaching, and program of action that, spread from mind to mind and will to will, would be capable of averting these evils.

The purpose of my life has been to share my experience with others—to shed light on the future panorama of history and metahistory, on the branching chain of alternatives we face or are bound to face, and on the landscape of variomaterial worlds that are closely linked with ours through good and evil. I have tried, and still try, to fulfill that task through fiction and poetry, but the limitations of those genres have prevented me from disclosing these ideas precisely and intelligibly in their entirety. The purpose of this book is to set out that worldview in an exhaustive manner, helping the reader to see how, though dealing with the preternatural, it at the same time holds the key to understanding current events and the fate of each of us. This is a book that, if God saves it from destruction, will be laid, as one of many bricks, in the foundation of the Rose of the World, at the base of a Community of all humanity.

There exists an entity that for many centuries has proclaimed itself the lone, steadfast unifier of all people, shielding them from the danger of all-out warfare and social chaos. That entity is the state. Since the end of the tribal period, the state has been of vital necessity at every historical stage. Even hierocracies, which attempted to replace it with religious rule, simply became variations of the selfsame state. The state bonded society together on the principle of coercion, and the level of moral development necessary to bond society together on some other principle was beyond reach. Of course, it has been beyond reach even until now, and the state has remained the only proven means against social chaos. But the existence of a higher order of moral principles is now becoming evident, principles capable not only of maintaining but also of increasing social harmony. More important, methods for accelerating the internalization of such principles are now taking shape.

In the political history of modern times, one can distinguish two international movements diametrically opposed to one another. One of them aims for the hypertrophy of state power and an increase in the individual's dependence on the state. To be more exact, this movement seeks to bestow ever greater power on the person or organization in whose hands the state apparatus lies: the Party, the Army, the Leader. Fascist and national socialist states are the most obvious examples of such movements.

The other movement, which appeared at least as far back as the eighteenth century, is the humanist. Its origins and major stages are English parliamentarianism, the French Declaration of the

Rights of Man, German social democracy, and in our days, the struggle for liberation from colonialism. The long-range goal of the movement is to weaken the bonding principle of coercion in the life of the people and transform what is largely a police state defending race or class interests into a system based on overall economic equilibrium and a guarantee of individual rights.

History has also witnessed examples of novel political arrangements that might appear to be hybrids of the two movements. Remaining in essence phenomena of the first type, they alter their appearance to the extent expedient for the achievement of their set goal. This is a tactic, a deception, but nothing more.

Nevertheless, despite the polarity of these movements, they are linked by one trait characteristic of the twentieth century: global ambitions. The ostensible motivation of the various twentieth century movements can be found in their political blueprints, but the underlying motivation in modern history is the instinctive pursuit of global dominion.

The most vigorous movement of the first half of this century was distinguished by its internationalist doctrines and global appeal. The Achilles heel of the movements vying with it—racism, national socialism—was their narrow nationalism, or to be more exact, the strictly racial or nationalist fences around their promised lands, the chimera of which they used to seduce and dazzle their followers. But they too strove for world dominion, and invested colossal energy toward that end. Now American cosmopolitanism is occupied with avoiding the mistakes of its predecessors.

What does that sign of the times point to? Does it not point to the fact that global unity has grown from an abstract concept into a universal need? Does it not point to the fact that the world has become smaller and more integrated than ever before? Finally, does it not point to the fact that the solution to all the problems of vital interest to humanity can be lasting and profound enough only if undertaken on a global scale?

Taking advantage of that fact, despotic regimes systematically actualize the principle of extreme coercion or partly camouflage it with a cunning blend of methods. The tempo of life is accelerating. Monolithic states are emerging that earlier would have taken centuries to erect. Each is predatory by nature, each strives to subjugate humanity to its sole rule. The military and technological power of these states boggles the mind. They have already more than once plunged the world into war and tyranny. Where is the guarantee that they will not do so again in the future? In the end, the strongest will conquer the globe, even at the cost of turning a third of the world's surface into a moonscape. The cycle of wars will then come to an end, but only to be replaced by the greatest of evils: a single dictatorship over the surviving two-thirds of the world. At first it will perhaps be an oligarchy. But, as often happens, eventually a single Leader will emerge. The threat of a global dictatorship—this is the deadliest of all threats hanging over humanity.

Consciously or unconsciously sensing the danger, the movements belonging to the humanist mold are trying to consolidate their efforts. They prattle about cultural cooperation, wave placards about pacifism and democratic freedoms, seek illusory security in neutrality, or, frightened by their adversary's aggression, they themselves embark on the same path. Not one of them has put forward the indisputable proposal that is capable of winning people's trust: the idea that some kind of moral supervision over the activities of the state is a vital necessity. Certain groups, traumatized by the horrors of the world wars, are trying to unite so that in the future their political federation will encompass the entire globe. But what would that lead to? The danger of wars, it is true, would be defused, at least temporarily. But who can guarantee that such a superstate, supported by large, morally backward segments of the populace (and such segments are far more numerous than one would wish) and rousing in humanity dormant impulses for power and violence, will not in the end develop into a dictatorship compared to which all previous tyrannies will seem like child's play?

It is worth noting that the same religious faiths that proclaimed the internationalist ideals of brotherhood earliest are now in the rearguard of humanity's push toward global unity. It is possible to attribute this to their characteristic emphasis on the inner self and their neglect of everything external, including sociopolitical issues. But if one delves deeper, if one says out loud for all to hear what is usually discussed only in certain small circles of people who lead a deeply spiritual life, then something not everyone takes into consideration is uncovered. That something is a mystical fear, originating during the age of the Roman Empire, of the future unification of the world. It is the indefatigable concern for the welfare of humanity felt by those who sense that in a single universal state lies a pitfall that will inevitably lead to an absolute dictatorship and the rule of the "prince of darkness," the result of which will be the final paroxysms and catastrophic end of history.

In actual fact, who can guarantee that a strong-willed egoist will not assume leadership of the superstate and, further, that science will not serve such a leader truthfully and faithfully as a means for turning the superstate into that exact kind of monstrous mechanism of violence and spiritual disfigurement I have been talking about? There is little doubt that theoretical models for blanket surveillance of people's behavior and thoughts are being developed at this very moment. What are the limits of the nightmarish scenarios that are conjured in our imagination as a result of the merger of a dictatorship of terror and twenty-first century technology? Such a tyranny would be all the more absolute because even the last, tragic means of casting it off would be closed—its overthrow from without by war. With every nation under one rule, there would be no one to war against. Global unity—the dream of so many generations, the cause of so many sacrifices—would then reveal its demonic side: *the impossibility of escape* if the servants of the dark forces were to seize control of the world government.

Bitter experience has already led humanity to the conviction that neither those socioeconomic movements guided solely by reason nor scientific progress in itself are capable of guiding humanity between the Charybdis of dictatorship and the Scylla of world war. On the contrary, new socioeconomic systems, in coming to power, themselves adopt the practices of political despotism and become the sowers and instigators of world war. Science becomes their lackey, far more obedient and reliable than the church was for the feudal barons. The root of the tragedy lies in the fact that the scientific professions were not from the very beginning coupled with a deeply formulated moral education. Regardless of their level of moral development, everyone is admitted into those professions. It should come as no surprise today that one side of every scientific and technical advance goes against the genuine interests of humanity. The internal combustion engine, radio, aviation, atomic energy—they all strike the bare flesh of the world's people with one end, while advances in communications and technology enable police states to establish surveillance over the private life and thoughts of each person, thus laying an iron foundation for life-sucking dictatorial states.

So, lessons drawn from history should lead humanity to realize that the dangers will not be averted and social harmony will not be achieved by scientific and technological progress alone. Nor shall it be accomplished by the hypertrophy of the state, by the dictatorship of a "strong leader," or by social democratic administrations that get buffeted by the winds of history, first right, then left, from inept starry-eyed idealism to revolutionary extremism. We must, rather, recognize the absolute necessity of the one and only path: the establishment, over a global federation of states, of an unsullied, incorruptible, highly respected body, a moral body standing outside of and above the state. For the state is, by its very nature, amoral.

What idea, what teaching will aid in the creation of such a supervisory body? What minds will formulate its guiding principles and make it acceptable to the overwhelming majority of people? By what paths will such a body—a body foreswearing the use of force—arrive at worldwide recognition, at a position even higher than a federation of states? If it can in fact introduce into leadership the policy of gradually replacing coercion with something else, then what would that something else be? And in what manner would it be introduced? And what doctrine would be able to solve the incredibly complex problems that will arise in connection with all that?

The present book attempts to give, to some extent, an answer to the above questions (although it shall also deal with wider issues). As a prologue to answering them, however, it is best to first clearly identify what this teaching sees as the irreconcilable enemy against which it is directed.

From the historical point of view, it sees its enemies in all states, parties, or doctrines that strive to enslave others and to establish any form of despotic political regime. From the meta-historical point of view, it has but a single foe: the Antigod, the Spirit of Tyranny, the Great Torturer, who takes many shapes and forms in the life of our planet. For the movement I am now talking about—both now, when it has barely begun to form, and later, when it will have become the decisive voice in history—there will be only one enemy: tyranny and coercion wherever it may arise, even within itself. Coercion will be admissible only in cases of absolute necessity, only in mitigated forms, and only until that time when the highest body, by means of a reformed educational system, has, with the help of millions of highly committed minds and wills, prepared humanity for the substitution of free will for force, the voice of deep-felt conscience for the decrees of human laws, and a community for the state. In other words, until the very essence of the state has been transformed and a living family of all peoples has replaced the soulless and coercive state apparatus.

One need not assume that such a process will require an enormous span of time. By systematically immersing the populations of huge countries in a single meticulously formulated system of education and social conditioning, powerful dictatorships have irrefutably proven what a powerful lever the molding of a generation's psyche can be. Each generation formed closer and closer to what the ruling powers considered desirable. Nazi Germany, for example, managed to achieve its goals in this area in the span of a single generation. Clearly its ideals can elicit no response in us other than anger and disgust. Its methods, as well, must be rejected almost wholesale. But we must take hold of the lever it discovered and not let go. The century of mass spiritual enlightenment, the century of decisive victories for a new, as yet barely discernible pedagogy is approaching. Even if only a few dozen schools are organized on its principles, a generation capable of doing its duty out of free will, not coercion, a generation acting out of creative impulses and love, not fear, would form there. That is the essence of *ennobling education*.

I picture an international organization, both political and cultural in nature, setting as its aim the transformation of the state through the consistent implementation of far-reaching reforms. The crucial stage in the fulfillment of that aim will be the founding of the Global Federation of Independent States. But this must carry the proviso that a special body be established over the Federation—the body I have already mentioned, which will oversee the activities of the states and guide them toward a bloodless and painless transformation from within. The key here is "bloodless and painless," for in that way it will differ from revolutionary doctrines of the past.

I consider it both premature and unnecessary to speculate on the structure and name of that organization. For now, so as to avoid constantly repeating a lengthy description, we will give it a provisional name: the League for the Transformation of the State. As for its structure, those who will be its founders will be both more experienced and more practical than I—they will be leaders of vision, not poets. I will only say that it seems to me personally that the League should establish branches in every country, with each branch consisting of several divisions: cultural, philanthropic, educational, and political. The political division in each country will assume the structural and organizational aspects of a national party of global religious and cultural reforms. All such parties will be linked and united in the League and by the League.

How, where, and among whom specifically the formation of the League will take place I, of course, do not and cannot know. But it is clear that the period of time from its inception until the establishment of the Federation of States and the moral supervisory body over it will be regarded as a preliminary stage, when the League will channel all of its energies into disseminating its ideas, recruiting new members, expanding its operations, educating younger generations, and forging within itself a future body that in time can be entrusted with a global leadership role.

The League's constitution will not restrict its membership to people of any particular philosophical or religious belief. All that will be required is an active commitment to realizing its program and a resolve not to violate its moral code, the cornerstone of the organization.

Despite all the vicissitudes of public service, the goals of the League must be attained not at the price of departure from its moral code but as a result of faithful adherence to it. Its reputation must be spotless, its disinterestedness not subject to doubt, its moral authority ever increasing, as the best and finest of humanity will be drawn to it and will constantly strengthen its ranks.

The path to global unification will proceed, in all likelihood, through various stages of international solidarity, through the unification and merger of regional blocs. The last stage would take the form of a global referendum or plebiscite—some form of free vote by every person. It may result in a victory for the League only in certain countries. But the inexorable march of history will be on the League's side. The unification of even half the globe will be the final step in a revolution of people's consciousness. A second referendum will be held, perhaps a third, and a decade or so later the borders of the Federation will encompass all of humanity. Then there will be a real possibility of implementing a series of wide-ranging measures aimed at transforming the conglomerate of states into a single state that will be gradually altered by two parallel programs: one external, concerned with political, social, and economic affairs, and one internal, focused on educational, moral, and religious matters.

From the above, it should be clear that the members of the League and its national parties will be able to wield as weapons only their words and their own example, and this only against those ideologies and doctrines that try to clear the path to power for a dictator or support a dictator already in power. Although the activities of the great Mahatma Gandhi and the political party he inspired were confined to the national scale, the League will see them as its historical predecessors. The first political leader/living saint in modern times, Gandhi consolidated a purely political movement on a foundation of high moral standards, refuting the prevailing attitude that politics and morality are incompatible. But the national borders within which the Indian National Congress acted will be expanded by the League to encompass the entire planet, and the goals of the League will be of a higher historical stage, or series of stages, than were the goals set by the great party that freed India.

Oh, there will of course be many people who will insist that the League's methods are impractical and unrealistic. I've met enough champions of political realism to last me a lifetime. There is no injustice or social villainy that has not tried to cover itself with that pitiful fig leaf. There is no weight more deadening, more earthbound, than talk of political realism as a counter to everything lofty, everything inspirational, everything spiritual. Such political realists are, incidentally, the same sort of people who in their time claimed, even in India, that Gandhi was a dreamer out of touch with reality. They were forced to eat their words when Gandhi and his party, while maintaining high moral standards, won freedom for their country and led it to prosperity. But this was not the kind of material prosperity that blinds people's eyes with the black soot of statistics on the increase in coal production or with radioactive dust from experimental tests of hydrogen bombs. This was cultural, ethical, aesthetic, and spiritual prosperity, which would slowly but surely give rise to material well-being.

Those who are unable to see the good in people—those whose outlook has coarsened and whose conscience has withered in the atmosphere of flagrant state violations of human rights—will also accuse the League of unrealistic methods. They will be joined by those who cannot see what revolutions in mass consciousness await us in the not too distant future. The trauma of wars, oppression, and every possible violation of human rights already has launched a grass roots movement for peaceful coexistence. Events that destroy our feeling of security, deprive us of all comfort and peace of mind, and uproot our faith in current ideologies and the social orders they uphold are constantly taking place and will continue to do so. The exposing of the unbelievable atrocities perpetrated behind the imposing facade of dictatorships, concrete proof of the foundation and price of their temporary victories and apparent successes, will parch the soul like a hot desert wind. People's spiritual thirst will become unbearable. The elimination of the threat of great wars, the discovery of paths to uniting the world without bloodshed, a spiritual leader and living saint who will head a united humanity in the future, the weakening of state coercion, and the growth of a global community spirit—this is what believers pray for and nonbelievers dream about in our century. And it is highly probable that a lofty, global teaching—moral, political, philosophical, and spiritual—will transform this generation's thirst into an international creative enthusiasm.

The fact that humanity's last major religious movement—the Protestant Reformation—took place four hundred years ago, and that the last religion of global impact, Islam, is in its thirteenth century of existence is sometimes cited in support of the argument that the religious era of humanity is past. But one should gauge the potential of religion as a whole, not by its specific forms. What matters is not how long ago the last major forms emerged but whether the evolution of religion has reached a dead-end: whether it is possible to integrate the indisputable laws of science into creative religious thought, whether there glimmers within such a worldview the possibility of making sense of our experience in the new era, and whether religion will be able to play a real and progressive role in such experience.

It is true that approximately four hundred years have passed since the last major religious movement of international scope. It is also true that for many centuries prior to the Protestant Reformation there had been no comparable movements. But is that even the point? Is it still not clear that a definite current of mental, creative work absorbed almost all of humanity's spiritual and intellectual energy during the last few centuries? It would be difficult to expect that while maintaining such a rapid pace of scientific, technical, and social progress and creating such cultural treasures in literature, music, philosophy, and art, humanity would, in the last centuries, find within itself the energy to create more universal religious systems as well.

But the turn of the century was the end of an era. The golden age of literature, art, music, and philosophy came to a close. The realm of sociopolitical activity has drawn to itself—and with time this has become more and more apparent—not the most, but the least, spiritual representatives of the human race. A gigantic spiritual vacuum has formed that did not exist even fifty years ago, and hypertrophied science has been powerless to fill it. If I may put it thus: colossal resources of the human genius have remained untapped. That is the womb of creative energy where the embryonic global interreligion is forming.

Will religion—not its old forms, but the sum religion that the world is now pregnant with—be able to eliminate the most dangerous threats hanging over the heads of humanity: world war and global tyranny? It will probably be unable to avert the next world war: if a third world war breaks out, it will likely take place even before the appearance of the League. But after the nucleus of the future interreligion has been formed, the League's first and foremost task will be to prevent all wars that threaten to break out and to prevent the rise of a global tyranny. Will that religion be able to achieve the greatest degree of harmony between individual freedom and the interests of humanity, a harmony conceivable only at the present stage of history? That is only another aspect of that same foremost task. Will it promote the balanced development of the creative impulses with which every person is gifted? Yes, except for demonic impulses—that is, impulses toward tyranny, violence, and self-assertion at the expense of other living beings. Will it, like other movements with similar global aspirations, require blood and victims in order to emerge triumphant? No—except in those cases when its faithful may be forced to prove their devotion to its message at the cost of their lives. Will its ideas contradict not only the philosophical doctrine of materialism (they will contradict that, of course, at all points from A to Z), but also the objective and indisputable laws of modern science? Not in the slightest. Is it possible to imagine a campaign during the period of its ascendancy wherein dissenters will be persecuted, when it will force its tenets on philosophy, science, and art? To the contrary, its proposed route leads from partial initial restrictions on freedom of expression to eventual unlimited freedom of expression. This being so, what remains of the argument that religion is incapable of responding and providing practical solutions to the most pressing problems of the day?

One has every right and justification to direct such a reproach not at religion but, alas, at science. It is that same system of views that fails to look beyond the limits circumscribed by contemporary scientific knowledge that is incapable of providing answers to the most fundamental and elementary questions. Does the Source, the Creator, God exist? Unknown. Does such a thing as a soul exist? If so, is it immortal? Science does not know the answer. What is time, space, matter, energy? Opinions are sharply divided. Is our world eternal and endless or, on the contrary, is it limited within time and space? Science does not possess the necessary data to give a definite answer. Why should I do good and not evil, if evil appeals to me and I can be sure of escaping punishment? The answers are totally unintelligible. How can science be used to avert the possibility of wars and tyranny? Silence. How can social harmony be attained with the least human cost? Mutually exclusive proposals are put forward that resemble each other only in that they are all equally unrelated to pure science. It is natural that on such shaky and subjective and, indeed, pseudo-scientific foundations doctrines have arisen based only on class, racial, nationalist, or party interests—that is, on those very systems whose purpose is the justification of dictatorships and wars. The distinguishing mark of such doctrines is their low level of spirituality. It follows, therefore, that the desired moral supervisory body cannot be organized on the basis of the so-called scientific worldview, for, in essence, such a worldview does not exist. Rather, it shall arise through communion with the world of spirit; through the reception of the rays of that world pouring out and into our hearts, reason, and conscience; and through the application of the precept of active and creative love to every facet of our lives. The moral level which incorporates all of the above traits is called sanctity.

There is yet another popular fallacy: a view of religion as a phenomenon that is reactionary by nature, particularly in our age. But it is just as ridiculous to speak of the reactionary nature of religion in general, irrespective of the specific forms it takes, as it is to try to prove the reactionary nature of art in general or philosophy in general. A dynamic thinker—one who perceives evolving sets of facts and the processes by which those sets are shaped—will be able to distinguish the telltale marks of reactionary and progressive forms in art, in religion, in all areas of human activity. One may find a large number of reactionary forms of religion, even more than one would like, but that fact has no relation whatsoever to the embryonic sum religion with which this book is concerned. For there have not been, nor are there, more progressive aims or methods in our century than those that will be fused together in that religion. As for the scientific method's claim to supremacy, it is powerless to stamp out the methods of art and religion, in their widest sense, just as an aggressive religiosity was powerless to stamp out science in its time. That is because their methods are differentiated not only by how they cognize but by what they cognize. In the last century, the rapid progress of science and technology gave rise to predictions about the death of art. A hundred years have passed and the constellation of arts has not only not faded away but has been brightened by yet another star—the art of cinema. Thirty or forty years ago many in Russia believed the demise of religion was inevitable as a result of scientific and social progress. And yet, despite all the resources mobilized against it, the constellation of religions has not only not faded away but scientific and social progress has caused it to be brightened by the ability to turn the world's religions from a collage of separate petals into one single, whole spiritual flower—the Rose of the World.

It follows from the above that a religious movement that integrates humanity's positive experience into its philosophy and praxis and draws conclusions from the negative experience that require too much courage and honesty to be made by other streams of social thought; a movement whose first and foremost tasks are the transformation of the state into a community, the unification of the entire world, and the ennobling education of humanity; a movement that will guard against the distortion of its ideals and methods with the indestructible shield of a higher morality—such a movement cannot but be recognized as progressive, promising, and creatively young.

A shield of morality! On what principles will such a morality be founded? I spoke of sanctity. But is it not simply utopian to think that entire segments of society, and not just single individuals, could be saintly?

It is necessary to state what exactly is meant here by the term "sanctity." An ascetic life spent in a monastery is not a prerequisite for the attainment of sanctity. Sanctity is the highest stage of moral development for a person. Whoever surpasses it is no longer just saintly, but is a prophet as well. Sanctity can take many different forms depending on time, place, and a person's character. If we generalize, sanctity, defined negatively, is the internal state of a person, constant and ending only with death, in which the will is free from egoistic impulses, the reason is free from slavery to materialistic desires, and the heart is free from bursts of random, turbid emotions that demean the soul. To define it positively, sanctity is the permeation of all one's inner and outer life with an active love for God, people, and the world.

It is doubtful that the necessary psychological climate for the emergence of a moral body founded on that same sanctity could be better prepared than in an organization whose meaning and purpose lie in the hope of this emergence. The League will be that very organization. Even atheists could number among its members. But the League's basic tenet—the necessity of a global moral body standing above all the states—will be the very thing to fuse the most committed, creative, energetic, and gifted of its members into a nucleus—a nucleus characterized by an atmosphere of unflagging spiritual creativity, active love, and purity; a nucleus composed of people enlightened enough to be aware not only of the danger threatening each of them if their ambitious impulses are unleashed but of the danger, as well, of a too superficial formulation of religious moral values, which can lead to ethical formalism, hypocrisy, spiritual staleness, and sanctimony.

No one but God knows where and when the Rose of the World's first flames will be kindled. The country—Russia—has only been designated; tragic events might still take place that could interfere with that mystical event and force it to be relocated to another country. The time—the sixties—has only been projected; disastrous cataclysms might take place that would move the date far ahead into the future. It is possible that the first flame will kindle not in the League for the Transformation of the State but in a different, as yet unknown group of people. But here or there, in this country or another, a decade earlier or later, the interreligious, global church of the new age—the Rose of the World—will appear as the sum total of the spiritual activity of many people, as the joint creation of people standing beneath the shower of heaven-sent revelation—it will appear, emerge, and embark on its historical journey.

Religion, interreligion, church—I cannot render the idea with the necessary exactitude using those words. Its many fundamental departures from previous religions and churches will in time require new words to be coined for use in reference to it. But even without them, it will be necessary to introduce such a large vocabulary of new words into the pages of this book that now, at the beginning, I think it best not to run to the aid of those words but to rely on a descriptive definition of the distinguishing features of what will be called the Rose of the World.

It will not be like any restricted religious faith, whether true or false. Nor will it be an international religious order like the Theosophists, the Anthroposophists, or the Masons, composed, like a bouquet, of various flowers of truth eclectically picked from every imaginable religious glade. It will be an interreligion or pan-religion, in that it will be a teaching that views all religions that appeared earlier as reflections of different layers of spiritual reality, different sets of variomaterial facts, and different segments of our planetary cosmos.[1] That point of view treats Shadanakar both

---

1. "Planetary cosmos" refers to the sum total of planes of differing materiality, dimensions, and time streams that are necessarily linked to the Earth. The planetary cosmos is the planet Earth with all the complexity of the material (and not just physical) planes of its existence. Many heavenly bodies possess such gigantic systems. They are called bramfaturas. The Earth's bramfatura is called Shadanakar.

A brief glossary appended at the end of the book gives definitions for those words that are either used here for the first time or altered by a new sense.

as a separate entity and as part of the divine universe. If the older religions are petals, then the Rose of the World will be a flower: with roots, stem, head, and the commonwealth of its petals.

The second distinction concerns the globality of the Rose of the World's aspirations and their historical concreteness. Not one religion, with the exception of medieval Catholicism, has made the reorganization of human society its aim. But the papacy, stubbornly trying to contain feudal chaos with the dams of hierocracy, was unable to weaken the exploitation of the have-nots by the haves, to lessen social inequality with wide-ranging reforms, or to raise the overall standard of living. Be that as it may, it would be unfair to blame the ruling Catholic hierarchy for its failure: the material resources, both economic and techno-logical, necessary for such large-scale transformations were still unavailable. It was no coincidence that evil in the world was felt to have existed from time immemorial (and right up to modern times has been considered eternal and unavoidable), and that Catholicism in essence focused, like all the other religions, on the "inner self" alone, teaching individual perfection. But times have changed, material resources have become available, and it is thanks to the entire historical process, and not to the Rose of the World, that the latter can now regard social justice not as something alien to its purposes, doomed to failure, and not worth the efforts, but can link it inseparably to the growth of the inner self: work on oneself and social justice will become two par-allel processes that should complement each other.

One often hears that Christianity has failed. If it were only a question of the past, one could say that from the social and over-all moral point of view it has failed. "Religion has failed." Yes, if humanity's religious creativity were spent by what has already been woven, religion in the above-mentioned sense truly could be said to have failed. But at present it is fair to say only this: the older religions could not substantially decrease the amount of social injustice, because they did not possess the necessary mate-rial resources, and the lack of those resources gave birth to a negative attitude toward all such attempts. In that way the ground was prepared for the secular stage of civilization.

In the eighteenth century social conscience awakened. Social disharmony was finally felt and perceived as something intolerable, demeaning, and to be overcome. That, of course, occurred in connection with the fact that the material resources that had been lacking began to appear. But the older religions were unable to grasp that fact. They did not want to take advantage of those resources, did not wish to direct the process of social transformation, and it is that same sluggishness, intellectual laziness, conceptual immobility, and closemindedness that is their greatest fault. Religion discredited itself by its centuries-long powerlessness in that respect, and it should come as no surprise that Europe, followed by other continents, fell into the opposite extreme: the transformation of society by purely mechanical means in conjunction with a complete renunciation of the spiritual side of the process. The result, too, should come as no surprise: upheavals the world has never before witnessed, loss of life that had never been envisaged even in our worst nightmares, and a decline in the overall moral level, whose very possibility many people in the twentieth century see as a grim and tragic enigma.

The responsibility for the depth and perseverance of the resulting secular stage rests to a large extent on the older religions. They also bear responsibility for the spiritual fate of millions of souls who, in the struggle for social justice, placed themselves in opposition to religion in general and thus tore the spiritual roots of their own existence loose from the soil of world spirituality. But genuine religious activity is a definite kind of social service, and genuine social service is at the same time religious activity. No religious act, even the self-abnegation of a monk, is done in isolation from the whole, and every such work contributes to worldwide enlightenment. No positive social activity can help but increase the amount of good in the world— that is, such activity cannot help but have religious meaning. The pulsing of social conscience, active compassion and concelebration, unflagging practical efforts for social justice—this is the second manner in which the Rose of the World is distinct from the older religions.

The third distinction concerns dynamism of outlook. There have already been religions that have incorporated concepts of metahistory—Judaism and early Christianity—but only in remote and brief periods during their formation did they try to formulate a spiritual framework to explain the historical processes taking place at the time. During those brief, half-forgotten times, the astonishing insights of the Apocalypse remained hidden from people's eyes by a blanket of allegories and innuendos; its code of images allowed for every imaginable interpretation. Thus, a genuine framework for understanding historical processes did not take shape. Historical knowledge was as yet scarce and limited in scope, geographical horizons were small, and the mystical mind was not yet ready to grasp the internal logic of metahistory and the incredible complexity of Shadanakar.

But the appearance of the Rose of the World has been preceded by the scientific era, an era that revolutionized humanity's view of the universe, of nations, of cultures, and of their fates. It has been preceded by yet another era: one of radical social changes and upheavals, of revolutions, and of world wars. Both kinds of phenomena have loosened humanity's psychological crust, which had remained for so many centuries unbroken. In that soil, plowed up by the iron teeth of historical catastrophes, the seeds of metahistorical revelation will fall. And the entire planetary cosmos will reveal itself to people's spiritual sight as a constantly evolving system of variegated worlds, a system speeding toward a blindingly brilliant goal, spiritualized and transformed from century to century and from day to day. Images from future eras are beginning to show through our reality—each in all its inimitable uniqueness, in its correlation of metahistorical forces battling within it. The goal of the Rose of the World is to become a receptor, fosterer, and interpreter of that knowledge. The collective mystical consciousness of all living humanity, it will illumine the meaning of the historical processes of the past, present, and future in order to assume creative guidance of those processes. If one may speak of any dogmas in its teaching, then those dogmas will be deeply dynamic, multifaceted, and capable of further enrichment, development, and long-range evolution.

From that follows the fourth distinction of the Rose of the World, which entails a program of consistent, spiritual-historical tasks that are entirely concrete and achievable in principle. I will list once again the foremost of them: the unification of the planet under a federation of states overseen by a moral supervisory body; the establishment of economic well-being and a high standard of living in every country; the ennobling education of younger generations; the reunification of the Christian churches and the creation of a free amalgamation of all religions of Light; the transformation of the planet into a garden and the state into a community. But those are merely tasks of the first order. Their realization will open the way to tasks of an even higher order—the spiritualization of nature.

Interreligiosity, the globality of its societal aspirations and their concrete nature, the dynamism of its outlook, and consistency in its global historical tasks—these are the characteristics that will distinguish the Rose of the World from all religions and churches of the past. The bloodlessness of its paths, the painlessness of its reforms, its kindness and consideration toward people, the waves of spiritual warmth that will emanate from it—these are the characteristics that will distinguish it from all sociopolitical movements of the past and present.

Obviously, the essence of the state, as well as the moral cast of society, cannot be transformed in the wink of an eye. An immediate and complete renunciation of coercion is pure fantasy. But that element will decrease over time and societal space. Every kind of discipline is made up of elements of coercion and consciousness, and one or another type of discipline results from the ratio of these two elements. Slave economies, prisons, and concentration camps boast a high percentage of coercion and an almost complete absence of consciousness. There is a slightly higher percentage of consciousness present during army drills. And further, to the extent that the element of coercion is weakened within disciplinary models, the categorical imperative of inner self-discipline grows and replaces it. The new pedagogy will be based on the fostering of that same impulse. Its principles and methods, as well as methods for the moral rehabilitation and rebirth of criminals, will be discussed in a later chapter. But it should be clear even now that the external stimulus of coercion will disappear quickest of all within the inner concentric circles of the Rose of the World, for those circles will be filled by the very people who have wed their entire life to its tasks and principles and no longer have any need of outside coercion. They will be its conscience, and who, if not they, should occupy the seats of the Upper Council?

Is it possible to overstate the edifying effect exerted by political systems where the worthiest people stand at the head of society, guiding and creating? Think not of those whose will is overdeveloped at the expense of other sides of their self and whose strength lies in their unscrupulous approach to means, but of those in whom will, reason, love, purity of thought, and a profound understanding of life are harmoniously developed and combined with conspicuous spiritual gifts—those we call living saints.

Recently we saw an example of just such a saint: we were witnesses to India's decisive hour and the great spirit of Gandhi. We were presented with an astonishing spectacle: a person wearing a loincloth, with no government authority, without a single soldier or servant at his command, without a roof over his head, became the conscience and the spiritual and political leader of three hundred million people. One soft-spoken word from him was enough to unite those millions in a massive, nonviolent struggle to free their country, in which the shedding of their enemy's blood gave rise to nationwide fasting and mourning.

It is easy to imagine how tragically the Indian people's historical course would have been altered if, instead of that saint, a person of a self-willed nature, like Mussolini or Stalin, had at that decisive minute stepped forward as leader—a so-called strong leader, a master of demagoguery and political intrigue, who masks his despotic nature behind fulsome speeches about the people's welfare! How skillfully he would have played on the baser instincts of the people, on their natural hatred for their conquerors, on their envy of the rich. What waves of fire and blood would have broken over India, flooding islands of high moral consciousness fostered and strengthened over thousands of years by the brightest children of that great people! And, in the end, what a tyranny such a person would have established over the exhausted country, taking advantage of the people's habit of obedience, formed through centuries of slavery. Gandhi channelled the country's thirst for self-determination and national identity down a different path. Here is the first example in modern times of the power that will gradually replace the sword and whip of state rule. That power is the loving trust a people have for whomever gives proof of the moral elevation upon which rests the authority of living saints.

I foresee a host of objections. One is as follows. Yes, such a thing was possible in India, with its unique characteristics, with its four-thousand-year religious history, with the moral stature of its people. Other peoples have different legacies, and India's experience is not applicable to any other country.

True, every people has its own historical legacy. And India's legacy has led to its people becoming a pioneer on that road. But almost every nation has encountered, either within or beside their borders, dictatorships and tyrannies of all imaginable colors and ideological masks, and each has had sufficient opportunity to realize into what a disastrous abyss a blind leadership—unenlightened by sanctity, not even meeting the minimum requirements of an average moral level—can plunge their country. After all, government leadership demands self-renunciation, and an average moral level is too low for that. Many nations, as well, have come to realize that where, in place of dictators, political parties alternate, faces change like a kaleidoscope. Diplomats and generals, bosses and lawyers, demagogues and business people—some are self-seekers, others are more principled, but none is capable of breathing a new, clean, and vibrant spirit into life or of solving problems of vital national interest. No one can trust a single one of them more than they trust themselves, because not one of them has paused even a moment to think about what sanctity and spirituality mean. They are fleeting shadows, fallen leaves blown about by the winds of history. If the Rose of the World does not make its appearance in time on the international scene, they will be scattered by the fiery breath of willful and merciless dictatorships. If the Rose of the World does appear, they will dissolve, melting under the rising sun of its great message, because the hearts of the people will trust one living saint more than a hundred modern-day politicians.

But an even greater and brighter effect will be exerted on the people and their destiny if three of the highest gifts—sanctity, religious vision, and artistic genius—are all combined in one person.

O, so many aspects of religion belong entirely to its past stages. One such aspect appears to be the power that strictly delineated, didactically formulated, law-like dogmas incapable of growth have had over people's minds. Human experience and the growth of individuality during the last centuries have led to human beings feeling cramped by and suspicious of any dogma. As a result, no matter how nondogmatic the Rose of the World's teachings will be, no matter how much they will be permeated by a spirit of religious dynamism, a great many people will have difficulty accepting them. On the other hand, many millions will respond to its call, as it will be addressed not so much to the intellect as to the heart, resounding in masterpieces of literature, music, theater, and architecture.

Works of art are more capacious and multifaceted than theosophical aphorisms or philosophical arguments. They leave more room for the imagination; they permit each person to interpret the teaching so that it is more understandable and in tune with his or her own individuality. Revelation flows down from many streams, and if art is not the purest then it is at least the widest of them. Therefore, every art form and a beautiful repertoire of ritual will outfit the Rose of the World with colorful and glittering habiliments. And for that same reason, it would be most natural for a person who possesses three of the greatest gifts—religious vision, sanctity, and artistic genius—to stand at the head of the Rose of the World.

Perhaps such a person will never come, or will come much later. It is possible that a collective of the worthiest, and not one single person, will lead the Rose of the World. But if Providence sends a person of such great spirit to our century—and it has sent them before—and the forces of evil are unable to thwart his or her mission, it will be the greatest of good fortune for the entire planet. For no one can exert a greater and brighter influence on humanity than a genius of the word who has become a visionary leader and living saint and who has been raised to the heights of being global guide of a cultural and social renaissance. That person, and only that person, can be entrusted with an extraordinary and unprecedented task: moral supervision of all the states of the Federation and guidance of nations with a view to transforming those states into a global community.

O, we Russians paid dearly for the unconditional trust we placed in a strong-willed man, whom many of us viewed as a benefactor of humanity. We will not repeat the same mistake! There are unmistakable signs that distinguish a person worthy of such a mission from an evil genius. The latter is gloomy; the former is bright with spiritual vitality. One consolidates power with executions and torture; the other will not spend a single day seeking power, and when that individual accepts power no one's blood will be spilled. One will cultivate the cult of personality across the land; the other will consider such glorification ridiculous and repellent. One is unapproachable; the other is open to all. One is wracked by an unquenchable thirst for life and power and hides from imagined dangers behind impenetrable walls; the other is free from worldly temptations and calm in the face of danger, with a clean conscience and unshakable faith. They are two antipodes, the ambassadors of two irreconcilable camps.

Of course, such elected leaders would be but the first among equals in an Upper Council. In everything they would rely on the cooperation of many, and their own activities would be monitored by many. They would be able to assume their extraordinary post only after undergoing rigorous tests. Such a post cannot be filled by the young, not even by the middle-aged, but only by those ripened by old age. Temptations and negative emotions must be long overcome. As for the election itself, it seems to me that it could be conducted only in the form of one or another kind of plebiscite. And even during the term of office of the High Mentors, the Council would be keeping watch on their activities. Departure from their path would result in the transfer of their powers to the worthiest. In general, all the issues involved could be carefully thought out, the dangers foreseen, decisions precisely weighed and later adjusted. But as long as the High Mentors keep to the preordained path, they will be the mystical links between humanity and the other worlds, the revealers of the will of Providence, the spiritual guides of billions and the guardians of their souls. There is nothing to fear by uniting all spiritual and secular power in the hands of such people.

Some will say that such people appear perhaps only once in every five hundred years. I will go one step further: individuals of such stature, who possess the sum of these above-mentioned gifts, could never have existed before. An Einstein could not have appeared among the Maoris of the nineteenth century. It would be ridiculous to expect to find a Dostoyevsky, such as we know him, among the subjects of Tutankhamen or Theodoric. He would have possessed a different sum of gifts then, and many of them would not have found outward expression in his life. People like those I am speaking of could not have realized the gifts they were endowed with even in the recent past, and their contemporaries would have remained in the dark as to their true stature and potential. The prerequisite conditions already seem to be taking shape as the new age begins; the Rose of the World will see them ripen in such a way that the social and cultural atmosphere will provide the High Mentor with a chain of successors worthy of the post.

Some will also say that even all the above-listed gifts are not enough for such an extraordinary position, that such people also need a versatile, sober, and practical political mind. No doubt. Such a leader will have to deal with thousands of the most varied problems; knowledge and experience—economic, financial, judicial, even technical—will be needed. But the age of Aristotle is long past; minds of encyclopedic breadth are unthinkable in our day and age. And the activities of those I am speaking of are just as unthinkable apart from the collective mind, from the Upper Council. The most profound minds, those wise in the vicissitudes of leadership, as well as specialists from every branch of knowledge, will take part in it. It is wisdom, not encyclopedic erudition or practical management skills, that will be demanded of the High Mentors: wisdom to understand people at first sight, to go instantly to the heart of complex issues, and never for a second to remain deaf to the voice of conscience. The High Mentors should be so elevated morally that love and trust in them will replace other methods of rule. The use of coercion or force will be a torment for them; they will resort to it only in the rarest of cases.

But that is only one possible option, although it is in my opinion the most desirable. It is easy to imagine an alternative: leadership of the Rose of the World, a relationship with the Federation government and legislative bodies, where the collective principle will be limited by nothing and no one. The task of working out a constitution belongs to the far future, and our fortunate descendants, not us, will have the chance to choose one option from the many possible.

But isn't that a theocracy? I dislike the word *theocracy*. Theocracy is the rule of God; to use it in reference to any kind of social or political system would be absurd from the point of view of atheists and blasphemous from the point of view of believers. History has never witnessed, nor will it witness, a theocracy. Not theocracy, but hierocracy, the rule of a priesthood, should be used in reference to the ecclesiastical states of the Pope or the Dalai Lama. The system I have described is the exact opposite of any type of hierocracy: the church will not disappear into the state, which swallows it up and rules in its name. Rather, the entire conglomerate of states and assembly of churches will gradually merge into a global community and interreligious church. Posts in the higher bodies—legislative, executive, and supervisory—will not be occupied by the upper hierarchy of a church but by the finest representatives of all nations, all faiths, all social classes, and all specialties.

Not a hierocracy, not a monarchy, not an oligarchy, not a republic: something qualitatively different from all that has come before will emerge. It will be a global-wide social system working toward sanctifying and enlightening all life on earth. I do not know what it will be called. The point is not in the name but in the essence. Its essence will consist of work in the name of spiritualizing individuals, all of humanity, and nature.

2 Perspective on Culture

LITTLE BY LITTLE a new attitude toward everything will arise: there would not be the slightest reason for the Rose of the World to come into being if it only repeated what has been said before. A new attitude and way of thinking will emerge in regard to every aspect of life, large and small: cosmic and historical processes, planetary laws and the links between variomaterial worlds, personal relationships and approaches to personal growth, states and religion, the animal world and the environment—in a word, everything that we group under the concepts *culture* and *nature*.

A new attitude toward everything will arise, but that does not mean that every old attitude will be discarded or vilified. In many cases a point of view will merely be presented whereby past attitudes will no longer contradict, but will complement, each other, revealing each as merely a different aspect of the same reality, or even of many realities. Such an approach is often effective, for example, when examining the older religions and the realities behind them. This book is devoted in its entirety to that new attitude. The subject matter is far too broad and complex to be even briefly outlined in one chapter. Although this chapter is entitled "Perspective on Culture" and the following chapter, "Perspective on Religion," one should not expect an exhaustive treatment of these subjects. All six books of this work are permeated with a new way of looking at various spheres of culture, various historical events, various religious systems, and various realms of nature. These first chapters are merely intended as a sort of introduction. They contain a synopsis of certain fundamental principles, no more.

In our century science has assumed the dominant role in culture. The scientific method lays claim to absolute supremacy; for that reason this chapter will begin with a description of the perspective offered by the Rose of the World on the scientific method itself. It must be stated promptly and plainly that no matter how many illusions the partisans of the scientific method have tried to create in that regard, it has never been, is not now, nor will it ever be the only mode of inquiry or the only means to know the material world. One need remember that besides the artistic method—with which the scientific method now condescendingly and grudgingly shares its preeminent status—the foundations for a mode of inquiry and a method to know the material world were laid long ago. The study of that method is inextricably linked to people's work on their spiritual selves and the enlightenment of their moral selves. There is even the possibility that it will become to a certain degree the dominant method in the future. I have in mind not so much magic or occultism, which have been discredited by a number of misunderstandings, but rather the concept of spiritual work. Various systems and schools of that type can be found in all religions with long spiritual traditions. Having in the course of centuries developed practical techniques for bringing the will to bear on the human organism and on external matter, and guiding a person to that level only after protracted moral preparation and manifold tests, they have elevated, and elevate now, hundreds, perhaps thousands, to what is in layman's terms called miracle working. That arduous method, which has aroused the intense hatred of modern-day philistines, is distinguished by one principle foreign to science: work on and transformation of one's own being, as a result of which the physical and ether coatings of one's self become more pliable, elastic, and obedient to one's will than is normally possible. That path leads to such allegedly legendary phenomena as passing bodily through three-dimensional objects, levitation, walking on water, teleportation, the healing of incurable diseases and of blindness and—that highest and rarest attainment—the resurrection of the dead.

What we are dealing with in such cases is the manipulation of laws that hold in our materiality, and the suspension of lower laws by higher ones, which as yet are unknown to us. And if, in the twentieth century, the majority of us live our entire lives without encountering indisputable examples of such phenomena, it does not necessarily follow that such phenomena do not occur, or that they are impossible in principle, but only that the prevailing conditions—cultural, social, and psychological—in the secular era (especially in the West, and even more so in the countries belonging to the socialist camp) have to such an extent impeded the study and mastery of that method that the number of such phenomena has been reduced to a handful of isolated cases.

Certain truly momentous events that took place nearly two thousand years ago (they will be discussed later) are responsible for the fact that it has become impossible to usher not individuals alone but whole masses of people onto that path of knowledge. With the passage of time, the psychological climate of the secular era obstructed more and more any movement along that path. Nowadays, enormous obstacles face anyone wishing to embark on study of the method. In certain countries such study has become, for all practical purposes, impossible. But there is no reason to suppose that the method will remain that slow and arduous forever. The areligious era is not endless; we are living at its close. It is difficult to imagine anything appearing more unwieldy, unrefined, crude, and impotent than do the achievements of modern technology when compared with the achievements of the method of which I am speaking. If the incalculable material and human resources that are now swallowed up for the advancement of the scientific method were invested in the development and study of this other method, then the panorama of human life—creative work, knowledge, the organization of society, and morality—would undergo radical changes. The psychological climate of the era of the Rose of the World will create conditions more conducive than ever before to the development of that method. But that belongs to the future, and not the near future at that. Until that time arrives we have no alternative but to use in the main a different method, much less refined and not leading very far, but dominant everywhere at the moment.

From that follows the Rose of the World's overall perspective on science and technology at the current stage of history. Laboriously

gathering facts, deducing regularities from them without understanding the nature or orientation of those regularities, manipu-
lating them mechanically without the ability to foretell what
inventions and social upheavals its discoveries will lead to, science
has long been open to everyone regardless of their moral level.
The consequences are in front of our eyes and above our heads.
The chief consequence is that not one person on Earth can be sure
that a hydrogen bomb or some other, more appalling scientific
achievement will not be dropped on them or their fellow citizens
at any moment by highly educated minds. It is therefore natural
that one of the first measures the Rose of the World will undertake
after it begins supervision of the states' activities will be the creation of an Upper Scientific Council—that is, a committee staffed
by members from the inner circles of the Rose of the World itself.
Consisting of people who combine the respect of the scientific
community with a high level of moral integrity, the Council will
assume executive management of all scientific and technological
work, serving both planning and regulatory functions.

What is involved in the protection of the vital interests of
humanity appears on the whole straightforward enough, at least
in its principles, and there is hardly a need to pause over it now.
As for the issues involved in the protection of the interests of the
animal and plant worlds, they will be discussed in those sections of
the book devoted to the animal world and the world of the elementals. That is perhaps the only area in which the outlook of the
Rose of the World and the views of the majority of contemporary
scientists cannot be reconciled. The conflict, however, does not
pertain to any scientific theory. Rather, it applies only to certain of
science's practical methods that are incompatible with the basic
demands of goodness not only in the view of the Rose of the
World but also in the view of nearly every religious moral teaching
and, indeed, of nearly every humane person.

Outside those purely methodological clashes, there are not, nor
can there be, any conflicts between the Rose of the World and science. There is nowhere for a conflict between them to arise. They
deal with *different things*. It can hardly be a coincidence that the
erudition of the majority of this century's scientific geniuses did

not prevent them from holding personal religious beliefs and from sharing and even creating bright, spiritual systems of philosophy. Einstein and Planck, Pavlov and Lemaître, Eddington and Milne—no matter what the field of their scientific inquiry, all remained, in their own way, people with a firm belief in God. I am, of course, disregarding here Russian scientists of the Soviet period, some of whom were forced to proclaim their materialism not out of any philosophical convictions but for completely different reasons, which are obvious to anyone.

Leaving aside philosophy and politics, we can say that in areas purely scientific the Rose of the World does not make any claim that science would have sufficient grounds to reject. What is being asserted is that science has been silent thus far about the realities the Rose of the World describes. But that is a situation that will not continue for long. As for the social, cultural, and moral tasks that the Rose of the World will attempt to carry out, it is impossible to imagine that they would meet with any objections in principle from authorities in the scientific community.

It is reasonable to suppose that it will not be the very idea of planning scientific activity that will be the subject of debate in the future but the limits of what will be subject to planning and of its practical methods. No doubt special study will be devoted to the planning and coordination of scientific work carried out in certain states of the midtwentieth century. But only individual features will be borrowed from their experience, if only because the Federation will be made up of many states, both large and small, that will have just been unified and will be at varying stages of economic development, states formed against the backdrop of different cultures and possessing different sociopolitical systems. Systems distinguished by greater economic centralization will find it easier to be assimilated into the inexorable process of global socialization; others, accustomed to a laissez-faire system, will be drawn into it more gradually. That, as well as the variety of cultural traditions, will result in an extremely mixed global economy and interplay of cultural heritages during the first stage.

Deep-rooted national antagonisms will also long continue to make their presence felt. It will take time to balance and harmonize the needs of different countries and different layers of society that will benefit from, say, the priority development of such and such a branch of industry in such and such a place or the sale of their products somewhere or other. In order to reach an equitable solution to those kinds of problems, a new psychological trait will be required from those who will head the Scientific Council and the Rose of the World itself: mastery of the inner sway of personal, as yet entirely natural, cultural-ethnic bonds—that is, a complete impartiality toward nations. What effort, what moral authority and even self-sacrifice, will be necessary just to weaken deep-seated antagonisms, such as Anglo-Arab, Russo-Polish, or Turko-Armenian! What will Germans, English, Russians, or Americans have to do to enable so many countries to forget the hostility those Western nations have aroused in them? What educational programs will be needed to soothe the wounded pride that prevents many small or middle-sized nations from being on friendly terms with their neighbors and that escalates into aggressive dreams of attaining greatness at the expense of other countries?

But that is only one side of the coin. Many Western nations will have to rid themselves of the slightest trace of their old feelings of superiority over others. Russians will have to realize that their country is not the crowning glory of creation and is in fact no better than many other nations. The English will be forced to perform colossal work on their inner selves so as to renounce their habit of favoring the interests of the inhabitants of the British Isles over the interests of citizens of Indonesia or Tanzania. From the French will be required the ability to take to heart the interests of Paraguay or Thailand just as passionately as they do their own. The Chinese and Arabs will liberate their hearts and minds from the once-justified, and now anachronistic, distrust of Europeans, which they have nursed for so many centuries, and will learn to bestow no less attention on the needs of Belgium or Greece than on those of Shanghai or the Sudan. The citizens of the republics of Central America will have to cease caring and complaining only about their own situation and take part in the distribution of the world's wealth, taking into account the needs of Afghanistan, Cambodia, and even Yakutia. The citizens of the United States will be expected to remember that they call themselves Christians and that Christianity is incompatible with a savage hate for any race, blacks included. This psychological remolding will be, as anyone can see, incredibly difficult, but it is the only way freedom from wars and tyranny can be won. As one would expect, nobody can hope to take part in the work of the global planning bodies without that remolding.

Nations will even have to learn to make sacrifices—not of their blood, not, of course, of the lives of their sons and daughters, but of dollars. For the more affluent nations will be faced with the necessity of sharing their resources with the peoples of the East and South, and disinterestedly at that, without an eye to turning such aid into big business. In short, all those in the leadership of the Rose of the World must be able to feel themselves as, above all, members of the entire cosmos, then as members of humanity, and only then as members of a nation.

The overall goal of the Rose of the World—or to be more exact, of the gigantic spiritual process that began thousands of years ago and of which the Rose of the World is but one stage—is the enlightenment of Shadanakar. And the foremost task of our age consists in establishing everywhere, without excluding a single human being, a standard of living worthy of humans, simple day-to-day well-being, and fundamentally decent moral relations between people. The idea that every person without exception should be assured of worthwhile work, rest, leisure, a comfortable old age, decent shelter, access to all democratic freedoms, and satisfaction of their basic material and spiritual needs will begin to be actualized more and more in everyday life.

Only much later, in the very last chapters, will I be able to shed light on concrete measures, on that program of integrated reform whereby these principles will, I believe, take on flesh and blood. For now, only the principles are under discussion. Thus, those in whom these principles awaken no sympathy will not waste their time and energy on further reading, while those in sympathy will be able to get a feel for the inner spirit of the Rose of the World before moving on to an investigation of the possible paths for making these ideals a reality.

The above is the basic attitude of the Rose of the World toward science and technology, as far as I can explain it without delving into metahistory and transphysics. That should also be the role played by the scientific method in the next few historical periods.

Several decades from now, the ever-increasing rate of economic growth will reach a level we will be fully justified in calling global prosperity. Living standards now enjoyed by citizens of the economically advanced nations will be established in the remotest corners of the globe. The rechanneling of the massive sums that are now spent on weapons into peaceful uses will impart almost unimaginable acceleration to economic growth. Universal elementary education will likely be achieved even before that. Eventually, even universal secondary education will be felt to be insufficient. The borders of the intelligentsia will encompass all of humanity. The development of newer and newer means of communication, along with their accessibility and practicability, will virtually eliminate the distance between nations and cultures. As the working day shrinks, new reserves of time will be freed up. Physiological science will devise technology that will enable the human brain to memorize input quicker and indelibly. Leisure time will increase. And those matters that now occupy the majority of people—the economy, politics, product improvement, technology, the further upgrading of material comforts—will lose their interest. It is entirely realistic to think that the generations of those times will find it baffling and strange that their ancestors could have been so engrossed by and emotional about decisions relating to such boring and trivial matters. Their energy will be channeled into the creation of riches of a higher order, since the economic base, being firmly grounded and global, will not be subject to any sharp fluctuations.

Issues connected with technology and economics will cease to engage people's overriding attention. They will be dealt with in their respective committees and will be subject to public scrutiny, just as issues of restaurant hygiene or sewage are now. Humanity's gifts will be put to a different use, dictated by the thirst for knowledge, a love for all living beings, a need for higher forms of creative work, and a passion for beauty.

The thirst for knowledge, which at one time drove explorers to embark on voyages through uncharted waters and to range over unopened continents, will send them first (perhaps even before the rise of the Rose of the World) into outer space. But the other planets are inhospitable. After several exploratory missions the launches will halt, and the thirst for knowledge itself will begin to shift in focus. Methods will be devised to activate and develop the dormant organs possessed by every human being: organs of spiritual sight, spiritual hearing, deep memory, and the ability to separate at will one's inner, variomaterial bodies from the physical body. Voyages around variomaterial worlds, around the unfolding planes of Shadanakar, will commence. It will be the age of cosmic Magellans and Columbuses of the spirit.

What systematic views on the individual's value, rights, obligations, and growth will help to create a new psychological climate and hasten the dawn of the golden age?

The absolute value of individuals lies in the fact that they share with God an innate capacity for creative work and love. The relative value of individuals depends on the level they have reached in their spiritual ascent, on the sum of efforts—both their own and Providence's—spent on the attainment of that level, and on the degree to which they manifest in their lives those gifts for divine creative work and love.

The terrestrial leg of the cosmic journey of an ascending monad is that stage when its gifts for creative work and love already can and should be brought to bear in elevating its natural and human environment—that is, lessening the tendency of individual parts and units within that environment to assert themselves at the expense of others. Evil consists of just that tendency. Its forms and magnitude are almost endless in their variety, but at its root it is always the same: the attempt to assert oneself at the expense of everyone and everything else.

The older religions judged the relative value of individuals by the degree to which they obeyed the prescriptions of a given religious-moral code. Religions with ascetic leanings believed the highest stage to be sainthood, defining it as either pure monastic service or as martyrdom for one's faith. In so doing they relegated love to the background. A monk's or martyr's self-denial were performed not out of love for humanity or for all living beings but out of a yearning to merge with God and to avoid the torments of hell. I am, of course, referring here to the predominant tendency, the prevalent attitude, and not to such astonishing individual apostles of love as St. Francis of Assisi, Ramajuna, or Milarepa.

Monstrous though it may seem to us, even the eternal suffering of sinners in hell did not arouse in the majority of adepts of those religions the desire to enlighten the world's laws, including the law of retribution, or karma. Eternal punishment for temporal sins appeared to them a just act of God or in any case (as in Brahmanism) an unalterable and absolutely immutable law. Buddha burned like a torch with the flame of compassion, but he, too, taught only how to free oneself from the wheel of iron laws and not how to enlighten and transform those laws. As for creative work, its intrinsic nature was not recognized at all—such a concept did not even exist—while little importance was attached to concrete forms of creative work accessible to ordinary people, with the exception of religious works in the narrow sense of the word: acts of charity, theology, missionary service, church architecture, and religious service.

Other religions that are not given to asceticism, such as Islam and Protestantism, modified the ideal of sanctity, broadening it and, at the same time, lowering it, making it more accessible, more popular, even going so far as to require the observance of commandments vis-a-vis God, the state, one's neighbor, one's family, and, lastly, oneself. It should be emphasized that neither one nor the other group of religions set themselves the task of transforming society, let alone nature. Accordingly, the conception of an individual's obligations also remained deficient and narrow.

It was only natural that such tasks were finally advocated by secular teachings, though in an extremely simplistic form. A lower, internally contradictory moral standard was proclaimed that blindly mixed progressive features with others that fell below a moral minimum one would have thought long beyond question. People dusted off the old formula "The end justifies the means" and, hesitating to proclaim it openly and honestly, began applying it in practice. The moral aspect of historical events was wholly ignored when the events were subjected to scrutiny or evaluation; verdicts were passed based only on consideration of the overall progressive or reactionary orientation of the given event. No one was disturbed by the fact that such a practice led to the justification of atrocities committed by many despots of the past, even such outrageous mass slaughters as the Jacobin terror or the activities of the Oprichnina. Many time-honored achievements in social progress—such as freedom of speech, the press, and conscience—were cast aside. Generations raised in such an atmosphere gradually ceased to feel even the need for those freedoms—a symptom that speaks far more eloquently than any tirade of society's shocking spiritual decline. Thus, as society further embraced that moral standard in the form it took in real life, those positive features that it did possess were nullified. For the future held only the prospect of the dominion of material satiety, purchased by a renunciation of spiritual freedom, by millions of human lives, and by the exile of billions of souls to the lower planes of Shadanakar, souls that had sold their divine birthright for a meager pottage.

One can only hope that humanity will learn from that terrible lesson.

The Rose of the World will teach the absolute *value* of individuals and their divine birthrights: the right to be free from the yoke of poverty and the oppression of power-hungry groups, the right to well-being, the right to all forms of free creative work and the public unveiling of the fruits of that work, the right to religious searchings, and the right to beauty. The right of people to a secure existence and to the enjoyment of the benefits of civilization is an inborn right that in itself does not necessitate a renunciation of freedom or spirituality. It would be leading people astray to assert that we are faced with a crucial dilemma here, that in order to attain what are only the natural and self-evident blessings of life we must sacrifice our spiritual and social freedom.

The Rose of the World will also teach the *obligations* of individuals: to consistently expand the area encompassed by their love and to foster, multiply, and enlighten what is born of their work. Thus, creative work is both a right and an obligation. Even now I am unable to comprehend how it was that that truly divine gift to humans did not receive due notice in any of the older religions, except for certain forms of polytheism, especially that of ancient Greece. If I am not mistaken, it was only in ancient Greece that creativity itself (and not productivity, as in other forms of polytheism) was deified. Great masters of the arts were even pantheonized.

It is a sad and puzzling fact that after the decline of ancient Greece the creative gift ceased to attract the notice of religions and was no longer conceptualized in ontological, metaphysical, or mystical terms. Under the influence of the shallowly interpreted Semitic idea that after six days of creation the Divine Creative Spirit rested, theology has preferred to circumvent the question of God's further creation. The words of God recorded in Revelations, "Behold, I will make all things new," has remained the lone flight of inspiration, the lone intuition in that regard. As for human creativity, an altogether suspicious attitude was formed toward it, as if the sin of pride to which a human creator could fall victim was more dangerous and deadlier than creative sterility. Unfortunately, the view on human creativity that formed in the religions of Indian origin was no less injurious.

The last few centuries of Western culture—so rich in works of genius in all spheres of art, science, and philosophy—have taught us much. They have taught us to hold human creativity in reverence and human labor in respect. But the secular spirit of these centuries has fostered just what the older religions feared: creators have become afflicted by pride in their creative gift, as if that gift had been forged by them themselves. True, that conceit has nested not so much in the hearts of real geniuses, let alone artistic visionaries, as in the hearts of lesser scientific and artistic figures. A series of chapters in this book will be specially devoted to a closer examination of that problem from the point of view of the Rose of the World's teachings.

In any case, creative work, like love, is not an exclusive gift bestowed on only a chosen few. A few now possess sanctity and moral vision, heroism and wisdom, genius and talent. But all that is merely activation of the potential dormant within every soul. A sea of love, an inexhaustible wellspring of creativity, bubbles behind the consciousness of each one of us. The sum religion will seek to remove that barrier and allow those healing waters to wash over our life. A creative attitude toward everything will appear among the generations raised under it, and even labor will cease to be a burden. Rather, it will become the outward expression of an unquenchable desire to create new things, better things, and to create of oneself. All the Rose of the World's followers will enjoy creative work, teaching its joys to children and teenagers. They will be creative in everything they do: writing, architecture, science, gardening, the decoration and tempering of daily life, religious service and religious drama, the love between man and woman, childrearing, physical exercise and dance, the enlightenment of nature, and play. For all creative work, except the demonic, that is done in its own name and for its own sake is divine in nature. Through it, people elevate themselves and fill their own hearts and the hearts of those around them with God.

When it comes to spiritual growth, the majority of people move along the slow and wide path. The path runs through marriage and childbearing, work and pastimes, through the fullness and variety of life's impressions, joys, and pleasures. But there is also a Narrow Path. It is a path for those who harbor in their soul a special gift that requires strict self-denial: the gift of sainthood. Religious teachings are wrong to claim that the Narrow Path is the one true path or the highest one. Equally wrong are those social or religious systems that deny it outright and erect barriers against those who feel called to that path and to it alone. It is doubtful that monasteries will be numerous in the era of the Rose of the World, but there will be some, so that all who are driven onto the Narrow Path by spiritual thirst will be able to work on activating powers within their soul that require years of inner work in silence and solitude to develop. If a person enters onto the Narrow Path out of fear of retribution or dreams of a personal, egoistic, and closed relationship with God, that person's victories will be meaningless. There is no such God Who rewards loyal slaves with the blissful contemplation of His glory. Contemplation of the highest spheres is the *release of one's self from oneself* to commune with the One, Who contains all monads and the entire world within Himself. Therefore, a follower of the Rose of the World will not feel compelled to embark on the Narrow Path by spiritual egoism or by a desire for personal salvation mingled with cool indifference toward the fate of others. Those who follow it will be motivated by the realization that gifts will be unveiled on the Narrow Path with which the living saint will be able to help the world more effectively from solitude than hundreds can in the outside world and, further, that after death these gifts will so grow in strength that even the powerful upper hierarchies of demons will bow before them.

There is no need whatsoever for heavy vows to accompany tonsure. There are no grounds whatsoever for condemning or vilifying someone who, after the lapse of several years, leaves the path. Those entering the path will at first take only a short-term vow: for three, five, or seven years. Only after successfully completing those stages will they, if they wish, be permitted to take a vow for a longer period of time. Yet even then the realization of the irrevocability of their decision, the fear of having made an irreparable mistake will not torment or haunt them, giving rise to despair and wild bursts of as yet unmastered negative emotions. They will know that with the expiration of the vow they will be free to return to the outside world, free to choose any lifestyle, any work, free to have a family without having to fear censure or scorn from anyone.

I have endeavored to provide a glimpse of the Rose of the World's perspective on the scientific and ascientific modes of inquiry, on individuals' rights and obligations, on human creativity and labor, and on the two basic types of spiritual paths: the Wide and the Narrow. In order to complete this overview of its perspective on culture, it would be sensible to dwell on the Rose of the World's views on art, in the broader sense of the word. But that subject is so important and touches on so many different levels, and is so close to my heart personally, that I have decided to devote a series of chapters to it in one of the later parts of the book. Therefore, before moving on to the question of the Rose of the World's perspective on other religions, I will jot down just a few words about art in the approaching era.

What features might distinguish the art to be created by people who have embraced the spirit of the Rose of the World in the near future, when the sun of the golden age will have only just begun to illumine the clouds on the horizon?

It would be naive to try to predict or summarize the variety of artistic trends, genres, schools, and styles with which that sphere of culture will scintillate toward the end of this century. But a certain dominant style will, I think, emerge. Of course, it will not exhaust all the different artistic movements (under the conditions of maximum freedom that would be impossible as well as unnecessary for the same reason). This style is destined to become the mainstream in art and literature in the last third of this century. The perception of reality intrinsic to the Rose of the World—*transparent* perception, which distinguishes variomaterial or spiritual planes through the physical plane—will find expression in that style. Such a perception of reality will be a far cry from a studied optimism that is afraid to shatter its own peace of mind in heeding the dark and tragic sides of existence. Creators of that style will not seek to ignore the distressing and frightening underside of the world. They will consider it cowardly to desire to forget about the bloody path of history; about the reality of the dreadful infraphysical planes of Shadanakar; about their merciless laws, which bind untold hosts of unfortunates in chains of inhuman torments; and about the ghastly fall that is being readied for the human spirit by the forces of the Antigod and that will almost certainly take place when the golden age has run its course. But a higher level of awareness will not tarnish their love for the world, it will not lessen the joy they receive from nature, culture, creative work, public service, love, and friendship. In fact, quite the contrary! Could the awareness of hidden dangers threatening the one you love ever extinguish the flame of that love? There will be wondrous, life-affirming works of unprecedented purity and joyfulness. There will appear in all the artistic genres—both those that already exist and those that will arise later—works that will sparkle like splashes of water on sunlit ponds, works by artists of the future about a love that is much more capacious than ours, works about youth, about the joys of family life and public service, about the broadening of human consciousness and the expansion of the frontiers of our perception, about friendship between people and elementals, about the daily proximity of the friends of our heart who are as yet unseen, as well as much more that will concern the people of those times and that we are incapable of imagining.

It seems to me that such a style—masculine in its fearlessness and feminine in its lovingness, a profound combination of joy and affection for people and the world, yet with a keen awareness of the world's darker depths—could be called either transparent realism or metarealism. And need I mention that a work of art will not necessarily have to be an example of transparent realism for people who have embraced the Rose of the World's spirit to be able to enjoy and delight in it? They will delight in everything that has the mark of talent and at least one of the following features: a sense of beauty, broad scope, profundity of thought, sharpness of insight, purity of heart, or a joyful spirit.

There will come a time when the moral and aesthetic level of society, and of artists themselves, will be such that the need for restrictions of any kind will disappear, and freedom of artistic, literary, philosophical, and scientific forms of expression will be absolute. But it will not be until several decades after the Rose of the World has assumed moral supervision over the states that the era of that ideal moral level arrives. It is not through wisdom but youthful naïveté that one could arrive at the idea that society has already reached those heights of maturity when absolute freedom will not give rise to critical, irreparable abuses.

At first it will be necessary to assign to local branches of the Global Artistic Council, besides more pleasant duties, that single checkpoint through which an artistic work will have to pass before its public unveiling. That will be, if you will, the censor's swan song. In the beginning, when national antagonisms and racial prejudice will have not yet been eliminated, and power-hungry organizations will continue to play on those prejudices, a ban will have to be laid on any form of hate propaganda against any segment of the populace. Censorship will be maintained longer over books and texts that popularize scientific and philosophical ideas that give inadequate, superficial, or distorted treatment to objective facts and thus lead uninformed readers astray. Censorship will persist over works of fiction, requiring from them, it seems to me, a minimum of artistic merit in order to protect the literary market from a flood of tasteless, aesthetically ignorant trash. Finally, an unconditional ban on pornography will likely be in place longest of all. With the removal of each of these restrictions another measure will take its place: the Global Artistic Council or the Global Scientific Council will, after the release of a work of poor quality, print an authoritative review of it. That will suffice.

Clearly, it will not be easy to devise a system to determine who will sit on such councils, a system that will ensure that people with party or conceptual biases, intolerant supporters of particular movements or philosophical schools, or champions of the creative interests of some single group, nation, or generation not interfere in any sphere of culture. I would think, however, that in the psychological atmosphere of the Rose of the World a system like that could be devised.

If, for the moment, we avoid entering into fine distinctions between the concepts of culture and civilization, we may say that culture is nothing other than the sum total of humanity's creative work. If creative work is the highest, most precious, and sanctified of human gifts, an expression of the human soul's divine prerogative, then there is not, nor can there be, anything more precious or sanctified than culture. Further, the more spiritual a given cultural level, a given cultural sphere, or a given creative work might be, the more valuable it is as well.

The culture of a united humanity is only now emerging. Until now the only cultures to reach individual maturity have been those of individual suprapeoples, a suprapeople being a group of nations that are bound by a distinct, jointly created culture. But none of these cultures is confined to that aspect that exists and evolves within our three-dimensional space. Those who participated in the building of that culture here continue their creative work in the afterlife as well, though the work is, of course, altered in accordance with the conditions of that world or those worlds through which the soul of the human creator is passing at the time. An awareness is growing of million-strong communities of such souls, of heavenly lands and cities above each of the world's suprapeoples, and of Arimoya, the emerging heavenly land of the culture of a united humanity. A perspective on culture based on such principles is new and startling. We would be right in even noting that with further crystallization and deepening it will grow to become a vast mythology, if in using the word "myth" we disaccustom ourselves from thinking of something that has no basis in reality. Here we are dealing with just the opposite: a colossal reality that is reflected hazily and superficially, but reflected all the same, in mythology.

The atmosphere established by the Rose of the World and its teachings will give rise to conditions necessary for that cultural mythology to be grasped by every mind. Even if only a limited number of minds are able to comprehend it in all its esoteric complexity, the spirit of the worldview, and not its letter, will gradually become accessible to almost everyone. And if we contemplate the prospect of instilling that worldview in the general populace, then devising a system of measures to safeguard all spheres of culture from interference by people who have no inner right to manage those spheres will cease to appear a hopeless task.

3 Perspective on Religion

HOW OFTEN WE USE THE WORD "truth" and how seldom we ponder its meaning. In pondering its meaning here, we will not, however, let ourselves be troubled by the fact that we are essentially repeating the question posed by Pilate. Rather, we will attempt, as best as we are able, to arrive at a deeper understanding of the concept.

We call "true" a theory or teaching that, in our opinion, presents an undistorted view on some object of knowledge. To be precise, truth is an undistorted reflection in our mind of an object of knowledge. There can exist as many truths as there are objects of knowledge.

But objects of knowledge are known *through us*, not *through themselves*. It thus follows that a truth about any object of knowledge known through us should be recognized as a *relative* truth. *Absolute* truth is the reflection of an object of knowledge that is known by some subject *in itself*. In principle, that kind of knowledge is possible only when the duality of object and subject is removed: when the subject of knowledge is the object.

Absolute universal truth is the undistorted reflection in a consciousness of the Greater Universe known in itself. *Absolute component truths* are undistorted reflections of some *part* of the Universe, also known in itself.

Naturally, absolute truth of the Greater Universe can exist only in the consciousness of a subject of knowledge commensurate with it, an omniscient subject capable of being the object, capable of knowing things not only through itself but also in itself. That subject of knowledge is called the Absolute, God, the Universal Sun.

God, as an object of knowledge, is knowable in Himself only by Himself. The Absolute Truth of God, as well as the Absolute Truth of the Universe, is attainable only by God.

Clearly, any *component* truth, no matter how small the object of knowledge, is attainable by us only in its *relative* form. But this sort of agnosticism should not be viewed as immutable. When any component subject of knowledge, any monad, ultimately merges with the Absolute Subject, it avails itself of the possibility of not only knowledge through itself, but also of knowledge in itself. It is therefore correct to speak of a *phased*, as distinct from an immutable, agnosticism.

There may be few or many versions of component truths—personal, individual varieties of one component relative truth. Objects of knowledge of smaller scale (in comparison with the subject) are, however, reflected in the consciousness of a number of like subjects in an identical, or almost identical, manner. It is that likeness between many subjects that dictates that their individual versions of one or another truth will be alike as well. If it were not so, it would be impossible for people to understand one another about anything. But the larger the object of knowledge (in comparison with the subject), the greater the number of versions that arise. The relative truth of the Universe and the relative truth of God give birth to as many individual versions as there are subjects of knowledge.

It should be clear that all our "truths" are, strictly speaking, only approximations of the truth. The smaller the object of knowledge, the better it can be grasped by our consciousness, and the narrower the gap between its absolute truth and our relative truth concerning it. There is, however, a lower limit in the ratio of scale between subject and object, below which the gap between the absolute and relative truth again begins to widen. For example, the gap between the absolute truth of an elementary particle and our relative truth concerning it is enormous. The gap between the absolute truth of the Universe, the absolute truth of God, and our relative truths concerning them is boundless.

One would think that, after Kant, these ideas should be universally known and acknowledged. But if they were internalized by every religiously feeling and thinking person, there would be no claims of individual or collective knowledge of the absolute truth, no claims of the absolute truth of some one theory or teaching.

As was shown above, only the Omniscient Subject is in possession of the absolute truth. If a human subject—for instance, the collective consciousness of some historical church—possessed that truth, it would be objectively revealed in the unqualified omniscience of that collective consciousness. But the fact that not one human collective or individual is invested with that omniscience proves yet again how groundless are the claims to absolute truth by any teaching. If the representatives of the Rose of the World ever think to assert the absolute truth of its teachings, such claims would be just as groundless and absurd.

But the claim that all teachings or some one teaching are false is just as groundless and absurd. There are not, nor can there be, any *wholly false* teachings. If there appeared an opinion that lacked even a grain of truth, it would never become a teaching, a system of ideas communicated to someone else. It would remain the invention of the person who brought it into being, as sometimes happens, for example, with the philosophical and pseudo-scientific imaginings of the mentally ill. Only individual *component* statements can be false, in the strict sense of the word. Such statements maintain the illusion of truth with light borrowed from true component statements that enter into the same system. There is, however, a certain ratio of quantity and weight between true component statements and false ones whereby the latter begin to nullify the grains of truth contained in the given teachings. There are, furthermore, teachings in which the false statements not only nullify the elements of truth but consign the whole system to the category of spiritual negatives. It is customary to call them "left-hand teachings." The future teaching of the Antigod, by which it appears the penultimate period of world history will be marked, will be formulated in such a manner that a minimal weight of component truths will by their light lend the appearance of truth to a maximum number of false statements. The end result will be that the teaching will entangle the human consciousness in webs of lies stronger and stickier than any other.

Religions that are not left-hand teachings differ from each other not by virtue of the truth of one and the falsity of all the rest, but rather in two altogether different respects. First, they differ by virtue of the varying stages of their ascent to absolute truth—that is, in accordance with the decrease of subjective, temporal elements within them. That *developmental* distinction can be provisionally labeled a *vertical* distinction. Second, they can differ by virtue of the fact that they speak of different things—they reflect different sets of objects of knowledge. This type of *segmental* distinction can be provisionally labeled a *horizontal* distinction.

One should always bear in mind these two types of distinctions as we examine the Rose of the World's perspective on other religions.

Scientific progress presents itself to us as a continuous process whereby relative component truths are accumulated, elaborated, and fine-tuned. At each successive stage it is the custom to repudiate not the set of facts accumulated earlier but merely their outdated interpretation. Instances when a previous set of facts was cast into doubt and repudiated—as happened, for example, with alchemy—are comparatively rare. But in the history of religion, other practices have unfortunately prevailed. Rather than seeing a continuous succession of interpretations of spiritual facts not subject to doubt, what we usually witness is that the repudiation of large numbers of relative component truths that were grasped earlier as a new set of truths, with the inclusion of a certain number of old ones, is presented as absolute. That is particularly true in regard to the supplantation of the so-called pagan religions by monotheistic systems.

It should be obvious to all that observance of such practices in the context of the expanding horizons of the twentieth century would at best lead to the creation of yet another religious sect. It would, of course, be ridiculous to apply the scientific method to religion, just as it would be ridiculous to apply the artistic method to the field of science. But it has long been time for us to adopt the scientist's good habit and not repudiate, but rethink sets of relative truths accumulated earlier.

From the above it follows that no teaching (except left-hand teachings, which are recognizable, above all, by their spiritually corrupting influence) can be rejected outright. They should be recognized as inadequate, as clouded with subjective, human contaminants of a temporal, classist, racist, or individual nature. Nevertheless, a grain of relative truth, a grain of knowledge "through us" of one or another aspect of the transphysical world, is present in each religion, and each of those truths is a precious jewel belonging to all humanity. At the same time, it is natural that the weight of truth in systems that take shape as the sum of the experience of a great many individuals is, as a rule, greater than the weight of truth in systems found only among small groups. An exception to the rule are new systems that might be in the process of gaining wider acceptance but naturally must first pass through an esoteric or infant stage.

In the worldview of the Rose of the World, such widely embraced systems are called myths, a point that will be explained in detail a little later. One or another transphysical reality always lies behind the myths, but it cannot help being distorted and muddied through contamination of the myth by the "all too human." It is hardly possible, at least at present, to formulate strictly and precisely a method to liberate the transphysical kernel of a myth from its human-made husk. The necessary set of criteria that would obtain in every case has not yet been devised. In addition, it is doubtful that such an intricate mystical task could be performed with the help of rational analysis alone. It is true that we could, by drawing on the teleology of history, devise a system of classification of religions that would allow us to group the highly developed religions together and thus convince ourselves that there are beliefs professed, though with different degrees of purity and stress, by the entire group. Among such beliefs are the oneness of God, the plurality of different spiritual hierarchies, the plurality of variomaterial worlds, the infinite plurality of evolving monads, and the existence of some universal moral law, which is characterized by the rewards or punishments people receive before or after death for what they do during their lives. As regards everything else, even the interpretation of the shared beliefs just listed, the myths either contradict one another or speak of different things.

If, however, in many cases the individuality of the subject contaminates the image of the object with something extraneous, something exclusively human, there are just as many instances when a spiritual truth can be intuited only by a mind of a definite cast. Individuality then becomes a factor that does not cloud intuition but, to the contrary, makes it possible. The teleological process in the history of human religions has partly consisted in readying the consciousness of individual persons, peoples, races, or eras by means of historical and biographical factors to enable it to intuit a given truth, a given transphysical reality. To other individuals, peoples, races, and eras, a consciousness readied in that manner and its religious experience may seem strange, distorted, or naive, and fraught with every sort of aberration.

From the hundreds of those possible, I will for the time being cite only one particularly illustrative example: the idea of reincarnation. An intrinsic part of Hinduism and Buddhism, and present in the Kabbala of esoteric Judaism, the idea of reincarnation is rejected by orthodox Christianity and Islam. But must one conclude on the basis of the idea's non-universality that it is no more than a racial or temporal-cultural aberration of the Indian consciousness? The problem is that in order to reconcile the beliefs of different religions one must, first of all, learn to sift out the primary from the secondary, the common from the particular. The common, primary aspect of any belief consists of the *seed* of the idea, a seed which displays remarkable tenacity over the centuries. Sowed in the soil of different cultural milieus, it sprouts in different ways, all of which are varieties of the given belief. If there is any teleological aspect to history at all, then, of course, that aspect should first and foremost inform the life of just those tenacious spiritual seeds—in the widely embraced *core of an idea* professed by millions of individuals.

The seed of the idea of reincarnation is the teaching about a certain *self* that completes its cosmic growth, or a segment of it, through stages of successive existences in our physical world. Everything else, such as the spiritual-material nature and structure of the reincarnating self, the dependence of reincarnation on the law of karma, the application of the principle of reincarnation to the animal world—all these are merely variations of the core idea. And it is easy to see that one will encounter genuine aberrations more often in those variations and details than in the seed, on whose intuition by the Indian people the teleological forces labored for many centuries, expending fantastic amounts of energy to weaken the partition between waking consciousness and deep memory—the repository of memories of the soul's journeys up to the moment of its last reincarnation.

The error of religious doctrines lies, for the most part, not in their contents but in their claim that the law stated by the doctrine is in universal force and must be professed by everyone who desires salvation. The above leads us to acknowledge the genuine nature of the spiritual experience that was molded into the idea of reincarnation. Yes, such a formative path does exist; there is in principle nothing in the essence of the idea unacceptable to Christianity and Islam, save perhaps the fact that no utterances by their founders about the idea have reached us. (Which, in any case, proves nothing in itself, since, as is known, far from everything they said found its way into the Gospels and Quran.) But it categorically does not follow that the path of reincarnation is the single possible and real formative path for an individual spirit. The Indian people's consciousness, readied in such a manner as to intuit that type of path, expressed its discovery, as often happens in such circumstances, in absolute terms and turned a deaf ear to intuitions of other types of formative paths. The exact opposite happened with the Jewish and Arab peoples. Intuiting the truth of other formative paths, on which incarnation on the physical plane occurs only once, the consciousness of these peoples expressed this second type of path in absolute terms that were just as unwarranted. The fact that one or the other path can, generally speaking, predominate in different human metacultures also led them to do so. As a result, an apparently irreconcilable dispute has arisen between the two groups of world religions. In actual fact, both these seemingly contradictory ideas are true at their core, having pinpointed two paths of those possible, and beyond a renunciation by each side of claims to the universal exclusivity of their ideas nothing is needed to resolve the "conflict."

Thus, one of the historical bases for supposedly irreconcilable conflicts between religions consists in the unwarranted expression of a belief in absolute terms. Another basis is as follows.

One of the fundamental doctrines of Christianity is of course the teaching of the Holy Trinity. The founder of Islam rejected that doctrine, because he suspected it of being a relapse into polytheism and, more importantly, because his own spiritual experience did not contain any positive indication of such a truth. But in this twentieth century there can hardly still be a need to reiterate the arguments of Christian theologians who in their time proved and explained the fundamental distinction between the doctrine of the Trinity and polytheism. It is a point so elementary that one can only suppose there are no longer any Muslim thinkers who, having studied the Christian creed, would persist in making that erroneous claim. As for the second argument—that Muhammad's spiritual experience contained no confirmation of the Trinity—it is logically unsound. No one person's experience can contain a confirmation of all truths that were arrived at earlier in the course of humanity's collective intuitions about God and the world. There is a limit to every individual's knowledge. Only the wisdom of the Omniscient encompasses the entirety of truth "within Himself." Therefore, the fact that Muhammad did not encounter anything in his personal spiritual experience that supported the Trinity doctrine should not in itself serve as sufficient grounds for rejecting the idea, even in the eyes of orthodox Muslims. Instead of the statement, "The Prophet, in intuiting the absolute oneness of God, recognized the falsity of the Trinity doctrine," one should, in all fairness, rephrase the statement thus: "The Prophet, in intuiting the absolute oneness of God, did not receive any indication of the truth of the Holy Trinity."

It is entirely natural that the Christian creed not only has no objections to the Muslim doctrine of the One God but wholly concurs with it. But Christianity supplements that belief with an idea whose persistence for two thousand years and whose acceptance by millions of individuals point to the truth of the *core concept*. So what does the conflict between these two fundamental doctrines of the two religions boil down to? Does it not boil down to the arbitrary and unwarranted denial of one's truth by the other, a truth that has no mention in the latter's own positive experience?

Now we see the second historical and psychological basis for deep-rooted disputes between different faiths: the unwarranted denial of the truth of a differing belief solely because we do not have any positive evidence for it.

Unfortunately, disputes founded solely on that logical and epistemological inconsistency are beyond count. Let's examine another well-known instance. Both the Sunni sect of Islam and Protestantism deny the truth of the cult of the saints, yet almost all other religions embrace it and in one or another form give expression to it. Objections to the cult can be reduced to two: first, people have no need of mediators between themselves and God; second, worship and prayer offered not to God but to those who were once human is sinful, as it leads to the deification of persons. But what exactly is meant by that famous statement that "people have no need of mediators"? If the one who gives voice to that thought has no need of them, then what right does he or she have to speak for others, even for all humanity? Who invested that individual with the authority? Certainly not the millions of people in almost every country and religion who have felt a vital, daily need for such mediators—a need that has made the existence of the cult of the saints psychologically possible. If we do not feel a need for something (there are people, for example, who do not feel a need for music) and become indignant with all those who do, regarding them as fatuous dreamers, self-interested liars, or unenlightened ignoramuses, what are we proving but our own ignorance?

The second argument concerns the sin of offering up divine worship and prayers to those who were humans. But divine worship, in the monotheistic sense, is not offered up to the saints; no one equates them with God. The very idea is ludicrous and, for people raised in Christian countries, inexcusably uninformed.

True, there is in Hinduism the concept of the avatar—-an incarnation of God in human form—but avatars are not saints. We kneel before saints as people who were able to overcome the human in themselves, or as instruments of God's will, as celestial messengers.

Protestantism denies the concept of sainthood altogether. But here we are dealing with an argument over particulars rather than the essence of the matter. For, in rejecting the ideal of monastic asceticism, Luther and Calvin did not belittle earthly sanctity, though they understood it, on the one hand, in a wider sense than did Catholicism and, on the other hand, in a somewhat lower sense: the Narrow Path as such was rejected.

The dying Muhammad forbade his followers to invoke his spirit in prayer. That shows the purity and sincerity of his purposes, but it goes directly counter to the basic principles of a religious-moral worldview. For if sanctity, as the highest form of self-sacrifice for the sake of humanity, is faultless and selfless service of God—and if we understand sanctity thus then it would be silly to deny that it exists on Earth and that it occurs, however rarely, in life—if that is so, then it is impossible to imagine the soul of a saint resting in idle bliss after death. Saints will help those still living and those below them in their ascent with all the powers of their souls, including those powers that are revealed only after death. It is as natural as an adult helping a child, and just as little does it diminish or demean those to whom the help is proffered. The Prophet Muhammad could hardly have been unaware of this. One can only suppose that certain abuses and excesses that he observed in the cult of the saints moved him to forbid his followers to establish anything of the sort. He may have thought that the prohibition would be balanced by the fact that deceased saints do not necessarily need reminders from people at prayer in order to extend them unseen help.

Every teaching that preaches the truth of the soul's immortality and of a higher moral law can suppose that the spirit of a saint will in the afterlife become indifferent and unresponsive to those still living only by going counter to all logic and its own principles. The denial of the truth of the cult of the saints makes sense only from the point of view of materialism. On the other hand, to express the cult of the saints in absolute terms as obligatory is unwarranted. There can be protracted legs in the journey of a soul, or in the journey of an entire people, when there is no need of "mediators," when a soul, consciously or unconsciously, feels that the growth of its independence, energy, freedom, and spiritual will precludes any need to appeal to anyone for help other than God Himself. On what basis and by what right will we force such an individual to take part in the cult of the saints?

A much greater difficulty is posed by the fundamental dispute between Christianity and other religions concerning the belief in the divinity of Jesus Christ and the worship of Him as the incarnation of one of the hypostases of the Trinity. It is well known that the other religions either recognize Jesus as a prophet among other prophets or ignore Him, sometimes even going so far as to positively deny His Providential mission. Christianity, for its part, citing the words of its Founder that no one can come to the Father except through the Son, denies all non-Christians the possibility of salvation.

It is possible, however, to avoid many misunderstandings and vulgarizations of ideas if we examine each utterance of Christ that has reached us, asking ourselves, Did Christ, in the present instance, speak as a person, as a concrete historical figure who lived in a particular country at a particular time, or does the voice of God that He hears in Himself become transformed through His mind and lips into human words? Every one of Christ's utterances requires examination in just such a vein. Does He speak in the present case as a person or as a Herald of truth from the spiritual world? For it is impossible to imagine that at every moment of his life Jesus spoke only as a Herald and never as a simple human being. There can hardly be any question that in His anguished cry on the cross, "My God, My God, why hast Thou forsaken me?" the pain of one of those minutes is recorded when he, Jesus the man, experienced the tragedy of separation, the tragedy of the cutting of the link between his human self and the Divine Spirit. On the other hand, in His teachings given at the Last Supper one hears clearly God the Son, the Planetary Logos behind the first-person-singular pronoun.

All Christ's words recorded in the Gospels should be grouped into one of these two categories. It then becomes perfectly clear that His saying that no one can come to the Father except through the Son should not be understood in the lower, narrow, literal, and merciless sense that no human souls besides Christians are saved. Rather, this must be heard in the majestic, truly spiritual, cosmic sense that every monad that reaches full spiritual maturity immerses itself in the depths of God the Son, the Heart and Demiurge of the Universe, and only after that crowning act returns to its source, to God the Father, and in a manner unfathomable for us merges with Him and the entire Holy Trinity.

Keshab Chandra Sen, one of the most prominent leaders of Brahmo Samaj, an Indian religious-philosophical society, voiced a profound insight when he said that the wisdom of the Hindus, the meekness of the Buddhists, the courage of the Muslims all come from Christ. In referring to Christ, Sen clearly meant not the historical figure Jesus, but the Logos, Who found expression chiefly, but not exclusively, in Jesus Christ. That idea, in my opinion, provides the intimations of a path to an outlook whereby Christians and many Eastern religious movements can arrive at mutual understanding.

Certain expressions that have become rooted in Christian theology, that are repeated almost automatically by us, and that are exactly what is unacceptable to other faiths also require reexamination and clarification. What is meant, for example, by the word *embodiment* in reference to Jesus Christ? Do we continue to think even now that the Universal Logos was contained within the form of a human body? Can we grant that a bodily instrument, an individual physical organism, a human brain capable of accommodating the Universal Reason was created after generations of teleological preparation? If so, then one must conclude that Jesus was omniscient in His human lifetime, which does not concur either with facts from the Gospels or with His own words. Do we not consider the disproportionate scale—the mixture of cosmic categories, in the very extreme sense of the word, with categories belonging to the local-planetary, the narrowly human—preposterous? And preposterous not because it *surpasses* the limits of our reason but, to the contrary, because it is all too obviously the product of thinking at a definite, long-past period of culture, when the universe appeared a billion times smaller than it is in reality, when it seemed quite possible for the solid firmament to fall upon the Earth, and for a dreadful hail of stars to come loose from the hooks on which they were hung. Would it not then be more precise to speak not of the embodiment of the Logos in the person of Jesus Christ but of the Logos's expression in Jesus through the medium of the great God-born monad that is the Planetary Logos of the Earth? We call Christ the *Word*. But a speaker does not after all take shape in a word but *expresses* himself or herself through it. Similarly, God is expressed, not embodied, in Christ. It is in that sense that Christ is in truth the Word of God, and thus yet another stumbling block to reconciling Christianity and certain other religious movements disappears.

I have touched on only four interreligious disputes. With the exception of the last one, which springs from a moot and insufficiently precise formulation, these disputes are founded on discrepancies in the spiritual experiences of the great prophets, on the fact that while viewing certain objects from different vantage points in Shadanakar, from different spiritual points of view, these visionaries see different aspects of the given objects. Such disputes can be provisionally labeled *horizontal* conflicts, meaning by that the validity of the points of view and their illusory contraposition.

Yet another example. Throughout their existence, Christianity and Islam have been battling with what they call paganism. Over the centuries the idea that monotheism and polytheism are irreconcilable and incompatible has become impressed on humanity as a kind of axiom. Discussion of why and how that came to be would lead us to digress too far. What is important is the question, On what basis did the religions of Semitic origin, while affirming the existence of spiritual hierarchies and devising a detailed description of them—both an angelogy and demonology—in the Middle Ages, restrict their number to those few that found a place in medieval schemata? Is there even a shadow of consistency in their denial in principle of truth to all other experience of spiritual hierarchies? There are absolutely no grounds for it, except references once again to the Gospels' and the Quran's silence on the subject. It was because there were insufficient grounds for a blanket denial that the Christian Church, in the first few centuries of its existence, did not so much deny the existence of the gods of the Olympic pantheon as identify them with the demons and devils of Semitic canonical texts. In doing so, the Church, contrary to the facts, ignored the character of the divinities as it was intuited by the polytheistic spiritual tradition, arbitrarily ascribing to them demeaning and shameful traits or deliberately overemphasizing the all too anthropomorphic element the subjects of knowledge—polytheistic humanity—had introduced into the images, an element which by that time had been preserved only in its lower, popular aspects. As if acknowledgment of the existence of hierarchies of nature, of great elementals, or of national guiding spirits could undermine the oneness of God—the Creator and Builder of the Universe, the source and estuary of the earthly flow of life— more than would acknowledgment of God's other beautiful children—angels and archangels, not to mention those demons of the Bible!

Unfortunately, even today that ancient misunderstanding has not been cleared up. For a long time now, nothing has remained of classical polytheism. But a hardened, narrow-minded intolerance lacking all wisdom is discernible every time the Christian churches—or at least those persons who speak in their names— have occasion to pass judgment on the Hindu, Chinese, Japanese, or Tibetan systems. The two other religions of Semitic origin are just as intolerant. What we are dealing with here is a typical example of horizontal differentiation between religions. Without contradicting each other in the essentials, without clashing with each other in the boundless spiritual cosmos, Christianity and Hinduism, Buddhism and Islam, Judaism and Shinto speak of different things, of different spiritual lands, of different parts of Shadanakar. But human ignorance interprets this as a contradiction and pronounces one of the teachings true and the rest false: "If there is one God, then other gods are nothing but shams. They are either devils or figments of the human imagination." How naive! God is One, but there are many gods. The writing of that word with both a capital and small *g* testifies in clear terms to the differing connotations attached to it in both cases. If someone is frightened of repeating the word in different senses, let that person substitute some other for it when speaking of polytheism—"great spirits" or "great hierarchies"—but nothing will be changed. That is, nothing will be changed if we discount the possibility that the use of the word "spirit" could in certain cases lead to misunderstandings, as many of those gods are more than spirits—they are powerful beings possessing material form, though they do so on other, transphysical planes of being.

All these disputes arising from misunderstandings between religions bring to mind an analogy I once saw in a religious text, though I do not remember which one. It told of several hikers who each climbed different slopes of one and the same mountain, saw and studied its different faces, and upon their return argued about who among them saw what really existed and who saw nothing but figments of the imagination. Each believed that the mountain was exactly as he or she had seen it, and that the testimonies of the other hikers about the other slopes were lies, absurdities, and traps to snare human souls. Thus, the first conclusion that follows from our examination of interreligious disputes reveals a path to eliminating those that arise either from a simple misunderstanding or from a discrepancy between the religious objects of knowledge experienced—that is, horizontal conflicts.

Not only polytheism but animism and proto-animism, too, consist of more than vague, random, subjective images that arose in the minds of prehistoric humans. Transphysical reality lies behind them as well. Providence is Providence for just the reason that it has never left peoples and races to be the dupes of fantasies and illusions without any possibility of contact with a higher reality. One would have to posit in place of God a dark, evil power as the true shepherd of humanity if one were to think that prehistoric humanity was barred for tens of thousands of years from the possibility of experiencing anything spiritual, or at the very least variomaterial, of coming into contact with something besides the physical world and our own fantasies.

But if this is so, how can the spiritual experience of so-called savages enrich us, who stand on such a high level of spiritual knowledge compared to them? By that which was intuited back then, in that milieu, by that inimitable psyche, but was not passed on and not included by succeeding spiritual traditions in their treasury. Research specifically devoted to theurgic beliefs and the tradition of protological thought could help not only to "rehabilitate" those ancient beliefs in their essential features but could also establish a place for them in the synthesized religious worldview that is now beginning to take shape. It would come to light, for example, that the belief of the Arunta tribe of Australia in a single living substance that flows between matter constantly and everywhere, from being to being, from object to object (and in essence the religion of that tribe consists entirely of such beliefs) is one of humanity's oldest revelations about the trans-physical cosmos. It is a vivid, brilliant revelation, more definitive than any later ones about that single life force. The Australians called it *arungvilta*, the more highly developed religion of Hin-duism calls it *prana*, and we have yet to hear what science will call it in twenty or thirty years from now.

That dispute—the belief in arungvilta-prana[1] by the oldest faiths and the denial of it by the overwhelming majority of later religious teachings—can be viewed as a *developmental* dispute, a vertical conflict between different levels of religious knowledge. But here we also encounter the same error, the same faulty approach to another tradition that we saw when we examined the question of Islam's denial of the cult of the saints and the concept of the Trinity. Here, too, behind all the arguments

---

1. Incidentally, if the Gospels do not speak of arungvilta-prana in so many words, they do recount in detail many cases when Christ and, later, the apostles put the substance to use. It is incomprehensible how orthodox Christian believers could account for the variomaterial mechanism that the performers of miraculous cures employed if they deny the existence of a life force flowing everywhere and through everything.

brought against those ancient revelations, lurks the same naive way of thinking: The canonical texts that are authoritative for me say nothing about arungvilta-prana. There is, therefore, no such thing. That way of thinking is, at the very least, foolhardy, because one is then forced to deny the existence not only of arungvilta-prana but of radio waves, elementary particles, a host of chemical elements, other galaxies, and even, for example, the planet Uranus, for the canonical texts maintain strict silence concerning all of them.

It also becomes clear that it is absolutely necessary to take into consideration what was disregarded back during the formation of the older, classical faiths: the experience of prehistoric spiritual revelation. In addition, we must consider something that could not be taken into account previously: the experience derived from the centuries-long evolution of religions on every continent, from world history, and from science. The material taken from those various experiences teaches us to treat all doctrines and beliefs dynamically, to see every belief as a link in the chain of religious-historical evolution, and to separate them into three layers. The deepest layer is the *core idea*, which contains the relative component truth. The next layer is the particular coloring, molding, or specification of the idea to the extent that its individual, racial, or temporal features are *justified*, since it was that and only that racial or temporal cast of mind that enabled the people to intuit the idea at all. The third and outermost layer is the husk, the aberrations, the unavoidable haze of the human mind through which the light of revelation passes. Therefore, experience from every stage of development, including polytheism, animism, and others, must be freed from its outermost layer, rethought, and included in the teachings of the *sum religion*.

The principles on which such work would be carried out have barely been outlined here. The set of criteria requires a great deal of work. Besides, such a reexamination of our religious legacy is a colossal undertaking requiring the combined labor of many, many people. At present, there are not enough people even qualified for the task, not to mention the absence of other necessary conditions. But if the task is huge, then it is better to undertake the preliminary work sooner rather than later. The difficulties should not be underestimated, but there is every reason to hope that with the commitment, energy, and initiative of those involved, the gulfs and rifts that now separate all religions will gradually be filled in and that, though each religion will preserve its uniqueness, a kind of spiritual amalgamation will in time unite all right-hand teachings.

It is well known that many Japanese who profess Christianity remain at the same time faithful to Shinto. An orthodox Catholic or Protestant, and a Russian Orthodox, too, are appalled by such a thing. They cannot comprehend how it is psychologically possible, and they even sense something blasphemous in it. But, far from any blasphemy, such a thing is possible and even natural, because the Christian tradition and the Shinto tradition differ from each other horizontally: they speak of different things. Shinto is a national myth. It is an aspect of the world religious revelation that was unveiled to the Japanese people, and to them alone. It is a conceptualization of the spiritual or, better yet, transphysical reality that presides over the Japanese people and them alone, manifesting itself in their history and culture. One will not find in Shinto answers to questions of a cosmic, planetary, or international nature—questions about the Creator, the origin of evil and suffering, or paths of cosmic growth. It deals only with Japan's metahistory, its metaculture, the hierarchies guiding it, and with the heavenly assembly of enlightened souls that have risen from Japan to the higher worlds of Shadanakar. The syncretism of the Japanese—that is, their simultaneous profession of Shinto and Catholicism or Shinto and Buddhism—is not a psychological contradiction. To the contrary, it is an intimation of how the traditions and truths of various religions will harmoniously complement each other.

Before the amalgamation of Christianity and other right-hand religions and faiths is realized—and that is one of the Rose of the World's historical tasks—it would of course be natural to bring about the reunification of the Christian churches. The Rose of the World will carry out the theological, philosophical, cultural, and organizational preparation for such a reunification with untiring commitment. Until the reunification of Christianity has taken place, until the Eighth Ecumenical Council (or several subsequent councils) has reexamined the entire mass of old doctrines and has adopted a number of beliefs based on the spiritual experience of the last one thousand years, until the highest authority of a reunified Christianity has sanctioned the Rose of the World's teachings—until that time those beliefs can be, of course, professed, propounded, and preached, but they should not be molded into a fixed, final form to be offered up for profession to all Christians.

The Rose of the World sees its surreligiosity and interreligiosity in the reunification of Christian faiths and in the further amalgamation of all religions of Light in order to focus their combined energies on fostering humanity's spiritual growth and on spiritualizing nature. Religious exclusivity will not only be foreign to its followers, it will be impossible. Co-belief with all peoples in their highest ideals—that is what its wisdom will teach.

The structure of the Rose of the World will therefore suggest a series of concentric circles. No followers of any right-hand religion should be considered outside the global church. Those who have not yet reached an awareness of surreligious unity will occupy the outer circles; the middle circles will be composed of the less active and creative of the Rose of the World's followers; the inner circles will be for those who have equated the meaning of their life with conscious and free divine creative work.

May a Christian enter a Buddhist temple with reverence and respect. Eastern peoples, separated from the centers of Christianity by deserts and mountain ranges, have over thousands of years intuited through the wisdom of their teachers the truth about different regions of the heavens. Glimmering through the smoke of incense are statues of the high guardians of other worlds and the great messengers who spoke to people of those worlds. Few Western people have had contact with those worlds. May the knowledge preserved in the East enrich their minds and souls.

May a Muslim enter a Hindu temple with a peaceful, pure, and solemn feeling. Those are not false gods that gaze on them there, but provisional images of great spirits perceived and passionately loved by the peoples of India. Other nations should accept testimony about them with joy and trust.

May an orthodox follower of Shinto not pass by the nondescript building of a synagogue with disdain or indifference. There, another great people that has enriched humanity with profound treasures preserves their knowledge of those truths through which the spiritual world revealed itself to them and no one else.

One can compare the Rose of the World to an upturned flower, the roots of which are in heaven and the petals here, among humanity, on Earth. Its stem is revelation, through which flow the spiritual juices that feed and strengthen its petals, our fragrant chorus of religions. Besides the petals, it has a heart: its own teachings. Its teaching is not a random blend of the highest beliefs of various theosophies of the past. In addition to a new perspective on our religious legacy, the Rose of the World will establish a new perspective on nature, history, the destiny of human cultures and their tasks, on creative work, love, the paths of cosmic ascent, and the gradual enlightenment of Shadanakar. In some cases the perspective will be new because, although various figures of the past have spoken of them before, they will be adopted and professed by a *religion*, by a *church*, for the first time. In other cases, a perspective of the Rose of the World will be new in the full sense of the word, because no one has ever voiced it before. These new perspectives flow from new spiritual experience, without which, instead of the Rose of the World, only a rational and sterile religious eclecticism would be possible.

But before moving on to the contents of that spiritual experience, to the principles of that teaching, we must first investigate by what paths of the soul that experience is acquired and by what methods we can facilitate or accelerate our acquisition of it.

BOOK II

On the Metahistorical and Transphysical Methods of Knowledge

1 Some Features of the Metahistorical Method

THE PHRASE *religious feeling* is a commonly used but misleading expression. There is no general religious feeling but, rather, a vast world of religious feelings and experiences, endless in their variety, which often contrast with one another, differing in emotion, focus, intensity, tone, and what we might call their tint. Those who have not had any personal religious experience and make inferences about it on the sole basis of others' testimony do not have the slightest idea of the breadth and variety of that world. Such third-party testimony, in conjunction with the absence of personal experience on the part of the listener, is almost always greeted with disbelief, preconceptions, and the tendency to interpret it in accordance not with the claims of the testifiers themselves but with the dogmatic tenets of areligious schools of thought.

The variety of religious feelings is matched by the variety of methods of religious knowledge. To set forth these methods would necessitate writing an exhaustive research work on the history and psychology of religion. Such a task in no way enters into the aim of this book. But one aim of this book is to help the reader arrive at an understanding of *those particular* methods of religious knowledge that seem to me to have the greatest creative potential at the current stage of history.

It would be most unfortunate if anyone suspected me of laying claim to the role of founder of a great historical, cultural, and social enterprise—that is, the creation of what we are calling the *Rose of the World*. The reality of the situation is altogether different. The Rose of the World can and will arise only as the result of the combined efforts of an enormous number of people. I am convinced that an identical process is taking place not only in Russia but also in many other parts of the globe, the foremost of which appear to be India and North America. The grandiose reality of other worlds is bursting into the human consciousness: at first the consciousness of isolated individuals, then of hundreds of people, and later of millions. Yes, now, at this very minute, people who as yet know nothing of each other, who are sometimes separated by great distances and national borders, and sometimes merely by the walls of a few houses, are experiencing startling breaches in their consciousness and are gazing on transphysical heights and depths. And some are endeavoring—in accord with their own abilities and inner cast—to express or depict their experience, if only approximately, in works of literature, art, or music. I do not know how many, but clearly already more than a few people are standing under that shower of revelation. As for my aim, it is to set forth that revelation exactly as I have been experiencing it—no more.

Therefore, this chapter will not deal with the scientific mode of thought and inquiry, or even with the artistic, but with things whose understanding requires a definite rethinking of the ideas that have reigned supreme in Russia for the past forty years.

I believe that serious investigation by researchers at the forefront of contemporary physiology and psychology into the large mass of apocalyptic literature, the autobiographical testimony of ecclesiastical authors and religious figures who underwent like experiences, and the unbiased study of material scattered throughout works on comparative religion will in time lead to the development of a scientific method on the basis of which it will be possible to lay the foundation for an epistemology of religious and, in particular, metahistorical knowledge. It is realistic to expect the emergence of an educational system geared toward mastering the mechanics of that knowledge, providing individuals, who will have theretofore played a passive role in that process, with techniques to initiate and control it, if only occasionally. But that all belongs to the future, and not the near future at that. The only thing certain for now is that the process varies in relation to both the subject and the object of knowledge.

It is impossible to encompass the compassless. I can speak here only of those varieties of the process with which my own life has brought me into contact. Although I would prefer to avoid it, I must, therefore, introduce to this book a greater autobiographical element. In doing so I will focus on three types of religious knowledge: metahistorical, transphysical, and ecumenical. However, it will be impossible, as well as unnecessary, to draw a clear boundary between them.

First of all, what exactly is meant here by metahistory? According to Sergei Bulgakov, perhaps the only Russian thinker to address the question openly, metahistory is "the noumenal side of that universal process, one aspect of which reveals itself to us as history."[1] However, I think that the application of Kantian terminology to questions of this type can hardly help to clarify the essence of the matter. The concepts of the noumenon and phenomenon were formulated by a different train of thought and engendered by different philosophical needs. Objects of metahistorical experience can be fit into the system of that terminology only through recourse to procrustean methods.

It would be just as ill-advised to equate metahistory with some variety of the philosophy of history. The philosophy of history is just that—philosophy—while metahistory is always concerned with myth.

In any case, in this book the term *metahistory* is used in two senses. First, it is the sum of processes—as yet outside the field of vision, interest, and methodology of science—that take place on planes of variobeing existing in other time streams and other dimensions and are sometimes discernible through the process we perceive as history. Those otherworldly processes are bound in the closest fashion to the historical process, and to a significant degree they determine it. But by no means are they identical with it. They are most fully revealed by means of that same method of knowledge that is called metahistorical.

---

1. S. Bulgakov, *Two Cities*, Moscow, 1911, p. 103.

The second meaning of the word *metahistory* refers to the teaching about those variobeing processes, a teaching, obviously, in the religious, not scientific, sense of the word.

It should come as no surprise that the ability to apprehend these processes varies from individual to individual in accordance with a number of psychological and perhaps even physiological factors. We are clearly dealing here with a kind of inborn predisposition; we have as little chance of summoning or destroying it as, for example, we do an inborn gift for music. Such a gift, however, can in the course of one's life be stifled or simply left unused like the talent buried in the ground. Or it can be fostered, sometimes in an extremely accelerated fashion. The educational system possible in the future would promote the development of that ability.

As it is now, we have little choice but to grope almost blindly for some means to influence that ability in a conscious fashion, and there would still probably be no noticeable progress toward that end in the whole course of one's lifetime if not for certain forces that, acting in concert with our efforts, take upon themselves the tremendous task of cultivating within us the corresponding organs of perception. Nevertheless, it appears quite probable that something else besides inborn traits and the active cooperation of Providential powers, something we ourselves must acquire—for example, a modest yet definite store of positive historical data—is necessary for the process of metahistorical knowledge to take place. The metahistorical method is closed to any person totally unaware of and having no opportunity to recognize his or her link with history, whether that person lives in the Australian desert or within the labyrinths of modern-day megalopolises. The role of science in the psychological process under examination (or to be more exact, in the preparation for the process) is for now limited to participation in the accumulation of that same store of historical data. The process itself, or at least that variation of it with which I am familiar, has no relation whatsoever to scientific forms of knowledge. I wish to repeat and emphasize that.

The process consists of three consecutive stages.

The first stage is a sudden inner experience that occurs involuntarily and, it would seem, without any preparation, although,
of course, in reality such preparation must have already taken
place beyond the limits of our consciousness. The experience
consists of revelations—lightning-quick yet encompassing enormous stretches of historical time—of the essence of great historical phenomena. This essence cannot be divided into categories or
expressed in words. The experience may take a *minute* or an *hour*,
and it overflows with dynamically bubbling images. The individual feels like a person long confined to a quiet, dark room who is
suddenly thrust outside at the peak of a storm—a storm terrifying
in its power and immensity, almost blinding, and at the same time
brimming with a feeling of breathless euphoria. Before such an
experience, an individual will have had no idea of the fullness of
life, of even the possibility of such fullness. Entire eras—in a manner of speaking, an entire metahistorical cosmos of those eras
with great powers battling within it—are simultaneously captured and synthesized. It would be a mistake to assume that these
images must always take visual form. A visual element and, perhaps, an aural element, as well, are a part of them. But the images
are to those elements what, for example, an ocean is to the hydrogen of which its water is composed. Because of the lack of close
analogies with anything more familiar, it is extremely difficult to
convey to the reader an idea of the experience.

The experience has a tremendous effect on one's whole inner
being. Its revelations so far surpass everything else that previously entered the range of the individual's consciousness that
they will nourish the inner world of the person who underwent
the experience for many years to come. They will become his or
her inner treasures.

This first stage of metahistorical knowledge might be called
metahistorical enlightenment. Such a designation, however,
should not be seen as an attempt to attach a positive connotation
to the said psychological phenomenon. I will speak more on that
a little later.

The yield of the enlightenment is stored in the depths of one's
mind, not as memories but as something vital and alive. From

there, individual images, ideas, and entire systems gradually, over many years, float up into the range of one's consciousness. But far more remain deep down, and the individual understands that no mental framework will ever be able to encompass and exhaust the cosmos of metahistory that has come ajar for him or her. It is these images and ideas that become the focus of the second stage of the process.

The second stage does not have the same momentary character as the first. It is a sort of chain of inner states—a chain running through weeks and months, its links appearing almost daily. It is inner contemplation, intense familiarization, rapt examination — sometimes joyful, sometimes painful—of historical images, which are perceived not in isolation but in the context of the second metahistorical reality that lies behind them. I am using the word *examination* here provisionally, while by the word *images* I again mean not merely visual perceptions, but synthesized perceptions that possess a visual element only in so far as what is being examined can have a visually perceptible form at all. In connection with this, it is extremely important to note that the objects of such contemplation consist of a significant number of phenomena from variodimensional planes of materiality. Clearly, these cannot be perceived with the physical organs of sight and hearing; they are perceived with other organs, which are part of our being but are usually separated from our waking consciousness by a thick wall. If the first stage of the process was characterized by the passive role of the individual, who became, as it were, the inadvertent witness to an astonishing spectacle, at the second stage it is to a certain extent possible to consciously manipulate the process. For example, one might choose one or another object for contemplation. But more often, and as it so happens, during the most rewarding hours, the images surface involuntarily, radiating, I would say, such mesmerizing power and revealing such multileveled meaning that the hours of contemplation turn into watered-down versions of the minutes of enlightenment. In the case of a subject with a creative bent, the images can become the source, lever, or axis of artistic works. And no matter how dark or bleak some of them might be, the power of the images is such that it would be difficult to find something equal to the pleasure afforded by their contemplation.

It seems to me that the second stage of the process might be called just that: metahistorical contemplation.

The composite arrived at in that manner is similar to a painting on which certain individual figures and perhaps the overall motif may be well-defined, but other figures are blurred, and there are gaps between them, while other sections of the background or individual details are missing altogether. The need then arises to explain the unclear links, to fill in the remaining blanks. The process enters its third stage, the one most independent of the influence of suprapersonal and suprarational powers. For that very reason, the most errors, unwarranted additions, and overly subjective interpretations will then occur. The main trouble is the inevitable distortion by reason. Its effects are almost impossible to escape entirely. But it is sometimes possible to discern the inner logic of metahistory and redirect even the work of the reason along its lines.

It would be natural to call that third stage metahistorical formulation.

Thus, metahistorical enlightenment, metahistorical contemplation, and metahistorical formulation are the three stages on the path to knowledge under question here.

I will mention yet another kind of possible state, one variety experienced during the first stage. It is a special kind of enlightenment associated with revelations of the demonic in metahistory. (Some demons have great power and a wide sphere of activity.) That state, which could accurately be called an "infraphysical breach of psyche," is extremely painful and is for the most part fraught with a feeling of singular horror. But, as in the other cases, it too is followed by stages of contemplation and formulation.

The books that I have written in a purely literary style are based on the metahistorical knowledge revealed personally to me. The worldview that forms the skeleton of this book has been derived in its entirety from those revelations. Where did I come up with its images? Who instilled these ideas in me, and how? What right do I have to speak with such confidence? Can I provide some kind of proof of the authenticity of my experiences? Now I will attempt to answer these questions as best I can. Going into autobiographical detail holds no attraction for me, so I will try to keep such details to a minimum. But that minimum will include, of course, a brief account of where, when, and under what circumstances I experienced my hours of metahistorical enlightenment.

The first experience of that kind—an experience that played a colossal and, in many respects, even decisive role in the growth of my inner world—took place in August of 1921, before I was fifteen years old. It happened in Moscow, as the day waned, when I, who by that time had come to very much love wandering aimlessly around the city daydreaming, stopped by a wall along one of the gardens that encircled the Church of Christ the Saviour and overlooked the river embankment. Muscovite old-timers will still recall what a wonderful view it gave onto the river, the Kremlin, and Zamoskvorechye, with its dozens of bell towers and colorful domes. It must have been already past six, for the church bells were ringing for vespers. The experience revealed before me, or, rather, above me, a raging, blinding, incomprehensible world that melded the historical reality of Russia into a strange oneness with something immeasurably larger above it.

For many years afterward, my inner self was nourished on the images and ideas that gradually floated within the range of my consciousness. My reason could long make no sense of them, attempting to create newer and newer constructs that were supposed to reconcile the contradictory nature of the ideas and interpret the images. The process entered the formulation stage too quickly, almost bypassing the intermediate stage of contemplation. The constructs turned out to be flawed, my reason proved unequal to the ideas bombarding it, and more than three decades of supplementary and illustrative revelation were needed for me to arrive at a correct understanding and explanation of the depths of what had been revealed to me in my youth.

I had a second experience of that nature in the spring of 1928, in the Church of Our Lady of Levshin, where I first stayed for the early liturgy after the Easter matins. That service, which begins at about two o'clock in the morning, is notable for the annual reading of the first chapter of the Gospel of John: "In the beginning was the Word." The Gospel is recited line by line in different languages—both living and dead—by all the serving priests and deacons in turn, who stand in different parts of the church. That early liturgy is one of the pinnacles of Russian Orthodoxy, of Christianity as a whole, and of religious services on Earth as a whole. If the matins that precede it can be compared to the sunrise, then the early liturgy is verily a spiritual midday, full of light and joy. The inner experience I am describing was altogether different from the first, both in tone and content. It was much broader, linked, as it were, with the entire panorama of humanity and with the apprehension of Global History as a single mystical stream. Through the exultant movements and sounds of the service being performed in front of me, I was able to perceive that higher region, that heavenly land in which our entire planet appears as the Great Church and where an eternal liturgy is celebrated without cease by enlightened humankind in splendor beyond our imagination.

In February of 1932, during my brief employment at a Moscow factory, I fell ill, and one night, while feverish, I was the recipient of a revelation that the majority of people will of course consider nothing more than delirium. But for me it was horrifying in content and unquestionably authentic. As in my previous books, I will use the expression "the Third Witzraor" to refer to the creature that the revelation concerned. I did not think up that strange, foreign-sounding name by myself. It came to me at the time. Simplified, I would define that gigantic creature, which somewhat resembles the monsters of ocean depths, yet far surpasses them in size, as a demon of state power. That night was to remain for a long time afterward one of the most painful experiences I have ever known. I think the term infraphysical breach of psyche would be quite applicable to that experience.

In November of 1933 I chanced to stop by a small church on Vlasevsky Lane. There, an acathistus to St. Serafim of Sarov was in progress. Hardly had I opened the door when a warm wave of choral music descended on me and surged straight to my heart. I was overcome by a state that is very difficult for me to write about, let alone describe without tears. Although I had previously disdained to engage in genuflection—my emotional immaturity having led me to suspect something servile in the custom—an irresistible impulse caused me to kneel. But even that was not enough. And when I prostrated myself on the rug, which was faded and worn by thousands of feet, some secret door in my soul swung open, and tears of blissful rapture, comparable to nothing else I had ever known, gushed forth uncontrollably. In truth, I do not really care how experts of various kinds of ecstasies label what then followed, and into what categories they place it. During those minutes I was raised to Heavenly Russia and presented before its Synclite of the enlightened. I felt the unearthly warmth of spiritual rays pouring from the center of the land, which is accurately and fittingly called the Heavenly Kremlin. The great spirit who had at one time lived on Earth in the person of Serafim of Sarov, and who is now one of the brightest lights on the Russian Synclite, approached and bent down to me, wrapping me, as if with a vestment, in streaming rays of light and gentle warmth. For almost a whole year, until the church was closed down, I went every Monday to the acathistus of St. Serafim and, incredibly, experienced that same state every time, again and again, with undiminished strength.

In early 1943 I took part in the crossing of the ice of Lake Ladoga by the 196th Rifle Division and, after a two-day journey across the Karelia Isthmus, entered besieged Leningrad late at night. During our march through the dark, deserted city to our station, I experienced a state whose content was reminiscent of the experience in my youth by the Church of the Saviour, but it was colored far differently. It was bleak and dark in tone. It burst through the distinctive nocturnal wartime setting, at first showing through it and then swallowing it up. Within it two irreconcilable camps—one of Darkness and one of Light—confronted each other. Their staggering size, and the great demonic being that glared at the rear of one of the camps, made me tremble with fear. I saw the Third Witzraor clearer than ever before, and only the first glimmers from its approaching enemy—our hope, our joy, our protector, the great national guiding spirit of our homeland—saved me from a complete mental breakdown.[2]

Lastly, something similar, but completely devoid of metahistorical terror, happened to me one night in September of 1949 in a small prison cell in Vladimir, while my lone cellmate was sleeping. The experience reoccurred several times between 1950 and 1953, again at night, and in a communal cell. The experience I had acquired on the previously described path of knowledge was insufficient to write *The Rose of the World*. But movement along that path brought me to the point where I was able from time to time to interact consciously with certain members of the Providential forces, and the hours of those spiritual meetings became a source of more precise metahistorical knowledge than the path I have just described.

The ether body's departure from its physical vessel and its travel through other planes of the planetary cosmos occurs comparatively often to many people during deep sleep. But on waking the traveler does not have any clear recollections of what was seen. These recollections are stored only in deep memory, which is sealed off tightly from the consciousness of the overwhelming majority of people. Deep memory (the anatomical center of which is located in the brain) is the repository of memories of the soul's prior existences and of transphysical journeys similar to the above. The psychological climate of certain cultures, such as those of India and the Buddhist countries, and the centuries-long religious-physiological study they have conducted have enabled them to weaken the barrier between deep memory and waking consciousness. If one puts aside easy skepticism, it is impossible to ignore the fact that in these same countries one can often hear

---

2. I tried to depict that experience in my poem "Leningrad Apocalypse," but the dictates of art forced me to unwind, as it were, the individual threads from the fabric of the experience. The opposing images that appeared simultaneously could only be portrayed in temporal succession, and a number of elements that, though they did not go counter to the essence of the experience, were in fact absent from it, were added to the general tableau. The bombing of the Engineer's Castle (at which I was not present) as well as the wounding of the protagonist of the poem can be numbered among those arbitrary additions.

claims, even from very simple folk, that knowledge of their prior lives is not completely closed to their waking consciousness. For Europeans—raised first on a Christianity that circumvented the issue, and then on secular science—there was nothing to weaken the barrier between deep memory and waking consciousness except the individual efforts of rare people.

I must say straight out that I personally have not made even these efforts, for the simple reason that I did not know where to begin and I had no teachers to consult. But for me there was something else instead, something that I no doubt owe to the efforts of unseen executors of Providential will: a small opening, a narrow crack, as it were, in the door between my deep memory and consciousness. No matter how unconvincing this may sound to the vast majority of people, I do not intend to hide the fact that weak, disjointed, yet indisputably genuine flashes from my deep memory began to inform my life from my childhood years, became more frequent in early adulthood, and finally, at the age of forty-seven, began to illumine the days of my existence with a new light. That does not mean that my organ of deep memory became completely unblocked—I am still a long way from that— but the meaning contained in the images that surfaced from it became so tangibly clear, and the images themselves sometimes so lucid, that their qualitative, fundamental distinction from ordinary memories and the work of the imagination is, for me, beyond question.

How can I not feel gratitude toward destiny, which consigned me for a whole decade to conditions that are cursed by almost all who experience them? Those conditions were hard for me, too, but they at the same time served as a powerful lever to budge open the spiritual organs of my being. It was in prison, in my isolation from the outside world, with my unlimited free time, my fifteen hundred nights spent lying awake in bed among sleeping cellmates—it was in prison that a new stage in metahistorical and transphysical knowledge began for me. The hours of metahistorical enlightenment became more frequent. Long rows of nights were transformed into sessions of uninterrupted contemplation and formulation. Deep memory began to transmit clearer and clearer images to my consciousness, illuminating with a new meaning both the events of my own life and those of history. Waking up in the morning after a short but deep sleep, I knew that my sleep had been full not of dreams but of something else, of transphysical journeys.

If one embarks on such travels through the demonic planes without a guide, while under the influence of the dark desires of one's soul or in answer to the treacherous call of the demonic, then, upon waking, one has no clear recollection of anything, bringing back from the journey only an alluring, seductive, sickeningly sweet sensation. Actions that will, in the afterlife, long bind the soul to those worlds may later sprout, as from a poisonous seed, from that sensation. There were occasions in my youth when I strayed onto those planes, and the journeys gave rise to such actions. I deserve no credit for the fact that the winding path of my life on Earth subsequently led me further and further away from those plunges into the abyss.

If the descent is undertaken with a guide—with one of the members of the national Synclite or the World Synclite—if it has a Providential purpose and function, then travelers, waking and experiencing sometimes the same sickeningly sweet, alluring sensation, are at the same time *aware of their temptation*. Moreover, they are able to find in their memories a counterweight to the temptation: the comprehension of the terrible meaning of those worlds and of the genuine face behind their mask. They do not try to return to those lower planes by means of *moral transgressions during their waking existence*. Instead, they turn the experience into an object of religious, philosophical, and mystical formulation, or even into material for their artistic works, which, along with other meanings, necessarily fulfill a cautionary function.

At forty-seven years of age I recalled and grasped the meaning of some of the transphysical journeys I had completed earlier. Until then my memories of them had been mostly vague, patchy, jumbled, and incoherent half-images. As for the more recent journeys, they frequently left a clear and authentic trace in my memory, exciting my whole being with the feeling of secrets revealed, as no dream, even the most vivid, can leave.

There is an even more advanced mode of travel through the planetary cosmos, involving the same departure of the ether body, the same journeys with a great guide through planes of ascent or descent, but with full maintenance of waking consciousness. Upon their return, such travelers bring back memories even more indisputable and, so to speak, exhaustive. This is possible only in those cases when the spiritual organs of the senses are already completely unblocked and the locks on deep memory are broken for good. This is true clairvoyance. I, of course, have not experienced such a thing.

As far as I know—and I may be mistaken—of European writers Dante alone was blessed with this gift. It was his mission to write *The Divine Comedy*. But his spiritual organs came completely unblocked only toward the end of his life, when the monumental labor on his poem was already nearing completion. He saw the numerous mistakes and inaccuracies, the vulgarization of meaning, and the gratuitous anthropomorphism of his images, but he had neither the time nor the energy to correct them. Nevertheless, the basic features of the framework he set out can be taken as a panoramic view of the variomaterial planes of the Roman Catholic metaculture.

Without daring even to dream of anything similar for myself, I did, however, have the greatest of good fortune to talk with some of those who left us long ago and at present belong to the Synclite of Russia. I hesitate to set down in writing the overwhelming experience of having them near. I will refrain from giving their names, but the presence of each of them was colored with an inimitable and individual tone of feelings. Our meetings occurred in the daytime as well as the night, and I in my crowded prison cell was forced to lie down on the bed with my face to the wall to hide the tears of breathless joy streaming from my eyes. The presence of one of the great brothers caused my heart to pound and my body to tremble with exultation and veneration. My whole being welcomed another with warm, tender love, as a dear friend who saw through my soul and loved it and brought me comfort and forgiveness. The approach of the third made me feel a need to kneel before him as someone powerful who had ascended incomparably higher than I, and his presence was accompanied by a solemn feeling and unusual sharpening of my attention. Lastly, the approach of the fourth gave rise to a feeling of joyful celebration and tears of rapture. There is much I can call into question and much I can doubt about the authenticity of my inner life, but not those meetings.

Did I actually see them during those meetings? No, I didn't. Did they speak with me? Yes, they did. Did I hear their words? Both yes and no. I heard them, but not with my physical sense of hearing. It was as if they spoke from somewhere in the depths of my heart. I repeated many of their words back to them, especially unfamiliar names of various planes and spiritual hierarchies in Shadanakar, trying as closely as possible to convey their sounds through physical speech, and then asking, "Is that right?" I was forced to repeat some names and words several times; there were also some that I was unable to reproduce accurately with the sounds of the Russian language. Many of the strange words pronounced by the great brothers were accompanied by light effects—not physical light, although one could compare them in some cases to flashes of lightning, in others, to a distant glow, and in still others, to moonlight. Sometimes they were not at all like words in the sense to which we are accustomed, but entire chords, as it were, of phonetic consonances and meanings. Translating such words into our language was out of the question, and all I could do was select one meaning and one syllable from all the meanings and all the harmoniously sounding syllables. But our talks consisted not of single words, but of questions and answers, of entire sentences expressing very complex ideas. Entire sentences undivided into words seemed to flash and imprint themselves on the silver paper of my consciousness, illuminating with an unusual light the gaps and ambiguities that my questions addressed. In truth, they were more like pure thoughts than sentences, thoughts that were transmitted to me directly, without words.

Thus, my path of metahistorical enlightenment, contemplation, and formulation was supplemented with transphysical journeys, meetings, and talks.

The spirit of our century will waste no time in responding: "Let's grant that what the author calls his experience appears genuine to him. But can it have any more objective significance than the "experience" of a resident of a mental asylum? Where is the proof?"

But there is something strange here. Do we demand proof for all manifestations of spiritual life and culture? And if not for all, then why for this particular one? We do not, after all, demand proof from an artist or composer for the "authenticity" of their artistic vision or musical inspiration. In the same way, there are no proofs in the communication of religious and, in particular, metahistorical experience. Those people whose inner world is even slightly consonant will believe the experience of another without any proof. Those to whom that inner world is foreign will not believe it and will demand proof, and even if they are given proof they will continue to disbelieve. Only science insists on faith in its testimony, forgetting at the same time how often today's conclusions are overturned by the conclusions of tomorrow. Other spheres of the human spirit—art, religion, metahistory—reject the necessity of such faith. They offer limitless inner freedom.

On the other hand, it would be the grossest of errors to mix these spheres together, to suppose, for example, that the metahistorical mode of knowledge is some unique and rare variety of artistic creativity. They may interact at certain stages, it is true. But it is possible for the metahistorical process of knowledge to be entirely free of elements of artistic creativity, while examples of artistic creativity that have no relation to metahistory are innumerable indeed.

But in the realm of religion, as well, there have been only a few varieties truly enriched by metahistorical knowledge. It is interesting to note that the word *revelation*, which is synonymous with the Greek *apokalypse*, has not prevented the latter from becoming firmly entrenched in the Russian language. Each word has traditionally carried a special shade of meaning. The word *revelation* possesses a more general meaning. If we do not confine ourselves within narrowly religious limits, we will have to include such events as the visions and ecstasies of Muhammad and even the enlightenment of Gautama Buddha in the list of historical instances of revelation. As for *apokalypse*, it is only one kind of revelation: the revelation not of regions of universal harmony, or of spheres of absolute wholeness, or even of groups of stellar or other cosmic hierarchies. It is revelation of the destinies of peoples, realms, churches, cultures, all humanity, and of those hierarchies that take part in these destinies in a most active and direct manner. It is the revelation of metahistory. *Apokalypse* is not as universal as ecumenical revelation; it is, *hierarchically speaking, lower*. It deals with the more particular, with what lies closer to us. But for that very reason it answers the burning questions of those people whose destiny it is to be thrown into the crucible of historical cataclysms. It fills the gap between one's apprehension of universal harmony and the dissonances of historical and individual existence.

As is known, only a few peoples at rare times were rich in such revelation: *apokalyptika* seems to have arisen among the Jews about the sixth century B.C., gripped early Christianity, and endured longest of all in medieval Judaism, feeding off the fiery spirit of its messianism.

As for Christianity, and in particular the Eastern Church, the apocalyptic mode of knowledge almost entirely disappeared as early as the beginning of the Middle Ages. It suddenly burst into small, wavering, smoking flames again in the first century of the Great Russian Schism. This is not the place to analyze the complex and numerous reasons for that tragedy, but it is impossible to ignore the link with the antihistorical attitude prevalent in the religious consciousness and in the world of religious feelings of that time. We can observe this attitude as far back as the time of the Byzantine Fathers of the Church. It is glaringly evident among even the greatest representatives of Russian Orthodoxy, those whose sanctity and higher spiritual experience is not subject to doubt. Antihistoricism approached the status of an obligatory canon of religious thought. It is instructive to recall the unresolved conflicts between the official antihistoricism of the Russian Church and the inherent, irrational pull toward the apocalyptic mode of knowledge and metahistory in the spiritual and artistic life of such lay Orthodox writers and thinkers as Gogol, Khomyakov, Leontyev, Dostoyevsky, Vladimir Solovyov, and Sergei Bulgakov.

But there is comfort in the fact that contact with metahistory can be made in ways altogether different from what has been discussed here. The *element of metahistorical experience* that one can uncover at times underneath the enormously thick layer of anti-historicism, be it seeming or genuine, testifies to that fact. Tyutchev wonderfully describes the feeling of being a participant in some kind of historical and mystical drama, a participant in the creative work and struggle of the great spiritual, or rather, trans-physical powers that most fully manifest themselves at crucial junctures in history. Could Joan of Arc have really performed her heroic deeds without having experienced that feeling? Could St. Sergi of Radonezh—an avowed hermit and ascetic in every other respect—really have taken upon himself such a decisive, leading role in the political tempest of his time? Without that feeling could the greatest of popes have tried, century after century, to bring the idea of a global hierocracy to fruition? Could Loyola have fathered an organization that consciously strove to gain control of the mechanism guiding the historical progress of humanity? Without that feeling, with reason alone, could Hegel have written *The Philosophy of History* and Goethe, the second part of *Faust*? Could the self-immolation of Old-Style Believers have been conceivable if the icy wind of eschatological, metahistorical horror had not chilled in them all attachment to this world, which, it seemed to them, had already fallen under the sway of the Antichrist?

A vague metahistorical feeling, unillumined by contemplation and formulation, often leads to distorted ideas and contradictory actions. Do we not sense a certain metahistorical fervor in the tirades of French Revolutionary leaders, in the doctrines of utopian socialism, in August Kont's cult of Humankind, or in the calls for global renewal by means of the destruction of all established order? (On the lips of Bakunin, such calls took on a tone reminiscent of the passionate appeals of the Jewish prophets, although the nineteenth-century orator attached a new meaning to those appeals, one directly counter to the ethic of those ancient prophets.) There are hundreds more similar questions one could ask. The answers that necessarily follow lead us to two important conclusions. First, it becomes clear that an undercurrent of apocalyptic experience can be uncovered throughout both Western and Russian culture in a countless number of phenomena that are at first glance even alien to it in spirit. Second, it becomes clear that metahistorical feeling, metahistorical experience—unconscious, vague, confused, contradictory—is from time to time woven into the creative process—artistic, religious, social, and even political.

In speaking of the metahistorical method of knowledge, I unintentionally touched upon the transphysical. The journeys and meetings I spoke of belong in part to the realm of transphysical knowledge. As I said earlier, it is by no means always possible to classify these phenomena into distinct categories. Indeed, were it not for the desire to introduce some clarity to a complex and little-studied group of problems, it would be entirely unnecessary.

Perhaps some readers are puzzled by my use of the term *transphysical* instead of the more common word *spiritual*. But in the strict sense of the word, *spiritual* properly refers only to God and monads. As for the term *transphysical*, it is used in reference to everything that possesses materiality, but materiality different from ours, and in reference to all those worlds that exist in different dimensions and time streams. By *transphysics* (in the sense of an object of knowledge) I mean the sum of those worlds, irrespective of the processes taking place within them. Metahistory comprises those processes that are linked with the evolution of Shadanakar; those linked with the evolution of the Universe make up metaevolution; the knowledge of metaevolution is *ecumenical* knowledge. *Transphysics*, in the sense of a religious teaching, refers to the teaching on the structure of Shadanakar. Objects of metahistorical knowledge are related to history and culture; those of transphysical knowledge are related to our plane's natural environment and the environment of other planes in Shadanakar; those of ecumenical knowledge relate to the Universe. Thus, those phenomena that I called transphysical journeys and meetings can be classified, depending on their content, either as metahistorical, transphysical, or ecumenical modes of knowledge.

Now, after that brief aside, nothing hinders us any longer from moving on to an examination of the two remaining types of religious knowledge—but only, of course, those varieties with which I am personally familiar.

2 A Brief Description of the Transphysical Method

THERE WOULD APPEAR to be among people an endless variety of attitudes toward nature—individual attitudes that sometimes harbor internal contradictions. But if we trace the evolution of those attitudes throughout the history of global culture, from the invention of writing up to the present day, we may detect a number of patterns, or rather, phases. I will permit myself here to outline, in a very simplified manner, the general features of three or four of the most important phases as I see them. It will not be a painstaking reproduction of how attitudes have changed over cultures and time but only a few quick brush strokes, the purpose of which is more to introduce the reader to the issues involved than to provide him or her with the necessary historical background.

The earliest phase was characterized by a conception of the universe as extremely small and of the Earth as the only inhabited planet. The world, however, possessed, besides our physical plane, a number of other planes, also material but with a materiality of a different nature and possessing different properties than ours. This was the first approximation of the transphysical reality of Shadanakar. None of the planes, including ours, were thought to evolve. They had been created once and for all and were inhabited by good and evil beings. Humans lay at the center of those beings' interests and were, so to speak, their apple of discord. Humans were not conscious of Nature as something distinct from themselves and did not contrast themselves with it. Individual natural phenomena evoked, of course, one or another feeling—fear, pleasure, awe—but it seems that Nature was almost never perceived as a whole, or was perceived so in a purely aesthetic sense, and even then only by individuals who were highly gifted artistically. For that reason, one rarely finds among artistic works of those eras lyrical poetry about Nature, and even more rarely does one find landscape painting. In the main, the cultures of antiquity, as well as certain later cultures in the East, belong to that phase. As for religion, polytheism was typical of this first phase.

Typical of the second phase were the monotheistic systems, which either ignored Nature or else were hostile to it. The growth of individuality led to the conception that humans could grow spiritually. Nature, on the other hand, showed no signs of spiritual growth. It was stagnant and static; it was amoral and irrational; it was under the power of the demonic; and if the spirit itself was not to be vanquished, that part of a person's being that was cosubstantial with Nature had to be vanquished by the spirit. This was the *antinature* phase. The Christian, Buddhist, and Hindu peoples all passed through it; Jewry (meaning believers in Judaism) still remains in it. The latter, however, like the Muslim peoples, did not so much declare war on Nature as simply snub it.

The Semitic attitude to nature has, generally speaking, been marked by a poverty of feeling. It has long been remarked how lacking the authors of the Bible and the Quran were in their feeling toward nature compared to those who wrote the great epics of ancient Greece and of India in particular. The Semites gave Nature what they considered its due, sanctioning procreation with the blessing of their religion, but in their religious philosophy and art they strove to ignore it, and with grave consequences. They virtually banned sculpture and portraiture because they feared anthropolatry and abhorred the deification of nature. Along with other Semitic elements, this anti-nature mindset spread to Europe with Christianity, stamped out the nature cults of Germanic and Slavic paganism, and reigned there until the end of the Middle Ages.

But the East was also to pass through that phase, though those societies colored it in their own way. The asceticism of radical varieties of Hinduism, the struggle of Buddhism to liberate the human self from the power of Nature—all this is too well known to dwell on here. Thus, we can say that in the first phase people were almost never conscious of Nature as a whole, and only poeticized and deified individual natural phenomena, while in the second phase they viewed it as hostile and under the sway of the demonic.

The third phase is associated with the era of scientific supremacy and with the impoverishment of the world of religious feelings. Having inherited a hostile attitude toward nature from Christianity, people of the third phase freed it of its religious overtones. They did not undertake to overcome the elements of Nature in their own being. They established a strictly utilitarian view of Nature. Nature was, first of all, an object of rational (scientific) research; second, it was a mass of lifeless powers to be harnessed for human use. Our physical horizons expanded immeasurably, knowledge of the structure and laws of our plane reached dizzying heights; that is the value of the third phase.

But there is no point in speaking of natural scientists' love of Nature. One can experience intellectual love only for products of the intellect: one can love with one's mind an idea, a thought, a theory, or a scientific field. In such a manner one can love physiology, microbiology, even parasitology but not a lymph node, or bacteria, or a flea. Love of Nature can be of a physiological nature, of an aesthetic nature, and lastly, of a moral and religious nature. But one thing it cannot be is intellectual. If individual specialists in the natural sciences do love Nature, then that feeling has no relation whatsoever to their specialty or, more generally, to the scientific method of knowledge of Nature. Rather, it is a feeling of a physiological or aesthetic nature.

Civilized (or at least, Western) humanity attained the greatest degree of alienation from Nature not, as it might seem, in the twentieth century but in the seventeenth, eighteenth, and early nineteenth centuries. Never were fashions so artificial as in the age of the powdered wig. Never were sections of Nature neighboring humanity disfigured so rationally and unnaturally as in the age of the Park at Versailles. It is just as impossible to picture an aristocrat from the age of Louis XIV sunbathing or walking barefoot as it is to imagine a Spartan woman from the period of the Greco-Persian wars wearing a corset and high-heeled shoes. The ascetic attitude toward Nature that had become ingrained in Christianity was wholly responsible, but it was an attitude that in the course of development had replaced spiritual snobbery with the snobbery of civilized society and replaced religious pride with the pride of reason, experiencing nothing but amused contempt for anything that did not bear the stamp of rationality.

The philosophy of Rousseau marks the turning point. But another century and a half had to pass and the world had to enter the age of the metropolis in order for most of humanity to experience a longing for Nature. The Lake poets of England, Goethe and the Romantics in Germany, Pushkin and, especially, Lermontov in Russia loved Nature with a higher aesthetic, and for some, pantheistic love. The Barbizon school of painting emerged, and by the end of the nineteenth century aesthetic love had become firmly established in culture.

In the twentieth century bodily love came into its own as well. Passive contemplation of Nature became insufficient; the need arose to experience it in a tactile, active manner, with one's whole body and through the exercise of one's muscles. The need was in part met by hiking and sports. Finally, in the first half of our century, the beach, with its physiological evaporation of people into a mixture of sunlight, warmth, water, and play, became an entrenched and lasting part of our everyday life. It is the same enjoyment of the beach that in the days of Ronsard and Watteau would have appeared to be the indecent eccentricities of lunatics and in the Middle Ages would have been equated with the witches' sabbat on Bald Mountain or with a Black Mass. If one imagines Torquemada suddenly transported as a spectator to the beach in Osten or Yalta, then there can hardly be a doubt that into the mind of that guardian of human souls would pop the thought of promptly organizing an auto-da-fé for those thousands of brazen heretics.

Perhaps nothing so graphically illustrates the narrowing of the rift between humans and Nature during the last hundred years as the evolution of fashion. Overcoats and headwear, at one time the inseparable accompaniments of "cultured" people, even on summer middays, began to be used only when climate dictated. Fifty years ago it seemed improper to leave the house without gloves; now people use them only in cold weather. In place of suits and starched fronts, which our grandfathers roasted in for the sake of decorum even in ninety-degree heat, people began going to work in short-sleeve shirts with open collars. Feet that had been cramped in fashionable boots were treated to the delight of slippers and sandals. Women were liberated from the nightmare of corsets. Dresses shortened at the legs and open at the neck became the fashion in summer, while long dresses survived only as evening wear. Boys whose great-grandfathers had at the same age paraded about wearing school blazers and a cap even in July now run about barefoot, with no top, kissed dark by the sun. People in large cities, separated from Nature as never before by such great distances and missing its warm embrace, have begun returning to it, as yet almost unconsciously, propelled by an instinctive bodily love, but carrying the seeds of a new, more mature relationship with Nature within the historical experience amassed in their hearts. That is the fourth phase.

Thus, there have been roughly four phases: the pagan, the ascetic, the scientific-utilitarian, and the instinctive-physiological.

We can summarize thus: by the second half of our century in the educated and semi-educated classes of those nations belonging to the Roman Catholic, German Protestant, and Russian spheres of cultural influence, two attitudes toward Nature that thus far have almost never conflicted with one another have become entrenched. One of them, the scientific-utilitarian attitude, which is utterly devoid of love, is older. It has focused its attention on exploiting the energy resources contained in Nature and measures everything against the criterion of material benefit for humanity or, what is still worse, for certain antagonistic groupings within it. From that point of view, it also approves of sport, the beach, and hiking. Partisans of that attitude calmly dissect live cats and dogs out of a desire to answer the question, "How does that work?" and shoot rabbits and partridge to satisfy an atavistic hunting instinct. Perhaps in the former case love for humanity is also involved. An Everest of canine corpses may yield, in the end, a grain of knowledge concerning, for example, conditional reflexes. That is the cost to be paid, as is said, to enlighten the inquisitive mind and spur medical progress. But there is not even a hint of love for Nature to be found there. I will go further: such an attitude toward Nature is immoral because, besides humans, the interests of no living being are taken into account, and because it leads to a view of all Nature as a cow to be milked. Fortunately, that attitude has begun to be tempered by a newer one: an unconscious egoistic-bodily love of nature, at times mixed with aesthetic elements.

But that evolution has not yet brought people to a recognition that it is possible and necessary, while maintaining the older shades of love of Nature (with the exception, of course, of the amoral utilitarian attitude), to infinitely enrich our attitude with moral and religious meaning. Not with pantheistic meaning, in which people have but a vague intuition of the presence of some impersonal, evenly distributed divine force in Nature. No. That stage is past, and prehistoric protoanimism is proof that the pantheistic feeling possessed by some people nowadays is nothing other than a modification of the ancient experience of *arungvilta-prana*. No! We are dealing with something different here. We are dealing with an attitude that is incomparably more moral and conscious, more coherent, developed, and refined, more joyful, more responsible. It can be founded only on the experience people have when they come into direct contact, through Nature, with the rich and multifarious worlds of the elementals. By "come into contact" I mean to enter into a relationship with the elementals, understanding better and better the opportunities for rewarding and creative friendship with them, our wonderful responsibility toward them, and our grievous, age-old guilt.

True, a vague feeling of guilt toward Nature, and animals in particular, has begun to have some effect. Societies for the humane treatment of animals have sprung up, love for them has even begun to be encouraged within the school curriculum, and that renowned wellspring of love known as the State has assumed guardianship of the environment. Unfortunately it is doing so only out of economic considerations. As for the humane treatment of animals, these charitable organizations were taught a brutal lesson by the natural scientists: after heated debate, vivisection without prior authorization has occupied a leading place among the methods of science. Citing the benefits to humanity as justification, scientists have firmly established this disgrace to all humanity in universities, laboratories, and even in those same high schools where children are taught to love cats and dogs.

What is the attitude toward Nature of the worldview that could serve as the foundation for the teachings of the Rose of the World?

This is a very broad question, but it is not difficult, I think, to deduce what the chief component of that attitude will be. The perspectives of the Rose of the World are, after all, distinguished first and foremost by *a sense of the transparency of the physical plane*, by the experience of the transphysical planes showing through it, by a passionate love of that experience and its painstaking cultivation. That sense of transparency, in encompassing the fields of culture and history, will be molded into a metahistorical teaching. In being directed toward the Sun, the Moon, and the starry sky, it will become the basis for an ecumenical—that is, metaevolutionary—teaching. In encompassing terrestrial Nature, it will find expression in the teaching about elementals. The teaching about elementals is but one branch of a broader teaching about the structure of Shadanakar—a transphysical teaching.

No matter how much the ancient beliefs about elementals (nature spirits in the broadest sense) were muddied by impurities introduced by the limitations of the human mind and imagination, no matter how many aberrations distorted the images of nature divinities in the pantheons of polytheistic religions—at the very heart of these beliefs lies the truth.

But it is our task, of course, to apprehend and show reverence for the worlds of elementals in a manner completely different from that of the peoples of antiquity. Subsequent experience has enriched us, broadened our knowledge, and sharpened our mystical awareness.

The chief distinctions between our belief in elementals and the belief of ancient peoples are as follows.

The ancients anthropomorphized their images of elemental divinities. We will no longer feel the need to attribute human forms to them.

The ancients viewed these worlds as forever constant and unchanging. We will recognize that they evolve, though in a manner unlike the evolution of our organic world, and we will strive to apprehend the path of their evolution.

The ancients were able to experience their link with individual planes of elementals but drew ill-defined boundaries between them, and they had no idea about the spiritual growth of these monads. Strictly speaking, they had no clear conception of the plurality of these planes. For us, the plurality of and interconnection between these planes and the spiritual growth of monads abiding on them will become objects of transphysical knowledge.

The ancients were incapable of drawing a rough map of our planetary cosmos. We will distinguish each plane in a much more precise manner and include it together with all its unique features in the overall panorama of Shadanakar.

The ancients were unable to reconcile belief in these worlds with belief in the One God. For us there will be no conflict between these two beliefs.

It should also be added that the ancients regarded propitiation and praise, and nothing else, as their spiritual duty toward elementals. For our part, we will strive to actualize our link with them through a readiness to participate in their play and creative work, through encouragement of their beneficent participation in our lives (possible paths to achieving that will be set forth in the relevant chapters) and last, through aid to elementals of Light and through work in enlightening dark elementals.

Such an attitude toward Nature combines a paganistic joy for life, monotheistic spirituality, and the breadth of knowledge of the scientific age. All these elements will come together in a higher synthesis through the spiritual experience of the emerging sum religion.

There is a widespread misconception that all religious outlooks are hostile to this life and that they substitute the values of the afterlife for the values of this world. There is no more justification for that generalization than for the claim, for example, that the art of painting distances one from this world, a claim based on the fact that it is partly true of the painting of the Middle Ages. Only religious credos of a particular phase have been hostile to life, and even then only in their more extreme manifestations. This outlook I am speaking of will not distance people from this world but will teach them to love it with a passionate and selfless love. It does not contrast "other worlds" with this one but sees them all as a magnificent whole, as a necklace on the breast of God. Do we like a crystal icon lamp less because it is transparent? Will we really love our world less because other worlds show through it? For people who feel that way, this life is good, and death is not an enemy but a dear guide, for a worthy life on earth predetermines an ascent to other worlds fuller, richer, and more wonderful.

But in what manner, on what paths, can humans achieve transparent perception of the world? Does it come independently of our will and efforts, like a lucky gift of fate, or can we knowingly cultivate it within ourselves and whole generations?

Until the combined efforts of a great many people are channeled into that cultivation, the joy of transparent perception will indeed remain a matter of the grace of God, and we will expend hardly any effort in acquiring it. Only through the protracted labor of the invisible friends of our heart, the executors of Providential will, do organs capable of such perception come unblocked in some of us, though often, much more often, the organs occasionally open a narrow crack and then close back up. But even these small cracks are enough for *transparent perception of the physical world* to begin and for those fortunate enough to experience it to resemble the blind who can see.

To initiate the process entirely at will—in oneself or others—is hardly possible, at least for the present. But we can work in such a way that in each one of us and in our children our labors will complement the labors of the Providential powers. Thus, a tunnel through the psychophysical strata will be dug, as it were, simultaneously from two ends: by us and by the friends of our heart.

The colossal task of creating such a pedagogy can at present only be designated as one of the tasks of a future civilization. An immense amount of preliminary work related to the study and systematization of experience in that area is still needed. I will treat that in greater detail in one of the last sections of the book. At this time I will only provide some necessary information concerning two or three possible varieties of that methodology. These varieties and many others not mentioned here can, of course, be combined to complement each other.

There is one prior condition without which efforts in this direction will lead nowhere. It is the desire personally to apprehend the transparency of that crystal vessel we call Nature. The process is therefore open either to those who themselves admit the possibility that worlds of elementals exist (otherwise one would not seek the transparency of the physical plane, but, to the contrary, would hope for nothing to happen, so that one's scientific skepticism could triumph) or to children, provided their trust of the elements and love of Nature is reinforced from an early age by the example of their elders. Naturally, they who deny beforehand the existence of those worlds will not waste time and energy on such experiments. And even if, for the sake of experiment, it entered their heads to make some efforts toward that end, they would achieve nothing, because their personal disbelief would constantly inform the results obtained. They would ascribe the results to self-suggestion or something of that sort. It would be no more than a step forward followed by a step backward, or running in place.

Thus, if that necessary inner condition is met, we must then concern ourselves with creating the necessary external conditions. It is easy to guess that what we are referring to here are those periods (six to eight weeks a year) when modern-day men and women are freed from earning a living and can permit themselves time alone in Nature. I would think that summer conditions are more conducive, because it is in summer, with its longer days, lush plant growth, and full awakening of earth and water, that the elementals' activity increases many times over as more and more planes become reanimated. Also, it is usually summertime when people go on vacation—that is, they have the chance, if only for a month, to spend time with Nature. But it should be stated from the start that one will not make much headway in a month, and there is no point whatsoever in embarking on such efforts during a two-week holiday. Of course, those who feel more affinity for the winter months should make allowances for that preference.

Someone might be expecting precise instructions from me: get up at such a time, go to bed at such a time, keep to such and such a daily schedule. I would prefer to avoid going into such niggling recommendations. What is our task? It is to immerse ourselves as deeply as possible in Nature, in the life of the elements, not as a sower of death or inquiring researcher but as a son or daughter who has returned home after years of wandering in foreign climes. To accomplish that task one individual will find it more natural and effective to do one thing, someone else, another. I would only like to relate what circumstances aided me personally.

Having secured for my summer holidays a "homebase," as they say, in a beautiful and, obviously, remote place, I first of all endeavored to avoid cluttering my heart and mind with sundry worldly cares. I minimized my links to the outside world, listened to the radio less often, and tried to get by as long as possible without newspapers, provided of course the world was not in the midst of a dangerous crisis. It was imperative to simplify my lifestyle, wear as little clothing as possible, and forget completely about the existence of shoes. I bathed two or three times a day in a river, lake, or the sea, finding a spot where it was possible to be alone with Nature.

I read books that induced a peaceful, benevolent mood and helped my thoughts attune themselves to Nature. Literature dealing with the natural sciences would be of no help during such times, as it puts one in a completely different frame of mind. The study of the exact sciences and technology would lead one even further astray. Best of all is good poetry and certain classics of prose: Turgenev, Dickens, Erckmann-Chatrian, Tagore (but not Stendhal, Zola, Swift, or Shedrin, and the like). It is a good time to reread children's classics, such as *Tom Sawyer* or *Treasure Island*, and books about children. All in all, spending lots of time with children and playing and talking with them can only help matters. I may scare off some with one injunction, but unfortunately it is firm: minimal consumption of meat and fish products and moderation in the use of alcohol. And one categorical requirement: no hunting or fishing whatsoever.

That was the atmosphere in which my travels began. It doesn't feel right to use the words "hike" or "excursion" to describe them. I would be gone for the entire day, from sunrise to sunset, or on a three-or four-day trip—in the forest, roving down country roads and field paths, over meadows, through woods, villages, farms, across rivers on slow ferries. These travels included chance meetings and casual conversations, and overnight camping, perhaps beside a campfire on the banks of a river, or in the fields, or in haystacks, or on some village hayloft. I tried to avoid any sort of contact with machines, conversations on technical topics, and reading of that sort, with the exception of occasionally resorting to mechanized transport. Then back to my remote homebase for a few days of rest and relaxation, listening to the crow of roosters, the rustle of tree tops, the voices of children and villagers, reading tranquil, deep, and innocent books—then off for more of the same roving.

That style of living can sometimes arouse in others puzzlement and snickering. One should not expect to be understood. People busy with farm work will even be inclined to view such eccentrics as no-good loafers: the majority of countryfolk are as yet capable of viewing only their own duties as real work. One should not take it too much to heart. One must know enough to ignore the opinions of others when sure of the rightness of one's actions.

But those are all external considerations. You can spend the whole summer tramping over hill and dale till you drop and still end up with nothing to show for it. Outside circumstances must be supplemented by efforts of the heart and mind. What sort of efforts are needed?

What people need to do is gradually train themselves to perceive the sounds of an ocean of trees, the swaying of the grass, the glide of clouds, and the flow of rivers, every voice and movement of the visible world, as *alive*, fully *aware*, and *kindly-disposed* toward them. A feeling that invariably oversees the emergence of new thoughts and feelings will grow stronger, gradually enveloping all one's days and nights: a feeling that, in lying down on your back, you are letting your head sink lower and lower into soothing depths that glimmer with soft light—loving, intimate depths that have existed since time immemorial. A feeling of simple joy, of profound calm will absorb the smallest spill of everyday cares. These are good times to lie on the bank of a river, oblivious to time, and gaze lazily at the cool water glittering in the sunlight. Or, lying somewhere under ancient pines to listen to the organ-like music of the treetops and the knocking of woodpeckers. One must have faith that the elementals of Liurna are overjoyed at your coming and will speak to your body as soon as it enters their flowing bodies, that the elementals of Faltora and Arashamf are even now singing you songs through the rustle of leaves, the buzzing of bees, and warm breaths of wind. When you are returning home from a long hike at dusk over fields smelling of freshly cut hay, climbing sun-warmed knolls and descending into the coolness of ravines, and a soft mist begins to flood over everything but the tops of haystacks—it feels good to take off your shirt and let your hot body be caressed through the mist by those who are fashioning the mist above the nodding meadows.

I could describe hundreds of other such times—from sunbathing on the sand to berry-picking, my mind divided between action and contemplation—but whoever embarks on that carefree and bright path will recognize them without any prior description. After all, such a path is possible not only in Central Russia but in the countryside of any country, from Norway to Ethiopia, from Portugal to the Philippines and Argentina. Only the specifics of the path will vary, but they can vary as well within the confines of a single region, depending on one's personal preferences. What is important is to generate that radiance and easygoing frame of mind within oneself and if possible to repeat those periods each year.

"What utter nonsense!" some will say. "As if we were not in possession of definite facts concerning why and how mists, the wind, or dew come about. As if we didn't know by what processes rain, rivers, and vegetation occur. To serve up such fairy tales with a straight face in the middle of the twentieth century! No wonder the author hints that he feels more at ease in the company of children: an adult would never put up with listening to such drivel!"

They are mistaken, those absolutists of the scientific method of knowledge: not the slightest contradiction of science is to be found here. To repeat: I mean here objective and critical science, as distinct from the philosophical doctrine of materialism. After all, if some rational microscopic being existed that was studying my body and was itself a part of it, it would be right in saying the moment I moved my arm that the arm is a lump of matter composed of such and such molecules that moved because certain of its parts—the muscles—contracted. They contracted because such and such a reaction occurred in the nerve centers and the reaction arose from such and such reasons of a chemical nature. And there you are! Clear as day. And naturally the researcher would be scandalized if it occurred to anyone to point out that the "lump" moved because such was the wish, free and conscious, of its owner, while the muscles, nerves, chemical processes, and the rest merely served to transmit the owner's will.

Physiology is concerned with the study of the mechanics of the process. That does not preclude the existence of psychology—the science dealing with the consciousness that puts the mechanics to use. Meteorology, aerodynamics, hydrology, and a number of other sciences concern themselves with the study of the mechanics of natural elements. That should not and will not interfere in time with the emergence of a teaching about elementals, about those consciousnesses that put the mechanics to use.

It all began for me personally near the town of Tripolye in the Ukraine on a sultry summer day in 1929. Weary but content after a hike of many miles through open fields and over slopes with windmills, from where a panoramic view opened onto the bright-blue branches of the Dnieper and the sandbars between them, I climbed the ridge of yet another hill and was all of a sudden literally blinded. Before me, motionless under the streaming rays of the sun, stretched a vast sea of sunflowers. At the same moment, I sensed an invisible ocean of vibrant joy quivering above that magnificent scene. I stepped up to the very edge of the field and, my heart pounding, pressed two bristly sunflowers to my cheeks. I stared at the thousands of earthbound suns, almost breathless with love for them and for the beings whose joy I felt above the field. I felt something strange: I felt that those invisible beings were leading me with joy and pride, like a guest of honor, to a fantastic celebration that resembled both a ceremony and a feast. I gingerly took a couple of steps into the midst of the flowers and, closing my eyes, listened to their touch, to their barely audible rustle, and to the celestial heat that was blazing all around.

It all began with that. True, I can recall experiences of that kind from my younger days, when I was a teenager, but they were not nearly as powerful. But both before and after the experience in Tripolye—not every year, but sometimes several times in the course of one summer—minutes of strange, inebriating joy came upon me while alone in Nature. They occurred, for the most part, when I had already covered hundreds of kilometers on foot and then chanced upon unfamiliar places distinguished by the lushness and wildness of vegetation growing unchecked. Transported by ecstasy and trembling from head to foot, I made my way, oblivious to everything, through dense thickets, sun-baked marshes, and prickly bushes, finally throwing myself down into the grass to feel it with my whole body. The most important thing was that during those minutes I was aware with all my senses that the invisible beings whose existence is mysteriously linked to the vegetation, water, and soil loved me and flowed through me.

In the years that followed, I spent the summers, for the most part, in the Bryansk Forest region. The memory of all that happened to me there is the joy of my life. But I am particularly fond of recalling my encounters with the elementals of Liurna, which at the time I called river spirits.

Once, during a drought, I set off alone on a one-week camping trip in the Bryansk Forest. The smoke of forest fires stretched out in fingers of bluish black, and sometimes whitish puffs of smoke, slowly curling and twisting, would rise above the huge fir forests. It so happened that I walked for several hours along a hot dirt road without seeing a spring or brook. The heat, as stifling as in a greenhouse, gave me an agonizing thirst. I had brought a detailed map of the area, and I knew that I would soon come across a small stream—one so small that even on my local map it did not have a name. Sure enough, the woods began taking on a different look: fir trees gave way to maples and alders. Suddenly the scorching road that was burning my feet began to slope down, the green of a meadow appeared up ahead, and skirting a clump of trees, I caught sight of a bend of the long-anticipated stream a dozen meters ahead. The road crossed it at a ford. What a pearl of creation, what a delightful child of God laughed at my coming! A few steps wide, shaded everywhere by the low-hanging branches of old willows and alders, it streamed as if through green caverns, softly gurgling and glittering with thousands of sparkles of sunlight.

Throwing my heavy knapsack down on the grass and tearing off my light clothing on the run, I entered the water up to my chest. When my overheated body plunged into the cool wetness, and dapples of shadow and sunlight flitted over my shoulders and face, I felt some invisible being, composed of what I don't know, embrace my soul with such innocent joy, with such laughing playfulness, as if it had long loved me and been waiting for me. It was like the rarefied soul of the river—all flowing, all trembling, all caressing, all coolness and light, carefree laughter and tenderness, joy and love. And when, after my body had long been in its body, and my soul in its soul, I lay down with eyes closed on the bank under the shady branches of the trees, my heart felt so refreshed, so cleansed, so purified, so blessed as it could only have been during the first days of Creation, at the dawn of time. And I realized that what had happened to me this time was no ordinary bathing in a river but a true ablution, in the very highest sense of the word.

Some might reply that they, too, have spent time in the forests and bathed in rivers, that they, too, have walked through woods and fields and, standing on the mating ground of grouse, have felt at one with Nature, but that they have never experienced anything resembling elementals. If it is a hunter speaking, it is no wonder: the elementals see only an enemy and desecrator in that destroyer of Nature, and there is no surer way of repelling them than taking a hunting rifle into the forest. If those who speak are not hunters, let them carefully reconstruct the weeks they spent in Nature and they will discover their own breaches of the conditions I set forth at the start.

It is impossible, of course, to predetermine the duration of the stages of that process of knowledge: the lengths of time vary depending on many circumstances, both objective and individual. But sooner or later the *first day* will arrive, and you will suddenly feel all of Nature as if it were the first day of Creation and the Earth were celebrating its heavenly beauty. It could happen at night by the campfire or during the day in the middle of a rye field, in the evening on the warm steps of a porch or in the morning in a dewy meadow, but the nature of the moment will everywhere be one and the same: the dizzying joy of one's first cosmic awakening. It will not yet mean that your inner vision has come unblocked for good. You will still see nothing besides the customary landscape, but you will experience with your whole being its multiplaned reality and permeation by spirit. The elementals will become even more accessible to those who undergo that first awakening. Such people will become more and more aware of the constant proximity of those wonderful beings through organs of the soul that have no names in our language.

But the essence of a first awakening lies in something else, something higher. It concerns not only transphysical knowledge but also what I am unable to find a name for other than the old word *ecumenical*. Many authors have attempted to throw light on similar states. William James calls it a breakthrough of cosmic consciousness. It can clearly take on very different shades for different people, but the experience of cosmic harmony lies at its heart. The methods I have described in this chapter are, to a certain extent, capable of hastening that hour, but there is no reason to hope that such joys will become frequent guests in the home of our soul. On the other hand, a soul can be overcome by such a state without any conscious preparation. Such an instance is described, for example, by Rabindranath Tagore in his *Memoirs*.

It is easy for people who have more than once experienced a feeling of general harmony with Nature to think that this is what I am referring to. No, far from it. A breakthrough of cosmic consciousness is an event of colossal personal significance, such as can occur in a person's lifetime only an extremely limited number of times. It comes on one suddenly. It is neither a mood nor pleasure nor happiness nor even a joy of astonishing dimensions—it is something bigger. Moreso than the breakthrough itself, recollections of it will have a powerful effect on one's being. The breakthrough itself is full of such bliss that it would be more accurate to speak of it not as astonishment but enlightenment.

Such states occur when the Universe—not the Earth alone, but the whole Universe—reveals itself in its higher aspect, reveals the divine spirituality that permeates and envelops it, erasing all the painful questions of suffering, conflict, and evil.

In my life such an experience took place on the moonlit night of July 29, 1931, on the banks of the Nerussa, a small river in the Bryansk Forest. I usually try to be alone when in Nature, but that time it so happened that I had taken part in a camping trip with a small group. It was composed of teenagers and young adults, including an aspiring artist. Each of us was carrying a knapsack with food, and the artist had also brought along a sketch pad. We wore nothing heavier than pants and shirts, and some had even taken off their shirts. We walked along quickly and silently, in single file, like tribespeople along the wild paths of Africa. We were not hunters or explorers or mineral prospectors—we were simply friends who wanted to camp by a fire on the famed banks of the Nerussa.

As always happens in the Bryansk Forest along the flats of a river, a fir forest as vast as the sea gave way to a deciduous wood. Century-old oaks, maples, and ashes rose up before us; aspens that resembled palm trees, with their crown of leaves at a dizzying height, enchanted us with their grace and stature; the roundish canopies of kindly willows shone silver as they hung over the water of creeks. In individual clumps, thickets, and glades, the forest approached the river as though with loving care. There were no villages, no signs of civilization. The wilderness spell was broken only by the barely distinguishable path left by mowers and by the rounded tops of haystacks, rising here and there in the fields in preparation for the winter, when they would be transported by sled to the villages of Chukhrai or Neporen.

We reached the banks of the river at the close of a hot, cloudless day. We took a leisurely dip, then gathered brush, and, building a fire two meters from the quietly flowing river under the canopy of three old willows, prepared a simple meal. The sky darkened. A low July full moon glided out from behind the oaks. Little by little the conversations and stories died down; one by one my companions fell asleep around the crackling wood. I was left awake at the fire, lazily waving a branch to ward off the mosquitoes.

When the moon, noiselessly moving behind the finely patterned, leafy branches of the willow, entered the range of my vision, those hours that come close to being the most wonderful of my entire life began. Breathing softly, having laid back on a handful of hay, I heard the Nerussa flowing not behind me, a few paces back, but as if through my own soul. That was the first unusual thing I noticed. Everything on Earth and everything that must exist in the heavens poured exultantly and noiselessly through me in a single stream. In bliss barely supportable by the human heart, I felt as if slowly revolving, graceful spheres glided through me in a universal dance, and everything I could think of or imagine merged in a jubilant oneness. The ancient forests and clear rivers, the people sleeping by the fire, the peoples of countries near and far, cities waking up and busy streets, cathedrals with sacred icons, seas tossing tirelessly, and steppes with blowing grass— everything indeed was within me that night, and I was within everything. I lay with eyes closed, and beautiful white stars, large and blossoming, not at all like those we are used to seeing, also floated along the world-turned-river like white water lilies. Although the sun was not visible, it was as if it, too, were flowing somewhere just outside the range of my vision. Everything was suffused not by its glow but by a different light, one I had never seen before. Everything flowed through me and at the same time rocked me, like a child in a cradle, with all-soothing love.

In trying to express in words such experiences, one understands better than ever the poverty of language. How many times have I attempted through poetry and prose to convey to others what happened to me that night! And I know that no attempt, including this one, will ever succeed in communicating to anyone else the true significance, dimensions, and profound effect that occurrence had on my life.

Afterward I tried with all my might to summon the experience again. I recreated all the same outside circumstances under which it took place in 1931. Many times in the years that followed I camped in the exact same spot on the very same nights. It was all in vain. But twenty years later, just as unexpectedly, it came on me again. This time it was not during a moonlit night by a forest river but in a prison cell.

Oh, that is only the beginning. It is not yet the enlightenment after which a person seems to become someone new, a person enlightened in the higher sense of the word, the sense attached to the word by the great peoples of the East. This is the holiest and most mysterious of enlightenments: it is the opening of one's spiritual eyes.

There is no greater joy *on Earth* than the complete opening of one's inner vision, hearing, and deep memory. The joy of people born deaf or blind who suddenly, in middle age, experience the opening of their physical eyes and ears is but a dim echo of it.

I can only repeat what I know of it by what others have said. There is a wonderful passage in Edwin Arnold's book *The Light of Asia* in which such a state is described, a state that turned one searcher of the truth into the one now known by all humanity as Gautama Buddha.

Here is the description. It deals with Buddha's entry into the state of *abhidjna*:

> insight vast
> ... to spheres unnamed,
> System on system, countless worlds and suns
> Moving in splendid measures, band by band
> Linked in division, one yet separate,
> The silver islands of a sapphire sea ...
> With waves which roll in restless tides of change.
> He saw those Lords of Light who hold their worlds
> By bonds invisible, how they themselves
> Circle obedient around mightier orbs ...
> ... star to star
> Flashing the ceaseless radiance of life
> From centers ever shifting unto cirques
> Knowing no uttermost. These he beheld
> With unsealed vision ...
> Cycle on epicycle, all their tale
> of Kalpas, Mahakalpas[1]—terms of time
> Which no man grasps ...
> Sakwal by Sakwal, depths and heights he passed ...
> Marking—behind all modes, above all spheres,
> Beyond the burning impulse of each orb—
> That fixed decree of silent work which wills
> Evolve the dark to light, the dead to life,
> To fullness void, to form the yet unformed,
> Good unto better, better unto best
> By wordless edict; having none to bid,
> None to forbid; for this is past all gods
> Immutable, unspeakable, supreme,
> A Power which builds, unbuilds and builds again,
> Ruling all things accordant to the rule
> Of virtue, which is beauty, truth, and use."

---

1. Universal periods of time. A kalpa is the period from the birth to destruction of a world.

What is there left to say? It would be not pride but sheer naïveté to hope even in the innermost corner of our heart that someday such an hour will strike for us as well. Yet comfort can be taken from the fact that every human monad without exception, sooner or later, even if after an almost endless period of time, perhaps in another, nonhuman form, in another world, will attain that state, surpass it, and continue on.

In the meantime it is our duty to share with others the best that we possess. My best is what I experienced on the paths of transphysical and metahistorical knowledge. That is why I am writing this book. In these last two chapters I have described as best I could the major signposts on my inner path. Everything that follows will be the presentation of what was understood on that path about God, about other worlds, and about humanity. I will try to avoid any further discussion of how it was understood; the time has come to speak of what was understood.

3 Points of Departure

Multiplaned Reality

OUR PHYSICAL PLANE—a concept synonymous with what astronomy calls the Universe—is characterized, as we know, by three-dimensional space and one time stream. In the terminology of the Rose of the World, the physical plane is called Enrof.

In modern science and philosophy debate continues about the infinity or finiteness of Enrof in time and space and whether the whole Universe is contained within Enrof, whether all forms of being are exhausted by its forms. The discovery of antimatter; the appearance and even extraction of physically material particles from out of a physical vacuum, particles that had hitherto existed in the world of negative energy; the experimental corroboration of the theory that the physical vacuum of space in Enrof is awash with oceans of particles of a different materiality—all these facts are signposts on the route that plodding science is following away from the ideas of classical materialism toward those that differ greatly both from them and from the views of the old idealistic philosophy. It is highly probable that the muddle the proponents of the philosophy of materialism have made of the issue by claiming that all its opponents are merely rehashing the old arguments of idealism is one of the tactics in the last stand of the materialistic consciousness before it "steps on the brakes," as they say, abandoning one position after another, and at the same time reassuring all that the classic thinkers of materialism had foreseen and long affirmed those very same things. It will be particularly interesting to see what acrobatics philosophy will have to resort to in the near future, when it is forced by the weight of evidence to incorporate antimatter into its system.

The primacy of matter over consciousness, the knowability in principle of the entire Universe, and at the same time, its infinite and eternal nature—these naïve doctrines of materialism, which were conceived during past stages of science, are still regarded as current owing only to contrived manipulations and, more important, to the intervention of authorities that are associated not so much with philosophy as with the police state. On the other hand, many doctrines of traditional religion will not bear up under the scrutiny of modern science to the same degree. The new methods of knowledge—metahistorical and transphysical—will not intrude on fields of scientific knowledge or in any way contradict science in its essentials. At the same time they will anticipate science's answers to certain questions.

A conception of the Universe as multiplaned lies at the heart of the Rose of the World's worldview. By *plane* is meant a material world whose materiality differs from that of other planes by virtue of the number of its dimensions and time streams. For example, there are interconnected planes neighboring ours, planes in which space has the same three dimensions but time has not one stream, as on our plane, but several. That means that on such planes time flows as several parallel streams of differing speed. On such a plane events take place simultaneously in all its time streams but their locus is situated in only one or two of them.

It is not easy, of course, to visualize what this means. The inhabitants of such a plane, although they act predominantly in one or two time streams, exist in and are aware of them all. The synchronicity of their being wakens them to the fullness of life to a degree unknown to us. At the risk of getting slightly ahead of myself, I will add that a large number of time streams in combination with a minimal number (one or two) of dimensions has the opposite effect, causing the inhabitants of such planes suffering. This suffering resembles an awareness of one's limitations, a searing feeling of powerless spite, a constant reminder of the enticing opportunities one is not in the position to take advantage of. Some of us would call it being "so close yet so far" or recognize it as the torment of Tantalus.

With a few exceptions, such as Enrof, the number of time streams on a plane far exceeds the number of dimensions. If I remember correctly, there are no planes in Shadanakar with more than six dimensions. As for the number of time streams on the highest of the planes in the bramfatura, it rises to an astronomical height of 236.

In extrapolating the specific features of Enrof onto other planes, it would be a mistake to think that all partitions separating plane from plane must be as difficult to pass through as the partitions separating Enrof from planes of different dimensions. True, there are partitions surrounding some planes that are even more difficult to pass through and that block them off from others even more securely. But such planes are few. There are far more groups of planes in which movement from plane to plane does not require death or a difficult material transformation, as with us, but only the attainment of special inner states. There are also those from which movement to neighboring planes requires no more effort than, say, travel from one country of terrestrial Enrof to another. Several of those planes together form a system. I am accustomed to using the Indian term *sakwala* when referring to each of those systems of planes or series of worlds. Along with sakwalas, however, there also exist solitary planes like Enrof.

Planes and entire sakwalas also differ from each other in the amount of space they occupy. Not all of them encompass the same cosmic area Enrof does. Difficult as it is to imagine, many of them do not extend beyond the limits of our solar system. Others are even more localized: they are immured, as it were, within the confines of our planet. There are even several that are linked not to the planet as a whole but to only one of its physical strata or regions. There is obviously nothing on those planes that can be likened to the sky.

Bound together by shared metahistorical processes, the majority having two rival spiritual poles, as it were, all the planes of every heavenly body together form a gigantic, tightly integrated system. I have already mentioned that such systems are called bramfaturas. In some of them the total number of planes does not exceed single digits, while in others it numbers several hundred. Besides Shadanakar, where the total number of planes now stands at 242, bramfaturas of the Sun, Jupiter, Saturn, Uranus, Neptune, the Moon, and certain moons orbiting the larger planets exist at present in the solar system. The bramfatura of Venus is in the embryonic stage. The remaining planets and moons are as lifeless on their other planes as they are in Enrof. They are either the ruins of former bramfaturas that were abandoned by all their monads or else they have never been bramfaturas.

Multiplaned systems of materiality somewhat analogous to bramfaturas, but incomparably larger, encompass certain solar systems—for example, the majority of the stars of Orion or the system of Antares' double suns and its many planets. Even larger are the galactic systems and the system of the entire Universe. They are macrobramfaturas. There are macrobramfaturas known to have an enormous number of variomaterial planes—up to eight thousand. There is nothing in the macrobramfaturas that can be likened to so-called vacuum, areas of extreme material paucity in Enrof. It is easy to see that macrobramfaturas are beyond the comprehension of even the greatest of the great human souls that now dwell in Enrof. No one can directly glean any concrete information about them except in the form of distant presentiments. Such information sometimes comes to us from the higher spirits of Shadanakar, those immeasurably greater than us, through the medium of the invisible friends of our heart. But even these accounts are extremely difficult for us to comprehend. Thus, it was nearly impossible for me to understand the strange and sorrowful communication that there is in the macrobramfatura of our Galaxy a material plane where space exists but time does not— a kind of hole in Time, where movement is yet possible. It is the plane of torment of great demons, the realm of eternal darkness. But it is eternal not in the sense of endlessly flowing time, but in the sense of the absence of any time.[1] That eternity is not

---

1. I would like to point out in passing that the difference between these two senses of the word eternity has thus far barely been grasped in our philosophical thought.

absolute, as Time can arise there, and therein lies one of the tasks of the grand cycles of cosmic evolution. For only the emergence of Time will make it possible to liberate the great sufferers imprisoned in their galactic hell.

Molecules and some types of atoms form microbramfaturas: minute systems, whose existence in our time is sometimes exceedingly brief. They are, however, quite complex worlds, and one should be aware of the fact that elementary particles are living beings, some of whom possess free will and intelligence. But it is practically impossible to communicate with them, let alone personally enter microbramfaturas directly. There is no being in any of the planes of Shadanakar who is capable of that at the present time: it surpasses for now even the power of the Planetary Logos. Only in the macrobramfaturas of the Galaxy are there spirits of such unimaginable power and grandeur that they are capable of descending simultaneously into multitudes of microbramfaturas. To do so such a spirit must, while maintaining its oneness, incarnate simultaneously in millions of those minuscule worlds, revealing itself in all its fullness in each one of them and within the tiniest fractions of time.

I have, in one way or another, been talking exclusively about material planes, since spiritual planes as such do not exist. The difference between matter and spirit is more a question of degree than of kind, although spirit is created by God alone and emanates from Him, while monads create materiality. In its initial state, free of any coating we could call material, spirit takes the form of a substance that we could roughly, and only as a first approximation, compare to the subtlest of energy. Only God and monads are of the spirit—monads being the countless hosts of God-born and God-created higher selves, indivisible spiritual entities. They differ from each other in the degree of their inborn potential, the inexhaustible variety of their material coatings, and the paths their lives take. A monad that has ascended to great heights can be here, there, at many points of the Universe at once, but it is not omnipresent. Only the Divine Spirit is truly omnipresent. It abides even where there are no monads—for example, in those ruins of bramfaturas abandoned by all monads. Nothing can exist without Him, not even matter we call dead. If the Divine Spirit left it, it would cease to be—not in the sense of a transformation into another form of matter or energy, but absolutely.

The Origin of Evil, Planetary Laws, Karma

If we examine the myth of the rebellion and fall of Lucifer within the context of the spiritual history of Shadanakar, it fails to shed light on anything. Never in the metahistory of our planet have any events taken place that could be said to have been mirrored in that myth. Something else did take place once, a long time ago, and recollections of it, though distorted, have been preserved in certain other myths—for example, in the legend of the revolt of the Titans. That will be discussed in more detail, however, in regard to something else. As for the legend of the rebellion and fall of Lucifer, those events took place at one time on an ecumenical scale, on the level of that macrobramfatura that encompasses the Universe, a level that surpasses all categories of our reason. What happened was translated by the seers of olden times into narrow human concepts specific to their era and took shape as the myth. Those time-specific conceptions have become outdated as the scope of our knowledge has broadened immeasurably, and if we now wish to discern the eternal and true seed of the idea within the myth, we must disregard all the time-specific features introduced into it and focus only on the one central fact affirmed by it.

It was only natural that the knowledge even the wisest of those times possessed concerning the magnitude and structure of the Universe lagged so far behind contemporary knowledge that the ecumenical information that filtered into their minds through the efforts of the invisible friends of their heart was flattened and compressed into the narrow confines of their empirical experience, of their powerful, but as yet unenlightened and unsubtle, minds. On the other hand, the task of anyone who attempts nowadays to convey in human words and concepts even an echo of the ecumenical mystery of the rebellion of the so-called Morning

Star could hardly be much easier. Such an attempt would consist of two stages: first, a search in the ocean of our concepts for words and phrases that mirror better than others that fantastic reality; second, a search in the ocean of our language for words and phrases that are capable of even slightly mirroring, in turn, those elusive concepts. But the success of such an undertaking is dependent on a person's inner growth and on his or her ecumenical insight. It cannot be accomplished on a whim.

I feel myself capable of only the beginning stages of such a work. I therefore cannot state anything concerning ecumenical events of that nature except to give simple confirmation of an event that at one time occurred. Back in the forgotten depths of time, a spirit, one of the greatest, whom we call Lucifer or Satan, in exercising his free will, which is the inalienable attribute of every monad, rejected its Creator in order to create another universe according to its own plan. He was joined by a host of other monads, both great and small. They began to create another universe within the confines of this one. They tried to create worlds, but those worlds proved unstable and collapsed, because, in rebelling, the monads that turned from God in so doing also renounced love—the single unifying, bonding principle.

The ecumenical plan of Providence leads a great many monads up to a higher oneness. As they ascend the steps of being, the forms of their unions evolve: love for God and for each other bring them closer and closer together. When each of them immerses itself in the Universal Sun and co-creates with Him, the most perfect of unions takes place: merger with God without the loss of one's unique self.

The ecumenical design of Lucifer is exactly the opposite. Each of the monads that allied themselves with Lucifer is but a temporary ally and a potential victim. Every demonic monad, from the greatest to the lowest, clings to the dream of becoming the ruler of the Universe; pride prompts it to think that it is the one with the potential to be the strongest of all. It is ruled in its actions by a kind of categorical imperative, which can to a certain extent be reduced to the formula, *There is I and not-I; all not-I must become I.* In other words, everything and everyone must be swallowed up by that single, absolutely self-asserting self. God gives of Himself; the powers that rejected God try to absorb everything into themselves. That is why they are first and foremost *vampires* and *tyrants*, and that is why a tyrannical tendency is not only inherent in any demonic self but is one of its essential attributes.

Therefore, demonic monads temporarily join forces, but deep down they are rivals to the death. That antagonism surfaces when some limited power is seized by their group. A free-for-all then begins, and the strongest triumphs.

The hopelessness of the demons' cosmic struggle also springs from the fact that God is always creating more and more monads and, since the demons are incapable of creating even one, the balance of power is constantly shifting against them. There are not nor will there ever again be any more falls. That is absolutely guaranteed, and I deeply regret that the extreme complexity of the question prevents me from finding the concepts necessary to present it in some kind of intelligible manner. In any case, all the demonic monads are of very ancient origin. They are all veterans of that great rebellion. True, something like a fall but in fact different has taken place since and takes place now: a highly-conscious being, sometimes even a whole group of them, temporarily choose to oppose Providential will. That choice against God is not made by the monad itself but by the lower self, by a limited mind. For that reason, its rejection of God takes place not in the spiritual world but in the material worlds, which are subject, by the will of those same demons, to the law of retribution. The mutiny is thus doomed to failure, and the mutineer embarks on a long road of atonement.

Gradually, in the course of their struggle, the futility of trying to create their own universe became apparent to the demonic forces. So while continuing to create individual worlds and expending incredible amounts of energy to stabilize them, those forces set themselves another goal: to take over worlds already in existence or in the process of being created by the Providential powers. Their goal is the takeover, not the destruction, of those worlds. But destruction is the objective end result. Bereft of the bonding principles of love and co-creation, held together only by the conflicting principle of coercion, such worlds cannot exist for any extended period of time. There are galaxies in the process of disintegration even now. And when astronomy begins to observe intergalactic nebulae over a longer period of time than it does now, the process of those galactic catastrophes will be revealed to science. There are planets either dead or dying—Mars, Mercury, Pluto—the ruins of bramfaturas. All the monads of Light were driven from those systems, which had fallen under demonic rule, after which a final catastrophe ensued, and the demon legions were left to roam homeless in space, seeking a new bramfatura to invade.

On the other hand, there are macrobramfaturas and whole galaxies where the legions of the rebel have been unable to force a breach. Orion—a macrobramfatura of extraordinary spiritual Light—is a solar system within our Galaxy that has entirely freed itself of the demonic. Those who gaze through a telescope at the great nebula of Andromeda will see with their own eyes a galaxy that has never been invaded by demons. It is a world that from start to finish has been ascending steps of ever-increasing bliss. There are many such worlds among the millions of galaxies in the Universe, but our Galaxy, unfortunately, is not one of them. Long ago expelled from the macrobramfatura of the Universe, the forces of the rebel are waging a continuous, relentless war against the forces of Light in the worlds of our Galaxy. This war has taken millions of forms. Shadanakar also came to be a war front.

Shadanakar became a front far back in those distant times when the Earth was no more than a semimolten globe in Enrof, while other planes in Shadanakar, as yet numbering in the single digits, had only just been created by the great hierarchies of macrobramfaturas. There was no law of survival on those planes. There, in the worlds of those beings now known to us by the generic term *angels,* the principles of love and friendship between all ruled. There was no law of death: everyone moved from plane to plane by means of a painless material transformation that did not rule out the possibility of returning. In those worlds—which at the time had only three dimensions and were consequently almost as dense as Enrof—there was no law of retribution: mistakes were

rectified with the help of the higher powers. A glimmer of recollections of that time, floating up into the consciousness of ancient
sages from their treasury of deep memory, but vulgarized and
simplified by that consciousness, became crystallized in the legend of paradise lost. In reality, it was not paradise but a gorgeous
dawn rising not over terrestrial Enrof, which back then was
devoid of organic life, but over the world that is now called
Olirna. The dawn glowed and was preserved in the memories of
those few human monads who did not, like most, come later to
Shadanakar, but who began their journey in times before the distant past—and not in Enrof, but in angelic Olirna. That community of protoangels can be called, in a certain sense, the first
humankind of Shadanakar.

A great demon, a cohort of Lucifer's named Gagtungr,
irrupted into Shadanakar with legions of lesser demons. The
long and fierce battle that ensued ended in a partial victory for
him. He was unable to drive the forces of Light from the bramfatura, but he did succeed in creating several demonic planes
and turning them into impregnable fortresses. He succeeded in
tampering with the emergence and evolution of life on terrestrial Enrof and in leaving his mark on the animal world. The
planetary laws that the forces of Light were using to create
organic life on Enrof were warped beyond recognition. It is
wrong and blasphemous to attribute the laws of survival, retribution, and death to the Godhead, for "God is Light and in Him
there is no darkness."

From God comes only salvation. From God comes only joy.
From God comes only grace. If we are shocked by the cruelty of
the world's laws, it is because the voice of God cries out in our soul
against the work of the Great Torturer. The infighting between
demonic monads, the victory of the strong over the right, and the
expulsion of the vanquished down into the chasm of torment—
that law of Lucifer's forces was carved on the face of organic life
in Enrof and took the form of the law of survival.

All the suffering that beings experience, all their pain and
agony, emit radiations—both here, in Enrof, and there, in the
worlds of the afterlife. Every feeling, every emotional response

necessarily emits corresponding radiations. Radiations from anger, hate, greed, or animal and human lust sink to the demonic planes, replenishing the energy of their various classes and groups of inhabitants. True, those radiations are barely sufficient to replenish the energy of individual demonic groups. But the radiation from suffering and pain, or *gavvakh*, is capable of satisfying hosts of demons of almost all types and sizes. Gavvakh is essentially their food.

In laying his claws on Shadanakar's laws, Gagtungr warped them in such a way as to generate and increase suffering. He made them onerous, cruel, and unbearable. He resisted the establishment of the law of transformation in Enrof; death arose as the resultant vector of the two opposing forces and became law. He resisted the principle of universal friendship: the law of survival arose as the resultant vector of the two forces and became a law of life. Finally, the demonic forces tampered with the life of other planes in Shadanakar—those planes through which travel beings who have incarnated at least once on terrestrial Enrof. Those planes were transformed into worlds of retribution, where tormentors reign and imbibe the pain of those who suffer there.

Among the various types of gavvakh, the one associated with the shedding of physical blood occupies a particularly significant place. When people and animals bleed, a burning radiation of especial intensity is released in the first few minutes. Therefore, certain categories of demons are not so much interested in the death of living beings in Enrof, or in the suffering of their souls in the afterlife, as they are in bloodshed. Not one bloodbath in history has occurred or will occur without the subliminal instigation of those bloodsuckers of the afterlife. Further, the bloody sacrificial rites of some ancient cultures were horrifying not only because of their cruelty but also because it was not gods but those very same demons that were feeding on them.

To replenish the power of Light, the Planetary Logos—the first and greatest of Shadanakar's monads—created a new plane and laid the foundations for a new humankind. Enrof was left to the animal world; the new plane was populated by *Titans*, whose external appearance was similar to ours, only larger and more majestic. In a world resembling Enrof, but one still wrapped in twilight, their glowing figures moved against the backdrop of a bluish-gray sky up the slopes and around the curves of the desert hills they worked on. The Titan humankind numbered a few thousand. They had no gender—the birth of new Titans was in no way connected with the sexual union of two adults. But Gagtungr succeeded in fomenting among them a mutiny against Providence. They were motivated by the idea that they were the seed and nucleus of a new universal power, a third power that opposed both God and the demons. They hungered for absolute freedom but despised the cruelty and malice of the demons. The mutiny ended with the forces of Gagtungr invoking the law of retribution to draw the Titan's souls down to deep planes of torment. Their suffering lasted more than a million years, until with the aid of the Providential powers they were able to break out of captivity. The majority of them are now completing their journeys among humanity, standing out from the general mass of people by the magnitude of their genius and its somber, though far from dark, tint. Their creative work is marked by dim recollections of their struggle against God, scorched, as it were, by an ancient fire. It is astonishing in its power. Their spirit differs from demonic monads in its striving for Light, its scorn for the base, and its thirst for divine love.[2]

In the last millennium before Christ, the power of Gagtungr was so great that retribution was stripped of its temporality in the afterlife planes of many of humanity's metacultures. All exits from the planes of torment were shut tight, and the sufferers there were deprived of all hope.

The law of retribution, the iron law of moral cause and effect—those effects that can manifest themselves in one's present life but most fully manifest themselves in the afterlife and even in subsequent reincarnations—can be referred to by the Indian term

---

2. I could name a few such people from among the number of giants of world culture: Aeschylus, Dante, Leonardo da Vinci, Michelangelo, Goethe, Beethoven, Wagner, Ibsen, Lermontov, and Lev Tolstoy.

karma. Karma is just as much a result of two opposing wills as are the law of death and the law of survival. If the demonic forces had not encountered continuous resistance from their enemies, the laws would be even harsher, because the demonic purpose of the laws is to generate gavvakh and paralyze any manifestation of Light by the souls that fall afoul of them. The laws have another side—their cleansing nature, a vestige of the ancient protolaws of Light laid down by the great hierarchies that created the world. The goal of those hierarchies, and of all the forces of Light in Shadanakar, was and is the mitigation and enlightenment of the laws. The goal of the demonic forces is their harshening.

Providence's design is to save all victims. Gagtungr's design is to turn all into victims. The theohumankind of the next global era will be a voluntary union in love of all. The satanohumankind—its rise at the end of the current era appears to be unavoidable—will be an absolute dictatorship of one.

The cosmos is the maturating ground of monads. The anticosmos is a universal union of rivals and a host of crippled monads of Light held captive by them in worlds over which demons rule. The captives have been deprived of the most sacrosanct of their attributes: freedom of choice.

Gagtungr is not dismayed by the disparity in magnitude between himself and Lucifer. He, like all demonic monads, sees his comparatively small stature as only temporary. Blind faith in his boundless growth and ultimate victory is an inseparable part of his self. Every one of those monads, no matter how minuscule it may be at present and no matter what lowly post it may occupy within the rebel hierarchy, believes in like manner in its future macrogalactic triumph. For that reason, all of them, including Gagtungr, are tyrants not only in their dreams and not only at a given moment, but at every stage of their path to the extent permitted by the power they wield at that stage.

Tyranny produces a more copious supply of gavvakh than any other form of rule. The ingestion of gavvakh increases the energy of demons. If they were to replenish their energy by imbibing other psychic radiations—from joy, love, self-sacrifice, religious devotion, ecstasy, or happiness—their essence would be transformed and they would cease to be demons. But that is exactly what they do not want. Through tyranny and tyranny alone can they bridle the centrifugal forces within the legions of demons subordinate to them. For that very reason, defections from and uprisings against Gagtungr by individual demonic monads sometimes take place in metahistory (and are reflected in history). The forces of Light cannot come to the aid of such uprisings, since any one of those monads has the potential to become just such a planetary demon. If it proved stronger than Gagtungr, it would become an even worse tormentor than he. One should bear in mind, however, that incidences of uprisings by individual demonic monads not against Gagtungr, as such, but against the demonic world order in general are not so rare. Such uprisings are nothing other than the conversion of demonic monads to Light, and it goes without saying that they are afforded every available means of help from the Providential powers.

Despite all the satanic cunning of Gagtungr's cosmic designs, those designs are flawed for the reasons given above. The chances that the planetary demon will be able to master all the demonic monads of the universe, and eventually Lucifer himself, are incredibly slim. But his relentless pursuit of dominion over the Universe affords him the only joy he can understand: he experiences such joy every time the smallest victory appears to bring him another step closer to the ultimate goal. Those victories consist of his enslavement of other monads or their souls: the demonic monads as half-allies, half-slaves, and the monads of Light as prisoners and objects of torment. As far as Gagtungr can picture the future of the cosmos, he sees himself as a kind of sun around which countless monads orbit, one after another falling into him and being swallowed up, with the entire Universe entering into orbit around him and being swallowed up, world by world, by the monstrously swollen hypermonad. The demonic mind is powerless to picture anything further. The smaller demonic monads are incapable of visualizing even that apotheosis. With unshakeable faith in their own ultimate victory over the Universe, they focus their will and thoughts on stages that are more immediate and easier to envision.

The Question of Free Will

There exists a misconception, a particular mindset held by a large number of people in our time, that has been assiduously inculcated into the minds of many peoples over the last four decades. It is a train of thought that leads the thinker to the conclusion, which in time grows into an axiom and dogma, that religion supposedly deprives people of their freedom, demands blind obedience to higher powers, and makes them wholly dependent on those powers. Furthermore, so the thinking goes, since those powers are only figments of the imagination, it is people's dependence on all the very real human institutions that endeavor to exploit the ignorance of the masses that is actually increased. That is the essence of "religious slavery," from which humanity is supposedly liberated by science and the philosophy of materialism.

To dispute this argument would require writing a tract refuting the basic tenets of materialistic philosophy. Such tracts have already been written, and if they have been insufficiently known in Russia, then the reason for that has more to do with politics than philosophy.

As for the claim that all religions demand submission to higher powers, there is no doubt that some religious doctrines have indeed preached predestination and the virtual absence of free will among humans. That is a fact, and I least of all am inclined to defend without discrimination any and all religious forms. But to make that charge against religion as a whole is no more justified than to claim, for instance, that literature is essentially reactionary, and to substantiate that claim by citing examples of individual reactionary writers and schools.

I would like to explain forthwith the fallaciousness of such an accusation in relation to the worldview of the Rose of the World.

First, I would like to voice some puzzlement: no science or philosophy (except subjective idealism), materialism included, disputes the assertion that the human will is dependent on a host of material factors. That very same philosophy of materialism even takes special pains to emphasize the will's heavy dependence on economic factors. Yet, no one is bothered by human subordination to natural and historical necessity. No one expresses outrage at humanity's bondage to the law of gravity, the law of the preservation of matter, the law of evolution, the laws of economic development, and so forth. Everyone understands that there is still enough room for the exercise of our will within the bounds of these laws.

The worldview of the Rose of the World, however, does not add a single new, supplementary factor to the list of factors that determine our will. What is important is their interpretation, not their number. That boundless and endlessly diverse something that is summed up by the phrase "the higher powers" acts on our will not so much through supernatural intrusions as through the medium of those same factors—those same laws of nature, evolution, and so forth—that we have just agreed to regard as objective facts. To a great extent those sets of factors determine not only our consciousness but our subconsciousness and superconsciousness as well. They are the origin of the voice of conscience, duty, instinct, and the like, which we hear within ourselves and which determine our behavior in a tangible manner. That is how the link between "the higher powers" and our will operates. True, there are some phenomena that could at first glance appear to be violations of the laws of nature by the higher powers. They are called miracles. But in cases when such phenomena, as opposed to tricks of the mind, do occur, they are not at all "arbitrary" violations of natural laws by the higher powers but the actions of those powers through a number of other laws as yet unknown to us.

What frequently appears to us to be the single, monolithic, and indivisible mover of our actions—for example, conscience—is in reality the extremely complex result of the interaction of various factors. Conscience is primarily the voice of our monad. But whether it gains access to our waking consciousness is determined by other factors—for example, some incident that serves as a shock to waken us to the monad's voice: a manifestation of Providence, the action of powers of a Providential nature.

Thus, people's choices are predetermined by three sets of forces: the Providential powers, which utilize the laws of nature and history to achieve their purposes and which gradually enlighten those laws; the demonic powers, which utilize those same laws and work to strengthen them more and more; and the will of our own monad, transmitted within the range of our consciousness by the voices of our heart and reason with the help of the Providential powers. Therefore, whether we view the laws of nature and history as mechanical, lifeless necessities or as the tools of living, individual, variomaterial or spiritual beings, the degree of our freedom will neither decrease nor increase.

It follows that the degree of our freedom of choice is no less from the point of view of the Rose of the World worldview than it is from the point of view of materialism. But the determining factors are interpreted differently and are more precisely broken down into their component parts.

If the materialist is not bothered by the limitations placed on our freedom by utterly impersonal and lifeless laws of nature, then how can we view as demeaning the limitations placed on our freedom by the will of the Providential powers? Only the limitations placed on our freedom by the will of the demonic powers can gall us. It does indeed gall us, but after all, they are those powers, those age-old enemies of ours, the disarming, conversion, and enlightenment of whom is our goal. We will cease to feel galled only when we render ourselves insusceptible to their influence. The evolution of life on Earth raises groups of beings up from a minimal degree of freedom among the simplest forms. The voice of a microbe's monad almost always fails to reach its embryonic consciousness, and its behavior is primarily determined by demonic powers acting on it through the medium of the laws of nature. The higher animals are much freer than a microbe; the amplitude of their conscious action is far greater. In humans conscious action is increased to an incomparable degree.

Opponents of religion as such argue that it demands the renunciation of our individual will and the subordination of that will to God's. In regard to some religions of the past, they are right. But the Rose of the World is not a religious teaching of the past. It is a religious and social-moral teaching of the future. The Rose of the

World will not demand submission to the will of God, for only what humans do voluntarily, not under compulsion, is of value.

It will not be demands for slavish submission to God's will that will sound from the churches of the sum religion. From there will sound forth a call to universal love and free divine co-creation.

The Divine Spirit is our unchanging, inexpressible, and highest yearning. It is the power that creates spirit, that is active in all souls, that is not silenced even in the depths of demonic monads, and that is directing worlds and worlds—from microbramfaturas to supergalaxies—toward something more perfect than good and something higher than bliss. The higher the stage reached by a monad, the closer its will coincides with the creative will of God. And when, having begun its cosmic journey from the simplest forms of animate matter, it passes through the stages of human being and national, planetary, stellar, and galactic demiurge, it merges, through the agency of God the Son, with God the Father, and its will completely coincides with God's will, its power with God's power, its image with God's image, and its work with the work of God.

Divine co-creation is the creative work of Light of all ascending monads of the Universe, from humans, elementals, and enlightened animals to giants of unimaginable grandeur, the galactic demiurges. That is why one sees here so often the word *demiurge*, a word almost never used in the older religions. Everyone who works for the greater glory of God, out of love for the world and its Creator, is a demiurge.

God is absolutely good. The old theology also asserted that God is omnipotent. But if God is omnipotent, He is then responsible for the evil and suffering in the world. Therefore, He is not good.

It would seem impossible to find a way out of that vicious circle.

But God creates of Himself. All the monads flowing out of His depths possess, as inalienable attributes, all the properties of those depths, including absolute freedom. Thus, divine creation itself limits the Creator, it fixes His power at a line beyond which the freedom and power of His creations begin. But freedom is freedom for the very reason that it offers the possibility of different choices. For many monads, it took the form of a negative choice, through their assertion of self only, through their rejection of God. That is the origin of what we call evil in the world, the origin of suffering, the origin of barbaric laws, and therein lies the possibility that evil and suffering can be overcome. The laws protect the world from descending into chaos. The demons, too, are forced to operate within them, if worlds are not to crumble into dust. For that reason, they do not try to overturn laws but to strengthen them. Laws are blind. And they cannot be enlightened in the blink of an eye, not by a miracle, not by divine intercession. They can be enlightened through the protracted cosmic process whereby monads that have rejected God renounce their evil will.

In God, all-embracing love and inexhaustible creativity are blended into one. All living beings, humans included, draw closer to God through the exercise of three divine properties innate to each: freedom, love, and divine co-creation. Divine co-creation is the goal, love is the means, and freedom is the condition.

Demonic monads are as free as all monads, but their love is grossly disfigured. It is directed exclusively inward: a demon loves only itself. And since the entire great reservoir of love in its spirit is focussed on that single object, a demon loves itself with a degree of intensity no human is capable of achieving.

Demonic monads have also not lost their ability to create. But divine co-creation evokes nothing in them but extreme hostility. Every demon creates for its own sake and in its own name only.

People's creative work becomes divine co-creation from the moment and to the extent that their irresistible creative impulse is guided by their will and faith not toward the attainment of one or another egoistic goal—fame, pleasure, riches, the service of a cruel and base teaching—but toward the service of the God of Love.

Freedom, love, and *divine co-creation* are the three words that sum up the Rose of the World's perspective on art, science, education, marriage, family, nature, and even on those aspects of modern life ignored by all religions: social justice and harmony.

Being and Consciousness

What I have said supplies us with a new point of view on the centuries-long debate over the primacy of being or consciousness.

"Consciousness determines being," was the formula of the idealistic schools. During the next, secular stage of culture, the formula was turned on its head, but its content remained untouched. It was the same juxtaposition of two components, and so the new formula inherited the simplism of its predecessor. The question is much more complex than those formulas. At the same time, it is simpler than the ungainly edifices of premises and conclusions constructed in the eighteenth and nineteenth centuries for the extraction of such modest gains.

"Being determines consciousness." "Consciousness determines being." Whose being? Whose consciousness? Of a specific individual? Of humanity? Of the world? Of living, conscious matter? Everything is so jumbled, so imprecise.

The consciousness of specific individuals (for simplicity's sake we will speak only of humans) is not determined by any one consciousness or by being in general but by a *set of factors*. These factors are (a) the individual's own physical being; (b) the being of the individual's natural and cultural environment; (c) the consciousness of a large number of people, both living and dead, for by their efforts these consciousnesses determine, to a significant extent, the cultural milieu in which the individuals live and that affect their being and consciousness; (d) the consciousness of x-number of other beings who influence the natural environment and transform it; (e) the being and consciousness of the hierarchies that create worlds; (f) the superconscious individuality inherent in the monad of the individual; (g) the being-consciousness of the One God, in Whom being and consciousness are one, rather than different, conflicting categories.

If the question refers not to individuals and their being and consciousness but to the Universe (or to be more exact, the emergence of consciousness in the organic matter of worlds in the Universe), then clearly, since the Universe is determined by the nature of the One God, the conflict between being and consciousness vanishes, for the above-mentioned reason. Since the Universe is determined by the work of God-created monads, the question concerning the emergence of consciousness after some period of unconscious existence becomes irrelevant. For if there were no God-created monads with their consciousness and being, then no matter, neither organic nor inorganic, could come into being either.

We could today afford to chuckle over the simplism of the classical formulas if one of them had not become the philosophical dogma of political despotism and caused untold harm, stifling the independent thought of a host of people and barring spirituality from access to their consciousness. The other formula, just as flawed, is nevertheless not as dangerous for the very reason that it is more spiritual. But that does not at all excuse the older religions and their philosophizing, their waste of so many centuries on intellectual speculation without coming a step closer to understanding the relationship between being and consciousness.

The Variomaterial Composition of Humans

Among the numerous planes of Shadanakar, there is a multi-dimensional world where human monads—indivisible and immortal spiritual entities, the higher selves of humans—abide. Created by God and God alone, with some (a very few) mysteriously born of ~~them~~ they enter Shadanakar, coating themselves in rarefied matter, or rather, energy. This is a substance that permeates all of Shadanakar; every individual spirit, in entering our bramfatura, must coat itself in it. The world where our monads abide is called *Iroln*.

Creative work toward the eventual enlightenment of the Universe is the task of every monad, except demonic ones. There are no demonic human monads. Human monads carry out that enlightening work in lower worlds assigned to them, creating material coatings for themselves there and acting on the environment of those planes by means of the coatings.

The monad first creates a *shelt* from five-dimensional materiality, then an *astral body* from four-dimensional materiality. We often group these two coatings together under the word *soul*. A shelt is the material vessel of the monad with all its divine properties and capacities. It is not the monad, which remains in five-dimensional Iroln, but the shelt that begins the journey on the lower planes. The shelt is created by the monad alone.

Mother Earth, the great elemental, takes part in the creation of the astral body. She takes part in the creation of astral bodies for all beings of Shadanakar: humans, angels, daemons, animals, elementals, demons, and even the great hierarchies, when the latter descend to planes where an astral body is required. The astral body is the higher instrument of the shelt. Concentrated within it are the gifts of spiritual sight, spiritual hearing, spiritual smell, deep memory, the ability to levitate, to communicate with the Synclites, daemons, elementals, and angels, and to perceive cosmic panoramas and perspectives.

Mother Earth, fertilized by the spirit of the Sun, next creates an *ether body* for the incarnating monad. No life in three and four dimensional worlds is possible without it. When the shelt with all its coatings, including the ether body, abandons the physical body—the last, outermost, and shortest-lived of its vessels—nothing but a corpse remains in Enrof. Our physical body is created for us by the angelic hierarchies—they create the matter—and by Lilith, the great elemental of humanity, who forges the family chain from three-dimensional materiality. The monad itself, through the shelt, contributes to the process by bestowing individuality on a given link in the chain.

Once the process of descent has concluded, the process of ascent begins. A monad can assume a physical body either just one time or over and over again. An ether body is created anew only if the bearer, in falling afoul of the law of retribution, is forced to embark on a journey through the great planes of torment. As for the path of ascent, the ether body accompanies the bearer through all the worlds of Enlightenment, all the way up to the zatomis—the abodes of enlightened humankind, the celestial cities of the metacultures. The ether body is composed of a living substance that is not everywhere uniform, differing as it does in all three and four dimensional worlds. It would be proper to call it, in recalling the ancient revelation given to humanity, arungvilta-prana.

The astral body accompanies the bearer higher, up to and including the sakwala of Higher Purpose. Higher than that, only the shelt is left to achieve final enlightenment and merge with the monad. Then the monad departs from Iroln and, coated with an extremely rarefied shelt, rises up the stairway to the highest worlds of Shadanakar.

All these planes will be discussed in later parts of the book; many of them will be described in as much detail as possible. But I am, unfortunately, incapable of throwing more light on the interaction between the various coatings of the monad and on their functions and structure.

Metacultures

The structure of Shadanakar (a vast area of investigation that we shall soon enter) will remain unintelligible at the most basic of levels if the meaning of the words *suprapeople, metaculture,* and *transmyth* is not firmly grasped beforehand.

The term *suprapeople* refers to a group of nations united by a common, jointly created culture, or to an individual nation, if that nation alone has created a culture that has reached a high level of distinction and maturity. It goes without saying that completely isolated cultures do not exist. Cultures interact with each other. But on the whole each culture is entirely unique and, despite the influence it exerts on other cultures, it remains, in all its fullness, the achievement of only one suprapeople, which is its creator.

It would not be necessary to introduce the suprapeople concept if it did not possess metahistorical, as well as historical, significance. Its metahistorical significance rests in the fact that the distinctiveness of a suprapeople is not limited to its own cultural sphere of influence in Enrof but also affects many variomaterial planes, both of ascent and descent, for certain parts of those planes are subject to the activities of one suprapeople alone. One should bear in mind that the term *suprapeople* not only includes those individuals, our contemporaries, who belong to it now. A great many of those who belonged to it earlier, even at the very dawn of its history, and who afterward, in the afterlife, have acted and act now on transphysical planes linked to that suprapeople. A staircase of planes common to all suprapeoples rises above humanity, but the complexion, landscape, and function of each plane varies above each suprapeople. There are even planes that only exist above a single suprapeople. The exact same is true of the demonic worlds of descent, which exist, as it were, *beneath* suprapeoples. Thus, a significant portion of Shadanakar consists of individual multiplaned segments. In each of those segments the Enrof plane is occupied by only one suprapeople and its culture. Those multiplaned segments of Shadanakar are called *metacultures*.

Every suprapeople has its own myth, which does not take shape in the culture's infant stage alone. Since the traditional use of the word *myth* does not match the meaning attached to it here, it is necessary to explain carefully in what sense I use the word.

When we speak of a tightly integrated system of rich symbols that embody some comprehensive international teaching and that find expression in legends and ritual, in theology and philosophy, in monuments of literature and art, and lastly, in a moral code, we are speaking of *myths of the great international religions*. There are four such myths: Hindu, Buddhist, Christian, and Muslim.

When we speak of a tightly integrated system of rich symbols that define the relationship of one suprapeople to Enrof and to the transphysical and spiritual worlds, a system molded into a definite religion that has played an enormously significant role in the history of the given suprapeople but has rarely spread beyond its boundaries, we are speaking of *national religious myths of individual suprapeoples*. Such are the Egyptian, ancient Iranian, Jewish, Germanic, Gallic, Aztec, Incan, Japanese, and some other myths.

When we are referring to symbols just as rich and perhaps also tied, although not as closely, to ideas of a religious and moral nature, which, though they have not evolved into a strictly formulated system, reflect, nonetheless, a group of common moral, transphysical, metahistorical, or cosmic truths in connection with the specific nature and role of that culture, we are dealing with *shared myths of suprapeoples*. Such are the myths of the South-Western (Roman Catholic) suprapeople, the North-Western (Germanic Protestant) suprapeople, or the Russian suprapeople.[3]

Last is the fourth and final group—*shared national myths*. They are myths of individual ethnic groups within a suprapeople that have created, as a supplement to the shared suprapeople myth, their own particular, very restricted variations of that myth, variations that have not evolved into any strictly formulated system or religion. One could cite as examples the pagan myths of the Slavic tribes, the Finnish tribes, the Turkish tribes, as well as the myths of some isolated and primal tribes in India. Ethnic myths in their embryonic state can be observed among many ethnic groups, but they rarely achieve any clear expression.

We will not use the word *myth* in reference to any other phenomenon in the history of culture.

The last three groups of myths are concerned with one specific culture. The first group—the myths of international religions—are (with one exception) mystically linked to planes in Shadanakar above those segmented sections called metacultures.

It seems to me that the concept of national religious myths can be grasped without too much difficulty. As for the shared myths of suprapeoples, for the sake of clarity, a pair of supplementary definitions are in order.

Defined inductively, the shared myth of a suprapeople is the sum of its beliefs concerning the transphysical cosmos and the part the given culture and each self belonging to that culture play within it.[4] The culture elaborates these beliefs, molding them into cycles of religious-philosophical ideas, iconography,

3. In some cultures, the Greco-Roman or Babylonian-Canaanite, for example, their myths had already passed the "shared" stage of development but did not take shape in a system strictly formulated enough to allow the Olympic or Babylonian myths to be numbered among the national religious myths of suprapeoples.
4. The very concept "given culture" can be no more precisely formulated than it was, for example, by the Greco-Romans, who distinguished between themselves and the rest of humanity, whom they lumped together as barbarians.

social-moral systems, state-political institutions, and cycles of national lifestyle manifested in ritual, daily routines, and tradition.

Defined deductively, the shared myth of a suprapeople is an *awakening by the suprapeople*, in the person of its most creative representatives, to *a second reality* above them, of which the suprapeople is a part and in which the direction of its growth and the roots of its fate are hidden. This awakening is made groggy by additives foreign to it issuing from unattuned human nature. We can give that second reality, which serves as the object of transphysical, metahistorical, artistic, and philosophical apprehensions, the provisional name of *transmyth*.

It goes without saying that the discrepancy between myth and transmyth can vary considerably. The limitations of those who apprehended the transmyth through intuition, dreams, artistic inspiration, religious meditation, or metahistorical enlightenment; the national, temporal, class, and individual peculiarities of their conscious and subconscious minds (the latter playing an active part in the process); the impossibility of finding words or three-dimensional images to convey precisely the reality of variodimensional worlds—can not all that lead to countless aberrations, to the cluttering of the myth with a mass of chance, inaccurate, anthropomorphic, simplistic, and even simply wrong ideas? But myths are dynamic. They exist in time, evolving and changing in appearance, and their later phases, as a rule, approach more closely the transmyth, because the minds that apprehend it have over the centuries become subtler, richer, keener, and broader.

But in the meantime, the transmyth is also evolving. The reality behind our reality is seething with movement, and there can be no question of it remaining static. The landscapes, edifices, and activities within a transmyth at the time of its emergence differ from those at the end of its metahistorical development as much as the city-fortresses of the Merovingians differ from modern-day Paris.

But two different realities, two different planes, two poles of the metacultural globe exist at every stage of the transmyth development together with the people on Enrof who apprehend it.

There are also other planes around those planes and between them, but each of them either appeared at a later time or has undergone radical changes. Some have even disappeared. Only three realms are stable and enduring. First, the suprapeople in Enrof; second, the abode of its enlightened souls, the holy cities and celestial land of its metaculture in the variodimensional space above them; and third, down below, in the worlds of descent, the antipode of the heavenly land—a bastion erected in worlds bound to strata deep within the planet's physical body. It is the focal point of the demonic in the given metaculture. The heavenly lands and everything contained within them are called *zatomis*; the subterranean bastions are called *shrastrs*.

Of these two poles, it is the zatomis that are usually reflected in a more detailed and distinct manner in myths. The images of shrastrs often do not take a finished form. As for the zatomis, the abode of the Synclites of metacultures, they can be found in the myths of every suprapeople, in both religious and shared myths. Such is Eanna of the Babylonians: the ziggurat in the city of Erech was, in the view of the Sumero-Akkadians, a model of the mountain of the gods, Heavenly Eanna. Later, the Babylonians saw an analogous meaning in the chief religious edifice of their great city—the seven-storied temple of Esagila. Such is Olympus of the Greeks and Romans. Such is Sumera, or Mount Meru, of the Indians—the Indian Olympus, on the slopes of which glitter the celestial cities of Hindu gods. Such are the images of Paradise and Eden in the Byzantine and Roman Catholic metacultures, Jannet in the Arab-Muslim metaculture, Shan Ti in the Chinese metaculture, Monsalvat in the North-Western metaculture, and Kitezh in the Russian metaculture.

As we attempt to descry the heavenly land of the North-Western metaculture through the thick haze of art, religion, mythology, and social systems, we should always bear in mind that suprapeoples, while they exist in Enrof, never cease creating their myths. The forms of expression change. New groups of people enter the historical scene as depictors of the myths. From the anonymous creators of folklore and customs, the task of myth-building passes to thinkers and artists, whose names are washed by waves of national love. But the myth lives on. It lives on, deepening, injected with new content, revealing new meaning in old symbols and introducing new symbols, in accordance with the higher level of overall cultural development of those apprehending it and, secondly, with the continuing metahistorical growth of the transmyth itself.

The heavenly land of the North-Western culture appears to us as Monsalvat, an eternally illuminated mountaintop where, through the centuries, righteous knights have guarded the Holy Grail, which contains the blood of the Logos Incarnate that Joseph of Arimathea collected at the Crucifixion and which was committed to the charge of the pilgrim Titurel, the founder of Monsalvat. In the distance towers an eerie castle built by the sorcerer Klingsor. This is the focal point of the forces that reject God and strive with dogged resolve to crush the power of the Monsalvat community—the keepers of the greatest of the holy relics and mysteries. These are the two poles of the shared myth of the North-Western suprapeople, which came down from the anonymous composers of Old Celtic legends, through Wolfram von Eschenbach, and down to Richard Wagner. The claim that Wagner's *Parsifal* is the last word on the myth is far from indisputable and surely premature. The Monsalvat transmyth is evolving; it is becoming ever more magnificent. We can only hope that thinkers and poets whose metahistorical enlightenment will allow them to apprehend and depict the heavenly land of Monsalvat as it is today will yet emerge from among the peoples of the North-West.

It is easy to see that the majority of even the greatest human images in the North-Western myth do not and cannot have a direct connection to the image of Monsalvat. To expect a direct connection in every case would be to reveal a narrow and formalistic approach to the question, even a complete failure to grasp what a shared myth of a suprapeople (not a national religious myth) is. Basically, every human image created by a great writer, artist, or composer, an image that continues to live on in the conscious and subconscious minds of millions of people and has become the inner acquisition of all who creatively perceive the image—every such image is a mythical image. Kriemhild and Ophelia, Macbeth and Brandt, Rembrandt's Esther and Goethe's Margaret, Egmont and Mr. Pickwick, Jean Christophe and Jolyon Forsyte are mythical to the same degree as Lohengrin and Parsifal. But what is the connection between the iconography, as well as the philosophical and social ideas, of the North-Western culture and the poles of the North-Western myth—Monsalvat and Klingsor's castle?

The poles of every suprapeople myth are ringed by a large number of circles, by whole worlds of images whose connection with the myth's focal point springs from their inner affinity with it—not from the role they play in the particular story—and from our ability to interpret and apprehend them through metahistorical contemplation within, or next to, the center of the myth.

Faust, of course, is not Merlin; Byron's Cain is not Klingsor; Peer Gynt is not Amfortas; and it would be strange indeed, at first glance, to compare Hauptmann's Emmanuel Quint with Parsifal. The image of Kundry, so central to the myth, has not been given equal treatment anywhere on the myth's outskirts. On the other hand, we will not find any prototypes of Hamlet or King Lear, of Margaret or Solveig within the center of the North-Western myth. But their gaze is directed toward it. One can make out a reddish glow on their clothing, a reflection of either the Holy Grail or the sorcerous fires of Klingsor. These colossal figures, rising up from various stages of artistic realism, at various stages of mystic illumination, resemble sculptures that guard the approach up the landings of the stairway to the sanctuary where the greatest mystery of the North-Western peoples is kept: the holy relic that sends out spiritual waves of Providence and grace to countries wrapped in thickening gloom.

Do we really discern the glow from the light of the holy relic—or from the light of the other pole of the myth, the satanic castle of Klingsor—on the legends of the Knights of the Round Table alone? Or on the Bayreuth operas alone? If Monsalvat ceased to be for us a mere poetic image among images, just an enchanting tale or musical melody, and assumed its true significance—the significance of a higher reality—we would discern its glow on Gothic abbeys and Baroque architecture, on the canvases of

Ruisdal and Dürer, in the landscapes of the Rhine and Danube, Bohemia and Bretagne, in the stained glass windows behind church altars, and in the austere liturgy and ritual of Lutheranism. The glow would be visible to us as well in the sanitized, soulless palace grounds of the Sun King and in the skylines of cities rising across the ocean like a Palmir of skyscrapers. We would see it in the lyrical poems of the Romantics and in the works of the great playwrights, in Masonry and Jacobism, in the systems of Fichte and Hegel, even in the doctrines of Sainte-Simon and Fourier. It would require a separate volume to illustrate how the power of contemporary science, the wonders of technology, and the ideas of socialism, even communism, on the one hand, and Nazism on the other, are contained within the myth of Monsalvat and Klingsor's castle. Nothing, no modern scientific discoveries, including the splitting of the atom, takes North-Western humanity outside the limits circumscribed by the prophetic symbolism of its myth. I imagine that other interconnections, as yet undisclosed, will reveal themselves to those who read through this book.

I have touched on one of the metacultures with its myth and transmyth only to help readers comprehend in a concrete manner the concept of the heavenly lands of humankind located on enlightened planes at the summits of the respective metacultures and to help them grasp the significance of their antipodes—the bastions of the powers that reject God, that are actively engaged in constructing their anticosmos and in struggling with the forces of Light within all the suprapeoples of Enrof, on every plane, and in every metacultural region.

But the stairway of planes in Shadanakar does not end where the segments of metacultures reach their zenith. Above them rise five and six-dimensional worlds, which have also been reflected, though hazily, in the religions and myths of humanity. The title *transmyth* is also used in that sense in reference to many of these planes. But the word *transmyth* is used in a narrower and higher sense in reference to one sakwala in particular: a system of five-dimensional worlds with an immense number of time streams. It consists of five magnificent, wondrous, translucent pyramids, which seem to glow with an inner light and which tower imposingly over Enrof. From there, not only Enrof but the heavenly lands of the metacultures, too, seem to be shrouded in murk far below. Those worlds are the highest aspects of three (not four) great international religions and of two religions that have, for a number of historical reasons, almost never broken out of their national confines, but that are illuminated by the glow from both their zatomis and that incomparably higher sakwala. More will be said about that sakwala in one of the later chapters.

I would also like to mention something as an aside. I imagine that many readers of this book are wondering why all the new words and names used to refer to the lands of the transphysical world and the planes of Shadanakar, even the names of almost all the hierarchies, do not sound Russian. That is because the Russian metaculture is one of the youngest. By the time its Synclite had begun to form, everything had already been named by others. One most often hears in these words sounds suggestive of Sanskrit, Latin, Greek, Hebrew, and Arabic, and sometimes even more ancient tongues of which no philologist as yet has any inkling. I don't know them either, of course. I have based my judgments concerning their strange phonetic construction only on individual words.

It now seems to me that everything necessary has been said to allow subsequent parts of the book to be fully intelligible. We have before us four parts almost wholly devoted to a description of the structure of Shadanakar—a kind of transphysical geography. Only by gaining an understanding, if only approximate, of the theater of and participants in the metahistorical drama can we proceed to those parts that are devoted to the metahistorical processes themselves—in particular, the metahistory of Russia and its culture, as well as the metahistory of modern times. This is connected with the tasks and concrete program of the Rose of the World and with an account of those historical paths that make possible the bloodless unification of humanity, global prosperity, the ennobling education of younger generations, and the transformation of the planet into a garden and the global state into a family. From there a bridge will be built to the final chapters: to certain distant historical prognoses, to the problem of the final catastrophe of global history, and to the inevitable, cataclysmic passage of Enrof to a higher materiality, a different plane of existence. The last few pages are devoted to the cosmic panorama that will unfold when that happens.

BOOK III

The Structure of Shadanakar:
Worlds of Ascent

1 The Sakwala of Enlightenment

I DO NOT KNOW when and where I will die this time, but I do know where and when I last died, prior to being born of Russian parents in 1906. Of course, that information is of no general import. It can be of interest only to those who are able to approach my testimony with trust and who feel a karmic bond with my fate. But my knowledge of certain legs of the journey from my previous existence to my current one is, from an objective viewpoint, wider in its interest. I can and should reveal the most essential things of what I gradually managed to remember, or rather, what I was helped to remember.

I have at times met people who have the same kind of crack-like opening in their deep memory, but not one of them has summoned the courage to speak of it with any but those closest to them. It has never even occurred to them to attempt to set those recollections down in writing. What has prevented them was both a conviction that such disclosures would evoke only ridicule and the natural diffidence of the inner self, which shrinks from holding up to the judgment of skeptical strangers what is intimate, inviolate, and at the same time unverifiable. For a long time I, too, viewed the matter in the same light, and even now I am undertaking the task without the least pleasure. But since positively everything I speak of in this book comes from the same unverifiable source, I see no reason to remain silent about the breaches in my deep memory. I should either have not begun the book at all or, once having started, I should, despite my apprehensions, speak of everything. In addition, I am encouraged by the hope that those readers who do not trust me stopped reading during the first chapters and that only people who are favorably disposed will continue to read further.

My last death occurred approximately three hundred years ago in a country at the head of a different, very old, and powerful metaculture. I have suffered my entire present life, since earliest childhood, from homesickness for my former homeland. It may be that I feel that homesickness so strongly and deeply because I lived not one but two lives in that country, and very full lives at that. But in departing from Enrof three hundred years ago, I was, for the first time in my entire journey through Shadanakar, free of the obligation of expiatory descents after death to the depths of planes where sinners unravel—sometimes for centuries, even millennia—the karmic knots they tie during their lives. For the first time, I succeeded in unraveling the knots in time—that is, while still in Enrof—having paid for the wrongs and mistakes of my youth with long years of suffering and painful personal losses. For the first time, I died with a light heart, though according to the religious beliefs of that country a truly horrific afterlife should have been awaiting me. But I already knew that, through expulsion from my caste and a forty-year life lived among the pariahs, I had atoned for everything. My death was replete with serenity and hope.

It was a prophetic hope, the kind that does not deceive. To the present day, I have been unable to recall anything about the first hours, even the first few days, of my new existence. But I do remember some sections of the new plane on which I existed for a long time afterward.

Although it is common to all the metacultures, this plane differs widely from one metaculture to another. In the ancient, tropical, immense metaculture that twice played host to my life on Earth, it resembled the metaculture's natural environment in Enrof, only milder, without its extremes of harshness and splendor, without its violent tropical storms and the deadly aridity of its deserts. I remember white clouds of unusually full and glorious forms on the horizon, towering almost motionless up to the middle of the sky. Days and nights passed, and still the gigantic, radiant towers hovered there, their outlines barely changing. The sky was not light or dark blue, but a deep green. And the sun there was more beautiful than here. It glittered with slowly and smoothly alternating colors, and I am unable to explain why the color of the light source had no effect on the color of what the light illuminated: the landscape looked almost the same as ours, the dominant colors being green, white, and gold.

There were rivers and lakes. There was an ocean, though I never did get a chance to see it: once or twice I made it only as far as the shore of a sea. There were mountains, forests, and wide open spaces reminiscent of the steppe. But the vegetation in these areas was almost transparent and as sparse as in the northern forests of Enrof in late spring, when plants have only just begun to don their leafy mantle. The mountain ranges and even the soil were just as airy and translucent, as if they were the ether bodies of those elements whose physical bodies we know so well in Enrof.

But there was no trace of bird, fish, or animal. Humans were the sole inhabitants. I say "humans," meaning not such as we are while in Enrof but such as we become after death in the first of the worlds of Enlightenment. On that plane I at last discovered firsthand that the comfort older religions offer us in the prospect of being reunited with loved ones in the afterlife is neither fable nor delusion, but it occurs only if our actions during our lifetime do not draw us down to the woeful planes of atonement. Some of my loved ones were there waiting to welcome me, and whole periods of my life on that plane were taken up by the joy of being with them. The plane is a very old one, at one time having been the home of the angelic protohumankind. It is called Olirna, and that melodious word seems to me a fitting choice for its name. Being with loved ones did not give rise to any of the tension, sorrow, petty worries, or misunderstandings that tarnish it here. The experience was true communion, sometimes accompanied by speech, but more often by silence, the kind we know here only at especially tender moments with the few to whom we are joined by an especially deep love.

Our life was entirely free of worries about the daily necessities of life, worries that play such a pivotal role in Enrof. The mildness of the climate eliminated any need for shelter. That may not be true in the Olirna of some other metacultures, but I cannot say for sure. The wonderful vegetation served as food, and springs and brooks, which, as I recall, tasted different from our water, served as drink. Clothing—or rather, that beautiful, living, softly glowing material that we try to replace in Enrof with garments of wool, silk, or linen—was produced by our very own body, by that same ether body of which we are here almost never aware, but which in the afterlife becomes just as visible and seems just as vital as the physical body is for us. Life is impossible without it both in the worlds of Enlightenment and in Enrof.

Nevertheless, my first while in Olirna was clouded by thoughts of those I had left behind in Enrof. I had left behind children and grandchildren, friends, and my elderly wife—the woman I treasured above all other people in Enrof, the woman for whom I had violated the laws of caste and become an untouchable. After our separation, I was constantly beset by anxiety for their fates, but I soon learned to distinguish their figures through the haze as they stumbled down thorny paths in Enrof. Some time later, it was my turn to welcome my wife, as young as she had once been, only more beautiful. Her journey in Enrof had come to an end a few years after mine, and now there was nothing to tarnish the joy of our reunion.

One after another new sense organs came unblocked: not those organs of sight and hearing that in the ether body coincide exactly with the corresponding organs of the physical body. No! These organs of sight and hearing had been working since the first minutes of my arrival, and it was with them that I perceived Olirna. What came unblocked were those organs we call spiritual vision, spiritual hearing, and deep memory; what the wisest of the wise strive to unblock in Enrof and what is successfully unblocked by only a few out of millions; what gradually comes unblocked in each one of us in Olirna. Spiritual vision and hearing can penetrate the partitions between many planes. It was with them that I perceived the life of those I had left behind on Earth—as yet hazily, but perceived nonetheless.

I enjoyed spending time in the enlightened natural surroundings—never have I seen such picturesque beauty in Enrof. But strangely enough, I felt there was something missing, and soon I realized what: a variety of life. With sadness I recalled the singing and chirping of birds, the buzzing of insects, the darting of fish, the graceful bodies and unconscious wisdom of the higher animals. Only then did I realize how much the animal world means for us and our relationship with nature. However, I was assured by those who knew more than I that humanity's ancient, vague dream about the existence of planes where animals are enlightened and intelligent is not a dream at all but an intuition of the truth. In time I, too, would be able to enter those planes.

Later—quite recently in fact—I was reminded about certain areas in the Olirna of all metacultures. They are regions that resemble rolling steppe, and those who were too engrossed in their own personal growth in Enrof, whose karmic knots have been unraveled but whose soul is too constricted and cramped, remain there for a time. Now nothing prevents them from redressing that inner imbalance amidst the transparent, silent hills and under the magnificent sky, absorbing the rays and voices of the cosmos and stretching the limits of their ever-expanding selves.

I was also reminded about areas in Olirna that resemble alpine country. Those who were able only after death to believe in—or to be more precise, to personally experience—the existence of a different reality, work on themselves there, in the valleys. From down below, they gaze up to the mountaintops, mountains that appear not as we see them but in their spiritual glory. The powerful spirits that hold sway there pour forth into the gazers streams of their own energy. And the faculties of the gazers' souls, which had been paralyzed by a lack of faith, come unblocked over days and years of direct contemplation of the multiplaned universe and of the glorious majesty of other worlds. But I have no clear recollection of all that, perhaps because I was only a guest there. Also, I cannot be entirely sure from the source of the information that the information itself was not simplified and thus distorted to facilitate my understanding of it.

Besides enjoying nature and the company of humans, I also spent time working on my own body. I needed to prepare it for transformation, as the path out of Olirna to the next, higher worlds lies not through death but through transfiguration. I understood that the verses in the Gospel that tell of the Ascension of Jesus Christ hint at something similar. His Resurrection from the dead altered the nature of His physical body. Upon His ascension out of Olirna, it was transfigured a second time, together with the ether body. I, like everyone else, was to undergo the transfiguration of my ether body alone, a transfiguration similar to the one the Apostles once saw with vision that penetrated into Olirna but could not yet reach the worlds lying beyond. How else could the Evangelists have expressed the passage of our Savior from Olirna to higher planes if not by calling the event His Ascension into heaven? And I, raised under strict Brahmanism, began to understand what strange and inexhaustible truth the Christian myth contained.

The image of the great betrayer, which I had hitherto taken to be mere legend, became reality in my eyes. I learned that he lives there in total seclusion, on a desert island amidst the seas of Olirna. His journey through the planes of torment took more than sixteen centuries. He was hurled down to the deepest of them all by the weight of his karma, a karma unparalleled in its gravity, and neither before nor after did he encounter a solitary human being. He was subsequently raised by the One he had betrayed on Earth, but only after the Betrayed had attained in His afterlife the incredible spiritual strength needed for it, strength that no one in Shadanakar had ever attained before. Raised higher and higher up the stairway of purgatories by the forces of Light, he finally reached Olirna, having atoned in full for his betrayal. Having not yet had any contact with its inhabitants, he is preparing himself on the island for his further ascent. I saw the island from a distance: it has a forbidding appearance. Strange cliffs, the tops of which all point in one direction, rise upon it. The tops are jagged, and the cliffs are a dark color, even black in places. But no one in Olirna has seen Judas himself: only the glow from his vigils can be seen above the island at night. In the future, when the rule of the one whom it has become customary to call the Antichrist has begun in Enrof, Judas, accepting an important mission from the hands of the Betrayed, will be born again on Earth and, after performing his task, will die a martyr's death at the hands of the Prince of Darkness.

But I am unable to say through what exact efforts I arrived at my own transformation and what actually happened to my body at that moment. At present, I am only able to recall what then took place before my eyes: a crowd of people, perhaps hundreds, gathered to see me off on my journey upward. The attainment of transformation by anyone living in Olirna is always a cause for celebration for others as well; a bright and joyous atmosphere surrounds the event. As I recall, it took place in the afternoon, on a height like a hill and, as with everything else in Indian Olirna, in the open air. I remember the rows of human faces turned toward me slowly beginning to blur as they seemingly receded into the distance, though it must have been I rising above the ground who was moving away from them. I could see a mountain range far away on the horizon, translucent as ever, as if it were of crystallite. Suddenly I noticed that the mountains had begun to radiate a marvelous light. Quivering rainbows crisscrossed the low horizon, out of nowhere wondrous luminaries of different colors appeared high above me, and the resplendent sun could not outshine them. I remember experiencing a mixed feeling of breathtaking beauty, incomparable joy, and astonishment. When my gaze wandered down, I saw that the crowd of well-wishers was no longer there beneath me; it was a different landscape altogether, and I realized that the moment of my passage to the next, higher plane was already past.

I had earlier been told that my stay on that plane would be very short, as all those passing through it leave after only a few hours. But during those hours the entire plane—it is called Faer—would be immersed in rejoicing for me, who had reached it. It is a great celebration prepared for every ascending soul— not only for human souls but also for those of other monads of Shadanakar that are climbing the stairway of Enlightenment, even those of higher animals. Faer is in a certain sense a parting of the ways: reincarnations in Enrof can still take place afterward, but only when there is a definite mission to perform. Subsequent falls or revolts are not precluded. Neither is a deeply conscious—and thus all the more grave—betrayal of God. A blind fall, however, will never be possible again, and spiritual paralysis is struck from the list of potentialities forevermore. This spiritual paralysis, which manifests itself in the psyche of those living, has through the centuries changed its complexion and name in Enrof. In our century it is primarily, but not exclusively, defined as materialism.

If one searches for a familiar image even distantly analogous to what one sees in Faer, it is impossible to settle for anything less than a holiday fireworks display. There is hardly a need to add that the most lavish fireworks display on Enrof compared to Faer are no more than a few lamps compared to the constellation Orion.

I saw a great many beings in their doubly and triply enlightened forms. They had come there from higher planes out of a desire to share in my joy. The enlightened are capable of sharing others' joy to an incomparably greater degree and intensity than we are. Every soul that reaches Faer arouses rejoicing in millions of those who have already passed through it. How can I convey my feelings when I saw hosts of the enlightened rejoicing because I, insignificant I, had reached that world? It was not gratitude, not embarrassed joy, not even shock—it was more like waves of that blissful emotion that causes mortals in Enrof to burst into silent tears.

I do not recall the time or manner of my passage to the next plane. The overpowering experience of Faer brought on a deep exhaustion and a relaxation, as it were, of the tissue of my entire soul. Everything that I can now reconstruct from my memory of the experiences at the next stage of my ascent can be reduced to a single state, yet one that lasted very long, perhaps for many years.

Radiant calm. Does it not sound like a contradiction in terms? We associate an abundance of light with activity, not rest—with movement, not calm. But that is here, in Enrof. It is not like that everywhere. Besides, the word "radiant" itself is not as precise as I would like. For the light of this next plane, called Nertis, is radiant and at the same time inexpressibly gentle. It combines the enchanting softness of moonlit nights with the bright airiness of blue springtime skies. As if lulled by something more soothing than the softest music, I sank into a contented sleep, feeling like a child who, after months of neglect, suffering, and undeserved pain, is cradled in his or her mother's lap. Feminine tenderness permeated everything, even the air, but it radiated with particular warmth from those who hovered around me, like caregivers who look after the sick and weary with inexhaustible love. They were beings who had earlier risen to even higher planes and had descended from there to Nertis, to such as me, to perform works of tenderness, love, and joy.

Nertis is the land of great rest. Imperceptibly, without any efforts on my part, but as a result only of the work of the friends of my heart, my ether body slowly underwent changes, becoming ever lighter, more permeated with spirit, and more obedient to my wishes. It is in Nertis that our ether body acquires the form it takes in the zatomis, the heavenly lands of metacultures. And if the loved ones I had left behind in Enrof could have seen me, they would have known it was I. They would have caught an elusive resemblance between my new appearance and the one they were familiar with, but they would have been astounded to the bottom of their hearts by the otherworldly brightness of my transfigured self.

What remained from before? My facial features? Yes, but now they shone with everlasting, unearthly youth. The organs of my body? Yes, but two soft blue flowers, as it were, glowed on my temples—my organs of spiritual hearing. My brow seemed to be decorated with a magical glittering jewel—my organ of spiritual sight. My organ of deep memory, located in the brain, was not visible. The changes that my internal organs underwent were also not visible, as all those adapted to feeding and procreation either disappeared altogether or were subjected to radical changes and took on new functions. Eating resembled breathing, and I replenished my energy by absorbing radiations of Light emanating from the elementals. Procreation as we know it is not to be found in any of the worlds of ascent. There is something else, and I will speak of it when we have reached the chapter on Heavenly Russia.

After a long period of time, I began to feel with joy my strength growing ever greater, as if mysterious and long-awaited wings were opening. The reader should not take me too literally: I am not referring to anything resembling the wings of flying beings on Enrof. I refer to the ability to move freely through four-dimensional space. It was still only something to look forward to—immobility lay on me as before—but the possibility of flight turned from a vague dream into a definite prospect.

I learned from the friends of my heart that my stay in Nertis was drawing to a close. It seemed to me that the cradle-like something in which I was resting began slowly to swing up and down, as it were, with every swing higher than the previous one. The motion aroused in me an eagerness to taste the even greater happiness I was soon to experience, and I realized that I was already on another plane, in Gotimna, the last of the worlds in the sakwala of Enlightenment. It was filled with gigantic flowers, as it were, whose size did not deprive them of a wonderful softness, and the spaces between them revealed endless heights and expanses of nine colors. All I can say about the two colors that lie outside our spectrum is that the impression produced by one of them is closest to a sky blue, and the impression from the other is distantly reminiscent of our gold.

Entire forests of the enormous flowers of Gotimna bob up and down, swing and sway, making sounds of unimaginable rhythm. Their rustling is like the softest of music, never wearying, as peaceful as the sound of forests on Earth. Yet it is full of inexhaustible meaning, affectionate love, and concern for all those living there. We moved with a lightness and ease no being in Enrof is capable of approaching, gliding, as it were, between the singing flowers in any one of the four directions of space or pausing to talk with them, for we came to understand their language and they understood ours. There, in sky-blue meadows or next to huge, softly glittering gold petals, we were visited by those who descend to Gotimna from the zatomis to prepare us, their younger brothers and sisters, for the next legs of our journey.

Gotimna is called the Garden of Higher Fate, for the destiny of souls for a long time to come is decided there. I arrived at a crossroads, one that lies on the path of all who ascend to that plane. For many centuries afterward it is impossible to change one's decision in any of the many worlds that are preordained there. I was free to choose one of two paths: either ascent up to Heavenly India, the end forever of my journey of reincarnations, which would be replaced by a journey of ascending transfigurations through variomaterial planes; or another, perhaps several, existences in Enrof, no longer as a consequence of karma left raveled—it had already been unraveled—but as a means to perform concrete, freely undertaken tasks entrusted to me alone.

Although the word "mission" sounds bookish and dry, I will use it from now on to refer to the special tasks entrusted to individual souls to be carried out in Enrof. For those who undertake missions, the burden of responsibility increases many times over, because the missions are never concerned merely with the fates of their agents, but with the fates of many souls, both during and after life. Indeed, these missions sometimes concern the fate of entire peoples or of all humanity. Retribution and expiation in the deepest and most terrible planes of torment await those who betray their trust, either by choice or out of weakness. There is no guarantee that a soul that has passed through the sakwala of Enlightenment will no longer be prone to falls, betrayals, or wrongful deeds. Only blind errors, founded on an ignorance of God's existence, are impossible. But things that sleep in the depths of the soul under the rays of Nertis and Gotimna can still waken in the nocturnal darkness of Enrof and draw the agent of the mission astray or downward. If these falls do not affect the essence of the mission, the Providential powers will help him or her up from any fall so that the mission can still be completed.

I was given the chance to descend back down, to the confines of another metaculture that had up till then been unfamiliar and alien to me, a metaculture still young but with a tremendous future. Something alarming, turbulent, and murky radiated from the immense, multiplaned land I could dimly make out in the distance. As for the task I was to undertake, it had bearing on a great task that went far beyond the borders of that metaculture and was meant to encompass the entire world in the distant future. Thousands of souls were already preparing to take part in the task.

That was the path I chose. I understood that I had agreed to shoulder a burden that would be impossible for me ever to throw off without serious repercussions for myself and others.

From the Indian Gotimna I was taken to the Russian Gotimna, where preparation for the mission my higher self had undertaken was to be completed. But falls, revolts, and betrayals are possible after moral lives of Light as well, because what slept in the sunlight can later awaken in the soul. Such falls also took place on my journey after Gotimna. I will have to shed light on that, however, in other chapters of the book. Now it is time to speak of the zatomis, the heavenly lands of the metacultures.

I have been able to speak of the sakwala of Enlightenment on the basis of what I have been able to recall from experience. In contrast, my memory contains only infrequent, sporadic images of the zatomis sakwala, images imprinted in my mind much later, during the transphysical travels I made while asleep here, in the Enrof of Russia. Those hazy images were supplemented by another, invaluable source of information: transphysical meetings and talks. The autobiographical style is not suited to the presentation of this material. Thus, the following chapters will unfortunately be formal and dry, like the chapter on points of departure.

2 The Zatomis

THE SUMMITS OF METACULTURES, the zatomis, to a certain extent follow the geographical contours of their respective cultures in Enrof. All zatomis have four dimensions, but they each differ in their number of time streams. The materiality of the sakwala is created by the Principalities, one of the angelic hierarchies. The zatomis themselves are slowly built through the combined efforts of hierarchies, heroes, geniuses, saints, and a broad spectrum of people capable of creative work, both while the suprapeople that produced them continues its historical journey and after, when that journey comes to an end and millions of its immortal monads continue to ascend from one height of universal knowledge and creative work to another. Each of the zatomis was founded by a great human spirit.

From a distance the planes bear a remote resemblance to our natural environment. The natural element on Earth that best describes the zatomis landscape is clouds in the sky. Regions of soft mist glowing with an inner light are the equivalent of our oceans and seas. They are the souls of marine elementals. The place of rivers of Enrof is taken by the rivers' own souls, forms of inexpressible beauty to which the words "shimmering mists" do not do justice. The vegetation bears little resemblance to ours: it is the souls of elementals, which we will speak of later. I think it sufficient for now to state that the souls of some elementals abide in the zatomis in the intervals between incarnations.

The alternation of night and day takes place on the planes in the exact same manner as here, resulting as it does from the identical rotation of the planet on its axis. The weather fluctuates between pleasant and gorgeous.

Higher humankind—the Synclites of metacultures—is our hope, our joy, our buttress, and our aspiration. Saints, as well as some visionaries and heroes, enter the zatomis almost immediately after their death in Enrof, quickly passing through the worlds of Enlightenment. History makes no mention of the overwhelming majority of such souls, those who lived quiet lives among the people, leaving no traces in chronicles or legend but only in the memory of those who knew them or heard of them from eyewitnesses. They are the unsung heroes of our life. To think otherwise—in other words, to picture the Synclite of a metaculture as a kind of "celebrity" gathering—would only go to show that our moral-mystical mind is still fast asleep.

Others, in particular the recipients of special gifts, who have fallen into the depths of purgatories after death are raised up by the forces of Light, which shorten the duration of their expiatory cleansing so they may join the Synclite. Some geniuses of the arts, many visionaries and heroes, and all saints unraveled their karmic knots while still in Enrof, having expiated the weight of their sins. For them, death was a wide-open gate to the zatomis.

Death caught others still burdened, and thus unprepared, for the higher planes. Such people must first pass through a series of planes in the upper purgatories (upper relative to the terrible circles of magma and the Earth's core, but lower relative to where we are). After finally reaching Gotimna, thousands of those souls do not choose to descend anew to Enrof, choosing instead to work and contribute to the great struggle from within the zatomis communities.

A third group of people did not burden their souls in Enrof with any mortal sins, but their outlook, the scope of their knowledge, and their sense of the cosmic—expanded though they were in Olirna—need to grow still more. For them departure from Olirna marks the beginning of travels, sometimes long, lasting even centuries, until they are capable of internalizing the tasks and wisdom of their Synclite. Thus, from the time of their death in Enrof until they join the Synclite, these souls do not undergo atonement but the expansion and enrichment of their selves.

Reincarnation is far from a universal law. The majority of monads do proceed along that path, however. They have already undergone a number of births among different peoples in Enrof, in different metacultures, even in different millennia in different corners of the globe, and many of them journeyed through other dominions of Shadanakar before their human cycle. Their shelts could even have presided over beings of the plant or animal worlds. Others have experienced, in times immemorial, incarnations as Titans, protoangels, or daemons. Recollections of their garland of births are stored in their deep memory, and the spiritual stature of such monads is especially great, the well of their memories is especially deep, and their future wisdom is distinguished by particular breadth. All recipients of a higher gift of artistic genius have woven such garlands of past reincarnations. Saints of Christian metacultures, unlike the saints of some Eastern metacultures, embark primarily on a different journey of ascent, one that brings them to Enrof but once. But during travels through other planes, that journey reveals to their eyes such heights of the universe that the memory burns within them like a star, and its rays disentangle their hearts from all webs of darkness during their one life in Enrof.

The activities of the Synclites are boundless in variety and scope and are in many respects beyond our power to comprehend. I can point to three branches of their activities: help, creative work, and struggle.

Help is for everyone who has not yet reached the zatomis. The angels of darkness, keepers of the purgatories, would not release their victims for centuries to come if not for the tireless efforts of the Synclites. Those suffering in the horrifying worlds of the magma and the Earth's core would be imprisoned there right up until the third global period. (We are now only approaching the end of the first.) If it were not for the Synclites, those living in Enrof would be encased in an almost impenetrable shell of spiritual darkness.

But that work—rescuing and relieving some, protecting and enriching others, and enlightening still others—is only one branch. Another branch is the creation of independent things of value, the significance of which cannot be exaggerated. But contemplating, let alone understanding, the works of the Synclites is possible for us only to a minimal degree. To convey their meaning using our concepts is completely out of the question.

Somewhat easier to grasp is the third branch of the Synclites's activities: their struggle with the demonic powers. One might say that they fight in the literal sense, but their weapons, of course, do not have a single thing in common with weapons in Enrof. They vary greatly according to both the degree of control they have over one's own being and those against whom they are directed. They all operate on the same principle, however, which is the concentration of volitional radiations to paralyze the adversary. Synclite members cannot die in battle. In the case of defeat, what can happen is prolonged captivity in the dungeons of demonic strongholds.

The zatomis landscapes are dotted with a sort of equivalent of cities. They bear little resemblance to ours, however, especially since there is no housing in the strict sense of the word. The buildings there serve a very special function: they are primarily meeting places for Synclite members and the spirits of other hierarchies from other worlds. The buildings where their enlightened meetings with monads of elementals take place are called sheritals.

Zatomis architecture is nevertheless suggestive of styles we are familiar with, only raised to an incomparably higher level. It is the result of two parallel processes that are difficult, but necessary, to understand. It so happens that the great architectural masterpieces of Enrof, in being saturated with the radiations of many human psyches, acquire a soul, or more precisely, an astral body. These astral bodies abide in the zatomis. But there are also buildings in the zatomis that have no twin in Enrof, for example, these same sheritals. There are also those structures that builders in Enrof envisioned, designed, and set about constructing on Earth, but history placed insurmountable barriers in their path.

Synclite members can penetrate as far down as the magma in the worlds of descent and can rise up to very high planes known as the Highest Aspects of the Transmyths of the Global Religions.

Oral communication takes place in each zatomis in the transfigured language of the corresponding country in Enrof, but it is a language both of sound and light. There would be nothing strange in applying our concept of "vocabulary" to these languages, but their vocabulary, with its distinct, incomparably richer store of concepts, differs greatly from ours. Besides these metacultural languages, there is also a lingua franca: the names of the planes, beings, and hierarchies have their origin in it. The speed and ease with which foreign languages are mastered there cannot be compared to the same process in Enrof, for it takes place effortlessly, by itself. It is customary to call the zatomis lingua franca the language of the World Synclite, though the name is not entirely accurate: the World Synclite, which we will speak of much later, possesses methods of communication that have nothing in common with any kind of oral language. But the members of the World Synclite descended from their heights to the zatomis of metacultures to oversee the creation of a common zatomis language, and that is why the provisional name of the language is associated with them.

Besides the Synclites, other beings abide in the zatomis: future angels. They are wondrous creations of God, and if we recall the Sirins and Alkonosts of Russian legends, we will approach an image of those whose presence adorns life in the Byzantine and Russian zatomis, an image of beings destined later to become "solar archangels." Other beings, no less beautiful, abide in other zatomis.

There are nineteen zatomis, and I shall say something here of each.

Maif is the oldest of the zatomis, the heavenly land and Synclite of the Atlantis metaculture, which existed in Enrof from approximately the twelfth to the ninth millennium B.C.

Atlantis was an archipelago; the largest and most important of its islands approached Sicily in size. It was populated by a so-called Red people. It was a slave-based society, which at first comprised a number of lesser states that were later unified under a dictatorship. Its worldview was polytheistic, with an important role reserved for magic. Its pantheon of gods and religious life were tainted by devil worship. Of those cultures known to us, Atlantis most closely resembled Egypt and, in part, the Aztec civilization, only grimmer. Architecture, sculpture, and dance were the principal art forms. Their civilization could by no means be called advanced, though its people, taking advantage of the chain of small islands running between Atlantis and America, maintained contact with the continent of their origin. Later they were to reach West Africa, and the legend of Atlantis subsequently came to Egypt via the ancient Sudanese civilization, which remains unknown to this day but whose ruins may still be unearthed in the future. Images of merciless and greedy divinities left their mark on the moral code of Atlantis, and ritual cannibalism played an important role in their religious life. In a late period of its history, semi-esoteric religious movements of Light emerged. But because of the active presence of the demonic, the overall spiritual picture was rather bleak.

The main island and the smaller ones surrounding it were destroyed by a series of catastrophic earthquakes. A few small groups of inhabitants escaped to America, and one group to Africa, where it was assimilated into the black population of Sudan. At present, Maif, which has already existed for almost fifteen millennia over a certain section of the Atlantic Ocean, has attained immense power of Light. Its emblem consists of a red temple on a black background; four white-clad figures stand in front of the temple with arms upraised. The figures represent the cults of the four divinities of Light. It was through these cults that spirituality flowed down into the Atlantis culture.

Linat is the name of the zatomis of Gondwana, by which I mean not the ancient continent that existed in the Indian Ocean long before the emergence of humans but rather the metaculture whose centers in Enrof were Java, Sumatra, South Hindustan, and certain cities that now lie on the ocean floor. The Gondwanese culture existed as late as the sixth millennium B.C.

This culture was composed of a federation of states—a commercial oligarchy with a slave-based economy. In addition, the advanced state of Gondwanese marine navigation enabled it to establish commercial and cultural links with the coast of

Indochina, Ceylon, and many Indonesian islands. As in Atlantis, polytheism was dominant, as were the same three art forms, though in Gondwana dance developed into religious drama. But the bloodthirstiness and demonic, mystic cruelty of Atlantis was alien to Gondwana. They were a sensuous, sanguine, life-loving people, richly gifted in the arts, and possessed of a very active sex life. Sexual mysticism permeated both their religious and everyday life, and attained genuine sumptuousness at the civilization's height. Not Atlantis, not even Babylon or Egypt knew such luxury. It seems to me that the Gondwanese race could be called proto-Malaysian. In any case, taut, brown skin covered their high cheekbones and full lips, their oblong eyes were slightly slanted, and their bodies were well proportioned and muscular, with broad shoulders, slender waists, and very strong calves. They were a people blessed with the full-blooded and passionate beauty of the south.

Some millennia later, the Indo-Malaysian culture arose in the same region, which in some ways resembled its predecessors, but was much more spiritually mature.

The emblem of Linat is a violet-clad woman and a green-clad man on a gold background. They are under the lower half of a red sun, their arms around each other's shoulders.

Violet here represents a mix of dark blue and red. Dark blue symbolizes the powers of Universal Femininity, Whose emanation into the Gondwanese metaculture marked the first time in the existence of humanity that such an event had taken place with such intensity. Red symbolizes the elements—not the elementals of Nature but the extremely active presence of certain elementals linked with humanity. Green represents the same intense activity by elementals of Nature. Gold is the hieratic background that speaks of the already developed spiritual reality existing behind the suprapeople.

Ialu is the zatomis of the metaculture of Ancient Egypt. (If I remember correctly, it also has another name, which sounds something like *Atkheam*.) This culture, which utterly eclipsed Atlantis in size and splendor, had created, even before the end of its historical existence, a huge Synclite and dazzling zatomis.

The demonic powers, however, dealt it a serious blow in the fourteenth century B.C., when the Providential powers, operating through the great visionary leader and prophet Akhenaton, made the first attempt in world history to enlighten the minds of the people with the truth of the One God. If Akhenaton's reforms had succeeded and met with worthy successors, Christ would have undertaken His mission several centuries earlier, and he would have done so not on the banks of the Jordan but in the Nile River valley.

I would like to mention that the Egyptian belief in the Heavenly Nile was based on experience of a higher reality. The magnificent river flowing through Ialu, the mythical Land of the Blessed—that is, the metaculture's zatomis—is multiplaned: it is both the great spiritualized elemental of the terrestrial Nile and the Collective Ideal Soul of the Egyptian people.

The emblem of Ialu depicts a white barge with sails on a blue river that flows into the sun.

Eanna is the zatomis of the ancient Babylonian-Assyrian-Canaanite metaculture, which arose, it appears, in the fourth millennium B.C. The seven-tiered temples/observatories, which were the centers and pinnacles of the great cities of the Tigris-Euphrates region, mirrored, like a terrestrial reflection, the grandiose heavenly city built by the Synclite of the zatomis. But the ziggurats in the cities of Babylonia and the collective of initiates who absorbed the radiations of the cosmic powers of Light on top of their mystical observatories were also not shielded from the extremely harmful radiations coming from the galactic anticosmos, whose center in Enrof is located in the Antares system. That tainted the already ambivalent religion even more and injected a subtle poison into the essence of those exposed, encrusting and weighting their inner self with doubt and pessimism.

The Babylonian metaculture was the first in which Gagtungr was able to effect the incarnation of a Witzraor, a powerful demonic being, in the subterranean four-dimensional plane bordering the Babylonian shrastr. The descendants of that demon have played and continue to play a huge and deadly role in the metahistory of humanity. To a significant degree the Witzraor was to blame for the general spiritual decline that distinguished the culture in Enrof. And although Ereshkigal, the goddess of the underworld, was defeated in the end by Astarte, the goddess of Light, who, in a burst of sacrificial love, descended to the Babylonian transphysical planes of torment, their beliefs about the afterlife of all human souls, excluding those of kings and priests, was nevertheless steeped in a pessimistic, almost nihilistic despondency: it was an intuitive understanding of the paralyzing power of the demonic.

The emblem of Eanna pictures a seven-tiered white ziggurat. The seven stories represent the seven planes that were clearly intuited by the religious consciousness of the Babylonian suprapeople.

Shan Ti is the zatomis of the Chinese metaculture, which has existed in Enrof since the second millennium B.C. It began to grow significantly in strength in the last centuries prior to Christ, when Confucianism created a lasting code of morality and everyday conduct that enabled the people's overall moral level to rise. However, a very low ceiling was placed on the free development of the higher aspects of the soul. Confucianist law, in gradually fossilizing, became not so much a vehicle for ascent as a brake to it. This explains why the size and strength of the Chinese zatomis, in spite of its long history, are not as great as one would expect. Another zatomis that coexists with Shan Ti encroached upon geographical China after the spread of Buddhism. In the last few centuries it has admitted many more enlightened souls than the national zatomis. The emblem of Shan Ti is the face of a beautiful woman wearing a lotus-shaped crown.

Sumera, or *Meru*, (I do not know which of these names should be considered correct) is the zatomis of the Indian metaculture, the most powerful of all zatomis in Shadanakar. In earliest mythology, the summit of Mount Sumera was topped by the city of Brahma and the cities of other Hindu deities were on its slopes. But Heavenly India was not limited to them, for it encompassed several large tracts of land separated by water.

At present Heavenly India overlooks a geographical area of Enrof that stretches far beyond the borders of the Indian state.

Over the course of 4,000 years the spiritual life of the Indian peoples, who are exceptionally gifted in the religious sense, has resulted in two metacultures separating from it and becoming independent systems of planes. In the meantime, Heavenly India itself has been reinforced by such a huge number of enlightened that by the twentieth century the influence of its Synclite had come to outweigh the power of all the demonic forces combined. India is the only culture in Enrof that has unwaveringly developed along a high moral path. Much earlier the power of the Indian Synclite prevented the forces of Gagtungr from creating, as they did in the other metacultures, planes of eternal torment. Before Christ, it was the one metaculture with purgatories and the only one whose lower extremity did not extend as far as the magmas.

Meru has two major centers—one above the Himalayas and one above the Nilgiri mountains in central India—and a host of lesser ones. In addition, the Indian Synclite possesses a stable base of support in Enrof in the form of a fluid collective of people that moves along a kind of geographical curve from age to age. Prior to the Second World War it was located in Pamir, and it is now located in south India.

The landscape of Heavenly India resembles that of Heavenly Russia, but the natural environment is lusher. Both the tropical character of the corresponding countries in Enrof and the zatomis' longer history account for this. The Heavenly Ganges, which has the same double meaning for the Indian metaculture as the Heavenly Nile has for Egypt, flows through the entire zatomis.

The emblem of Sumeru depicts three white mountain chains, each higher than the previous one, each topped by golden cities. The first chain is the zatomis, and the second and third are very high worlds, the highest aspect of the Hindu transmyth.

Zurvan is the zatomis of the ancient Iranian (Zoroastrian) metaculture.

The insufficiently precise formulation of the idea of the One God in this nevertheless lofty and pure religion did not allow it to lay the necessary groundwork for Christ's mission to take place in Iran. A later attempt by the Iranian metaculture to make up for that failure through the creation of a new international religion—Manichaeanism—ended in a second failure, when demonic emanations gained access to the creative consciousness of its founders. By the time of the Muslim conquest, the Iranian culture had exhausted its forward momentum. During the centuries that followed, its only base of support in Enrof has been a Parsi community in India. As one would expect, the number of people entering Zurvan through the worlds of Enlightenment is now extremely small, while Zurvan itself has almost detached from its geographical area in Enrof.

Zurvan's emblem: a sacrificial altar with a burning fire.

Olympus is the zatomis of the ancient Greco-Roman metaculture. The name Olympus refers both to the center of the zatomis, a great city of the enlightened that is indeed connected to the geographical site of Mount Olympus, and to the entire heavenly land of the Greco-Roman metaculture. Having been, at the time of ancient Greece and Rome, the abode and theater of activity of those nonhuman hierarchies that were reflected in the persona of the Greco-Roman pantheon, the zatomis gradually became, in the millennium after Christ, the abode of the Synclite. The hierarchies that at one time abided there have, in the course of centuries, completed a great journey of ascent. They now abide and work in incomparably higher worlds, and at the same time they overlook Olympus and emanate beneficent energy to its Synclite.

Apollo is the name of the demiurge of the Greco-Roman metaculture. Pallas Athena is the name of the Collective Ideal Soul of the suprapeople.

The emblem of Olympus is a white temple, in the classical style, on a mountain against a blue sky.

Nikhord is the zatomis of the Jewish metaculture. It is the lower plane of the Synclite of Israel.

The great human spirit Abraham was the founder of Nikhord. The ancient teachers of Judaism were inspired by the demiurge of the suprapeople, but the purity of the inspiration was tainted first by elemental emanations from the "genius" of the Sinai mountains and then by emanations from the Jewish Witzraor.

Nonetheless, one should still regard the *I* of the Old Testament as the Almighty. Monotheism, as the soil without which Christ's task could not be carried out in Enrof, was essential for all humanity. Nikhord was able to instill the idea of the One God into the people's consciousness at the cost of a massive expenditure of energy, which exhausted it for a long time afterward. That is the reason for their not always successful struggle with the demonic and of the tragic nature of Jewish history. In the century that witnessed the life and death of Jesus, that geographically small region was the site of a ferocious battle between the forces of Gagtungr and God. That will be discussed in more detail elsewhere. Christ's Resurrection was greeted in Nikhord with great rejoicing. The attitude of the Jewish Synclite toward the Planetary Logos is the same as in all other zatomis—there can be no question of any other. But the revelation of Christ's truth awaits those in Olirna who are destined to enter Nikhord later. They did not accept this truth while on Earth and it is so astonishing that many are unable to come to terms with it for a long time afterward.

The destruction of Jerusalem and the Jewish kingdom gave rise to mourning in Nikhord, but with an awareness of the logic of events. No other fate was possible for the aggressive but weak Jewish Witzraor after it entered into irreconcilable battle with the demiurge of the suprapeople during the years of Christ's mission on Earth. There have been no more Jewish Witzraors since the final defeat of the Jews by Hadrian. But behind the Witzraor stood another, more terrible demonic hierarchy—the spawn of Gagtungr and true rival of the demiurge—which continued to influence Jewry even during the diaspora. Medieval Judaism continued to develop under the influence of two opposing wills: that demon and Nikhord. At present, Nikhord admits a very small number of new members, who do nevertheless enter the worlds of Enlightenment through Judaism.

Geographically, Nikhord is still linked to the Palestine region. But the refounding of the state of Israel in the twentieth century has nothing whatsoever to do with Nikhord. The restored temple is a showpiece, no more. No new Israeli Witzraor has appeared, but a similar role is being played by one of the beings to be discussed in the chapter on *egregors*. It is under the powerful influence of the main camp of demonic forces.

Nikhord's emblem depicts a tentlike structure surrounded by trees with large red fruit. The tent is the Ark of the Covenant, the symbol of the first enduring revelation in history of the One God; the fruit-laden trees are the Promised Land, which awaits the suprapeople not on Earth but in the zatomis.

Paradise is the provisional name of the zatomis of the Byzantine metaculture. Like the other zatomis of Christian metacultures, it is one of the staircases rising from different directions to an extremely high world called Heavenly Jerusalem, which is nothing other than the Higher Aspect of the Christian Transmyth. This will be discussed more a little later.

Paradise is an ancient, powerful plane, a section of which exists in part over Russia as well. Its founder is the great human spirit who in Enrof was John the Baptist.

The victory of Jesus Christ, though only partial, gave rise to a great mobilization of forces in the demonic worlds. In particular, their efforts were aimed at preventing the planes of torment of the Byzantine metaculture from being turned into temporary purgatories. Their efforts were crowned with success, but the end result was the collapse of the Byzantine culture in Enrof. The lack of purgatories and the unavoidable descent by sinners after death to the endless tortures of the magma and core gave rise among the more spiritually gifted of the Byzantine people to a constant feeling of horror toward the most venial sin. To a significant extent that was what led to their extreme asceticism.

Metahistorically, the southern Slavs are located in a transitional area bordering the Byzantine, Russian, Roman Catholic, and Muslim metacultures. Their Synclites are in Paradise.

The emblem of Paradise is of a stream running through a garden in blossom, in which people are clad in golden garments. Their clothing symbolizes the transfigured body, and the color gold represents the body's permeation by the power of the Creator of the Universe.

Eden is the provisional name of the zatomis of the Roman Catholic metaculture, and it is one of the staircases to Heavenly

Jerusalem. Several peoples of various ethnic roots belong to the metaculture: Poles, Hungarians, Czechs, Irish, Croats.

The founder of Eden is the great human spirit who in Enrof was the Apostle Peter.

The emblem is the same as for Paradise, but the dominant color is light blue. Light blue represents the dense permeation of Catholicism by the spirit of Universal Femininity.

Monsalvat is the zatomis of the metaculture of North-Western Europe, North America, Australia, and some parts of Africa. Geographically, it is the largest and most dispersed of all the zatomis. The founder of Monsalvat is the great human spirit Titurel, who had close ties with Christ long before our Savior's incarnation in Palestine. Like Lohengrin and Parsifal, he is not a fictional hero but a person who did at one time live in Enrof (though not in Palestine). The Holy Grail contains the ether blood that Christ shed on Golgotha.

The division of the planes of Eden and Monsalvat is based for the most part on national and cultural distinctions between the Romanic and Germanic peoples. But the greater or lesser part played by the ecclesiastic or lay segments of the populace led to a host of changes taking place in the afterlife fates of the people of Western Europe, especially since Monsalvat appeared several centuries after Eden. France is in an interim stage; its tragedy lies in the fact that it has no Synclite of its own. Some of the ascending monads from France rise to Eden after death, and others to Monsalvat.

The center of Monsalvat, which had earlier been connected with the Alps, was relocated far to the East at the end of the Middle Ages and is now located near Pamir. (The reasons for this are very complex.) But a host of other, lesser metacities shine above Europe and America. Some of them overlook centers in Enrof that are small in size but spiritually powerful, such as Heidelberg, Cambridge, and Weimar.

Monsalvat's emblem is a Gothic cathedral, white in color, on a mountain peak. In the foreground is a cup glowing red.

Zhunfleya is the zatomis of the Ethiopian metaculture, which for two thousand years has struggled to survive under exceptionally unfavorable historical and geographical conditions: a small island of Christianity between two hostile oceans, Islam and the paganism of African tribes. The metaculture has not been able to realize even one-tenth of its potential. At present, a distressing metahistorical process is taking place: Zhunfleya is being relocated to another sakwala, the sakwala of developmentally arrested metacultures in Enrof. An exceptionally fortunate combination of historical circumstances could still reverse the process.

Its emblem is a white circular building draped in fluttering cloths. The building represents the zatomis, and the cloths represent subtle materiality.

The zatomis of the Islamic metaculture is *Jannet*. Islam differs from the other global religions in that it lacks a higher aspect of its transmyth—that is, there is no world dedicated specifically to Islam in the very high sakwala of the worlds of the higher transmyths of the global religions. That accounts for the poverty of Muslim mythology, for the lack of originality of most transphysical images and themes formulated in it, which were borrowed primarily from Judaism and Christianity. Islam, which is in many respects a regression in relation to Christianity, nevertheless offers a soul the possibility of ascent, enables spiritual energy to flow through it into our world, and in the course of its history has created a very bright, if not powerful, zatomis and a dazzling Synclite.

Its emblem is a white mosque between two symmetrically bending palms with people clad in green and white. The mosque represents the zatomis; the palms represent the two chief branches of Islam.

Sukhavati—which is in Buddhist mythology the western paradise of Amitabha Buddha—is the zatomis of the metaculture associated with northern Buddhism, known as the Mahayana. It overlooks Tibet and Mongolia and coexists over China and Japan with Shan-Ti and Nikisaka, the Japanese national zatomis.

Sukhavati separated from its parent Indian metaculture in the ninth century A.D., when the centers of Buddhism moved once and for all out of India into Tibet and China. It particularly grew in strength three to four centuries later, when the Himalayan metaculture, which had had a brilliant beginning, started to show signs of a premature decline, and the leading role of the Tibetan and Chinese centers of Buddhism was reaffirmed.

The zatomis of Sukhavati is one of the most populous and strongest. It is one of two staircases to the high world of the Higher Aspect of the Buddhist Transmyth which is called Nirvana and of which we will speak later.

The emblem of Sukhavati is the sun dawning over lotus flowers.

Aireng-Dalyang is the zatomis of the prodigious Indo-Malaysian metaculture, which is as yet relatively unknown here in Russia. Having separated from the Indian metaculture around the fifth century A.D., it encompassed the Hindu-Buddhist kingdoms of Java, Indochina, and Ceylon, at one point taking historical form as the Shailendra Empire. The metaculture was later seriously weakened both by the succession of Java, which fell under Islamic control, and by predatory demons—the European Witzraors—at the end of the nineteenth century. The metaculture is still smoldering within the Indochinese kingdoms, but a favorable historical climate could give rise to a renewed blossoming.

Its emblem depicts laughing children in the garden of a temple-palace.

Heavenly Russia will be described in more detail than the others a few paragraphs below.

Unfortunately I know virtually nothing about the zatomis of the *Black* metaculture, not even its name. I know that it is young and still very weak. After the collapse of the Sudanese culture, together with its religion, which had enabled spirituality to flow down not only among the elite but even among the masses of the Black peoples of equatorial Africa, Blacks were for a long time deprived of the possibility of ascent after death. The possibility arose for them again only a few centuries ago in connection with the fact that some tribes had reached the stage where their hazily formulated polytheistic systems became capable of assimilating the first manifestations of spirituality. The door to an ascending afterlife was opened to the Black peoples to an even greater extent by the spread among them—unfortunately weak—of

Islam and Christianity. The founding of Liberia was also of metahistorical significance, establishing as it did a small but stable center of Christian spirituality in equatorial Africa. The Black population of North America is also connected with the Black zatomis. White people rise to the zatomis only in rare instances. Harriet Beecher Stowe, for example, after having reached Monsalvat, left it for the Black zatomis, where her work has for a long time been of great significance, and her position has partly resembled that of a queen and partly that of a high priestess.

Its emblem is a stairway leading from a lake to an orange circular building. The lake represents the materiality of the suprapeople and the building represents the zatomis. The color orange is a blend of the gold of the sun with the scarlet of elementals linked not with the natural realms but with humanity.

The last of the great zatomis is in the midst of construction. It is *Arimoya*, the future zatomis of the global metaculture, which is connected with the appearance and dominion of the Rose of the World, the future interreligion. As in the other zatomis, the materiality of Arimoya is being created by the Principalities, one of the angelic hierarchies. The great human spirit who was Zoroaster in his last reincarnation on Earth is overseeing the creation of what I will provisionally designate with the term *great design*.

The emblem of Arimoya is a white, multitowered cathedral, with one main central tower, colonnades, and stairways. It is surrounded by a number of large string instruments resembling golden lyres. The towers represent the zatomis of humanity; the central tower is Arimoya; the colonnades are the worlds of daemons, angels, elementals, and enlightened animals; the lyres represent all the peoples of the Earth.

Heavenly Russia. Its emblem is a pink-white city of many churches on a high bank overlooking the dark blue bend of a river.

Like the other zatomis, Heavenly Russia, or Holy Russia, is linked with the three-dimensional territory that roughly follows the contours of our country. Its great centers correspond to certain of our cities; between them are beautiful regions of enlightened nature. The principal center is the Heavenly Kremlin, which overlooks Moscow. Its cathedrals shine with unearthly gold and white. And high above meta-Petersburg, in the clouds of that world, soars the lofty white sculpture of a galloping horseman. It is not intended to be a representation of anyone in particular; it is, rather, a symbol of the direction of our metahistorical journey. Lesser centers are scattered throughout the entire zatomis, including the metacultural summits of other nations that together with Russia form a single suprapeople. There abide the Synclites of the Ukraine, Georgia, and Armenia. Recently the Synclite of the Bulgarian people, along with its own heavenly cities, has begun to merge with the zatomis. I do not know the total population of Heavenly Russia, but I do know that about half a million enlightened souls now abide in the Heavenly Kremlin.

Yarosvet, the Demiurge, takes the form of a transparent ocean of energy in the air of that world, passing from horizon to horizon and flooding all hearts with Light. His power is concentrated in the temples of the demiurge. There he assumes individual features, his voice becomes audible, and interaction takes place between him and the enlightened, interaction that imparts to them strength and higher wisdom.

Another hierarchy similar to the demiurge manifest themselves in the same way. They are the great guiding spirits of the individual nations that are also part of our metaculture. Ones older than Yarosvet can be found among them, as can the young guiding spirit of the Ukraine.

But neither Navna—the Collective Ideal Soul of the Russian people—nor her sisters—the Collective Souls of the other peoples—are there. They are prisoners behind thick walls of state power in the citadel of the Witzraor, the state demon, in the underworld of Russian antihumankind. Only their distant voices and weak light reach Heavenly Russia.

There, seas of glowing ether—the souls of elementals, which shine with colors beyond our imagination—lap against structures that bear a remote resemblance to the azure and white hulks of mountains. The Russian church sings of that world when it sends the deceased on their final journey, so that the

Lord may give them rest in "a place of light, a place of plenty, a place of calm, so they may know neither sorrow, nor grief, but life everlasting."

Newcomers to Heavenly Russia materialize in special sanctuaries as children, not infants. Their inner world is similar to that of children. As for aging, it is replaced by growth in enlightenment and spiritual strength. There is neither conception nor birth. Guardians, not parents, make provision for the conditions necessary for the enlightenment of souls rising up from Gotimna.

One can discern in the external appearance of some Synclite members features that their lives in Enrof have made famous: now those features are radiant and dazzling. Rarefied and softened, they shine with spiritual glory. Their clothing, produced by their transfigured body, glows of itself. They move freely in all four directions of space in a manner that is vaguely reminiscent of the soaring of birds, but which surpasses it in ease, freedom, and speed. They have no wings. A great many planes are within the sight and hearing of the enlightened. Among the planes of descent are purgatories, the magma, and terrible Gashsharva. The worlds of Enlightenment, the circles of angels, daemons, and elementals, the worlds of emanations from other bramfaturas, and the worlds of the Higher Aspects of Global Transmyths are among the planes of ascent. Synclite members can enter the dark shrastrs, the worlds of antihumankind, where the inhabitants can see them but are powerless to destroy them. They can enter our Enrof as well, but humans can perceive them only with spiritual sight.

The love between man and woman in Enrof, which is worthy of the title of greatness, continues there as well, growing and deepening, liberated from all things that may burden it here. There is bodily intimacy between some as well, but it has been freed of any procreative function and has nothing whatsoever in common with physical intimacy in Enrof. Many bodily organs have by that time undergone radical alterations in their structure, function, and purpose, including organs concerned with the consumption and digestion of food, since the replenishment of bodily energy there resembles breathing. Growth in spirituality eventually brings the enlightened to the next great transfiguration of the body, which leads to higher worlds, to Heavenly Jerusalem, and still higher—all the way to the World Synclite and the Elite of Shadanakar.

There is nothing in the zatomis resembling our technology; its place is taken by something extremely difficult to grasp. I can nevertheless state with surety that, instead of creating mechanical devices from external matter, it operates on the principle of developing the manifold abilities of one's own essence. There, only that which is to a certain extent comparable to our works of architecture is created from external matter.

The souls of churches that were built on Earth, or were supposed to have been built, gleam everywhere there. Many temples, however, serve a function difficult for us to comprehend. There are sanctuaries for interaction with angels, the World Synclite, daemons, and the upper hierarchies. A few large temples are reserved for meetings with Jesus Christ, Who descends there from time to time, assuming a visible, humanlike form. Other temples are for meetings with the Virgin Mary. A magnificent temple is now being erected, destined to be the sanctum of the Great Feminine Spirit, Who will take on an astral and ether body from the marriage of the Russian demiurge with the Collective Ideal Soul of Russia. I have been accustomed since childhood to calling it the Temple of the Universal Sun, but the name is wrong. It properly refers to a different and even more majestic building, the one destined to be built in Arimoya. As for the temple being erected in the Heavenly Kremlin, it is called the Sanctum of Zventa-Sventana, and I will later explain the meaning of that name. That great Feminine Essence has by now already entered one of the highest worlds of Shadanakar. She will never incarnate physically in Enrof but will be born in Heavenly Russia and assume human form. She will not be our queen or goddess; she will be Light, divine grace, and celestial beauty.

Staircases of wondrous worlds, each visible through the other, rise from the altars in the Temple of Femininity, the Temples of Christ, and the Temples of Yarosvet, the demiurge. The staircases rise up through Heavenly Jerusalem to the threshold of the World Salvaterra.

From time to time, great human spirits are born in Heavenly Russia: those who have completed their journey in Shadanakar, having reached its highest worlds, and who now co-create with the Planetary Logos. They leave the Elite of Shadanakar to help those below and, in order to carry out missions beyond the comprehension of the greatest mystical minds of humanity, they materialize in the zatomis. There they assume the same enlightened bodies as the Synclite members but far surpass them in the speed with which they reach full spiritual maturity and in their inner stature. Their paths in the zatomis resemble the lives of geniuses among the masses of humanity. The Synclites are notified ahead of time of their arrival and await them with gladness and rejoicing.

Those who were geniuses and messengers on Earth continue their work in the zatomis after atonement, enlightenment, and transformations.

The bliss of the Gamayuns and Sirins themselves increases when they see the masterpieces being wrought by great spirits that last walked the Earth in the persons of Derzhavin and Pushkin, Lermontov and Gogol, Tolstoy and Dostoyevsky, Rublev and Surikov, Glinka and Mussorgsky, Kazakov and Bazhenov. Shining waves of inconceivable sounds swell in places as if from out of the heart of the celestial mountains. They usher souls into a state of such spiritual joy that a heart on Earth would burst from it, and, rising and twisting like clouds of glory, they plunge down into love and quiet bliss.

The great architect who at one time undertook construction of the Church of the Body, Soul, and Spirit on the Vorobyov Hills in Moscow, and who lived through the death of his dream, exile, oblivion, and impoverishment, is now at work on the most sacred of all things in the Heavenly Kremlin: the inner chapel of the Sanctum of Zventa-Sventana.

Only a handful of enlightened souls in Heavenly Russia would be recognized by those of us familiar with the history of our Motherland. The names of the rest will mean nothing to us.

In the monasteries of Kievan and Muscovite Russia, as well as in those of later times, quiet souls, not gifted enough to blaze forth like saints, lived their lives unnoticed, silently and humbly contributing in their small way to religious work and to the collective labor of the spirit.

Down the roads of Russia throughout the centuries roamed pilgrims and searchers, raconteurs and minstrels, the anonymous authors of fairy tales and uplifting poetry, of songs and legends, of unrecorded stories, now lost, about the heroes and ideals of those times. The brilliant masters of spinning, engraving, and icon-painting; the carpenters and builders of splendid terems, humble wooden churches, and brightly decorated houses; masons, cabinetmakers, potters, weavers, jewelers, and copiers; people who loved their work and pursued it in studios, shops, monastery cells, and in the open air; whose works, stamped with the joy of the creative process and a passionate love for life, have pleased and delighted entire generations—where else can those creators be and what could they be creating now if not the everlasting treasures of Holy Russia?

Throughout every period in Russian history thousands of peasants—land-clearers, farmers, hired hands, serfs and free alike, have lived simple and pure lives, have carried out the sowing and reaping as a duty laid on them by God, with veneration for and gratitude to Mother Earth, and have died simply and peacefully, believing in God and forgiving everyone.

Throughout those centuries thousands of mothers have borne their cross, raising children worthy of the name "human" and seeing their life's purpose in that calling. Is that not one of the highest forms of creative work?

When schools began to be built, hundreds of people abandoned their customary surroundings and way of life and left for (one could say descended into) the lower levels of society, shutting themselves off for their whole life in remote areas, amidst chronic ignorance, where there was no one with whom to exchange an intelligent word: all for the sake of educating the uneducated.

And what of medical practitioners who worked one to an entire district? And doctors who displayed their heroism during epidemics? And those revolutionaries who were motivated not by fanaticism, hate, and a thirst for power but by a genuine love for the people and by anguish at seeing their anguish? And those priests who, to the extent the gifts given them by God allowed, were models of a pure and simple life, cultivating in many the best that was in their simple hearts? It is impossible to list all the paths by which travelers on Earth arrive sooner or later at the Synclite. It is only a question of time, of stages still to be passed through on the way to that goal. It is a goal that people are not fully conscious of but that is known to their immortal monads and thus draws them onward.

Oh, it is pointless to imagine Heavenly Russia as a never-ending, monotonous series of solemn liturgies and prayer sessions. We have no idea of the spiritual delights they enjoy there or of the jokes, laughter, and even games, especially among the children.

I could list the names of some Russian cultural and historical figures who have entered Heavenly Russia in the last forty years. Let those-who-will laugh over the information. After all, I have long been accustomed to having a reputation of a lunatic. So here are the names of some of those who did not descend in their afterlife, and instead entered the Synclite through the worlds of Enlightenment immediately upon their death in Enrof: Leskov, Rimsky-Korsakov, Kluchevsky, Gumilov, Voloshin, Rachmaninov, Anna Pavlova, Sergei Bulgakov, John of Kronshtadt, Patriarch Tikhon, Prince Alexei Nikolayevich, several masters of the arts, and thousands of heroes who died at the hands of Stalin. Here are the names of only a very few of those who joined the Synclite after a brief time in the upper purgatories: Fet, L. Andreyev, Alexander Blok, Shalyapin, Alexander II, Konstantin Romanov, Professor Pavlov.

I know, as well, the names of some among the enlightened who have risen to special heights in Heavenly Russia: Pushkin, Lermontov, Gogol, Lev Tolstoy, A. K. Tolstoy, Dostoyevsky, the Aksakovs, Vitberg, Kutuzov, and Chemezov, a little-known engraver of the eighteenth century who died young.

The following are at present closer than the rest to the great transformation that will raise them to Heavenly Jerusalem and the World Synclite: Lermontov, Vladimir Solovyov, the Emperor Ivan VI, as well as two spirits whose names surprised me but which were twice repeated: Shevchenko and Pavel Florensky.

During the whole existence of the Russian zatomis, a few dozen people have risen through it to the World Synclite. Of these the following names are known to me: Saint Vladimir, Yaroslav the Wise, Antony and Feodosy of Pechery, Nestor the Chronicler, Sergi the soldier, who was the author of *The Lay of the Host of Igor*, Alexander Nevsky, Sergi of Radonezh, Andrei Rublev, Nil of Sory, Lomonosov, Alexander I, Ambrosius of Optina, and Serafim of Sarov.

Our sight, once it bursts the fetters of our space, can discern the heavenly lands of other metacultures in the distance, beyond the borders of the Russian metaculture, lands just as radiant and full of unique variety. Preparations through love and mutual understanding for the creation of holy Arimoya, the heavenly land of all humanity—that is the bond that now joins the Synclites and cities of different metacultures. The greatest of the children of humanity, after completing their work in their holy cities, leave their metaculture. Rising up to the World Synclite from different directions, as it were, they come together at last, but still long before they have reached that world. The world where they meet is called *Gridruttva*, the white chamber where they devise the overall plan for the ascent of humanity. Their further ascent takes them to planes where their wisdom and power surpass those of demiurges. The Higher Providential Plan, which we can sometimes distinguish in history as the pattern behind the individual plans of the demiurges, is the product of their creative work. They are the World Synclite. While maintaining full clarity of spiritual consciousness, they co-create with the Planetary Logos Himself.

Work on Arimoya in four-dimensional worlds has only just begun; its historical reflection on Earth will constitute the meaning and goal of the coming century. It is for that very purpose that the energy of the Eternal Virgin Mother, energy that is concentrated within one divine monad, flowed down from transcosmic spheres into the highest planes of Shadanakar. It is also for that purpose that a fabulous temple is being erected in Heavenly Russia—in order to receive Her, Whose birth in the four-dimensional worlds is the goal and purpose of the future marriage of the Russian demiurge and Collective Soul. In historical terms, it is through the manifestation of the Great Feminine Spirit in the Rose of the World that the transformation of the governments of all peoples into a global community will begin. In all that, the Russian Synclite is being helped and will be helped by the Synclites of all the metacultures. In turn, the World Synclite will inherit and continue their work, so as to crown it with the appearance of a global theohumankind.

There is, however, another sakwala of zatomis in Shadanakar besides the nineteen great ones. These are the zatomis of metacultures whose development was tragically arrested in Enrof. If it becomes clear that the Providential forces of a given metaculture cannot withstand the onslaught of the demonic, its zatomis is transferred to a plane in that other sakwala. Its cultural and sometimes its state institutions in Enrof dissolve little by little into the cultures surrounding it, its Witzraors die, the underworld shrastrs hunger in miserable inactivity and eventually die off. But the zatomis continues to develop; its Synclite continues and intensifies its creative work. Souls that have not yet attained a level at which the zatomis of such a metaculture opens its doors to them may complete the necessary stages of growth outside of Enrof or undergo incarnations in other metacultures and countries. But in the end they always ascend to their own zatomis. There are also instances when the cultural-historical base in Enrof continues to exist while experiencing gradual decay, and the zatomis maintains an active link with it. In such cases, it is still possible, under favorable circumstances, for the zatomis to be restored to its former sakwala, and its suprapeople to historical life. Something like that is now taking place with Zhunfleya, as I have already mentioned.

It remains for me to list briefly the fifteen zatomis of that second sakwala.

Nambata is the zatomis of the Ancient Sudanese metaculture, which developed very slowly, barely smoldering under very unfavorable conditions in the Niger Valley, in the vicinity of Lake Chad, and in Cordophan between the ninth and fifth millennia B.C. It collapsed under the centrifugal forces that exhausted it during continuous internecine wars. That first attempt in the history of humanity to unite antagonistic and ethnographically diverse peoples through a common interethnic religion (polytheistic, of course) failed because of the intense demonic influence emanating from the religion's extremely ambivalent pantheon. Archaeological ruins of the culture may still be unearthed.

Its emblem is a circle of naked black dancers on an emerald-green background.

Tsen-Tin is the zatomis of the proto-Mongolian metaculture (proto-Mongolian in the geographical, not ethnographic, sense). Its people were Asiatic, but both anthropologically and spiritually they were more closely related to the peoples of Gondwana than to those of later Mongolia. Its people settled northern China and the Amur region in the fourth or third millennium B.C. and were in the process of converting from a nomadic to a settled way of life. Small cities had already begun to spring up. The culture had a remarkable beginning. It was not a demiurge of the suprapeople at the head of their hierarchy but a powerful demonic being that was to convert and had already begun to convert to Light. The being was thrown down by Gagtungr and the suprapeople were crushed by hordes sweeping over from Central Asia.

Its emblem is a winged dragon with its head thrown up to the sun, all awash with the sun's rays.

Pred is the zatomis of the Dravidian metaculture, which is a provisional designation, as it comprised peoples of various ethnic roots, including some closely related to the Sumerians. The cities of Mohenjo-Daro and Harappa belong to the later stages of the metaculture. Its collapse (at the beginning of the second millennium B.C.) resulted from factors both internal (I have no idea of their nature) and external (the invasion of the Aryans).

I did not see clearly the emblem of Pred. But I did see a pink pagoda.

Asgard, which is sometimes incorrectly referred to by the more popular name Valhalla, is the zatomis of the ancient Germanic metaculture, which was crippled by the spread of historical Christianity. Disaster overtook it in the twelfth century A.D.

Its emblem is a golden hall in the clouds.

Tokka is the zatomis of the ancient Peruvian (pre-Inca) metaculture, which developed historically in the centuries immediately prior to and after the birth of Christ. There is, perhaps, no reason to bewail the collapse of the culture in Enrof, for the influence of the demonic was very strong in it.[1]

Its emblem depicts the stone statue of a seated puma.

Bon is the zatomis of the ancient Tibetan metaculture, which was destroyed by Buddhism, but elements of it were assimilated by the Mahayana culture.

The Bon emblem depicts red and blue bolts of lightning crisscrossing above the orange tent of a king. The blue lightning represents Buddhism and its spirituality; the red represents the pre-Buddhist Tibetan religion, which was tainted to a very great extent by demonism. The tent represents royalty, which fell as a result of the meeting of those two powers.

Gauripur is the zatomis of the small Himalayan metaculture, which separated from India too soon, yet had immense potential. It was there that the brightest centers of Buddhism were at one time kindled. There, in the context of the teaching, those metahistorical processes took place that fashioned it into a religion in the full sense of the word—that is, a teaching that was not only moral but transphysical and spiritual as well. The moral aspect of Buddhism was raised in the Himalayas to a height known only in the purest forms of Christianity.

The Himalayan metaculture collapsed under the two-pronged onslaught of state demons: the Turkic Witzraors from the north and west, and the Witzraors of the Great Mogul Empire from the south. At present the metaculture is dying out in Nepal.

---

1. That culture was supposed to have greatly advanced the task of enlightening the animal world, but historically it came to deify it and degenerate into widespread cannibalism.

Its emblem is a crowned mountain peak beneath the constellation Orion.

Yunkif is the zatomis of the Mongolian metaculture, which immediately fell prey to an unusually powerful Witzraor. Disaster overtook it in the thirteenth century.

Yunkif's emblem is a rolling line of hills, with two flocks, white and red, battling above them.

Yiru is the zatomis of the ancient Australian metaculture, which for two thousand years existed in central Australia in total isolation from the rest of humanity. Their society reached the level of a slave state. The metaculture collapsed as the result of the extremely active role played by demonic elementals—the spirits of deserts and impenetrable thickets. For many centuries two religions—"right hand" and "left hand," polytheistic and demonic— were locked in struggle within the culture. The latter offered human sacrifices to those same malevolent elementals that were engaged in destroying the metaculture. Toward the end, it was that religion that prevailed, and resistance to the encroachment of the desert and thickets was proclaimed taboo. The culture in Enrof died out from internal dessication. The most refined of their arts was painting. It was to a certain extent reminiscent of Cretan painting but was more distinctive and imaginative. The ruins to be unearthed will not be extensive enough to permit a picture of the civilization to be reconstructed.

Its emblem is a cloud above a volcano, representing the suprapeople and its Synclite.

Taltnom is the zatomis of the Tolteko-Aztec metaculture. Its emblem is the face of a hero crowned by the sun.

Kertu is the zatomis of the Yucatan (Mayan) metaculture. Its emblem depicts a blue serpent twined around a golden tree. Not every people has regarded the serpent as a dark symbol. The golden tree represents the spiritual (transphysical) world. The blue serpent symbolizes the suprapeople, who through spiral-like growth rise into the spirit.

Intil is the zatomis of the Incan metaculture, whose collapse in Enrof, strange as it may seem, saved the world from great peril. (This will be discussed in another part of the book.) Its emblem is a red-clad figure, wearing a miter, with arms uplifted to the sun. Red here symbolizes majesty, and the miter, the high priesthood.

Daffam is the zatomis of the metaculture of the Great Lakes Indians.[2] Its emblem is a group of warriors pointing their spears at the crescent of a waning moon.

Lea is the zatomis of the Polynesian metaculture, which was doomed by its extreme geographical dispersion. Embers of that metaculture are still smouldering on Hawaii, Tahiti, and other archipelagoes. Its emblem is a golden mountain on an island in a blue sea.

Nikisaka is the zatomis of the Japanese metaculture, which was seriously wounded twice—by Buddhism and by Europeanism—and thus has not been able to realize its full potential. Shinto is in essence the veneration of Nikisaka as the Japanese Synclite. The goddess Amaterasu, properly understood, is none other than the Navna of Japan. The transfer of Nikisaka to the sakwala of developmentally arrested metacultures in Enrof is now taking place. The Rose of the World will be able to provide real assistance in revitalizing the zatomis: it is still entirely possible for the process to be reversed.

Its emblem is a blossoming cherry tree beside a pond.

---

2. That culture was specially charged with combating Voglea, the female lunar demon. That accounts for the suprapeople's exceptional chasteness and their rejection of urban-based civilization.

3 The Middle Planes
of Shadanakar

BEFORE ATTEMPTING TO DRAW a general picture of the demonic sakwalas, which play such a colossal role in the transphysics and metahistory of Shadanakar, as well as the sakwalas of elementals, some of which are closely bound with the demonic, I consider it advisable to give the reader some notion of certain sakwalas of ascent that succeed, as it were, the zatomis sakwalas. These sakwalas are extremely diverse, but together they comprise the middle planes of Shadanakar.

It is only natural that the higher the planes, the more difficult it becomes to apprehend them, and the fewer analogies with Enrof can be found in their landscapes, in the form and appearance of the beings abiding there, and in the manner of life they lead. Nine-tenths of what is seen or otherwise perceived remains beyond our comprehension. In the majority of cases, one has no choice but to confine oneself to a straightforward presentation of the essential facts, without attempting to reveal their consistency or deeper meaning. Therefore, this chapter promises to be virtually nothing more than the dry enumeration of the names of a few sakwalas and the planes they comprise.

I seem to recall, for example, that within Jewish mysticism can be found the concept of the *egregor*; however, it is difficult for me to judge how closely the term corresponds to the meaning given to it here, if only because of my less than superficial knowledge of Jewish theosophy. In any case, what is meant here by *egregors* are variomaterial formations that take shape over large collectives from certain emanations of the human psyche. Egregors do not have monads, but they possess a volitional charge of limited duration and the equivalent of consciousness. Every state, even

Luxembourg, has its own egregor. They are essentially static, passive beings. The majority of egregors do not take part in the struggle between the demonic and Providential forces in Shadanakar. There are some, however, that side with the demonic camp.

When egregors disintegrate, their equivalent of consciousness disappears as well, dispersing into space. They do not experience any pain at such times.

To the extent that it is possible to speak of the landscape of those planes, the sakwalas of egregors are characterized by yellowish swirls of space in which the egregors themselves stand out as somewhat denser than their surroundings.

The seven planes that compose that sakwala can be listed in the following order:

Zativ is the region of the egregors of primal tribes, which die out as the tribes are assimilated by larger nations or are destroyed physically. The egregors of humanity's oldest cultural-political formations used to abide there, egregors that have by now already dissolved into space.

Zhag is the region of state egregors. In addition, egregors of certain large contemporary social-political organizations, like the Indian National Congress Party, can also be found there.

Foraun is the plane of the egregors of churches. They form from the dark-ether radiations that issue from the mass of humans belonging to some church, radiations released by every person who has not reached the level of sanctity. The radiations arise when a soul's religious feelings become tainted with mundane preoccupations, material concerns, acquisitiveness, negative emotions—in general, with what the Fathers of the Church termed *worldly cares*. It often happens that egregors act as serious brakes or weights on the ascending path of churches. In time there will also be in Foraun an egregor of the Rose of the World. It is unavoidable, since the interreligious church of the future will be composed not only of saints but of hundreds of millions of people at different stages of their spiritual growth.

Udgrogr is the plane of egregors of the anti-churches and the power-hungry mass parties of modern times.

One plane, whose name I do not know, is inhabited by egregors generated by the psychic activity of the shrastrs' demonic populace. I also do not know the name of the plane of egregors that form from the psychic activities of the world of daemons— that second, brighter humankind to be briefly discussed below.

The last of the egregor planes is called Tsebrumr. It is as yet empty. In time there will appear there the egregor of the future Anti-Church, the church in which will be carried out the quasi- religious, demonic worship of Gagtungr. This will be, at the end of the first eon, the nucleus and foundation of the future satano- humankind.

A different, higher humankind of Shadanakar abides in a sak- wala of three- and four-dimensional planes with an immense number of time streams. Unfortunately, my knowledge of them is meager to say the least. A host of unanswered questions that arise in connection with them has left a large gap in the picture I have been drawing of Shadanakar. These beings are called daemons. They are proceeding along a path of development similar to ours, but they began it much earlier and have achieved greater success in their spiritual growth. It appears that the key to this is the fact that Jesus Christ's mission, which in Enrof was curtailed almost at the start through the efforts of Gagtungr and which ended in only a partial victory, was brought to a successful conclusion in the daemon world. That occurred at a much ear- lier time than when Christ was incarnated in the person of Jesus. His victory in the daemon world removed the burdensome obstacles Gagtungr had placed on their path of ascent, and at present these beings have left us far behind. The length of time and number of trials necessary for them to reach spiritual matu- rity have been reduced many times over. There have been no signs of social disharmony among them for a long time, and their energy is channeled into spiritual and moral growth and into helping other planes, particularly the humanity of Enrof.

Daemons are winged people who, though they partly resemble angels in their external appearance, are different from them. In addition to many distinguishing characteristics, daemons are divided into two sexes. The chief plane of their existence, which corresponds to our Enrof, is called *Zheram*. Its natural environ- ment, which is similar to ours, has been elevated to artistic and moral excellence, while their technology is spiritualized by an inner wisdom concerning the various energies and planes of Shadanakar and by the cultivation of higher abilities within their own being. The daemons are aware of everything essential about humanity in Enrof.

Ever since the completion of Christ's mission in Zheram, the daemons have been freed from the necessity of descent into the demonic worlds of retribution after death. The multiplaned sakwala of purgatories, which the majority of us know from experience but have forgotten, has been replaced for them by a single plane, called *Urm*, where some of them undergo expiatory cleansing after death. *Kartiala*, the world of enlightened daemons, their heavenly land, parallels the zatomis of our humanity. From there a staircase opens to the sakwala of Higher Purpose, and, lastly, to the World Synclite.

The daemons' active involvement in the struggle against Witzraors and antihumankind in the shrastrs constitutes one of the many tasks undertaken by the daemons of Kartiala in relation to other worlds in Shadanakar. Their inspirational and guiding influence upon the creators of our artistic culture constitutes another. The apostrophe some poets use to address their daemon, and others their Muse, is by no means a poetic device. It is testimony to genuine transphysical facts. I do not know if the nine sisters of Apollo ever existed in the Olympus zatomis—it is entirely possible that they did—but there can be no doubt that the female daemons (muses) or the male daemons (Socratic daemons in the narrow sense of the word) have aided our artists and thinkers in plumbing their inner creative depths. Only the blindness of materialism could cause us to pass over the countless testimonies to this fact given by our poets, writers, musicians, and philosophers, beginning even before Socrates and ending with Gogol and Alexander Blok.

Once they have completed their task, the majority of daemons/inspirers leave those they inspired. Sometimes a kind of union occurs, an extremely rare phenomenon very difficult to explain.

It is common for human shelts to weave an incarnation in the daemon world into their garlands. They are ordained such an incarnation so as to consolidate the gains their souls have made on their paths of Light.

But there is also another race that abides in the daemon sak-wala, one that is less in number and has lagged behind in development. They are the wards, as it were, of the daemons. I do not have a clear notion of how they came to be in those worlds. It seems that they, too, are daemons, ones who at some time in the distant past went astray, lost their wings, and are now undoing the harm they caused themselves on a special road of atonement. These wingless beings barely differ in appearance from humans.

Here I come to a fact that will inevitably evoke scoffs and even exasperation in most readers of this book. But if it is true that a song suffers from the loss of a single word, then this book will suffer from the loss of a single thought. Those beings whom I referred to as a lower race of daemons can in part be characterized as the metaprototypes of certain heroes and heroines of global literature and art in Enrof. It sometimes happens that the intuition of artists in Enrof—albeit, an intuition of geniuses alone—penetrates to Zheram, sees one of those beings, and records its image in human art. The image becomes a kind of magic crystal that acts as a locus for radiations people emit at times of active perception. These radiations rise up to Zheram and supply the metaprototype with energy to grow. If such an image is not created, the metaprototype's growth slows and in some cases it may even have to leave the daemon sakwala and embark on a lengthy journey through Enrof.

The majority of human representations in our painting and sculpture have no metaprototypes: they are portraits of people, no more. But works of art like the *Mona Lisa*, for example, are, in addition to their human prototype, connected with prototypes in Zheram that have been apprehended by the intuition of the genius. This is the origin of the extraordinary eloquence and power of these masterpieces. It is regrettable that the *Mona Lisa* was painted by Leonardo da Vinci in such a way that the prototype ended up debased, with the portrait absorbing certain elements from Duggur—one of the worlds of demonic elementals—as a result of which the prototype fell from Zheram to Urm, for that plane serves as a purgatory for metaprototypes as well as for daemons. The proto-Mona Lisa, raised back up to Zheram and higher through the afterlife efforts of Leonardo da

Vinci, now abides in one of the planes of Higher Purpose. Venus de Milo is already in the World Synclite, since it was to the daemon Kartiala that the soul of the Greek woman who posed for the sculptor rose up through Olympus after the historical demise of Greco-Roman culture. Merging in Kartiala with her metaprototype, she began to climb the staircase of ascent through the upper planes. In time, the same will happen with all the souls of such metaprototypes.

The situation is even more complex and various with paintings of the mythological, psychological, historical, and folk genres. Morozova, the noblewoman in Surikov's painting, had a metaprototype in Zheram, as did some of the secondary figures on the canvas, and the metaprototype has been raised up to Kartiala thanks to the artist's work. In addition, Surikov is at present working in the Heavenly Kremlin on a dazzling variation on the picture.

Repin's depiction of Ivan the Terrible's murder of his son tied a knot that Repin has been unable to unravel to the present day. This he must do in Drukkarg—the shrastr of Russian antihumankind counterposed to the Heavenly Kremlin, where Ivan the Terrible now abides as captive and slave.

The situation is worse still for the *Fallen Demon* of Vrubel—a stunning, unprecedented case of a demonic infraportrait. To unravel the knot, Vrubel was forced to descend to Gashsharva, to the angels of darkness. It is a terrible thing to have to say, but it might be better, despite the brilliance of the work, if it were destroyed in Enrof.

Landscape painting, in spite of its immense cultural and psychological importance, very rarely possesses any transphysical meaning. Such meaning is present either in those cases when the artist is able to communicate to the viewer his or her feeling for the worlds of elementals visible in Enrof through nature, or to hint at the landscapes of some other plane through the use of unique combinations of lines and colors. In my personal opinion, the Russian artist who succeeded best in that was Roerich, and at times the dubious, scorned, even untalented artist Churlonis.

As for literature, in the overwhelming majority of works, there are no metaprototypes behind the characters. For example, almost all Soviet literature, with a few exceptions, has none. As well, characters of a historical nature—for example, Pushkin's Boris Godunov or Shakespeare's Julius Caesar—cannot have a metaprototype. But Macbeth has one, because the work is not historical. Generally speaking, the presence of a metaprototype in a work entails a sharp departure from historical accuracy in attributing particular depth to the personage and a greatness of character that does not have any basis in the historical prototype. That is not to be found either in Pushkin's play or *Julius Caesar*, which is proof of the lack of metahistorical depth in those works.

After the death of artistic geniuses in Enrof, the metaprototypes of their works in Zheram meet and spend time with them, as the karma of artistic creation draws them together. Many great artistic geniuses have in their afterlife had to assist the prototypes of their heroes or heroines in their ascent. Dostoyevsky spent an enormous amount of time and energy to raise up his metaprototypes, for the suicides of Stavrogin and Svidrigailov, dictated by creative and mystical logic, threw proto-Stravogin and proto-Svidrigailov down into Urm. At present, all Dostoyevsky's heroes have been raised up by him: for example, Svidrigailov has been raised to Kartiala, and Ivan Karamazov and Smerdyakov to Magirna, one of the worlds of Higher Purpose. Also there are Sobakevich, Chichikov, and other heroes of Gogol, and Tolstoy's Pierre Bezukhov, Andrei Bolkonsky, Princess Maria, and Natasha Rostova, whom Tolstoy raised from Urm at the cost of tremendous exertions. Goethe's Margaret already abides on one of the upper planes of Shadanakar, while Don Quixote long ago joined the World Synclite, which Faust, too, will soon enter.

I would like to take this opportunity to say a few words about the transphysical meaning of the dramatic arts. Christianity's traditionally negative attitude toward such forms (regardless of how it has been explained by cultural historians and even religious teachers) arose because the early and medieval Christians, in a manner of speaking, sensed unconsciously with their religious intuition the close relationship between the dramatic arts and the ancient organism that is partly linked with Lilith, and partly with an even darker demonic world, called Duggur. (In a later chapter I will describe that world in more detail.) Duggur is bound up with human sexuality, and although it was not discerned clearly in the Middle Ages, its diabolical radiations evoked fear, disgust, and shame in the people of that time. Properly speaking, theater can possess, on a transphysical level, widely varying, even contradictory, meanings. Shaliapin was fully justified in fasting and praying after performing the role of Mephistopheles. The play *The Life of a Man* was harmful for the playwright, the cast, and the audience because it lacked what the ancients called *catharsis*. All drama that takes actors and the audience through catharsis—that is, spiritual elevation and enlightenment, however brief—is deeply vindicated. As for metaprototypes, the effect of performances in Enrof are like that experienced by Dostoyevsky's Smerdyakov. While he was in Urm, thrown down there by the mystical-creative impulses of Dostoyevsky, the performance of his role on stage pained, burdened, and slowed him. Now it is of no consequence. The performance of morally uplifting roles or roles leading to catharsis are good for everyone, including metaprototypes.

With the daemon sakwala, my account will for a time leave the four-dimensional worlds. *Fongaranda*, a lone five-dimensional plane that is not a part of any sakwala, is now before us.

A warning is in order here: we are about to deal with concepts that are far from customary. For Fongaranda is the abode of shelts of masterpieces of architecture. There they possess the ability to move and grow; they evolve in the sense of spiritual maturation. Their external appearance closely resembles that of enlightened elementals, but they are not fluid in form as those spirits are, nor are their bodies interpenetrable. The reader should bear in mind that the construction of their images in Enrof by architects of genius, whose intuition caught their gleam in Fongaranda, gives them an ether body, which forms inside the physical body of the buildings after many years of receiving radiations from thousands and millions of people. If enough time has passed for such an ether body to form, the destruction of the physical body in Enrof is no longer of any transphysical consequence. The shelt in Fongaranda dons the ether body and moves to one of the zatomis. After the turn of the eon (the global period when the zatomis will cease to exist as such) the shelts of those monads, together with their coatings, which by then will have been completely transformed, will merge with their monads on one of the planes of Higher Purpose and subsequently enter the Elite of Shadanakar.

It is primarily the shelts of churches and palaces that abide in Fongaranda. There are, for example, spectacular prototypes of an Orthodox monastery, an Egyptian pyramid, a ziggurat, a *gopuram* of South India, a Catholic abbey, and a Rhenish castle. But there are also shelts of some individual buildings, for instance, St. Peter's Cathedral, the Cathedral of St. Basil the Blessed, the Temple of Heaven in China, even the palaces at Versailles and Pushkin. There are also shelts such as those of the Parliament buildings in London and the Admiralty in St. Petersburg.

After a strange world like Fongaranda, the concept of a sakwala of angels will probably seem familiar and like nothing out of the ordinary. There are two such sakwalas. The first and lower of the two comprises three planes. It is called Angels of the Lower Circle. In essence they are, chronologically speaking, the first humankind of Shadanakar, who at one time lived on planes of denser materiality, though not in Enrof. Their era preceded the era of the Titans. It is beyond our capacity to fully comprehend the manner of their lives now, in their enlightened worlds. We can only apprehend that aspect of their work that has a direct bearing on us. The first of these planes is inhabited by *cherubim*, the guardians of people performing missions of Light. They are just that—guardians; it is the daemons who are the inspirers! We have heard of guardian angels since childhood, and it is not our fault if we thought that such an angel hovered over the right shoulder of every one of us. They have the same external appearance described in tradition, and their world is a landscape of gorgeous colors that we cannot perceive but that are vaguely reminiscent of pink and violet.

Another plane—a land of white-gold pierced everywhere by beams of light—belongs to *seraphim*, the guardians of certain human communities: churches, religious groups, some charitable organizations, and those very few cities whose spiritual integrity and moral purity are of particular importance in the eyes of the Providential powers. There are times when a guard of seraphim encircles a city because taking place within it is one or another metahistorical event or transphysical process that requires special assistance or protection. When the process or event is completed, and a new era begins, the guard of seraphim is withdrawn. There were guards over Kiev during the reign of St. Vladimir, over Moscow during the reigns of Prince Daniil and Ivan Kalita, and several times over Jerusalem, Rome, and many other cities. Benares, a city of tremendous metahistorical significance, is one of those rare instances when the guard of seraphim does not leave a city for several centuries. Of course, from a narrowly Christian point of view, statements like the preceding can only give rise to perplexity. In appearance seraphim resemble six-winged angels.

The sakwala concludes with the world of the so-called *Thrones*, whose appearance nearly matches our image of archangels, and whose abode is greenish blue, pierced by playful beams of light. The Thrones are the guardians of nations. There are many of them—the spiritual maturation of every nation is overseen by a host of those resplendent beings.

Moving on to the second sakwala—the Angels of the Upper Circle—I find I cannot even resort to such meager visual images as I used for the first sakwala to help the reader form an idea of this one. All I can say is that they are the abodes of hierarchies of Light of tremendous power, those same ones who create the materiality of the three-, four-, and five-dimensional planes in Shadanakar.

First come the Astrals, known in Christian mysticism as the Principalities. They are the creators of materiality for Enrof. Next come the Powers, creators of materiality for the daemon sakwalas, and the Dominions, creators of materiality for the worlds of Enlightenment (except Olirna). The sakwala of Angels of the Upper Circle concludes with the world of the Virtues, who create materiality for the zatomis, and the Archangels, those same beings who were Sirins, Alkonosts, and Gamayuns before their transformation in Paradise, Eden, Monsalvat, Zhunfleya, and Holy Russia—all the zatomis of Christian metacultures. They create materiality for the worlds of Higher Purpose. The materiality of the angelic worlds themselves, as well as that of the upper planes of Shadanakar, is created by the hierarchies of the metabramfatura.

I realize that, despite the similarity in nomenclature, the above is not concordant with traditional Christian angelology. I am sorry that it is so. But I am not writing on the basis of my own knowledge and cannot make any alterations until that single Voice I trust with all my heart tells me otherwise.

Our survey has arrived at the sakwala of Higher Purpose. These worlds are common to people, angels, daemons, elementals, and even to enlightened animals. They soar far above those distinct segments of Shadanakar called metacultures. Naturally, my knowledge of them is scant, if not to say beggarly.

I am not even sure of the name of the first of these worlds. It sounds something like *Usnorm*, but I can't make it out more clearly. The spinning of the planet on its axis is evident there as it is here. It must have been nightfall at the time I was there, because I vaguely remember seeing a glowing mist of stunning majesty, as though the creative heart of our Universe had revealed itself to me in visible form for the first time. It was Astrafire, the great center of our Galaxy, which is hidden from our sight in Enrof by dark clouds of cosmic matter.

I also saw a scattering of countless stars, but not as we see them here. Indeed, they were not stars, but bramfaturas. They were not bright pinpricks in the sky but systems of concentric spheres visible through each other. When my gaze rested on one of them, it grew huge and distinct, just like a cinematic close-up. It seems to me now that they were all spinning slowly, harmoniously sounding and calling to each other with multi-toned voices. But that may only seem so now, and may be the result of preconceptions about the harmony of the celestial spheres, an idea that came to me not from experience but from human legends. In any case, those harmonies could barely be heard above the surges of an incredible choir that was sounding right there around me, rising from depths to heights that I could neither comprehend nor measure with my eyes. All this is my recollection of the plane/temple reserved for the eternal liturgy of humankind.

Oh, not only humankind! There were, I guess, millions of beings there, and—I don't know how many exactly—probably more than half of them had never been nor were destined to be human. There were enlightened souls of elementals and animals, wondrous daemons, and angels of various circles. When we read the prophecy in the Apocalypse about animals gifted with intelligence performing the liturgy around the altar in another world, it may be a symbol, but it is also a hint at reality, a reality that did not yet exist at the time the author of the Apocalypse was living. For Usnorm, the temple common to all, is the brainchild of that same great human spirit who was John the Evangelist in his last incarnation on Earth.

While there were millions worshipping, those performing the service at the church altar numbered in the thousands. Everyone who reaches the sakwala of Higher Purpose eventually performs the liturgy in Usnorm, and is then followed by the next in order.

The most uplifting and joyous services in the churches and temples of the higher religions are but dim reflections and echoes of the eternal liturgy of Usnorm. There is indeed an oral element in the liturgy, but the words are in the language of the World Synclite, which we cannot reproduce, and in which words are not simply individual sounds but chords of meaning, as it were, and some appear at the same time as flashes and waves of light. There is an element of movement in the liturgy, the heavenly prototype of sacred dance. But as Usnorm is five-dimensional, movement occurs not along a horizontal surface, as it does here, but in all five dimensions. There are elements of light and color in the liturgy, but it is impossible to convey a description of these colors outside the seven visible to us. What can I say that would do justice to the symphonies of light, beside which even the fireworks of Faer seem monotone and feeble? What can I say about the spiritual fragrances? About the incense of Usnorm, which rises from gigantic floating and swinging thuribles up to Astrafire itself?

Usnorm is the first world where those who are ascending no longer absorb material radiations but rather purely spiritual ones. These issue from the very highest transcosmic spheres, which one could call the Empyrean, if that ancient word is not taken to mean a fantastic "world of motionless stars" but rather the all-embracing abode of pure Spirit—that is, the Holy Trinity.

The worlds of Higher Purpose are way stations between the zatomis, Kartiala of the daemons, and Hangvilla of enlightened animals on the one hand, and the worlds of the Higher Transmyths of the Global Religions on the other. Above Usnorm is Gridruttva, the white chamber where the great creative plan for humanity is devised. After it comes Alikanda, which resembles the heart of a flower; Tovia, which resembles foam, hoarfrost, a white garden, or falling snow; and Ro, which resembles huge singing crystals. The most beautiful works of music in Enrof, in Olirna, among the daemons, even in the zatomis are but echoes of these crystals. These three planes are the abode of human monads that have merged with their mature souls.

Magirn, a plane that resembles illumined ocean depths, is the abode of monads and metaprototypes that have merged with their shelts and transfigured astral bodies. The monads of animals merge with their mature souls in Kaermis, which could be described as a land of living sphinxes. The same happens in Deitrast to the monads of daemons and in Sibran to the monads of angels, about which I can only say that it is an unbelievable choir of rejoicing. The monads of elementals abide in Flauros, of which the words "solar flares" can give an intimation. The sakwala of the world of Higher Purpose also includes Niatos: violet heights where the monads of our former enemies—demons who have converted to Light—merge with their shelts. I have already mentioned the powerful demonic spirit, the great "dragon" of the proto-Mongolian culture. Cast down by Gagtungr into a plane of torment known as the Rain of Endless Misery, it was long ago rescued from there by the Providential powers and now shines in the world of violet heights as one of its most beautiful lights.

As far as I can recall, Iroln, splendid and immense, is also a part of the sakwala. It is the abode of human monads before they merge with their mature souls. Iroln is the initial destination of the individual spirit of each person when it leaves the heart of the Creator and enters Shadanakar. It resembles a multitude of suns gliding and spinning. And now I am not sure: it seems to me that Iroln is not five but six-dimensional, and my inclusion of it into the sakwala of Higher Purpose is a mistake, an aberration on my part.

Higher on the staircase of hierarchies in Shadanakar are situated, one after another, the sakwalas of cosmic emanations. What are they? Other bramfaturas have been acting on Shadanakar in a tangible manner throughout its multimillion-year history. These bramfaturas are either more powerful than ours, or more advanced, or commensurate with us in size and level of ascent, but because they are located not too far from us in space they therefore interact with our bramfatura. The materiality of the worlds of emanations is created by the forces of Light of other bramfaturas. The bramfaturas are inhabited by higher beings who can travel great cosmic distances without difficulty. These visitors from other bramfaturas are the great allies and friends of the forces of Light of Shadanakar.

Other than to list a few names, I have literally nothing to say about some sakwalas of emanations. For example, there is a sakwala of emanations from Orion. Orion is a system of bramfaturas of immense power that has freed itself completely from the demonic, and it plays a prominent role in the life of the Galaxy. Of course, listing the names of the ten planes that make up the sakwala cannot evoke in the reader anything but disappointment in its meagerness. But how do I know? Perhaps even these names will be of some use in the future: Yumaroya, Odgiana, Ramn, Vualra, Ligeya, Fianna, Eramo, Veatnor, Zaolita, and Natolis.

Despite the huge disparity between our conditions and those that reign on the physical plane of Jupiter or Neptune, we must accustom ourselves to the idea that many of the planets and their moons possess bramfaturas. Jupiter is even inhabited on our plane, in Enrof, by intelligent life forms, but they are so different from us and live under conditions so unthinkable that no contact will ever occur between us and them in Enrof. But contact does take place on the five-dimensional planes of both bramfaturas. The Elite of Jupiter and its moons have created two planes of emanations within Shadanakar, one plane has been created by Saturn and its moons, and one each by Uranus and Neptune. All of them together make up the sakwala of planetary emanations.

A special place is occupied by the three planes of Iora, Achnos, and Gebn. They form the sakwala of emanations from the transfigured planet Daiya, which no longer exists in Enrof. The planet used to be situated between Mars and Jupiter. Long ago, the efforts of its demiurges led to the expulsion of the demonic powers to the bramfatura of Daiya's moon. Daiya entered its third eon—that is, it underwent a physical transformation and disappeared from cosmic Enrof. As for the moon, it suffered a catastrophic break-up (the asteroids are fragments of it) and the demonic hordes were scattered into outer space. When our scientific instruments become powerful enough to observe planets in other solar systems, we will sometimes witness the sudden disappearance, in the space of a few hours, of some of these planets. No doubt scientists will advance a number of clever hypotheses to explain away the phenomenon before they admit that the same thing that is happening in these cases at one time happened to the planet Daiya.

The sakwala of solar emanations numbers nine planes. Again, I can give only names: Raos, Flermos, Tramnos, Gimnos, Areya, Nigveya, Trimoya, Derayn, and Iordis.

I can also list the names of the four planes of emanations from Astrafire, the center of the Galaxy: Grezuar, Malein, Viruana, and Luvarn.

One particular system is in part connected with the sakwalas of emanations. It would be more correct to call this system a bramfatura, though at present it is part of Shadanakar, being encompassed within its five- and six-dimensional planes. It is the Lunar Bramfatura.

I do not know when exactly the development of lunar humankind—Selenites—came to an end in Enrof. In any case, it was in the very distant past, almost a million years ago. But evolution there proceeded at a much slower pace, though the time required between the appearance of organic life on the surface of the Moon and the emergence of intelligent life forms was far less than for the corresponding process on Earth. Generally speaking, the idea that physically smaller worlds should in every case evolve more quickly is not always true of individual periods of development of organic life, let alone of the tempo of the evolution of intelligent life. But H. G. Wells's intuition of the external appearance of these beings, which he describes in his fascinating book, is amazing, especially if one considers the rationalist complexion and scientific-like superficiality of his thinking. He correctly envisioned their overall insect-like appearance: the soft, elastic consistency of their physical tissue, their bodies' ability to metamorphose in accordance with the task at hand, the advanced state of their technology, and even the fact that toward the end of their civilization they had begun partly to exploit the interior of the Moon.

The Selenites' tragic end resulted from the victory of Voglea, the female lunar demon. One might well wonder how it was that the activities of a female demon found an outlet in their rationalistic society. But there exists a particular variety of rationality, one that can be denoted as female, and not everywhere is its expression so weak as among our humanity. It took root among the Selenites with special resiliency, and its effects could particularly be seen in the fact that their technology was based far more than ours on the principles of magic.

The stages of the Selenites' spiritual and cultural decline went from satanohumankind to degeneration to death under the weight of their technology. Their deepening spiritual bankruptcy caused the Selenite society to descend into anarchy, lose the ability to run their own machines, and finally die of cold and hunger. But to this day, the world of Voglea remains a part of the Lunar Bramfatura. For an extremely long time it maintained a singular kind of neutrality, at times warring with both the powers of Light and Gagtungr. But in the last while the planetary demons of Shadanakar and Voglea have been moving toward a truce and, in fact, an alliance to join forces and drive the powers of Light out of Shadanakar. One demonic plane in Shadanakar, Duggur, is closely linked with the emanations of Voglea. At present, the bewitching, vampire-like, blue-gray female demon is rebuilding a special plane—the lunar hell. There, with Gagtungr's consent, the victims of Duggur will descend. Until now, some of those victims have met with an even worse fate: ejection from Shadanakar into the emptiness of the Galaxy.

The three other planes of the Lunar sakwala counterpose Voglea's world. Soldbis can be seen on the surface of the Moon from the zatomis; it is the abode of a great many of those enlightened ones whose spiritual growth was too slow and who therefore met with tragedy. Their last incarnation in Enrof occurred during the period of the lunar satanohumankind and degeneration, and since then they have spent a vast length of time on rehabilitation and gradual enlightenment in Soldbis. Another world, Laal, is for the Lunar Elite. A great many Selenites have already risen even higher, to the Elite of Shadanakar. Finally, there is Tanit, the abode of the lunar goddess and the third and brightest of the lunar worlds.

If through careful observation we unravel into separate strands what we feel at nights when the moon is full, we will awaken to certain threads of feeling. First is a sense of harmony, which is the effect Soldbis and Laal have on us. Second is a subtle nostalgia for the heavens, which is Tanit calling to us. Third is the lure of sexual transgression, which is Voglea haunting and tempting us. She fears the Sun, always retreating from its light to the dark side of the Moon. During a full moon, only diminished emanations from Voglea—those that pass through the Moon's crust—reach us. But when the Moon is waning, Voglea moves together with the darkness to the side facing the Earth. That is why the waning of the Moon and a new moon have for many such a sickening, sinister, and depressing effect on the subconscious.

Our survey of the structure of Shadanakar has at last arrived at the grandiose sakwala that I am forced to refer to by the painfully cumbersome title of the Worlds of the Highest Aspects of the Global Religions. It is the world of their purest transmyths.

Many years ago, long before the Second World War, when I was still quite young, a mysterious, beautiful, and persistent vision began appearing to me. Seen from an endless distance away, it looked like a bluish crystal pyramid with the sun shining through it. I sensed the magnitude of its significance, the waves of grace, power, and beauty pouring forth from that shining center, but I had no idea what the vision could mean. Later I even thought that it was a glimmer of the World Salvaterra refracted by my limited human mind. How naive! Those whose souls are illumined by a glimmer of the World Salvaterra become saints and prophets. And, of course, its glimmer can in no way be likened to anything earthly.

It was only many years later, quite recently in fact, that I learned that the pyramid is not alone, that there are others in tandem, as it were, with it, five in all, and there will never be a sixth in Shadanakar. But there is only one blue pyramid. The rest are other colors, and it is impossible to say which is the most beautiful. Of course, for us, transmyths are in themselves transcendental. It may very well be that "in themselves" they bear no resemblance to any geometric forms. But it was in the form of those gigantic crystal pyramids that they imprinted themselves on my mind, and the adoption of just those images must contain some deeper meaning.

Later I was struck by something else. One of the pyramids, smaller in size but of a wondrous, unearthly white, is the higher transmyth of a religion that I personally would never have thought to include among the global or higher religions: the transmyth of Zoroastrianism. My puzzlement has yet to be dispelled. To this day I have been unable to learn how that local religion, which left the historical scene a long time ago and, it seems to me, is not, mythologically speaking, all that rich, could prove to be a reflection of an immense reality professed by it alone. My puzzlement notwithstanding, its world is called Azur.

Another pyramid, which I better understand, is also comparatively small in size, but it is gold in color. It is the highest aspect of Judaism, the aspect that has left far below the anti-Christian intransigence of its lackluster and turbid earthly twin. It is the golden world of heavenly glory, whose light penetrated into the visions of the great mystics of the Kabbala and the prophets, and for which the winding thread of the Talmud is as the dust of valleys is for a lord of mountain heights. The name of the golden pyramid is Ae.

The highest aspect of the Hindu transmyth is a huge pyramid whose color is reminiscent of our violet. That complex world is layered, the outermost of its layers being the ultimate goals of Vedanta and yoga, and the highest layer being the ultimate goal of the Synclite of India, an intimation of which we might find in Indian philosophy under the name of Nirukta. Concerning another layer, Eroya, and yet another, whose name I do not have the right to pronounce, I can only say that, though they who were once humans also abide in those worlds, they are more like guests there. Shatrittva, the last layer of the violet pyramid, is the abode of many hierarchies of the Hindu pantheon. But one can speak of the exact correspondence of the pantheon images to the hierarchies of the transmyth only in part, in certain individual cases. For example, hierarchies of entirely different heights, powers, and cosmic levels—from "the National Aphrodite" of India to the Virgin Mother of the Universe—are worshiped in Enrof under one and the same name, Kali-Durga.

No less huge is the green pyramid, the world of the higher aspect of Buddhism, which comprises two layers. There is a popular misconception that Buddhism, or at least its southern variety, is atheistic. In reality, there is of course no atheism to be found at the highest levels of Hinayana or Jainism. But beginning with Gautama and Mahavira, thinkers and disseminators have judged that it is in the best interests of the masses to emphasize the immateriality of the question of God in one's spiritual salvation, so that the efforts people themselves have to make are not shunted onto God. And how could they not believe in God, they whose Nirvana is the first of the two layers of the great green pyramid? The second layer belongs to the Dhyani Bodhisattvas, the hierarchies that guide the peoples of Buddhist metacultures. We should treat with caution the claim made by the spiritual shepherds of Tibet that the majority of Dalai Lamas are reincarnations of the Dhyani Bodhisattva Avalokitesvara. To take that claim literally would show that the clarity of our thinking has not yet risen above the clarity that is attainable within definite religious limits. But we will not be far from the truth if we regard the proposition that Avalokitesvara is reincarnated in a successive series of Dalai Lamas as a sort of intimation that most Dalai Lamas are inspired by that great hierarchy, an intimation designed to accord with the level of mass understanding. The second to last of the Tibetan spiritual leaders was not wholly inspired, while the one ruling at present (1957) is nothing other than an imposter, which accounts for his behavior.

As for the blue pyramid that has been beckoning to me for the last twenty years—it is Heavenly Jerusalem, the higher trans-myth of Christianity. It is what lies behind the Christian creeds shared by Catholics, Orthodox believers, Protestants, Ethiopians, and the future followers of the Rose of the World. I said "creeds," but that is not precise, because it is almost impossible to express that single, common truth in words. Heavenly Jerusalem is the highest plane of the Synclites of Christian metacultures, and yet it is still not the Church. The Church is the highest plane of Shadanakar. And before undertaking to describe it, we must do an about-face and go down, far down into fire and darkness. For without a notion of the frightful and dread demonic sakwalas, we will also be unable to gain a proper notion of the higher planes of Shadanakar.

BOOK IV

The Structure of Shadanakar: The Infraphysical Planes

1 The Demonic Base

ONE FACT that our religious consciousness has failed to take into account to this day is that the Trinity intrinsic to God recurs or is duplicated in some of the monads He creates. The crude saying, "The Devil is the ape of God" has a profound and multifaceted meaning. The warped, inverted imitation of the Trinity, the inner mystery of the Divine Spirit, by the great demonic monads constitutes one of its most important senses. I cannot, of course, shed any light on the triune of Lucifer. It is on a level so infinitely beyond all the powers of our comprehension that it is scarcely possible to apprehend anything about it other than the very fact of its existence, the fact of its fall in times immemorial, and its continuous struggle against God.

Despite the tremendous gap between the dimensions of his being and ours, the nature of Gagtungr, the great demon of Shadanakar, may, under favorable circumstances, be apprehended to a somewhat greater extent. Most important, his tri-unity becomes evident, though the cause, origin, and purpose of that triunity (if it does indeed have a purpose) remain a mystery.

What comes to light first of all is that we are dealing with a kind of blasphemous parody of the hypostases of the Holy Trinity. But the nature of the Divine Triune—arguably the most complex issue in theology—will be discussed, if only briefly, in another section of the book. Thus, for now it is impossible to shed light on the nature of the parody I have just mentioned. I will only say that Gagtungr endeavors to counterpose his first person, the Great Torturer, to the First Hypostasis of the Divine Trinity; his second person, who could best be described by the

name the Great Harlot, to the Second Hypostasis; and the antipode called Urparp to the Third Hypostasis of the Trinity.
Urparp is the implementer of the demonic plan and in a certain
sense might be called *the principle of form*. It is that aspect of the
great demonic being that manifests itself in the life of various
planes in Shadanakar as a power that actively works toward
transforming their nature in accordance with the designs and
purposes of the Torturer. It is the formative power. Fokerma,
the Great Harlot, is that aspect of the demonic being that pulls
and draws souls and fates within Gagtungr's compass. The first
aspect, Gisturg, the Great Torturer, is the ultimate depth of the
demonic self, the repository of its higher will, power, and desire.

His external appearance, as seen by the spiritual vision of
those few humans who have gained entry to the dark heights of
Digm, his abode, is dreadful beyond all description. Reclining, as
it were, over a raging purple ocean, with black wings stretched
from horizon to horizon, he raises his dark grey face up to where
a blaze of infrapurple light pulses and flares, while above it all
blazes a luminary of an inconceivable color vaguely reminiscent
of violet. Woe to those whom Gagtungr fixes with his gaze and
who return that gaze with open eyes. If I remember correctly, of
all the human agents of dark missions later brought to Digm,
only one, Torquemada, found the strength at that moment to
call to mind the name of God. All the other monads became
slaves to the devil for untold centuries to come.

Besides Gagtungr, the elect of evil also abide in Digm. They
are the monads of a very few humans that have merged with
their demonized shelts and the few souls of certain beings of a
demonic nature, including the grand igvas, the dark leaders of
antihumankind who have already completed their journey on
various denser material planes. There they together devise the
plan for the struggle against God; there they prostrate themselves before Gisturg, are intimate with the Great Harlot, and
are initiated into depths of knowledge in contemplating the face
of Urparp.

There is yet an even higher demonic plane in Shadanakar:
multidimensional Shog, whose materiality was created by the

great demons of the macrobramfatura. Powerful currents of dark energy flow out of the depths of the Universe into the plane, and no one other than Gagtungr can enter it. All others are only able to see it from the outside, and even then only at rare moments. At those moments, they no longer perceive as spherical that same luminary of indescribable color that blazes over Digm. Rather, they perceive it as a pulsating arc stretching from one end of the plane to the other, with its light still akin to violet. It is the galactic anticosmos, the seat of power within the Galaxy of Lucifer himself. At times, the arc sags inward, as it were, and Lucifer's energy pours into Shog. Thereupon Gagtungr, imbibing it, raises his wings up to the black sky. That, at least, is how those who see Shog from the outside perceive it. The manifestations and forms of that world themselves are in actuality transcendental for us.

There are, however, other planes in Shadanakar from where the galactic anticosmos is visible, though in a different aspect. The anticosmos of all bramfaturas, Shadanakar included, are two-dimensional: they are endless geometrical planes, as it were. They all intersect along the same line, which could be called the demonic axis of the Galaxy. To help the reader visualize it, I will employ a kind of structural model. Take a book, stand it up vertically on its spine, open it and spread its pages out, and in your mind imagine the two dimensional plane of each of its pages extending on to infinity. All the planes will intersect at different angles, but all along the same vertical line somewhere on the spine. The demonic axis of the Galaxy, its anticosmos, is the cosmic prototype for the line of intersection of all these planes. Naturally, it will be visible to any being abiding on any of these two-dimensional worlds, including the corresponding plane in Shadanakar.

The two-dimensional plane in Shadanakar is sometimes called hell, but the term is not entirely appropriate. The plane is not where human souls suffer in the afterlife; rather, it is the abode of most of the demonic beings of our planet. It could be called the anticosmos of Shadanakar, but that is not quite correct either, because the anticosmos is not that one plane alone but all the demonic worlds that counterpose the Divine Cosmos. It is only, so to speak, the chief demonic stronghold. Its real name is Gashsharva.

One could, if one likes, consider the beings there to be incarnated. On the other hand, the concept of incarnation is extremely relative. Their monads always remain high up in Digm and Shog, while their shelts, for the most part, languish between incarnations in the Pit of Shadanakar, a horrible one-dimensional world.

Gashsharva is the nucleus of the system of worlds created by the demonic powers of Shadanakar to counter the Divine Cosmos and eventually subvert it. No human being could help viewing that dismal yet awesome world as anything but horrific. The combination of a large number of time streams with only two dimensions produces a peculiar spiritually stifling atmosphere. Every monad experiences great pain when its shelt enters that world, a pain reminiscent of the sensation that would arise if a body were forced into a tight iron corset. The fewer the dimensions, the denser the materiality of the world. The atmosphere of that world, however, still resembles air, while the completely flat and uniform ground is harder than any matter in Enrof. There is no equivalent of our vegetation. The radiation of the beings themselves and certain mechanical devices serve as light sources. Blue and green are not visible here, though two kinds of infrared are. I will give one of them the provisional name of infrapurple, stressing as I do so that it has no relation to infraviolet. The impression it produces is like that of a very thick, dark, and intense purple.

The galactic anticosmos, which is visible from Digm as a luminary of an absolutely inconceivable and indescribable color, and from Shog in the form of a titanic blazing and pulsating infrapurple arc stretching across the sky, appears to Gashsharva as a section of the horizon that emits infrapurple light of uniform strength from infinitely distant regions.

All the inhabitants of Gashsharva are bound together by the tyranny of Gagtungr and, at the same time, by a kind of union of shared interests. They hate Gagtungr, yet not as much, of course, as they hate God. The keepers of the lower purgatories, magma, and core—the three sakwalas of Retribution—abide there.

Vrubel's *The Fallen Demon* has a twofold meaning. It is both a memory of Digm, of Gagtungr with wings stretched to the horizons, and a metaportrait, or rather, an infraportrait, of a lesser demon: a keeper of one of the purgatories. They are called angels of darkness, and the name captures their appearance perfectly. There is something human-like about them, they have large wings of astonishing beauty, and one senses something regal in the purplish and reddish color of their wings. But in Vrubel's picture these extraordinary wings are broken. The artist's brilliant intuition conveyed through this detail the chief disability crippling Gashsharva's inhabitants. Their wings are in actuality undamaged, but the possibility of using them is painfully limited, for they can only struggle laboriously, but not fly, through the plane's dense yet transparent atmosphere. The ashen pallor of their faces is loathsome and terrible; their predatory and merciless nature is wholly revealed in their facial features. These keepers of the lower purgatories replenish their energy by imbibing the gavvakh of humans drawn down to the purgatories by their karma. In passing from Gashsharva to those purgatories, they enter a less dense atmosphere in which crooked, uneven flight, all zigzags and jerks, is nevertheless possible.

Other inhabitants of Gashsharva, *ryphras*, the keepers of the magma, bear absolutely no resemblance to humans. Each of them individually resembles most closely a moving ridge of hills. They have something like a face, but the features are very indistinct.

The reader might criticize me next for my lack of imagination or for faithfulness to Christian tradition just where it is the most suspect. But it is that very same free play of the imagination that I am trying to banish from these pages, and the fewer the fancies they contain the better. As for Christian tradition, what is retained here does not depend on my personal preferences but on corroboration by my spiritual experience. Unfortunately, the existence of certain beings popularized in Christian demonology has also received such corroboration. Strange as it may seem, beings resembling the devils of our legends do in fact exist, complete with, believe it or not, horns and tail. They abide in Gashsharva, where they have the dubious pleasure of being the keepers of the Core—the sakwala comprising the most horrific planes of torment in Shadanakar. Generally speaking, many of the legends we are accustomed to treating with a smile or, at best, regarding as symbolic should be taken quite literally. Now there is a challenge that is beyond the powers of the modern rational mind!

Gashsharva is inhabited by a wide range of fantastic beings. Among them I also know of powerful female demons, to whom I am accustomed to giving the provisional name of *velgas*. They are giants. They sometimes manifest themselves in human history as fomentors of violence and anarchy. In no way do they resemble humans or even the monsters of our world here. They are more like huge, coiling, blanketing cloaks of black and purple. Every people, as I recall, has only one velga. In any case, in Russia, there is only one, a very ancient one. Their incarnations in Gashsharva—if we can consider them incarnations—last for centuries.

At one time all those beings lived on the Earth's surface—not in Enrof, but on a plane of approximately the same density and even remotely resembling it. Created by Gagtungr at the very beginning of Shadanakar's history, that plane has long ceased to exist. The demonic beings were smaller in size in that world and were, on the whole, somewhat different in appearance. But they were unable to feel at ease there. They were pressed and cowed by the light. Their essence would have been transformed under its influence and would eventually have ceased to conform to their demonic natures. They do not have an easy life now in Gashsharva, but there they nevertheless remain who they are.

Still other beings make that plane their home, but I know nothing about them, though I do know that some of those who were humans in Enrof abide there. They are the agents of special dark missions. Contrary to expectation, they experience virtually no suffering there. They have a different purpose for being there. In Gashsharva they are meticulously groomed by the powers of Gagtungr for their next incarnation among humanity.

What could bring a human shelt to accept such a mission? Danton accepted his out of fear. Having descended after death through all the planes to the Pit of Shadanakar, he was, through the efforts of Urparp, taken up from there to Gashsharva and some time later was born yet again in Enrof. I don't know if he has died yet this time, but quite recently he was living in Russia, where in performing a new dark mission he brought several greatly gifted people to ruin. Sometimes a dark mission is accepted voluntarily, out of a thirst for power or blood, out of an inborn predisposition for evil. Such was the case, for example, with Tamerlane, who after death passed through the same circles as Danton, only more slowly. Raised up finally to Gashsharva, he had no choice but to accept a new mission. That mission was of far less importance than the first. Gagtungr loves to make a mockery of everyone, including his puppets.

The forces of Light are frequently forced to descend to Gashsharva. To descend thus is very painful but necessary: events in the struggle with Gagtungr's legions require it. The inhabitants of Gashsharva see their enemies penetrating into their world, but they are powerless to prevent it.

The Demonic Base comprises yet another world, a world of one time stream and one dimension. It is the Pit of Shadanakar, the plane of torment for demonic shelts and for those few people who have performed dark missions.

The Pit came into being at the very dawn of our bramfatura through the efforts of Gagtungr and other, more powerful dark forces. It is composed of the densest materiality possible. In Enrof, only the materiality of stellar cores or that of the monstrous bodies of our Galaxy known as "white dwarfs" can to any extent be likened to it. It is difficult to imagine how movement could take place under such conditions. It does, though it is movement that is painful to the highest degree. It is necessary for the maintenance of their level of energy; otherwise they are sucked into a kind of cavity that leads to an even more wretched place: the Pit of the Galaxy.

That all serves to clarify once and for all the relativity of the concept of incarnation. Demons, having incarnated in Gashsharva or on certain other planes of three and even four dimensions, sink to the Pit after death, where a new body, the densest possible, awaits them. That is the law of karma, whose double edge is turned back on the demons themselves. To replenish his energy, Gagtungr himself imbibes the radiations of their sufferings in the Pit. Why not rebel against the law of karma? It is that same karmic law which supplies them with energy during their incarnations on all the other planes. To fight the law would be tantamount to renouncing gavvakh as food, tantamount to entering into conflict with the entire demonic camp and the whole anticosmos—that is, it would be tantamount to ceasing to be a demon.

There is such a pit in every bramfatura in our Universe, except in those that are free of the demonic. Thus, there are millions of such pits in the Galaxy. Just as the two-dimensional cosmic planes of many anticosmoses or gashsharvas intersect along a common line, all the cosmic lines of galactic pits converge at a single point. The point is located in the Antares solar system. It is no coincidence that the star, also called the Heart of the Scorpion, served as the embodiment of sinister, even diabolical, powers in many mythologies of antiquity and the Middle Ages. That immense solar system is the focal point of the Galaxy's anti-God forces, their abode in the three-dimensional world. It is also a gigantic metabramfatura of demons, the anticosmos of our Milky Way to the degree that the anticosmos is manifested at all in Enrof. I have already said that bramfaturas in which demons have been victorious are not long-lived, and the large planet revolving around Antares that is presently energizing the Pit of Shadanakar will soon break up, but another will take its place. The one that energized the Pit at the time of Shadanakar's founding perished millions of years ago.

Antares is visible in our latitudes low on the southern horizon in late spring and summer, and many may remember well its brightly pulsating wine-red rays. Neither the sun nor any other heavenly bodies are visible from the Pit of Shadanakar—only motionless Antares, on which one end of the Pit rests. In the Pit, it appears infrared. In the opposite direction, the one-dimensional world fades as it approaches the surface of the Earth.

Nothing is visible in that direction. That is where the cavity to the timeless Pit of the Galaxy lies concealed.

It is difficult to imagine how a body, denser than any other, could resemble the simplest thing we are capable of imagining: a kind of black line. It is even more difficult to conceive how it is that those beings retain the equivalent of sight and even touch. The most incomprehensible thing, I would think, is how they are able to see at all through that densest of atmospheres. It is from that atmosphere that they replenish their energy. Interaction between them is possible but extremely limited. Their suffering is beyond description.

Not only the Pit but all the worlds of the Demonic Base appeared, as I have mentioned, while the physical body of Shadanakar was cooling. Before the emergence of organic life in Enrof, Gagtungr centered his activities around attempts to establish a demonic plane on the surface of the Earth and, when that failed, to reinforce and expand Gashsharva and other planes connected with the lower layers of the crust, the magma, and the core of the planet. When organic life did emerge in Enrof, he focused his efforts on gaining sway over the animal realm—efforts that were in part successful—and on making the demiurges' laws more oppressive. The resultant of those two forces formed the basis for the laws of Nature and karma under which we live.

The Semitic religions are disposed to attribute to God responsibility for the severity of the laws. Surprising as it is, their severity itself, at least the severity of the laws of retribution, did not arouse any protest, and were not even recognized as overly harsh. Even the saints of Christian metacultures reconciled themselves with inscrutable calm to the idea of eternal suffering for sinners. Their minds were not troubled by the absurdity of eternal retribution for temporal evil, while their conscience—how I don't know—was appeased by the idea of everlasting immutability, that is, the inevitability of these laws. But that mode of reasoning and conscience is long past. The idea that the Law, in the form it has taken, was created according to God's will should seem blasphemous to us now.

Yes, not a hair of your head will be lost nor will a single leaf on a tree rustle except through the will of God. But we should understand that to mean not that the universal Law in its entirety is the manifestation of God's will but that the maturation of free wills that make up the Universe is sanctioned by God. The existence of a great many free wills gave rise to the possibility that some of them would deny God. Their denial led to their struggle with the forces of Light and to their creation of an anti-cosmos counterposed to the Cosmos of the Creator.

From the very moment life emerged in Enrof, Gagtungr and his horde left their imprint on the laws governing that life. They were unable to change the laws of the middle planes of Shadan-akar, but many species and classes of animals and some planes of elementals fell under their sway, either wholly or in part. That is the origin of the duality of what we call Nature: beauty, spiritual-ity, harmony, and peacefulness on the one hand; living beings killing each other on the other. Is it not obvious that both these aspects are equally real? Is there even one person with a brain and conscience, no matter how deeply he or she might love Nature, who would venture to say that its harmony eclipses and alleviates the boundless sea of suffering that is evident to the unprejudiced eye? And could even one person be found who, despite that sea of suffering—so glaring, so indisputable, so inces-santly bombarding our ears with the groans and cries of living beings—has not even once in a while still experienced the inex-plicable harmony and incomparable beauty of Nature? How is it that to this day people have failed to understand and resolve that crucial paradox? Is it not because in the West religious thought for more than twenty centuries has been held in thrall by the idea of God's absolute omnipotence and by consequent preconcep-tions about the oneness of Nature? And in the East, is it not because a deep-rooted philosophical monism has not permitted people to approach an understanding of Nature's duality?

2 The Worlds of Retribution

DURING THE PREHISTORIC ERA, the demonic powers were occupied with slowing human development and preparing the planes of transphysical magma and the core to receive millions of human souls in the future. Later, during historical times, the *shrastrs* and *Witzraor sakwalas* were created. The majority of purgatories appeared at even later times.

Our survey of the worlds of retribution begins with the purgatories, because they are closer to us than the other planes. They are more commensurate with our customary notions, and in the case of a descent after death, it is in the purgatories that the descent begins. In the majority of cases, it ends there as well.

The word *purgatory* is borrowed from Catholicism, but many of the Catholic beliefs invested in it do not coincide with the overall picture of what is to be described. The term *sheol* could also have been used in reference to those planes, but the Judaic images of those shadowy lands of the dead will also find no parallel in my description.

The purgatories of the various metacultures differ somewhat from each other. Taken separately, each of them also undergoes substantial changes over the course of centuries. In addition, they took shape in different historical periods. There were none at all in the metacultures of antiquity, the Byzantine metaculture included. To be more precise, worlds of eternal suffering existed in their place, and a distinct echo of the mystical knowledge about planes of eternal suffering can be heard in the majority of ancient religions.

The oldest of the purgatories belongs to the Indian metaculture. It was the Indian Synclite that first attained the power of

Light necessary to prevent Gagtungr's forces from turning into planes of torment their sakwala of afterlife atonement—a sakwala that the Indian metaculture had inherited from the daemons and Titans, the most ancient of humankind. Later some planes in the metacultures of Judaism, Christianity, and Islam were converted into purgatories. The key role in that was played by the Resurrection of Jesus Christ, His descent into the demonic worlds, and the struggle that ensued over several centuries between the Christian Synclites and the demons over mitigation of the Law of Retribution. But the struggle did not end in victory in the Byzantine metaculture. The enemy camp offered stubborn resistance. As a result, the Byzantine metaculture broke away from Enrof.

I mentioned before, in passing, the implications of the Byzantine Orthodox Church's refusal to embrace the idea of purgatories when it arose in the Western Church. The horrifying prospect of the eternal torments awaiting the soul of a sinner should be regarded as the impulse for the extreme asceticism with which the Byzantine religious spirit burned to the very end of its history. Yes, the eschatological depths, with all the extremes of its demonic cruelty, unfolded before the eyes of Byzantine prophets. One can only be surprised not at the desperate ascetic excesses of that culture but at the fact that such excesses did not take place in all the metacultures that lacked purgatories.

The first sheol in the Russian metaculture was created in the twelfth century, after having been converted from a plane of torment through the efforts of Christ. Its appearance has changed somewhat over time, and the karmic weights that draw the dead down into that world have changed as well. Be that as it may, the mechanics of the Law of Retribution have, of course, remained always and everywhere the same: it dictates that a violation of moral laws encumbers the ether body of the perpetrator. While such a person is still alive, the encumbered ether body remains afloat, as it were, on the surface of the three-dimensional world, with the physical body playing the role of life preserver. But as soon as that person's link is severed by death, the ether body begins to sink deeper and deeper, from plane to plane, until it reaches equilibrium with its surroundings.

These are the basic mechanics. But there are also beings who oversee its smooth operation: the *enforcers of karma*. Among the various demons of Shadanakar, they are a class unto themselves. They are newcomers. When the demonic hordes of the planet Daiya were expelled to the bramfatura of its moon, and the moon soon after broke up into a mass of dead fragments (asteroids), its demonic inhabitants scattered into space in search of a new haven. A group of them entered Shadanakar after concluding a sort of pact with Gagtungr's forces. They are beings of superior intellect, but they are as cold as ice emotionally. They know neither hate nor love, malice nor compassion. They assumed supervision of the mechanics of karma, replenishing their energy with emanations from the mental suffering of people who have been forced to descend to Skrivnus, Ladref, and Morod—the upper planes of the purgatories—after their life in Enrof. The enforcers of karma are immense in size, they are as translucent and grey as frosted glass, their bodies are rectangular, and, strangely enough, their faces somewhat resemble those of guard dogs: pointy ears and alert eyes. They enter into battle with the forces of Light only when those forces undertake to mitigate the laws of karma and to transform purgatories.

The first of the purgatories is called *Skrivnus*. It is the very picture of a stark, Godless world and society: a colorless landscape, a leaden grey sea that is always calm. Withered grass, stunted bushes, and moss call to mind our tundra. But at least in the spring, the tundra is covered with flowers. Not a single flower has sprouted from the soil of Skrivnus. Hollows surrounded by short but unscalable slopes serve as the dwelling places of the millions who were once people.

Skrivnus knows neither love nor hope nor joy nor religion nor art. Nor has it ever seen children. Interminable labor is interrupted only by sleep, but the sleep is without dreams and the labor is without creativity. Huge, frightful beings keep watch on the other side of the slopes. From time to time they toss out piles of objects that seem to float through the air. On its own, each object finds the one who is to work on it: mending old clothes no one needs, washing things that look like bottles caked in grease and dirt, stripping pieces of broken metal. Both work and sleep take place primarily in long barracks, sectioned off inside by waist-high partitions.

The inhabitants fully retain their human appearance, but their facial features are smudged and flattened. They remind one of identical-looking pancakes. Be that as it may, the memory of life in Enrof is not only preserved in the hearts of the inhabitants; it gnaws at them like the dream of paradise lost. The most relentless of the torments of Skrivnus is the weariness of interminable slavery, the tedium of the labor, and the absence of any hope for the future.

It is not a hopeful prospect, but the nightmare of an ever-present threat that offers the only seemingly realistic way out of that place. A black, box-like ship appears on the sea and quickly and noiselessly glides into shore. Its sighting sends the inhabitants into a horrified panic, since none of them can be sure that they will not be swallowed up in the pitch black of the ship's hold. Having rounded up a number of them—they whose karmic weight condemns them to suffer on deeper planes—the ship casts off. Those confined in the hold do not see the route being taken. They only sense their horizontal motion giving way to a spiraling descent, as if the ship were being sucked into a whirling maelstrom.

Skrivnus is restricted to the expiatory suffering of those whose conscience has not been sullied by the memory of grave sins or crimes but whose consciousness in Enrof was insulated from the will and influence of its shelt by a thick wall of worldly cares and exclusively material concerns.

The next plane resembles the previous one, but it is darker, as if it were suspended in nebulous murk on the edge of everlasting night. There are neither buildings nor crowds here. Everyone, however, is aware of the unseen proximity of a great many others: tracks like footprints betray their presence. That purgatory is called *Ladref*, and tens of millions spend a brief time there. Descent to Ladref is the consequence of religious skepticism, which does not give spirituality the power to penetrate into a person's essence and lighten his or her ether body.

They who are doomed to a further descent have the impression of falling asleep and then suddenly waking up in unfamiliar surroundings. In actual fact, demonic beings—the enforcers of karma—transport them while they are in a stupor into a different time stream, though the number of dimensions—three— remains constant in all the sheols.

Those expiating their karma find themselves in a darkness where only the soil and sparse equivalents of vegetation emit a dim phosphorescent light. Glowing cliffs do lend a grim beauty to the landscape in places. That is the last plane with vestiges of what we group under the name Nature. The planes that follow will consist solely of urban settings.

In *Morod*, that next plane, absolute silence reigns. Everyone in that world is convinced they are utterly alone, there being no signs of any other inhabitants. An overpowering feeling of forsakenness encases them like a suit of armor. In vain do they scramble about, pray, call for help, or seek out others—all are left alone with their own soul. But their souls are corrupt, their memories are sullied by the wrongs they did on Earth, and there is nothing more frightening for such souls than solitude and quiet. There, everyone comes to a full realization of the meaning and repercussions of the wrongs they committed on Earth and drains the cup of horror their sins instill. Nothing distracts the unfortunates from that endless internal monologue, not even the struggle for survival. There is no struggle—there is food all around in abundance in the form of certain kinds of soil. As for clothing, in the majority of planes, Morod included, the ether body itself radiates a material coating—a coating for which clothes are a substitute in our world. And if, in the worlds of Enlightenment, this coating is beautiful and radiant, the creative handicap of the inhabitants of Morod allows only for the creation of ether rags. In point of fact, the astral-ether essence of those undergoing expiation was already clothed in such tatters back in Ladref.

They whose conscience Morod does not cleanse can no longer expect a smooth passage into the next plane. Instead, they experience a sudden and terrifying plunge down into it. It is as if a quagmire opens up underneath the unfortunates and sucks them down: first their legs, then their bodies, and last their heads.

Our survey of the purgatories has arrived at *Agr*, a plane of black vapors, where the dark mirror images of the great cities of Enrof dot the landscape like islands. Agr, like all the purgatories, does not extend into outer space, so neither sun nor stars nor moon can be seen there. The sky appears as a solid firmament wrapped in constant night. Some objects glow of themselves; the ground also emits a dull glow, as if it were saturated with blood. There is one dominant color there, but we in Enrof are unable to see it. It gives an impression close to dark crimson and might well be the color we know as infrared.

I am only slightly acquainted with infra-Petersburg. As I recall, it also has a large river, but it is as black as ink, and there are buildings that emit a blood-red glow. It could, in a way, be likened to the light given off by the fires on Vasilievsky Island on national holidays, but it is a ghastly likeness. Those who have fallen into that world have retained their human features, but their bodies are deformed and repulsive. They are short in height and their movements have slowed. Their bodies no longer radiate any kind of material substitute for clothes, and unrelieved nakedness reigns everywhere. One of the torments of Agr is a feeling of impotent shame and a constant awareness of one's own wretched state. The inhabitants are also tormented by the beginnings of a stinging pity for others like them, as it dawns on them that they share the blame for their tragic fate.

The unfortunates are afflicted by a third torment: fear. It is instilled by *volgras*, demonic predators also present in Agr. When we had come near the building that constitutes the dark-ether body of the Engineer's Castle, I saw a huge creature the size of a dinosaur sitting motionless on its roof. It was a female, one droopy and flabby with grey, porous skin. Forlornly pressing a cheek to the tower and hugging it with its right paw, the poor thing was staring blankly into the distance with what appeared to be empty eye sockets. It seemed very unhappy. I had the impression it desperately wanted to cry out or howl, but it had no mouth or orifice of any kind. To feel pity for it, however, was in itself very dangerous. The crafty predator was on the lookout for prey, and any of those who had been humans were potential victims. The poor beings, wild with fear of the volgras and hardly daring to breathe, were hiding behind corners or skulking at the base of the buildings the monsters had chosen to rest on. To be eaten, or rather, to be sucked in by a volgra through its porous skin, is to die in Agr, but only to reappear even lower, in *Bustvich* or in horrible *Rafag*.

I later learned that there were a great many volgras, that they are to some degree intelligent, and that the primitive, dark civilization that characterizes Agr is their creation. They had virtually no mechanical devices to facilitate their labor. They erected the buildings that I saw all around by hand, using material similar to the trunks of California's giant redwoods, and every piece of that material, once it had been fixed to the other pieces, began to glow with a dull crimson light that illuminated virtually nothing. What connection exists between the buildings in the human cities of Enrof and the volgras' buildings in Agr remains a mystery to me.

They have no oral language, of course, but they do use a kind of sign language. They must have built the buildings for shelter from the brief showers that poured down every few minutes. The rain was black.

Also strange is the fact that volgras have three sexes, not two. The male impregnates the neuter, who carries the embryo for a period of time and then passes it on to the future mother.

But here and there silent buildings that do not glow at all dot the civilization like islands. The volgras did not go anywhere near them. There must have been something I could not see that was hindering them. Such buildings were standing on the site of St. Isaac's Cathedral and certain other churches in St. Petersburg. They are the only refuge where the tormented of Agr can feel safe from the volgras, if only for a short time. Who built them? When? Out of what? I do not know. Hunger did not permit the unfortunates to hide long in those shelters, but drove them out in search of the edible mold that grows on the base of buildings in that bleak city.

If those who were human are not doomed by a heavy karma to fall prey to a volgra and come to in the next world of descent, then they are destined sooner or later to undergo a transformation that will lift them up. The bodies of those who are nearing completion of their atonement gradually begin to change. They grow in height, the facial features they used to have begin to form anew, and the volgras do not dare go near them. The transformation itself takes place with the assistance of brothers and sisters from Heavenly Russia. Descending to Agr, they surround the ones who have completed their ordeal. Only those others who themselves will soon be raised from there in the same way are allowed to be in attendance. While they watch from the wings, it seems to them that the members of the Synclite lift those freed onto their wings or into the folds of glittering sheets. The volgras, gripped by mystic fear and trembling, watch from a distance, unable to understand what is happening.

The staircase of ascent is not closed to a single demonic monad, not even to volgras. But such a conversion requires a high level of consciousness, which is hardly ever in evidence there.

Something completely different is sometimes in evidence there instead. The landscape is broken in places by glowing puddles that resemble small pools of waste. There is something nauseating about the green in them. It is Bustvich, the next lowest plane, visible through Agr. Everything there is rotting, but nothing decomposes completely. The sensation of rotting alive combined with a spiritual lethargy constitutes the torment of Bustvich. They whose soul, encumbered by indulgence of unenlightened physical desires, did not fashion any kind of counterweight during life on Earth, unravel the knots of their karma in Bustvich. There the prisoner is gnawed at by an overpowering feeling of self-disgust, because its ether body has taken the form of excrement. For, horrifying and revolting as it may be, Bustvich is essentially nothing more than the volgras' cesspool.

Physical torments begin to commingle with mental ones. The prisoners are extremely restricted in their mobility, and in their means of self-defense. But self-defense is of primary necessity for every one of them, for abiding with them there, between incarnations in one of the worlds of demonic elementals, are the souls of small, human-like demons coated in a dark ether body. They look like human worms, and are about the size of cats. They eat alive those who at one time were humans in Enrof, and they do it slowly, a little at a time.

At that time (that is, in 1949), the Emperor Paul I was in that plane's twin copy of the Engineer's Castle. (There is one in Bustvich as well.) He had already passed through a cycle of torments on deeper planes and was being slowly raised up to Drukkarg, the shrastr of Russian antihumankind. I was astonished by the harshness of his fate. But it was explained to me that if the agony of his murder on the night of March 12th had not relieved him of a part of his karmic weight and if instead he had continued to tyrannize the country right up until a death by natural causes, the weight of his crimes would have drawn him down even deeper, until he had reached *Propulk*, one of the most horrific of the planes of torment.

Bustvich is followed by the purgatory of Rafag, where the karmic consequences of betrayals and self-serving loyalty to tyrants are expunged. Rafag is the torment of constant affliction by debilitating illness of a sort that might find on our plane a distant parallel in cholera. Rafag is the last plane in which the landscape is even faintly reminiscent of our cities, but there are no shelters such as were scattered throughout Bustvich and Agr. The mantle of humanity's prayers does not reach Rafag; only the powers of the Synclites and upper hierarchies of Shadanakar can penetrate beyond it.

Angels of darkness rule over the lowest three purgatories.

Shim-big, the first of these planes, is a slow stream flowing through an inexpressibly oppressive world enclosed under a high vault. It is hard to tell what the source of its drab, colorless half-light is. A drizzle sprinkles on the stream, raising tiny bubbles on its surface. It is no longer the covering of the souls being tormented there but the souls themselves, in their decomposed ether bodies, that resemble wispy brown rags. They stumble

back and forth, grabbing hold of whatever they can to keep
from falling into the stream. It is not only fear that torments
them. They are afflicted even more by a feeling of shame of
unsurpassed intensity and by a desperate longing for their real
body and for the soft, warm world—memories of the joys of life
on Earth.

The feeling of pity also intensifies there.

In the meantime, the mouth of the stream can be seen up
ahead. The stream itself, and the entire tunnel-shaped world,
breaks off just as a subway tunnel breaks off where a trestle
begins. But the water does not fall anywhere: the water and the
banks and the vault—everything—dissolves into a grey, fea-
tureless void. Nobody can exist there, and there is not even a
hint of any kind of ground or atmosphere. Only one thing does
not disappear there: the spark of self-consciousness. In that
purgatory, *Dromn*, the soul experiences the terrifying illusion of
non-existence.

In Shim-big, atonement is done by those who were responsible
for a few human deaths (even the deaths of criminals), whether
by passing death sentences or by denouncing someone to the
authorities. In Dromn can be found those whose violation of the
Law would seem, in our view, incomparably lesser. The arith-
metic of karma is strange indeed! What draws one down to
Dromn is not heinous crimes or bloodshed but only the karmic
consequences of a zealous atheism, an aggressive repudiation of
spirituality, the active promotion of the false idea of the soul's
mortality. The secret behind that surprising and seemingly disproportionate punishment is that those acts of will corked tight,
as it were, the breathing holes of the soul while it was still in
Enrof, resulting in an even greater encumbering of the ether
essence than occurs even as the result of individual crimes taken
separately. To prisoners of Dromn, it appears that nothing exists
anywhere, that they themselves do not exist—just as they imagined it during their lives. Only after tremendous efforts taking
up no brief span of time are they able to come to grips with the
astonishing fact that, contrary to all reason and common sense,
their conscious self does not disappear even there, in the void.

In so doing, they begin to understand, vaguely at first, that it could all have been very different if they had not chosen that nonexistence, or semi-nonexistence, themselves.

But the misery of self-inflicted aloneness that colors their stay in Dromn begins to give way, little by little, to alarm. The self feels as if it is being drawn somewhere down and to the side and as if it is turning from a dot into an elongated body pointed downward. The absence of any points of reference prevents it from knowing whether it is falling slowly or descending at a rapid speed. The only orientation it has is an inner voice, which howls louder than any logical thought, that it is moving neither up nor horizontally, but down.

Down below, an area of pink comes into view. For several seconds the color may even appear inviting. But then a blood-chilling guess takes hold of the unfortunate self: it realizes that it is falling helplessly into a calm sea of molten iron. It gains in weight, and it hits the molten-red surface of *Fukabirn*, the last plane in the sakwala of purgatories, and plunges deep down into it. Besides the burning sensation, the torment consists of a feeling of horror at descending into eternal torture, a descent that rings of finality.

Commencing after Fukabirn is the sakwala of transphysical magma. These circumscribed worlds coexist in three-dimensional space, though in different time streams, with belts of molten rock within the planet's crust. I would like to repeat and stress that in all the metacultures, except the Indian, the suffering in those worlds was without end until Jesus Christ carried out His liberating descent into them, which in Church tradition is called the descent of the Savior into the dead. From that moment on, it became possible, though only at the cost of tremendous efforts, for the forces of Light to extricate sufferers from those abysses after the period of time necessary for them to unravel the knots of their personal karma.

The first of the magmas is *Okrus*, the muddy bottom of Fukabirn.

As far back as in Dromn, the shelt had been left without any of its old coatings and a new bodily essence had begun to form. Its formation nears completion in Okrus, but there is nothing even remotely human in its appearance. It is a spherical object of animate inframetal.

Who are the torments of Fukabirn and Okrus for? There are actually few such sufferers. Millions suffered in Skrivnus and Ladref, but hundreds, perhaps only dozens, suffer here. The condemnation of ideological enemies to horrible tortures, the condemnation of the innocent, the torment of the defenseless, the torture of children—that is what is expiated through suffering in Okrus and Fukabirn.

There, the tormented remember well the religious teachings and the warnings they were given on Earth. They are sensible of bodily pain as retribution but have already begun to recognize the dual nature of the Law and the demonic, not Divine, responsibility for its harshness. Their consciousness begins to waken. That is the Providential side of the Law, the ancient basis for it that was established by the demiurges back before Gagtungr's invasion of Shadanakar. The wakening of consciousness, the wakening of conscience, and the growth of spiritual thirst are those aspects of the Law of Retribution that the forces of Light did not cede to the dark forces and thanks to which the Law, despite everything, has not become an absolute evil.

In its infraphysical state, the magma is very similar to its physical counterpart. Prisoners there at first retain their freedom of movement, but there is as yet no need to make efforts to sustain their existence. They absorb energy from their surroundings automatically. The same is true of *Gvegr*, the second belt of magma, a motionless lava sea.

I would, however, like to remind the reader that suffering of any kind in Enrof alleviates torments in the afterlife, primarily by reducing their time span, but sometimes also through a change in their "quality." On the whole, the length of a soul's expiatory punishments after death is determined by the number of the victims that suffered from its actions in Enrof. Mass crimes result in descent to a lower plane of retribution. For example, *Urkarvire* can take the place of Okrus, or *Propulk* can take the place of Gvegr. For the bodily suffering that began in Fukabirn and increased in Okrus and Gvegr reaches its zenith on the next plane, the seething magma of Urkarvire. There, the corrupters of lofty and enlightened ideas, who bear the blame for warping the transphysical paths of thousands and millions, do atonement. Urkarvire likewise harbors those who are guilty of those heinous deeds known, in our dry, lifeless language, as conscious sadism—that is, not only did the criminals experience a feeling of pleasure from causing others suffering but they were fully aware of the immorality of the pleasure at the time. They were aware, but that did not prevent them from enjoying it, nor from indulging in it time and again.

Fortunately, time flows much more quickly there. For example, a world famous writer of modern times, who was not guilty of conscious sadism, of course, but of corrupting ideals, of perverting ideas and poisoning a great many minds with lies, had the impression that he had spent only a few days there, and not the ten years it was in Enrof time.

Next comes the hard magma of Propulk, the world of expiatory suffering for mass butchers, the instigators of bloody wars, and the torturers of entire peoples. All freedom of movement is lost. Their bodies feel as if they were lodged in a hard substance and pressed from all sides. But even this horrible bodily suffering is surpassed by the suffering of the soul. They feel a stinging remorse and longing for God that is impossible on any of the planes above it. Fortunately, few descend to Propulk. Need I say that Yezhov or Beria's cohorts are there? Amazingly, only a short while ago, Malyuta Skuratov was still suffering there. In the Propulk of the Western metacultures, not only Robespierre and Saint-Just but even some of the sixteenth-century inquisitors were still unraveling their karma.

The magma sakwala concludes with the superheavy magma of *Yrl*. The bodily suffering there is completely overshadowed by spiritual torment. Yrl was created for the punishment of those who in our legal tongue are called "repeat offenders": those who, having once already fallen to the magma and returned to Enrof, again encumbered themselves with unspeakable crimes. The magmas end there.

Below the magmas begins the sakwala of worlds corresponding to the physical core of the planet, worlds common to all metacultures.

First come the infrared caves of *Biask*, the direst of the red infernos, as we might designate the entire staircase of planes from Fukabirn down to Biask. There, the body again metamorphoses, sprouting the semblance of a head and four limbs. But the gift of speech is lost, for there is no one with whom to converse. Each of the prisoners is held in solitary confinement and sees only his or her tormentors, who, strangely enough, resemble the devils of our legends. Sitting here in Enrof in relative security, we can afford to chuckle as much as we like about people believing in those horned villains, but do not wish even your sworn enemy a closer acquaintance with them. The victims that fall to Biask number at most in the dozens, but because there is a great throng of devils in need of their gavvakh, these devils wring gavvakh out of their victims by every means they are capable of devising.

The victims of Biask are those who in Enrof were tempters of the spirit. Such crimes are judged so harshly because they do great karmic damage to thousands of human souls. Even butchers at whose hands hundreds of people have died physically do not do as much harm as those about whom it is said in the Gospels: "Whoever causes one of these little ones who believe in me to sin, it would be better for him to have a great millstone fastened round his neck and to be drowned in the depth of the sea" (Matt.18:6). And even if Yaroslavsky or Bedny had been good people in their private lives, it would not have saved them from the fate that awaits tempters of the spirit in the afterlife.

Beneath Biask gape the vertical cracks of *Amiuts*. Those who fall there get snagged, as it were, and hang there completely helpless. And since the cracks lead down to Gashsharva, the unfortunates finds themselves hanging right over the lair of the demonic powers in Shadanakar. In Amiuts are those who combined conscious sadism with an immensity of heinous deeds.

But there are side tunnels leading from the vertical cracks of Amiuts. They are Ytrech, the planetary night which will last until the end of our planet's existence in Enrof—that is, until the end of the second (future) eon. There have been very few there, Ivan the Terrible, for instance. Further, there is yet another, very special plane. Only this plane could be equal to the crime of Judas Iscariot. It is called *Zhursh*, and no one except Judas has ever entered it.

It goes without saying that we do not have even the slightest inkling of the suffering experienced on the planes of the Core.

Our survey has now arrived at the graveyard of Shadanakar, the last of the planes. I could not clearly make out its name. Sometimes it sounded like *Sufel*, sometimes I thought it was closer to *Sufetkh*, and the question has remained unresolved in my mind. Those who persist in doing evil descend there from the lower planes of torment. Their shelts—what is left of them— are abandoned by their monads. The monads leave Shadanakar for good, to start anew in places, times, and forms beyond our conception. Yet that is still better than falling through the Pit of Shadanakar into the Pit of the Galaxy. At least in the former case the monad does not leave cosmic time.

But the shelt is alive. It is a conscious, albeit lesser, self. It is barely stirring in Sufetkh, as little by little the last of its energy expires. It is that same second death mentioned in the Holy Scriptures. A spark of consciousness flickers to the end, and the magnitude of its suffering surpasses even the imagination of the demons themselves. To this day, no one of Light, not even the Planetary Logos, has been able to penetrate into Sufetkh. It is sometimes visible to members of the Synclites, but from neighboring planes, not from within. At those times they can make out a desert, over which glows the dim purple sun of Gashsharva, Gagtungr's anticosmos.

Fortunately, in the entire history of humanity, the total number of monads that has fallen to Sufetkh does not exceed a few hundred. Of them, only a few have left any trace in history, for all the prominent chronically descending monads are brought to Gashsharva. Those for whom even Gagtungr has no use go to Sufetkh. I know of only one historical figure among them: Domitian, who in the incarnation following his fall to Propulk became

Marshal Gilles de Retz, the one who at first was a comrade-in-arms of Joan of Arc but was later a villain and sadist, who bathed in tubs made from the innards of children he had murdered. Cast down to Yrl, he soiled himself again in his next incarnation in Enrof with atrocities committed during the Inquisition. After his third death, he sliced through all the planes of the inferno for the third time, reached Sufetkh, and was ejected from Shadanakar like slag.

I know full well that the humanitarian spirit of our age would prefer to be presented with a very different picture from the one I have described in this chapter. Some will find it objectionable that, departures notwithstanding, my testimony seems to resemble too closely traditional images from historical Christianity. Others will be shocked by the savagery of the laws and by the bodily character of the horrible agonies endured on the planes of torment. But I am prepared to ask of the former: Did you seriously think that the teachings of the Fathers of the Church were based on nothing but figments of a spooked imagination? Only a mind as empty of spirit as a tractor or a rolling mill could suppose, for example, that we can reduce *The Divine Comedy* to a collection of artistic techniques, political diatribe, and poetic fantasy. In the first part of his book, Dante revealed the staircase of infraphysical planes extant in the Roman Catholic metaculture in the Middle Ages. One must learn to separate the impurities introduced into the picture to satisfy artistic demands or as the result of aberrations inherent to the age from the expression of genuine, unparalleled, and staggering transphysical revelation. And I do not consider it out of place to mention that the one who was Dante now numbers among the few great human spirits that have it within their power to penetrate unhindered down to the very Pit of Shadanakar.

As for those who are upset at the severity of the laws, I have only one thing to say: Work to enlighten them! Of course, it would be easier to sell the intellectual mindset of the humanitarian age on an image of so-called spiritual, rather than physical, torments: pangs of conscience, despair over the inability to love, and the like. Unfortunately, these barbaric laws were clearly established without consideration for the sentiments of the twen-tieth-century intelligentsia. It is true that spiritual suffering also plays a large role in the planes of descent. Essentially, only the great criminals of history are primarily subjected to bodily suf-fering, suffering that is, in addition, worse than any physical pain of ours, because ether pain surpasses the physical both in intensity and length. But we could also ask: Given the amount of pain these people caused their victims in Enrof, what pangs of conscience or, as Dostoyevsky thought, despair at not being able to love could counterbalance that mountain of suffering on the scales of the impartial Law of karma?

And each of us is free to join those who are working to mitigate that Law.

3 Shrastrs and Witzraors

I AM ABOUT TO DESCRIBE worlds of special significance for humanity, its history, and for all of Shadanakar. These are the worlds designed by the demonic forces to be frontline weapons in the realization of Gagtungr's global plan. They are, properly speaking, two sets of worlds, two sakwalas of infraphysical planes closely linked to one another.

I have already mentioned that within every metaculture there is a sort of antipode to its zatomis, a sort of demonic stronghold where the holy cities of the Synclites are reflected upside-down, as it were, in black mirrors. I am referring to shrastrs, the abodes of antihumankind.

Shrastrs are separate regions of a single four-dimensional world, but each region possesses its own unique number of time streams. The ring of shrastrs is metageologically connected with the lower layers of the Earth's crust, with its countervailing prominences, and they are the dark twins/antipodes to Eanna, Olympus, Paradise, Monsalvat, Heavenly Russia, and the other zatomis. The peaks and ridges of the countervailing prominences, which offset mountain ranges on the Earth's surface, point to the center of the planet. In Enrof, those regions are devoid of life: there is basalt, lava, and nothing else. But that is not true of the four-dimensional world. Below them, toward the center, is empty space—a reddish and pale orange cavity that blazes with darting waves of light and heat. The resultant of two gravities operates on the Earth's inner surface: gravity toward the crust and toward the core. The inhabitants' conception of up and down differs from ours. Infrapurple and infrared, almost black, luminaries glow motionless in the subterranean orange-reddish sky—this is how Gashsharva and the planes of torment of the Core appear to the eye from the shrastrs. By the rays of those moons, the populous societies and monstrous hierarchies that manifest themselves before our eyes in the form of great states, tyrannical regimes, and the faceless vampires of global history live and fortify their strongholds.

What is Nature like there? What is the predominant landscape on the underside of the world? There are no blues and greens; they would not be visible to the inhabitants. Instead, they have two colors not visible to our eyes. There is also something resembling vegetation, but it is fiery and dreadful: clumps of huge, dark crimson bushes and large, waving flowers of flame that stand alone in places. The land is very rugged. Lakes and seas of white and pink lava dot the crust's surface. On the whole, the landscape has a distinctive geologic-urban character: gigantic cities with populations in the millions. In infra-Russia, for example, the chief city encompasses almost the entire countervailing prominence of the anti-Urals, another corresponds to the Caucasus, and cities are now under construction on the prominences countervailing the mountains of Kazakhstan and the Tien Shan. There are also cities situated beneath our lowlands, but they are less common, as those areas are for the most part flooded by lava.

Antihumankind basically consists of two very different races or species. The principal race is composed of small but highly intelligent beings that proceed through a circle of reincarnations in the shrastrs, where they assume a four-dimensional form somewhat reminiscent of ours. That form, the equivalent of our physical body, is called karrokh. It is composed of the materiality of those planes, which was created by the great demonic hierarchies. The shrastr inhabitants have upper and lower pairs of limbs, though they have a different number of fingers and toes than we do. In addition, they are equipped with something like wing membranes. Their stalked red eyes, bulging cylindrical heads, mouse-gray skin, and puckered, tube-like mouth might evoke disgust in humans. But they are beings of keen intellect and the builders of a civilization that in certain respects is more advanced than ours. They are called igvas.

Igvas first appeared in the shrastr of the Babylonian-Assyrian metaculture. Another race, the ancestors of the contemporary *raruggs*, of whom I will speak a little later, inhabited the older shrastrs. But I do not have a very clear notion of the actual origin of the igvas: we are dealing here with concepts so strange that they lie beyond the grasp of our reason. Thus, although no human monads are demonic by nature, it sometimes happens—albeit very seldom—that a person will at some point in his or her journey voluntarily become an igva. To do so requires a strong desire, tremendous clarity of mind, and singular ability in specific areas. Such was the founder of antihumankind, an individual who lived in a very real sense in Erech and Babylon, where he was a priest of Nergal, and behind whom stretched a long chain of incarnations in more ancient cultures and in the Titan humankind.

The igvas originated from the union of that person with Lilith. She is sometimes capable—though very rarely and only at the bidding of Gagtungr—of assuming a female form in denser worlds. When she appeared in Babylon, for human eyes it was as if she had suddenly materialized out of nowhere. Three people saw her: the future father of the igvas, and two others, one of whom went insane, the other of whom was put to death. The one for whom she had assumed that ghost-like physical form joined his astral, and then ether, body with hers. She then descended, all wrapped in flame, to an empty infraphysical plane where she disgorged the first pair of igvas. The father of the race did not incarnate again in the shrastrs or Enrof. He is now in Digm, and his contribution to the design and realization of the demonic plan is great indeed.

The igvas have a unisyllabic oral language. The human language it most closely resembles phonetically is probably Chinese, but because of the tube-like shape of the igvas' mouths, vowel sounds like "o," "u," and "ü" predominate.

The igvas sometimes wear clothes, but they more often go about naked. Their extreme intellectualism has completely sterilized their sex life. Their method of procreation resembles the human method, but it is more unsightly. They copulate almost on the run, without feeling any need for privacy, for they have no feeling of shame. Their feelings of love, affection, and pity have remained in the embryonic stage. Brief unions take the place of families, and children are raised in minutely equipped and scrupulously systematized educational institutions.

Theirs is a slave-based society. It is composed of two classes: the upper intelligentsia—which includes scientists, engineers, clergy, and, if such a word can be used, administrators—and the subservient majority, who act only on the directions of the leadership. Yet even the leadership is strictly subordinate to the will of the so-called *grand igvas* (a kind of succession of high priests/emperors) and the monsters of the neighboring plane—the Witzraors.

The grand igvas are virtually the absolute rulers in every shrastr. A shrastr is neither a monarchy nor, of course, a theocracy; it is a satanocracy. The principle of dynastic succession is entirely alien to the igvas. Successors are systematically selected and prepared over the course of decades with astonishing forethought. The grand igvas' clarity of mind is immense, though they have an inverted—that is, demonic—conception of the world. They can see as far down as the anticosmos of the Universe. They are constantly being energized by Gagtungr himself. After their death, the grand igvas rise straight up to Digm.

It would be incorrect to say that the equivalent of our science and technology can be found in the shrastrs. Rather, it is our science and technology that are the equivalent of the igvas'. The different conditions and natural laws on that plane have dictated a scientific approach different from ours, but our scientific research methods and technological principles are very similar. Having far outstripped us in the field, they have knowledge of techniques and methods that smack of magic and that would seem like sorcery to many of us. But they also apply the principles of the screw, the wheel, and the rocket engine. They have vessels for traveling on the lakes of infralava. Ridiculous as it may seem, scheduled flights between shrastrs have long been in operation, and even hiking is popular—for exploration, not aesthetic, purposes, of course. Aviation is also advanced, though the igvas themselves can fly at great speeds, often hovering upside-down and clinging like flies to the ceilings and walls of buildings.

Science has allowed the igvas to penetrate to the Earth's surface as well. The surface is as lifeless and desolate on their infraphysical plane as the Moon's surface is on ours. Since the shrastr sakwala does not extend beyond the limits of our solar system, there are no stars in the sky. But the igvas have seen the planets and the Sun, though to them they look very different. The temperature in the shrastrs is very high (it would be unbearable for us) and therefore the Sun, which appears to the igvas as a pale infrared spot, emits far from sufficient heat for them. In spite of all the protective measures taken against the cold, the igva explorers suffered horribly on the Earth's surface, which is just as inhospitable for them as Antarctica is for us. They do have the prospect, however, of settling the surface of the planet, and not on their own plane, but on ours.

Their scientific instruments have already registered echoes of Enrof. It is possible, even almost inevitable, that in time they will make their presence known to us, and exchanges and contact will arise. In that way, they will of course try to manipulate humanity, for their most cherished hope, the dream that binds them, is to expand their realm, with the help of the Witzraors and Gagtungr, to include all the planes of Shadanakar. What is envisioned is the great Antigod of the future, who is being readied in Gashsharva for birth as a human in the not too distant future, and who will produce a pair of half-people, half-igvas in Enrof. They will be the origin of the igva race on our plane. Multiplying like flies, they are gradually to replace people, turning the Earth's surface into the abode of satanohumankind.

Igvas proceed through a circle of incarnations in the shrastrs, but in the intervals between them they all endure the same fate: their shelt and astral body fall into the Pit (no incarnation is possible in the superheavy materiality of the Pit without an astral body), speeding through the magma and Gashsharva down a tangent, as it were, so that they barely come into contact with them. During the descent, their ether body rapidly flakes apart. Cases of enlightenment among igvas are so rare as to be almost nonexistent, but in those cases they of course undergo a different fate in the afterlife. All of them, except some of the grand igvas, have an inverted view of God as a universal tyrant more terrible than Gagtungr. Christ, Who they hear of from the grand igvas, takes the place in their minds of the Antichrist—a violent and very dangerous despot. Generally speaking, everything is turned on its head. It is therefore natural that their religion primarily consists of ecstatic demon worship, radiations of which rise up to Gagtungr.

Do not think that the igvas' civilization is limited to science and technology. It also possesses some art forms. A gargantuan sculpture soars in front of the grandiose, cone-shaped temple in Drukkarg, the capital city of Russian antihumankind, a city situated in a hollowed-out mountain. It is a sculpture of a proto-igva riding a rarugg. If we apply our standards of measurement (and it is quite legitimate to do so in many cases), we could say that the eyes of the igva in that sculpture are vermilion-red stones the size of a two-storey house, while the dark crimson eyes of the rarugg are many times larger than that.

But the rational cast of the igvas' mind and their sterile emotional life have impeded the development of art. In conjunction with the overall grotesqueness of their tastes, all this has led their art down paths on which our aesthetic standards are not applicable. Architecture is the furthest advanced of art forms in the shrastrs. Their cities are composed of structures of superhuman size but bare geometric forms. Part of the cities are mountain sides, hollow inside and finished on the outside. Cubes, rhombuses, and truncated pyramids shine with finishes of red, gray, and brown. The constructivist school in human architecture may provide the reader with a mental picture of the style in the shrastrs. The powers of Light in Fongaranda needed to greatly intensify their inspiration of peoples' creative subconscious in order to keep human architecture from succumbing to the emanations rising out of the shrastrs and from turning the cities of Enrof into pitiful imitations of the igvas' stereometrical cities.

Music, predominantly percussion, blares in these cities as well. To our ears, it would sound like cacophony, but it does sometimes achieve rhythmic melodies capable of mesmerizing some of us, too. Dance plays an even bigger role in the life of the igvas, if we can speak of their appalling bacchanalias as dance. And their demon worship, which combines stunning light effects, the deafening roar of enormous instruments, and ecstatic flights of dance in four-dimensional space, turns into mass frenzies that attract angels of darkness. The energy radiated from it is imbibed by Gagtungr himself.

Besides the igvas, there are other beings dwelling in the shrastrs: raruggs. They are the aborigines of that inverted world, an ancient race who in part resemble centaurs, in part angels of darkness, but most of all, I think, flying dinosaurs. They fly, but not as pterodactyls once flew on their bat-like wings in Enrof. The raruggs' wings are powerful and jut straight out from the sides of their inordinately huge bodies. A creature of such size could not fly under the laws of gravity operating in Enrof.

It is no coincidence that they resemble dinosaurs, for raruggs are those same dinosaurs. After a protracted cycle of incarnations in the bodies of allosaurs, tyrannosaurs, and pterodactyls, some of them—the most predatory species—embarked on a path of further development on the infraphysical planes. Over millions of years they have achieved a degree of intelligence, but it is still a far cry from the acute intellectualism of the igvas. On the other hand, their physical strength and unbelievable emotional intensity are such that after a lengthy battle for that plane of existence the igvas were forced to reconcile themselves to coexistence with the raruggs. Soon after, a unique modus vivendi was drawn up between the two races, which subsequently grew into an alliance. The raruggs are now something like the intelligent warhorses of the igvas, their cavalry. The igvas themselves take part in wars only as a last resort. Under normal circumstances they exercise command, especially in the field of military technology. The clumsy brains of the raruggs have as yet been unable to rise to the challenge of military technology. But their incredible bloodthirstiness, belligerence, and fearlessness are indispensable for victory in war on that plane. The ancient legends of the winged steeds of hell are echoes of the knowledge of the existence of raruggs.

There are two kinds of wars on the underside of the world. In the past, the history of those satanocracies to a significant extent boiled down to mutual rivalry and armed conflict. Of course, not all of humanity's wars were connected with battles in that dark world, but our great wars undoubtedly were. During major wars some shrastrs suffered catastrophic damage and even destruction. The situation has now become more complex: the higher demonic powers are making every effort to secure peace between the shrastrs. The reasons for that are very complex and will gradually be explained as we continue. The truly implacable war is being fought not between shrastrs but between igvas, raruggs, and Witzraors, on the one side, and the zatomis Synclites, angels, daemons, and demiurges of the suprapeoples on the other.

After a metaculture has concluded its historical cycle on Enrof, its shrastr is doomed to a bleak existence resembling a constant agony of hunger. Such shrastrs are no longer of any use to Gagtungr and are left to their fate.[1] The igvas and raruggs degenerate, and scientific and technological progress loses momentum. The destruction of the corresponding power-hungry state institutions in Enrof leads to a stoppage in the supply of the Witzraors' and igvas' food staple—which I will discuss in more detail a little further on. The starving shrastr inhabitants are forced to get by on petty theft, stealing food from their more prosperous neighbors, or else they struggle to survive on a "vegetarian diet." That is also the fate of some shrastrs whose metacultures still exist in Enrof, but whose Witzraors have been killed

---

1. The following are the names of shrastrs of metacultures that have concluded their cycle in Enrof: Dabb—the shrastr of Atlantis, Bubgish—the shrastr of Gondwana, Setkh—the shrastr of ancient Egypt, Tartarus—the shrastr of the Greco-Romans, Nergal—the Babylonian-Assyrian shrastr, Devan—the shrastr of Iran, Zing—the shrastr of the Jews, Babylon—the shrastr of Byzantine. The last name is apparently based on a misinterpretation of symbols in the Apocalypse. The "Babylon" of Revelation refers to the future satanohumankind, not to the Byzantine shrastr.

during internecine wars and whose great subterranean cities have been destroyed.[2]

There are four strong shrastrs still active today. They are Fu-Chzhu, the Chinese shrastr, which is very old but has recently received a new boost in development; Yunukamn, the shrastr of the Roman Catholic metaculture, which has experienced a serious decline and is now quite backward but still active;[3] Drukkarg, the shrastr of the Russian metaculture; and Mudgabr, the most powerful of the shrastrs, the underside of the great North-Western culture. The founder of Mudgabr was the human/igva Klingsor. In his last incarnation in Enrof, Klingsor was one of the anonymous instigators of Jesus Christ's crucifixion, the witting ally of Gagtungr behind the mask of a Pharisee and patriot. The anti-Monsalvat that he subsequently founded in no way resembles today those fanciful patriarchal images that belatedly entered Wagner's musical dramas from medieval legends. Nowhere has progress in igva science and civilization reached such heights as in Mudgabr. I may add that it was the igvas of that shrastr who first penetrated to the lifeless and desolate surface of the Earth on their plane.

But life in the shrastrs is very tightly intertwined with the existence of demonic beings of a completely different genus and scale, whose home planes form an adjoining sakwala, which closely interacts with the shrastr sakwala. Igvas and raruggs are unable to enter those planes, but the inhabitants of the adjoining sakwala—Witzraors—can and do cross—or to be more exact, slither—over into the igvas' cities.

---

2. Aru—the shrastr of the Indomalaysian metaculture; Alfokk—the shrastr of the Muslim metaculture; and Tugibd—the shrastr of the Indian metaculture. The last two could still experience a renaissance in connection with the appearance of neo-Indian and neo-Muslim Witzraors.

3. An unprecedented metahistorical phenomenon was behind the Inquisition—the most horrible of all Gagtungr's progeny. There has been nothing like it before or since in any of the metacultures. It abided in Gashsharva, and a host of the forces of Light were engaged in battle with it. It was only in the eighteenth century that the coup de grace was administered by the great human spirit John the Evangelist, whereupon it was expelled from Shadanakar into the Pit of the Universe. The papacy is still not wholly impervious to the emanations of the demonic forces and thus even today has yet to fully condemn that terrible period of history.

They are powerful beings who play a role in history and meta-history as huge as their bodily dimensions. If we imagined the head of one of the creatures where Moscow is, its tentacles would reach to the sea. They move with breathtaking speed and are endowed with speech and great cunning. Their genesis is complex and double-sided. Every dynasty of Witzraors began as the fruit of the union between a *karossa*—that is, the individual national manifestations of Lilith, the *Aphrodite Universalis* of humanity—and the demiurges of suprapeoples. In the majority of metacultures, those beings were engendered by the will of the demiurges as defenders of the suprapeople from outside enemies. They first appeared in the Babylonian metaculture, whose demiurge attempted to set that progeny of his against the war-like egregors of Egypt and Media, who were threatening the very existence of the Babylonian suprapeople. But karossas carry the cursed seed of Gagtungr, which he planted long ago in the ether body of Lilith, whose individual national-cultural expressions they are. And the seed of Gagtungr doomed the first Witzraor, who at first obeyed the demiurge's will, to metamorphose soon after into the transphysical agent of Babylonian state power. Its belligerency in turn forced the demiurges of other suprapeoples to resort to extreme measures to defend their countries in Enrof against the attacker. Those measures consisted of engendering the same kind of beings capable of withstanding the Babylonian Witzraor. In that way the monsters appeared in the Iranian and Jewish metacultures, and then in all the rest.

The procreation of these extremely aggressive and wretched beings takes place in a fashion reminiscent of budding. They have no gender. Immediately upon being budded, each child becomes the sworn enemy and potential slayer of its parent. That is how a sort of dynasty of Witzraors became established in metacultures—a child succeeding the parent after the latter is murdered and its heart devoured. Either a lone Witzraor or a parent Witzraor plus one or more of its progeny who fight a battle to the death with their sire exist simultaneously in the majority of metacultures. Witzraors battling and killing one another is one of the most monstrous spectacles of metahistory.

In the course of Russia's history, three ruling Witzraors have been supplanted, but each of them, before they died, had children that they managed to devour. In the North-Western metaculture, a different situation arose. There were, and are, several concurrent Witzraor dynasties, and that circumstance has had immense historical consequences for the whole world, for the existence of several such dynasties has hindered, and hinders now, the unification of the North-Western suprapeople into one whole. It was also the decisive factor in the outbreak of all the great European wars, as well as the two world wars.

Witzraors abide in a barren world similar to a steaming tundra. It is broken into individual regions in accordance with the borders of the metacultures. Every Witzraor can enter not only neighboring regions (only after first vanquishing the neighboring Witzraors, of course) but the shrastrs as well. It slithers in like a mountain of mist. At the sound of its voice, the igvas and raruggs quake as before a sovereign and despot, but at the same time they regard the Witzraor as their great champion against both other shrastrs and the forces of Light. How could they battle the hosts of the Synclites and the demiurge himself without it? It is these various conflicts—between Witzraors, and between each Witzraor and the demiurge and Synclite of the given metaculture—that represent, to a significant degree, the transphysical aspect of that process we perceive as politics and history.

Witzraors can see Enrof dimly, and they see our people and landscapes hazily and distortedly, but they love our world with a burning, unsatiable passion. They would like to incarnate here, but they cannot. They can see Gagtungr clearly and tremble before him like slaves. In their ignorance they consider the grand igvas mere agents of their will. In reality, the grand igvas see farther and deeper and know more than the Witzraors, and they endeavor to manipulate the Witzraors' greed, belligerence, and power in the interests of antihumankind.

How do the Witzraors replenish their energy? The mechanics of the process is difficult to explain. A Witzraor radiates a singular kind of psychic energy that penetrates into Enrof in huge quantities. Absorbed by the human subconscious, it manifests

itself in human affairs as the spectrum of nationalist-state sentiments. Veneration of one's government (not of one's people or
homeland, but of the government and its power), the identifica-
tion of oneself as a participant in the grandiose life of the state,
the worship of kings or leaders, a burning hatred for the enemy,
pride in the material wealth and conquests of one's state, nationalism, belligerency, blood thirstiness, jingoism—all those feelings that enter into the range of human consciousness can only
grow, swell, and hypertrophize thanks to the Witzraor's energy.
But at the same time, human psyches, in a manner of speaking,
enrich those discharges of energy with their own distinct additives. A unique mass psychoradiation of dual nature and reverse
impetus results. It sinks through the Earth's crust, penetrates to
the neighboring infraplanes, and forms a slimy red dew on the
shrastr's soil. The igvas harvest it for the Witzraors—that is their
chief duty in relation to them—and help themselves to the left-
overs. Making do on a vegetarian diet is not only wearisome for
them, but it also does not keep them from degenerating.

It is entirely possible that I have oversimplified or misrepre-
sented the mechanics of the process. But its essence—Witzraors
feeding off the psychoradiations of the masses, radiations specifically connected with human emotions directed toward the
state—is not only a very real fact, but it is also the source of
untold misfortunes.

Igvas cannot enter the Witzraors' planes, but see them from
the outside, dimly, in shadows. Lying low in the shrastrs, they
follow the battles between the Witzraor and demiurge and try
with all their might to supply the infuriated demon with more
energy-giving dew. They cannot see the demiurge, but the invis-
ibility of a powerful being of Light capable of battling with the
state demon itself instills them with terror and a keen hatred.
They know that the death of the Witzraor will entail, besides the
fall of the regime in Enrof (which might even cause them to
rejoice, if a young, stronger regime were to succeed in its place),
the failure of the Witzraor dynasty or the destruction of the
shrastr. That would doom any belligerent regimes in the given
metaculture to destruction, at least for many centuries to come.

Since I am seeking to share everything I know, even trivial details that would seem to be of no consequence, I will list the names of fallen Witzraor dynasties in a footnote,[4] while the names of dynasties still in existence today are as follows: Istarra is the Witzraor of Spain; Nissush, of the Mongolian-Manchurian-Japanese dynasty; Lai-Chzhoi, the crossbreed of Nissush with Zhrugr of Russia, is at present coexisting with Nissush; Zhrugr itself; and lastly, Vaggag, the overall name for the North-Western Witzraors, several of whom, as I have mentioned, abide on the same plane simultaneously. There are now three: the English Ustr, the French Bartrad, and the Yugoslavian Charmich, a bud of Zhrugr that was cast onto their plane.

These Witzraors are not the first in their line—their dynasties arose in past centuries. But in the twentieth century, entirely new dynasties have also arisen from the union of the demiurges with karossas of metacultures existing in modern times. They are as follows: Shostr, the neo-Arab Witzraor, which was engendered after the collapse of the Ottoman Empire and which has sought to assert itself in various Muslim states, beginning with Kemal's Turkey; Avardal, the neo-Indian Witzraor, engendered a few years ago out of that same crucial necessity of defending the metaculture; Stebing, the Witzraor of the United States of America, which has something tigerish about its appearance and wears a golden cone on its head; and Ukurmia, the neo-German Witzraor, engendered after the collapse of the Third Reich and the fall of the old Witzraor dynasty. The North-Western demiurge was forced to undertake that desperate measure as a last resort. The new Witzraor is less truculent than its predecessor; unheard-of efforts are being made to inspire it from very high worlds of Light. It is the first Witzraor

---

4. Unidr—the Witzraor of Babylon, Assyria, and Carthage; Forsuth—the Witzroar of Macedonia and Rome; Foshts—the Jewish Witzraor; Ariman—the Witzraor of Iran (strange as it may seem to use that name in reference to the state demon); Kharada—the Witzraor of India; Efror—the Witzraor of the caliphates, premodern Turkey, and the Turko-Muslim Empire. I do not know the name of the Witzraors of Byzantium, or of the fairly weak Witzraors of the medieval states of Southeast Asia connected with the shrastr Aru.

to be given the opportunity to ascend, and there is something noble, even leonine, in its appearance.

To this day, no Witzraor has experienced anything in its afterlife other than falling to Uppum, the Rain of Eternal Misery. This is the hell reserved for Witzraors, which was created long ago by Gagtungr for the dragon of the proto-Mongolian metaculture, who had converted to Light. Later Uppum was locked tight, and rescue from there is impossible, at least in this eon.

It remains for me to say a few words about Drukkarg, the only shrastr that comes within range of my waking memory. A temple of approximately one kilometer in height stands in the center of the capital city of Drukkarg. I have already mentioned the statue of the proto-igva riding on a rarugg with outspread wings, and if we must consider the statue of the Bronze Horseman in St. Petersburg to be a distant likeness of that statue, then something entirely different yet familiar is transphysically connected with the temple: the mausoleum.

The capital city is girded by a ring-shaped citadel of concentric circles. Navna, the Collective Ideal Soul of Russia, languishes in one of them. Her plight has worsened under the third Zhrugr: a thick vault has been built over her. Now her radiant voice, a bluish glow the igvas and raruggs cannot see, shows but dimly here and there on the surface of the cyclopean walls. Outside Drukkarg, only the faithful in terrestrial Russia and the enlightened in Heavenly Russia can hear her voice.

Who is Navna? She is what unites Russians into one country; what calls and draws individual Russian souls higher and higher; what imparts to Russian art its inimitable fragrance; what stands behind the purest and most sublime female images in Russian fables, literature, and music; what evokes a longing in Russian hearts for the sublime, special charge entrusted to Russia alone—all that is Navna. Her collectivity resides in the fact that something from every Russian soul rises up to Navna, enters her, finds shelter in her, and merges with her self. Or to express it another way: a kind of spirit-energy present in every Russian person abides in Navna. Navna is the future bride of the Russian demiurge and the prisoner of Zhrugr.

Zhrugr, like all Witzraors, cannot have any children besides the Zhrugr juniors that it sometimes buds. But something distantly resembling a union between it and Dingra, the Russian karossa, takes place when it imbibes individual Russian souls—or to be more exact, shelts—during physical sleep and casts them into the bosom of Dingra, where they are subjected to a crippling and spiritually sterilizing transformation. We perceive the effects of that in the psychic rebirth of those of our compatriots who have taken active part in the construction of the citadel.

Drukkarg has other inhabitants besides the raruggs and igvas: they whose life and work in Russian Enrof were tightly bound with the aggrandizement of the state, they who wielded great power and left their stamp on the fates of millions of souls. In Drukkarg they are captives and slaves, who are put to work on nonstop construction of the igvas' citadel. Nothing short of the death of Zhrugr and the destruction of Drukkarg will liberate them. Ivan III, for example, has been there since the very beginning of his afterlife, as have almost all the other monarchs, commanders, and state figures.

Are there any exceptions? Yes, there are. On the one hand are the tyrants: before entering Drukkarg they must spend centuries expiating their individual karma on deep planes of torment. Some of them, such as Ivan the Terrible, have already passed through those circles and are now in Drukkarg. Others, such as Paul I and Arakcheyev, are only now being raised from the depths of the magma. But there is also another category of exceptions, one insignificant in number: those monarchs who fashioned a counterweight to their individual state karma while still alive, doing so through passionate faith, divine mercy, kindness, or even suffering. Recall St. Vladimir, Vladimir Monomakh, Alexander Nevsky, Fyodor Ioannovich. Recall those for whom power, which was hardly in their grasp, proved to be a source of only suffering, loss, and even death: Fyodor Godunov, Ioann Antonovich. Many will be surprised to hear that Nicholas II was saved from Drukkarg by the suffering he underwent in Yekaterinburg. Alexander I, one of the most important figures in Russian metahistory, is in a category by himself. A separate chapter will be devoted to him.

There are approximately three hundred such prisoners in Drukkarg. They are human-like beings of immense size who resemble the ancient Titans. But there is no light in their faces as there was in the faces of the Titans. To the contrary, their faces seem to be consumed by a deep inner fire, and their bodies are coated in coarse, dark crimson material. They are chained to each other, and their work resembles the laying of stone, and this for the erection of ever more wings for the citadel. They are allowed time for only hurried naps. They feed on the infravegetation. Fear grips them in the presence of the Witzraor, who in the case of disobedience or rebellion can cast them down, like the igvas, into the Pit of Shadanakar. The history of Drukkarg has witnessed such incidents.

In the same way, Karl V, Napoleon, and almost all the monarchs, commanders, and state figures of North-West Europe and North America are Titan captives in Mudgabr. Gregory VII, Loyola, and the majority of the popes work as stone-layers in Yunukamn. Torquemada, who spent many centuries in Biask and Propulk, has only just been raised up to the lower purgatories.

In a special, impregnable dungeon, the rulers of Drukkarg incarcerate those Synclite members who were taken prisoner during battles between the shrastr forces and the forces of Light. No one can kill them—not Witzraors, not igvas. They languish there in a kind of life imprisonment, waiting for the inevitable fall, sooner or later, of that bastion of antihumankind.

BOOK V
The Structure of Shadanakar:
Elementals

1 Demonic Elementals

AMONG THE DIFFERENT variomaterial planes that make up Shadanakar, there are four sakwalas linked with what we call the natural elements. But in what way are they linked?

We are dealing here with a concept that almost defies rational explanation. It so happens that any area of the three-dimensional world, an area, say, of snow-covered mountain peaks, is not at all limited in purpose and meaning to what we perceive through our five senses—that is, it is not limited to those mountain peaks composed of gneiss, granite, and other rocks and covered by snow and ice. That three-dimensional area is, above and beyond that, a kind of hemisphere attached to another area that could also be called a hemisphere, but one with a different number of dimensions. Snow-covered mountain ranges, lifeless, inhospitable, and barren in their sterile magnificence, represent but one of two hemispheres, or one of two closely integrated planes. The other hemisphere (or, to be more precise, plane) differs in the number of its dimensions. It is a land of embodied spirits of stunning majesty, the monarchs of snowy peaks.

This plane is called Orliontana. It is Orliontana radiating through the three-dimensional rock and ice that evokes the feeling of august calm, power, and resplendence that snow-covered mountain peaks evoke in all who are even slightly susceptive to infusions of energy from the transphysical world through the medium of beauty. Viewed with spiritual vision, Orliontana is a land of mountain peaks in their spiritual glory. As for the summits visible to the naked eye, they are no less than the product of the awesome, multimillion-year creative life of those elementals of Orliontana. When human souls bearing the marks of prolonged exposure to atheism withdraw into seclusion amidst the translucent mountains of Olirna, it is the unobstructed view of the plane of Orliontana that enables them to rid themselves of the last vestiges of closeted ignorance and inner inertia and arrive at an understanding of the multiplaned reality and spiritual majesty of the Universe.

But in contrast to Orliontana, most of the planes of elementals are localized—that is, they do not extend far into outer space. To be more precise, they do not even extend as far as the limits of our solar system, as the worlds of the shrastrs do. For that reason no sky is visible from most of these planes. The planes of elementals themselves resemble oases in the midst of voids of space. Like the shrastrs, they are demarcated from each other by differences in the number of their time streams.

Elementals are those monads that proceed along their path of maturation in Shadanakar primarily within the realms of Nature. That fact notwithstanding, one should bear in mind that humanity in one of its aspects also represents a distinct realm of Nature. That aspect is manifested, though not exhausted, in those elemental forces seething within it and without which its existence is unthinkable. It should thus come as no surprise that there are also elementals linked not with Nature in the customary sense of the word but with humanity, with its elemental, natural aspect.

There are among elementals a great many spiritual entities of Light, there are demonic elementals, and there are also transitional groups whose essence has been tarnished in the course of their development. But one thing unites them all: more than anyone else, they follow a path closely bound to the realms of Nature. That does not mean, however, that no elemental monad can ever incarnate in the form of a human, daemon, or angel during any leg of its journey. It is entirely possible, just as in times immemorial some human monads began to fashion forms for themselves from denser materialities not on human planes but in the sakwala of elementals or angels. But for them it was a comparatively brief phase. For individual elementals, incarnation in human or any other form is just as brief.

Excluding the animal realm and the tree world, we could say that elementals assume their densest form, their true embodiment, in those sakwalas that bear their name. The natural elements in Enrof—water, air, earth, vegetation, the mineral layers of magma, and lastly, arungvilta-prana, that "life force" that is a necessary component of all organic life in Enrof—are, for the most part, not the bodies of elementals but rather the outermost concentric circle of their habitats, which is permeated, manipulated, and trans-formed by them. The natural elements are the theater and source material for their creative work, for their fun and anger, for their battles, games, and love. The body proper of elementals is, for most, fluid: their bodily contours are changeable and interpenetra-ble. However, that is not true of all elementals, and in every such case I will make the necessary qualifications.

I am beginning with demonic elementals only because they are contiguous, through that same demonic nature of theirs, with the infraphysical planes, the description of which, thank heavens, we are preparing to take our leave of. Then, after a few words concerning the transitional group, we will with a measure of relief be able to bring this description of woeful or darkened planes to an end. We can then, after a description of the planes of elementals of Light, conclude our survey of the bramfatura with the very highest worlds, spiritually blazing in their unattain-able heights, in the holy of holies of Shadanakar.

There exists a region—*Shartamakhum*—of rampageous and ter-rifying elementals of magma, which are to be virtually the last to undergo enlightenment. Shartamakhum should be regarded as the plane of embodiment of beings whose shelts go between incarnations to the infra-iron ocean of Fukabirn, though they do so without experiencing the suffering that is the lot of human souls that have fallen there. The physical magma is, as I have said, the outermost circle of their habitat during their incarnation in Shartamakhum, the theater and source material for their creative work, anger, and battles. During volcanic activity, earthquakes, or geological upheavals, the elementals of Shartamakhum shoot up from the subterranean depths of that plane to its surface, as it were. In so doing, they draw lava up to Enrof from under the ground, bringing death to all living things. But that is only an indirect, almost incidental consequence of their activities. They have no concern for living things. In fact, they are not even aware of their existence, and if they were, they would not know what to make of them. The real function of their activities should be looked for on an altogether different level, and it will become more evident if we imagine the effect on the Earth if activity in Shartamakhum had ceased millions of years ago.

Subjectively, the elementals' activities consist of only violent rampages and wild, uncontrollable frenzies that afford them pleasure simply through the consciousness of their power and impunity. Objectively, their rampages have given rise to geological changes in terrestrial Enrof, set in motion mountain-forming processes, and provided impetus for shifts in the prevailing continental and oceanic configurations and thus to the consequent evolution of plants and animals, and, in the end, to the creation of the necessary preconditions for the emergence of *Homo sapiens*. The Providential powers have partly succeeded in channeling the malicious and furious actions of those demonic elementals into good and extracting from them a certain positive result.

But there are also elementals from whose activities they have to this day failed to extract anything positive. Such are, for example, the elementals of quagmires, swamps, and tropical jungles. *Gannix*, their plane, resembles the murk of ocean depths. Between incarnations in Gannix, their souls abide in Ytrech, the darkest of the worlds of the terrestrial Core. As for Gannix, have not many peoples at the dawn of their history felt its influence, until other aspirations of the spirit eclipsed or stifled that experience? And do not some peoples feel the influence of Gannix even now? The legends of many-faced, or rather, faceless, guileful beings that don a mask to lure people into peril have their roots in that same world. It not only lurks behind three-dimensional areas of bog and swamp but also in the thin ice that covers rivers in the Siberian taiga and in the moosekeg and mudholes of central Russia. It is the black, swirling, beguiling elementals of Gannix, together with desert elementals, that were to blame for the tragic demise of the original Australian culture.

No less hostile to humans and all living beings are the elementals of sandy regions, whose plane, *Svix*, resembles a desert during a sandstorm. Between incarnations on that plane, the desert elementals abide in Shim-big, where in the form of whirlwinds they exacerbate the suffering of human souls passing through that infraphysical tunnel by latching onto them. Becalmed deserts, when the elementals of Svix have exhausted themselves or are immersed in slumber, present the human eye with such majestic expanses, with such a peaceful and pure vastness, and sky that opens up above it with such manifest sublimity, that there is probably no other place in Enrof that better facilitates contemplation of the One God. It is easy to see why a clearly formulated monotheism arose and established itself in countries with great deserts. But the desert is two-sided. And one can distinguish the traces of desert squalls obscuring the face of the heavens and the traces of elementals of Svix darkening the face of the One God even on the pages of such monuments of world revelation as the Bible and the Quran.

The souls of yet other elementals abide in the pitch-black worlds of the terrestrial Core between incarnations: the grim, torpid, dark, and grasping elementals of ocean depths. *Nugurt*, their plane of incarnation, is not due to be enlightened for a long, long time, toward the end of the second eon. But if the forces of Shartamakhum shoot up to the surface during eruptions, the radiations of Nugurt, to the contrary, inch their way up from the gloomy depths through the sun-lit world of the beautiful elementals of the topmost layers of the sea. The radiations of Nugurt are stronger out on the open sea, because the dark layers are deeper there than in the shallow waters closer to shore. Their radiations do not pose any physical danger to us, but our psyche is subject to their wasting, oppressive action. Many sailors would be able to retrace the stages of that process in themselves if their minds were equipped with the tools of transphysical analysis.

There is yet another world of demonic elementals that stands apart, as it were, since it is not linked with the natural elements but with elements of humanity. The plane is called Duggur, and it is of vital importance to remember that name, for the demons of the great cities of Enrof rule there, demons who pose a very real danger to our psyche.

Like Agr and Bustvich, Duggur is an ocean-like area of uninhabited dark vapors with infrequent islands linked geographically with the metropolises of our three-dimensional world. The landscape is extremely urbanized, even more urbanized than in the shrastrs, because there are no mountains, lava seas, or vegetation in Duggur. But the glow of black and crimson light is not to be found there either. The entire color spectrum of our world is visible there, the dominant colors being pale blue, blue-gray and moon blue. Even the sky is visible from Duggur, but the Moon is the only luminary, for the plane does not extend far beyond the limits of the lunar bramfatura. Be that as it may, the Moon does not look at all like we are accustomed to seeing it, because the inhabitants of Duggur can only see the plane of the Moon's bramfatura on which Voglea, the great lunar demon, abides. There is no feminine form of the word "demon," but such a word becomes necessary when speaking of worlds like Duggur. And though the word "demoness" sounds strange and clumsy, I have no choice but to use it.

The demonesses of the great cities of our plane are saddled with a huge bulk in Duggur. Their incarnations are partly human-like, but only as far as immense carcasses barely able to move resemble humans. There is only one such demoness in each city in Duggur. The urban populace is made up of lesser demons of both sexes, who are barely distinguishable from humans in size and appearance. They swarm around their empress like drones around a queen bee, but their purpose in doing so is only partly to serve her. Their main purpose is carnal pleasure, while her function and purpose is not propagation of the species (it propagates without her), but the gratification of her subjects' lust. Grandiose residences are erected for the demonesses. In each of Duggur's cities there is only one such residence, which is in the form of a truncated pyramid. It is reminiscent of an enormous sacrificial altar. Duggur is not only grandiose; it is, in its own way, even stately and, in any case, luxurious.

Like the shrastrs, the inhabitants of Duggur also possess the equivalent of human technology, though its level is comparable to the level of technology found in the great cities of antiquity. Society there is advancing very slowly, and is slowly beginning to exhibit certain signs of what we call self-determination. But slavery remains at the foundation of the socioeconomic structure, the slaves being those who fell there from humanity or from certain worlds of elementals. The status of the lesser demons is reminiscent of the status of the patricians and charioteers of ancient Rome. One could not say that the Duggur inhabitants were particularly cruel in any way, but they are sensual beyond all bounds, more sensual than any other being in Enrof. No revolt will ever shake the foundations of the great demonesses' power, for it is a power founded not on fear but on the lust that the millions of their subjects feel for them and on the pleasure given to them as a reward for their obedience and love.

The demonesses of Duggur give themselves to whole crowds at a time, and a continuous orgy almost beyond our comprehension takes place in their residences, their palace-temples. This orgy is in honor of the demonic empress of the Moon, the same demoness whose influence we humans sometimes feel on moonlit nights in cities, where it blends with the inspirational and pure influence of Tanit, the lunar plane of Light, arousing a longing for sexual forms of pleasure that do not exist in Enrof. They do, however, exist in Duggur. An almost endless array of such forms has been devised in Duggur, an array richer in variety than anywhere else in Shadanakar. The influence of Tanit does not penetrate to Duggur at all, and they have no idea even of what sunlight is. Everything is plunged in the blue-gray murk or the pale bluish moonlight that sparkles with violet. There is nothing there to inhibit the raging of passions aroused by Voglea, the lunar demoness. Swirls of vapor rise up to her from the continuous orgies in the palace altars of Duggur, and she imbibes them. But nothing can satisfy the desire of the countless inhabitants of those cities, for they are haunted by a deeper kind of lust few of us can comprehend—a mystical lust that beckons them toward something beyond their power to attain: the Great

Harlot. She is their supreme deity, the object of their longing and dreams. Their highest cult is devoted to her. On her feast days the demoness rulers give themselves to slaves. But that mystical lust can only be satisfied in Digm, in Gagtungr's abode, and only a select few are deemed worthy of it.

The huge population of Duggur replenishes its energy at the expense of our plane. Radiations from human, and sometimes animal, lust, called *eiphos*, flow on the streets of Duggur in slow and gooey streams of whitish liquid, which the inhabitants consume. Such food suits their own essence: lust is the meaning, purpose, chief pursuit, and passion of their lives. The orgasmic intensity of pleasure that they experience is many times stronger then we are capable of experiencing. They proceed along a truly vicious circle of reincarnations, for during every interval between incarnations their souls sink down to Bustvich and take the form of human worms that devour sufferers alive in that eternally decaying world. Yet the pleasure afforded them by their lust, even by their unquenchable mystical lust for the Great Harlot, is so great in their eyes that they are prepared to pay for their frenzies and orgies in Duggur by serving time in Bustvich.

The Moon serves as the only luminary in Duggur. Therefore most of the time the plane is plunged in deep murk. At those times artificial lighting—long chains of pale-blue and purple street lamps—takes over. They stretch in endless rows beside massive, sumptuous buildings. The curve is the dominant motif in their architecture, but that does not rescue it from ponderousness. The buildings' outer and inner furnishings are tasteless and crude, but stunning in their richness, in their ostentatious splendor. Architects, artists, scientists, and workers all belong to the slave class. The main, demonic population is just as impotent intellectually and artistically as they are gifted in lust.

A fall to Duggur poses a grave danger to a human soul. A fall occurs if an otherworldly lust—that same mystical lust that the lesser demons of Duggur feel for the Great Harlot—haunts and corrupts a soul during its life in Enrof. Even a spell in Bustvich cannot restore the natural balance between the encumbered ether body and its surroundings. The soul and its coatings plunge down into Rafag, where yet another fall awaits it, this time into the same world that troubled it like a vague dream on Earth. There, in Duggur, it is encased in *karrokh*—a densely material body resembling the physical body but made from the materiality of demonic worlds generated by the dark hierarchies of the metabramfatura and by Gagtungr.

In trying to rescue souls from slavery in Duggur, the powers of Light meet with exceptional difficulties. There is, however, one act, an act dependent on the will of the human soul itself, that can open the door to its rescue: suicide. A sin in Enrof, where materiality is created by the Providential powers and is being prepared for eventual enlightenment, suicide is sanctioned on the demonic planes, as it results in the destruction of the karrokh and the liberation of the soul. But if that step is not taken, and the powers of Light are frustrated in their rescue attempts, the soul, after dying in Duggur, goes to Bustvich again, then back to Duggur—no longer as a slave but as a member of the privileged class. The shelt gradually becomes demonized, trapped in the wheel of incarnations from Duggur to Bustvich and back again, and the monad may in the end renounce it. It then falls to Sufetkh, the graveyard of Shadanakar, and dies there once and for all, while the monad departs from our bramfatura to begin its journey anew somewhere at the other end of the Universe. Of those few souls that have died forever in Sufetkh, the majority were victims of Duggur.

We shall conclude the description of Duggur with a short poem. In Duggur-Petersburg, just as in Drukkarg and Heavenly Russia, there is a twin—or rather, a triplet—of the large statue of the Bronze Horseman. But in Duggur the horseman does not ride on a rarugg, as in the capital of Russian antihumankind, nor, of course, does he ride on a dazzling white steed, as in Heavenly Petersburg. There, the sculpture is of the founder of that netherworld city, with a blazing, smoking torch in his outstretched hand. The figure also differs from the others in that it is riding a giant snake, not a horse. The reader may now be able to understand what Alexander Blok was referring to in the following poem, which is full of transphysical insight.

Still evenings will fall
The snake uncoils over the streets.
In the outstretched hand of Peter
The flame of a torch will flicker.

Lines of streetlamps will be lit
Shop windows and sidewalks will gleam
In the glow of dull squares
Lines of couples will file out.
Darkness will cover all like cloaks
Looks will be lost in beckoning looks.
May innocence from the cornerside
Beg in slow murmurs to be spared.

There on the slope the cheery tsar
Swung the stinking censer
And burning smoke from city fires
Cloaked the beckoning street light in vestments.

Everyone come running!
To the intersections of moonlit streets!
The whole city is full of voices,
Voices rough of men, voices musical of women.

He will guard his city
And turning scarlet beneath the morning star
In his outstretched hand will flash a sword
As the capital drifts off to sleep.

That, instead of a torch, a sword of retribution, of karma, will
sooner or later flash in the hand of the founder of Duggur
instead of a torch is clear enough. And every human soul that
has been in that moon-dark city cannot help recalling, even if
only dimly, their sojourn there. What is not clear is to what
extent Blok himself understood the connection between Duggur
and our world. I will try to make some observations about that
in those chapters devoted to the question of the metahistorical
meaning behind artistic genius.

There are also planes of elementals that belong to a transitional, not demonic, group, but are connected in certain ways to Duggur. Their monads, like those of all elementals of Light, abide in *Flauros*, one of the beautiful worlds of Higher Purpose. But because their nature was tarnished in the course of their development, their journey of incarnations takes them to the planes of the Nibrusks, Maniku, Kattaram, and Ron, while Duggur, where they languish in slavery, serves as both their purgatory and plane of torment. An ascending afterlife takes them first to *Shalem*—their Olirna—and higher, through Faer and Usnorm and up to Flauros, where they merge with their monads.

Nibrusks are beings somewhere between the lesser demons of Duggur and what the ancient Romans referred to as *genii loci*. Not a single human settlement can exist without Nibrusks. I still don't quite understand how and why those beings are concerned with the physical aspects of human love, especially with childbearing. Perhaps the Nibrusks replenish their energy from some kind of radiation the human soul emits in states peculiar to infancy and early childhood. In any case, there is no question of their concern. They see to matters in their own little way, helping to bring together men and women on our plane. They make a big fuss over our children, hustling and bustling all around them, and even trying to guard them from dangers we cannot see. But they are capricious, impulsive, and vengeful. One cannot always trust them.

Let the wise of our century who have locked themselves into a prison cell of materialism scoff from the heights of their ignorance at the superstitions of savages, but there is a profound truth in the legends about gremlins, penates, and lares, those good-hearted and mischievous tiny spirits of the home. Ancient paganism was far more aware of that truth than we, more than Jews and Muslims, more than Christians, all of whom heaped slander and lies on those harmless creatures. One cannot help but be amazed at the injustice of the tales told of gremlins. Such fables were born of one spirit alone—the same spirit peculiar to fanatic believers in monotheism, hypocrites and dry moralists who proclaim as evil everything that does not enter into their canon. How much more fairly did the ancients treat those beings, regarding lares and penates as their loyal friends!

The land of those small elementals who nestle in human dwellings is called *Maniku*. The landscape of that world resembles a room and has a certain coziness about it. But it is dark and cold outside, and heaven forbid that those beings be driven from their warm shelters. The form they take is unlike the form possessed by the majority of elementals: there is nothing fluid or flowing about them. To the contrary, like the Nibrusks and the inhabitants of Duggur, they have a solid, sharply defined body, or rather, bodikins. They are tiny, fun-loving, and mischievous, and some go out of their way to be kind. They are a singular kind of philanthropist and love to do people small services in such a way that no one notices it. Others, it is true, permit themselves more or less harmless pranks on people. Generally speaking, they treat us case by case. But they try to protect and take care of the home as best they can, because if it is destroyed their shelter on the plane of Maniku is destroyed as well, and the little ones, left homeless, will in most cases perish. Only a few ever manage to reach another shelter.

I have virtually nothing to say about *Kattaram*, the land of mineral elementals connected to the upper layer of the Earth's crust. I have not had any personal experience of it, while my invisible friends told me only a little about their world. All I learned was that the landscape of Kattaram consists of self-illuminating minerals amid pockets of underground space. It has a fairy-tale beauty but would nevertheless appear lifeless to us. The population of Kattaram is rich in variety (think of *The Mistress of Copper Mountain*, on the one hand, and trolls on the other), and interaction with these elementals can sometimes pose many otherworldly dangers. I know even less of *Ron*. Its landscape resembles that of Kattaram, but it is enlivened by a reflection—just a reflection—of the sky. It is the land of mountain elementals, a motley world of beings who are often battling with each other.

Shalem—the Olirna of the elementals of the four previous planes—should be regarded as the highest of the planes in that sakwala. Its landscape could in part be likened to huge oaks standing in the middle of a desert. Where the oaks are concentrated, the dominant color is blue-green, with yellow and gray on the outskirts. There the elementals acquire full Light and majesty. Awaiting them is not death but a transformation leading to Faer and Usnorm, though almost complete immobility is the price they pay for it. They are compensated for their immobility by the deep and focused character of the spiritual meditation in which they are immersed. Some peoples in Enrof, sensing the existence of those beings, regarded them as the spirits of individual mountains, waterfalls, springs, or other natural landmarks. In reality they are not spirits but fully embodied beings, and the perpetual link between them and the natural landmarks of Enrof is only an appearance, conditional upon their immobility, all of which the ancients interpreted in concordance with their level of understanding similar truths. The truth is that even if a spring dries up, a waterfall is blocked, or a mountain is thrown down by an earthquake, the elementals of Shalem will remain unwavering at their spots until the inner work on their own beings has finally readied them for transformation.

2 Elementals of Light

I AM WEARY of listing more and more new names and introducing more and more new planes. True, there are only a few left, for we are approaching the end of our survey of the structure of Shadanakar. But I would like to point out that I have not been introducing all these names for my own amusement or on a whim. No matter how strange they may sound now, and no matter how much they may seem empty figments of the imagination to the overwhelming majority of people, a time will come when every high school student will know these names as surely as they now know the names of the republics of Central America or the provinces of China. Had I thought differently, I would never have presumed to draw the reader's attention to these names. What is the point of compiling a "geography" or "geology" of some planet in the Aldebaran system if no one will ever go there, and if even our descendants only see it as a faint star in the sky? What need is there for such intellectual exercises? But a handful of people now have need of the metageography of Shadanakar, soon hundreds will, and some day, no doubt, millions will discover a need for it. After all, some two hundred years ago, in the age of Madame Prostakova, only a handful of people had any use for ordinary geography.

How glad I am that our descent into the demonic worlds is at an end and that we can now look forward to planes of beautiful beings who are undoubtedly well-disposed toward humanity. But it is always a great deal more difficult to describe things of Light, especially things of other worlds, than that which is dark or monstrous. I am afraid that I too will suffer the fate of the majority of those who write, finding graphic words for dark and woeful images, yet suffering from writer's block when faced with brilliant radiance.

Radiant and shining indeed are the monads of elementals of Light in lofty Flauros, as they send out their shelts like rays to the zatomis, where they wrap their souls in astral coatings. The souls remain there in the intervals between incarnations. When incarnating in the worlds of elementals of Light, they in turn wrap themselves in the materiality of ether, a denser substance. It is those worlds that will be described in the present chapter. None of the elementals of Light, with the exception of the elementals of Arashamf, engage in procreation, just as they do not experience incarnation in Enrof. Each independently coats itself in the matter of the four-dimensional worlds. Such is incarnation without procreation. After a chain of incarnations, every elemental, instead of the death we are accustomed to, undergoes a transfiguration that takes it to Faer and Usnorm.

They perceive Enrof, and particularly humans, through touch and another sense that we do not possess. They are not indifferent, of course, to humans. Their attitude toward each of us is determined by our own attitude toward Nature. As mentioned earlier, the natural elements in Enrof are best understood as the outermost concentric circle of their habitat. It seems that only music and poetry have thus far succeeded in conveying the interconnection between elementals and the natural elements, their wondrous life of frolic, games, love, and joy. One need only recall Wagner's brilliant score—the so-called *Rustling Forest*—where it is no longer the case that the wind speeds over a sea of trees and blooming meadows, but through the wind the elementals themselves kiss each other and the beautiful Earth.

German fairy tales about elves are not fairy tales at all. There really is a plane of kindly, endearing little beings that resemble elves. It could be called just that: the Land of the Elves.

The uppermost thin layer of earth, where roots and seeds nestle, has a corresponding plane in the transphysical world: the wondrous land of *Darainna*, the land of good spirits that care for roots and seeds. It might seem like a fairyland to us. The seeds and roots glimmer in the softest tones of blue, silver, and green, and a living aura glows softly around each seed. The inhabitants of Darainna are tiny beings that look like white caps, and on top of each there is another cap, smaller, like a head. They have a pair of gentle yet dexterous limbs—a cross between arms and wings. They quietly glide through the air, rustling the folds of their caps (which is their means of communication with each other) and weaving spells over the seeds and roots like fairy god-mothers do over cradles. Those mysterious processes by which a great tree in all its complexity grows from a tiny seed are known to them. If not for their help, the dark powers would long ago have gained access to those cradles and turned the Earth's sur-face into an impenetrable jungle of nightmarish plants, vampir-ish and gruesome counterparts to our vegetation.

If one descends deeper into the soil of Darainna, one will sooner or later reach Ron or Kattaram.

A plane by the name of *Murohamma* corresponds to the lower-lying vegetation of forests--moss, grasses, bushes—everything we call underbrush.

The abode of elementals of trees is called *Arashamf*. They are not dryads. There might well be beings like those the ancient Greeks called dryads, but I have no knowledge of them. The elementals of Murohamma and Arashamf do not bear the slightest resemblance to humans or to any being on our plane. The souls of individual trees dwell in the zatomis, where they possess intelligence and are beautiful and wise. The Synclite members interact with them to the fullest degree. They engage in a mutual exchange of ideas, feel-ings, and experiences. But in Arashamf, the elementals coat them-selves in ether bodies and sink into a reverie. The trees of Enrof are their physical bodies. Every elemental of Arashamf has gone through a large number of incarnations; for many of them the number of years lived in Enrof is in the six digits, sometimes almost a million years. The landscape in Arashamf resembles greenish tongues of fragrant, cool, gently swaying flames. Some of these ele-mentals are full of goodness, like saints, and favorably disposed toward us. They are patient, serene, and humble in their wisdom. At times, something breathtaking takes place among them: they all bow down to each other in the same direction. The entire ether forest turns into a mass of flames that gently bend and straighten, flowing into each other, and in chorus they offer up something like hymns of praise. The plane of Murohamma sometimes takes part in it too. Murohamma is the same greenish color, but thicker, darker, warmer, and more gentle.

Everyone should find it easy to recall soft breezes kissing the Earth during summer sunsets or a spring afternoon. They kiss the Earth and its grasses, fields of grain, paths, trees, the surface of rivers and oceans, people and animals. The elementals of the plane called *Vayita* take delight in life. They take delight in us and in plants, water, and the sun; they take delight in cool, hot, soft, hard, bright, or shadowy ground, stroking and caressing it. If we could see Vayita with our own eyes, we would have the impression that we were immersed in verdant, fragrant, playful waves that are completely transparent, pleasant in temperature, and, most important, alive, intelligent, and bubbling with delight over us.

When you plunge face first on a hot day into the grass of a meadow in bloom, and your head spins from the smell of pollen and from the aroma coming from the warm ground and leaves, while barely audible breaths of light and warmth glide over the meadow, you can be sure that it is the elementals of Vayita playing and celebrating with the children of *Faltora*—the land of elementals of field and meadow. We are left without a single clouded thought in our mind. It might seem to us that we have found paradise lost. The dust of worldly cares is blown from our souls by clean breaths of wind, and we are incapable of feeling anything but an all-consuming love for Nature.

A world of truly inexpressible delight shines through the streaming water of the Earth's rivers. There exists a special hierarchy that I have long been accustomed to calling river spirits, though I now see that the name is imprecise. Each river has a single, unique spirit. The outermost layer of its ever-flowing body is visible to us as the currents of a river, but its real soul is in Heavenly Russia, or another heavenly land if it flows through the territory of another culture in Enrof. But the inner, ether layer of its body, which its essence permeates incomparably more fully and in which it is embodied with almost full consciousness, is located in a world adjoining ours called *Liurna*. The fact that it is continuously surrendering the currents of both its flowing bodies to a larger river, and that river, to the sea, but doing so without any diminishment in its body as it flows on from source to mouth, constitutes the greatest joy of its life. It is impossible to find words to describe the charm of those beings, beings so joyful, playful, sweet, pure, and peaceful that no human tenderness is comparable to theirs, except perhaps the tenderness of the most giving and loving daughters of humanity. And if we are fortunate enough to experience Liurna in body and soul by immersing our body in a river stream, our ether body in the streams of Liurna, and our soul in its soul, which shines in the zatomis, then we will climb out onto the bank with a cleansed, brightened, and joyful heart such as humans might have had before the Fall.

Vlanmim, the land of elementals of the upper regions of the sea, partly resembles Liurna in the effect it has on the human soul. The landscape of that world resembles a rhythmically rolling ocean of bright blue (such a softly radiant, ravishing blue does not exist in Enrof), its waves capped not by foam but by milky white, lacy spheres that look like large flowers. These flowers bloom and melt before one's eyes, and then bloom and melt anew. The elementals of Liurna are feminine, and those of Vlanmim are masculine, but that has no relation whatsoever to procreation, although the union of river with sea is an expression of the love between the elementals of these two worlds. Vlanmim can also make us wiser and purer in heart, but because it is open from below to the influence of the grim elementals of Nugurt, the ocean depths, it is not as gentle as Liurna. Its influence is noticeable on the moral fiber and even the physical appearance of people—fishermen and, in part, sailors—who come into daily contact with it, even if that contact takes place on a level beyond their consciousness. On sailors, however, the mark of other elementals, ones not of Light, is all too apparent. Sailors are influenced by, on the one hand, the inhabitants of Nugurt, and on the other, the Nibrusks and the inhabitants of Duggur, the elementals of large port cities. As for fishermen, they receive from

Vlanmim the traits that set them apart from other people: the combination of purity, courage, and a crude, slightly brutal strength with childlike integrity.

Everywhere over land and sea stretches *Zunguf*—the land of elementals of atmospheric moisture, which produce clouds, rain, dew, and mists. There is no clear boundary between Zunguf and *Irudrana*—the land of elementals whose activity in Enrof takes the form of thunderstorms and sometimes hurricanes. Both these planes blend with each other, just as their inhabitants do. That same transmyth is revealed that glimmered in the mythologies of ancient peoples, giving rise in their creative imagination to the titanic images of the thunder gods: Indra, Perun, Thor. If only the ancients, who ascribed, as with everything, human features to these images, had known how infinitely distant these beings are from even the slightest resemblance to humans! When rain showers down to the ground and the tempestuous and frolicsome children of Zunguf give themselves up to rejoicing, bouncing from the earth and the surface of water back up into the air, which seethes with drops of water, above, in Irudrana, armies of beings like Thor or Indra only in their playful competitiveness battle away. For them, thunder and lightning are creative work, and hurricanes are life at its fullest.

If a light snow floats down on a cool night, or trees and buildings are whitened by frost, the robust, clear, almost ecstatic joy we feel testifies to the proximity of the wondrous elementals of *Nivenna*. White expanses immaculate with a special, inexpressible purity—that is Nivenna, the land of elementals of frost, snowflakes, and fresh snowfalls. Frolicking in unearthly fun like that of the elves, they cover their beloved Earth with their veil. Why are we filled with such joy for life when myriads of silent white stars softly descend all around us? And why, when we see a wood or city park white with frost, do we experience a feeling that unites solemnity and lightness of heart, a rush of energy and delight, veneration and childlike joy? The elementals of Nivenna have a particularly tender love for those of us who have kept the eternal child alive in our heart; they greet such people with gladness and try to play with them. Even the excitement, youthful vigor, and rush of blood in the veins of children during snowball fights or tobogganing gives them pleasure.

Beside Nivenna is stern and somber *Ahash*, the plane of arctic and antarctic elementals, which are connected to the polar regions of our planet. Ahash extends into outer space, and from it is visible the Milky Way. The borders of both polar regions creep toward and away from the tropics as the seasons change.

The untamed spirit of those beings, with their penchant for jumping from crystal clear meditation to fury, with their sudden urges to build whole worlds of transphysical ice, with their love of gazing eye to eye into the endless depths of the metagalaxy, has left a striking mark on the physical environment of the polar basins. When the revolution of the Earth around the Sun brings winter to the Northern hemisphere and gives the elementals of Ahash access to the more populated parts of those continents, they come pouring in with physical masses of arctic air in train, battling with snowstorms and blizzards over field and forest, giving free reign to their joy from the heights of anti-cyclones.

They do not perceive Enrof in the same way we do. Nor do they perceive humans with the faculty of sight. But some among them are as predatory and as cold emotionally as Andersen's Snow Queen, and they represent a danger to humans. There are others that intuit the inner spirit of those of us who are akin to them in courage, daring, and fearlessness. They can love such people with a strange love incommensurate with ours. They cradle them on their snowy laps, open the way to the depths of their lands, guide them through the terrible majesty of the physical layers of their realm, and forgetting the incommensurability between their immensity and our physical smallness, are prepared to wrap them in a blanket of white to the lullabies of howling blizzards.

The last two planes also extend, like Ahash, into outer space: *Diramn*, which is connected to the stratospheric ocean of air and the belt of lower temperatures, and *Sianna*—the world visible to inner vision through the high-temperature zones that encompass our planet in the upper atmosphere. But the elementals that abide there are so immense and so alien to our way of thinking that it is extremely difficult to gain an understanding of their essence. They are elementals of Light, but their light is a searing, perilous light. Only a human soul that has already risen to exceptional heights can gain admittance to their realm.

That concludes the sakwala of Lesser Elementals. They are, of course, lesser not in comparison with humans—many of them are far mightier than any individual human—but rather in comparison with the elementals of another sakwala, with the ascending staircase of Greater Elementals, the true planetary divinities, the sovereigns of our world. The lesser elementals tremble with joy at their breath. The majority of them are beautiful, supremely good beings of inexpressible majesty. But it is nearly impossible to speak of the landscapes of those planes and of the forms of those great beings, for they all exist simultaneously at a multitude of points on their planes.

The dominion of *Vayumn*, "the Lord of Blessed Wings," the embodied spirit of the air, stretches from the upper reaches of the atmosphere down to the deepest chasms. His brother, *Ea* (if I remember correctly, his other name is *Vlarol*), "the Lord of Life-Giving Waters," was worshiped long ago by the Greeks as Poseidon and by the Romans as Neptune. But the Babylonians grasped his grace and cosmic dimensions best of all, dedicating a magnificent cult to the guardian and keeper of the Earth's waters. Both spirits are on eternal guard over the sources of life all over the world—not only in Enrof but in many other sakwalas as well. Both are as old as water and air, and just as immaculate.

Povurn, the third brother, "the Lord of Flaming Body," is even older, for there is a profound reality behind the ancients' belief in Pluto and Yama. That terrifying lord of the subterranean magma is not the servant of Gagtungr; he will, however, be the last, it seems, of the Greater Elementals to undergo transformation, which occur at the end of the second eon.

There is also a fourth great brother, the youngest, *Zaranda*, "the Lord of the Animal World." The tragic history of the animal realm in Enrof has left a deep, truly global mark of sorrow on his form. And no matter how historians try to explain the symbolism behind the Egyptian sphinx, metahistory will always regard it as an image of the one who combines in himself the nature of the "Great Animal" with wisdom far beyond the reach of human beings.

There are seven Greater Elementals in all. Two divine sisters divide the remaining spheres of power between themselves: *Estira*, "the Queen of Eternal Gardens," the mistress of the plant realms of Shadanakar, and *Lilith*, "the Aphrodite Universalis of Humanity."

Lilith plays an immense role in our lives. Like all the Greater Elementals, her abode is incommensurate with any of our forms and is indescribable, while her own form is boundless. Her vario-material body exists simultaneously at a multitude of points on her plane, and only in rare instances does it assume a form that can be seen by human spiritual vision. I do not know the mechanics of the process, but I do know that the formation of any body in the worlds of dense materiality is impossible without the involvement of Lilith, with the exception of animals, whose species are forged by Zaranda. In all the other realms, it is Lilith that discharges that duty. She forges the family chain for humanity, and daemons, and for raruggs, igvas, and the inhabitants of Duggur in the demonic worlds. Every densely material body created with her assistance in the dark worlds is made of karrokh. That is why she is fully deserving of being considered the sculptress of our flesh. Human sexuality is inextricably bound with her being and influence. Whether it is she or her karossas, that power always presides over every act of human copulation, and while the embryo is in the womb, she is there.

At one time, long, long ago, that elemental became the spouse of the Prime Angel—that great Spirit that subsequently became the Logos of Shadanakar. Their union took place during the creation of the angelic planes, and Lilith became the proto-mother of that first humankind. But Gagtungr was able to infiltrate Lilith's world, and her body of subtle materiality absorbed a demonic element. This was a disaster of catastrophic proportions. From that time on, all family chains forged by her, be they Titan, daemon, or human, acquire something of that element. There is a term in Jewish mysticism—*yetzer hara*—that refers to the demon seed in humans. We will try using it in reference to that cursed seed planted in humans through Lilith, who carries it within herself and in her karossas to this day.

Only Lilith has a monad and complete consciousness. The karossas, her localized manifestations, notwithstanding their power and longevity, possess only the equivalent of consciousness and lack a monad, Dingra of Russia included. Incidentally, we are indebted to those sculptresses of the human flesh for the visible, at times almost elusive, physical resemblance that distinguishes the members of a common nation or kinship group.

It is known that the cult of the goddess of love on ancient Cyprus eventually split into two diametrically opposed sects: the lofty cult of Aphrodite Urania, the goddess of spiritual, creative, poeticized, and poetic love, and the cult of Aphrodite Pandemos, "the Common Aphrodite." The latter cult gained widespread appeal among the lower classes, taking the form of orgiastic rites and the blessing of sexual excesses as a holy offering to the goddess. Some other cultures have experienced analogous processes of bifurcation and polarization of previously unified principles. There are even more cultures where the historian is presented with a later phase: cults of sexual perversion and the random blend of demonic and elemental properties behind the false mask of the divine. Ritual prostitution in Canaan, Babylon, India, and other countries is a phenomenon of that nature. The karossas of nations or suprapeoples presided over such institutions, and they preside over the rites of orgiastic sects and mass fornication even now. It is also clear that such phenomena require the involvement of the lunar demoness and the dark powers of Duggur. But when, in battling those who threaten his people with physical destruction, a demiurge seeks a way to create a powerful and combative champion, he is forced to descend to the karossa of the people and unite with her. The cursed yetzer hara unavoidably infects their joint offspring, and the poisoned body of the karossa produces a two-faced monster. That is the origin of the first born of every line of Witzraor. It will only be possible, it appears, to rid the karossas and Lilith herself of the yetzer hara in the second eon.

The first and last of the Greater Elementals, *Earth*, is the mother of all the others, and not only of them, but of every living thing in Shadanakar: every elemental, every animal, human, daemon, angel, demon, and even every great hierarchy. An inexhaustible wellspring, she is the one who creates the ether body of all beings and takes part along with the individual monads in the creation of their astral bodies. She is endowed with warm, inexhaustible love for everything, even demons: she grieves for them, but forgives them. Everyone, even angels of darkness and the monsters of Gashsharva, call her Mother. She loves all and everything, but she reveres only the highest hierarchies of Shadanakar, especially Christ. She is fertilized by the great radiant spirit of the Sun both in Enrof and in her own indescribable world. She perceives people and their inner world, she hears and responds to the call of our heart, and she answers through love and Nature. May her name be blessed! Prayer can and should be offered up to her in great humility.

May the beautiful Moon, the daughter of Earth and Sun, be blessed. And may the Sun be thrice blessed. All of us, our future body and soul, together with all of Shadanakar, at one time abided in its immaculate heart. Great god of light! They sang your glory in the temples of Egypt and ancient Greece, on the banks of the Ganges and on top of the ziggurats of Ur, in the Land of the Rising Sun, and in the far West, on the Andean plateaus. We all love you—good and bad, wise and ignorant, believers and nonbelievers, those who feel the infinite goodness of your heart, and those who simply enjoy your light and warmth. Your brilliant Elite has already created a staircase of radiant planes in Shadanakar and cascades of spiritual grace pour down it, lower and lower, into the angelic worlds, the worlds of the elementals, and the worlds of humanity. Beautiful spirit, the origin and sire of all living matter, the visible image and likeness of the Universal Sun, the living icon of the One God, allow me too to join my voice, audible to you alone, to the global chorus of your praise. Love us, O radiant one!

3 Perspective on the Animal World

WE ARE OFTEN UNAWARE that our utilitarian view on all living beings has become almost second nature to us. Everything is valued strictly according to the degree it is useful to humans. But if we have long considered barbaric that historical-cultural provincialism, elevated to the status of political theory, known as nationalism, then humanity's cosmic provincialism will appear just as ridiculous to our descendants. The myth of "the crowning glory of Creation," a legacy of medieval ignorance and primitive egoism, should in time dissipate like smoke, together with the supremacy of the materialist doctrine that endorses it.

We are witnessing the emergence of a new worldview, in which humans are one link in a great chain of living beings. We are higher than many, but we are also lower than a great many more. And every one of these beings has an autonomous value independent of its usefulness to humanity. But how do we determine that value in every specific case? What criteria do we use? On which standard of values should we base our judgements?

We can first of all state that the material or spiritual value of anything, whether it be material or spiritual, increases in direct proportion to the total efforts expended on its becoming what it is now. Of course, when we try to apply that principle to the valuation of living beings, we soon arrive at the conclusion that it is impossible for us to ascertain the exact amount of those efforts. But it is possible to realize that the higher the being on the cosmic staircase, the greater the amount of efforts (its own efforts, those of Nature, or those of the Providential powers) expended on it. The development of intellect and of all the faculties that distinguish humanity from animals demanded an incredible amount of work—by humanity itself and by the Providential powers—an amount greater than was needed earlier to raise animals from lower to higher life forms. That is the basis, as best as we can grasp it, of the cosmic standard of values. It thus follows that the value of a protozoan is less than that of an insect, the value of an insect less than that of a mammal, the value of a non-human mammal far less than that of a human, the value of a human tiny compared with that of an archangel or national demiurge, while the value of the latter, notwithstanding all its grandeur, pales next to the value of the Elite of Light, the demiurges of the Universe.

If we examine that principle in isolation, we might draw the conclusion that humans bear practically no responsibility toward anything below them: if the value of humans is higher, it must mean that Nature itself dictates that humans utilize beings lower than them in a way useful for the race.

But no moral principle should be examined in isolation, for they are not sufficient unto themselves. Rather, they enter into a general system of principles that currently define the reality that is Shadanakar. The principle of moral duty could be considered a counterweight to the principle of spiritual value. It has not yet been intuited at levels below humanity; nor was it even intuited at the early stages of humanity. But it can now be given a fairly accurate formulation as follows: *Beginning at the level of humans, the duty of a being toward beings below it increases in direct proportion to the level of the higher being's ascent.*

A duty toward domesticated animals had been laid on humans as early as prehistoric times. This was not merely because humans had to feed and protect them. This was but a simple exchange, a duty in the lowest, material (not moral) sense. In return for providing the animal with food and shelter, people either put the animal to work or took its milk or wool or even its life (in the latter case, of course, they violated the natural rate of exchange). The moral duty of early humans was to love the animal they had domesticated and put to use. Riders of ancient times who felt a deep bond to their horses, shepherds who displayed not only solicitude but also affection for their flocks, peasants or hunters who loved their cow or dog—all of them carried out their moral duty.

That elementary duty has remained the norm for all humanity to this day. It is true that higher individual souls—those we call saints and to whom Hindus refer using the more precise word *mahatma*, "great soul"—intuited a new, much higher level of duty that issued naturally from their spiritual greatness. *The Lives of the Saints* is full of stories of friendships between monks or hermits and bears, wolves, or lions. In some cases they may be legends, but in other cases, such as that of St. Francis of Assisi or St. Serafim of Sarov, facts of that nature have been verified by eyewitness accounts.

Of course, only sainthood is capable of such a level of duty toward animals. It is not the lot of the greater part of humanity now, just as it was not three thousand years ago. But three thousand years is a long time. And there is no justification for the claim that we are doomed to remain at the same level of primitive duty as our distant ancestors. If people groping their way through a finite and mist-shrouded animistic world could find it within themselves to love their horse or dog, then for us that is no longer sufficient. Does the lengthy road that we have traveled since then not oblige us to strive for more? Is it not within us to love those other, wild animals—at least those that do us no harm—from whom we receive no direct benefit?

All living beings, including protozoa, possess what we have provisionally termed shelts, or, if the reader prefers, souls—that is to say, a fine variomaterial coating that the immortal monad fashions for itself. Material existence is impossible without a shelt, just as any existence whatsoever is impossible without a monad. The monads of animals abide in Kaermis, one of the worlds of Higher Purpose, while their souls complete a lengthy journey up an ascending spiral through a special sakwala of several planes. They incarnate here, in Enrof, but many of them do not undergo a descent after death. They, too, live under the law of karma, but it works differently for them. It is only in Enrof that they unravel their knots at an extremely slow pace during journeys of countless incarnations within the limits of their class.

The Providential powers had originally intended Enrof to be the exclusive abode of the animal realm—that is, of the host of monads that had descended here in shelts to undertake the great creative task of enlightening the materiality of the three-dimensional plane. Gagtungr's meddling wrecked that original design, increased the complexity of the task, twisted fates, and lengthened time frames to a horrifying degree. That was all accomplished primarily by subjecting organic life in Enrof from its very beginnings to the law of the jungle.

Why are almost all baby animals so endearing and cute? Why do even piglets and baby hyenas, let alone wolf or lion cubs, evoke such warmth and tenderness? Because the demonic in animals only begins to make its presence known the minute they are forced to enter into the struggle for survival—that is, when they fall under the law of the jungle. Baby animals in Enrof resemble animals as they appeared in the adjacent world they left when they first came to Enrof. Even snakes were beautiful, vibrant, and extremely playful beings on that plane. They danced, giving glory to God. If not for Gagtungr, in Enrof they would have become even more beautiful, intelligent, and wiser.

Gagtungr's activities caused a sharp line to be drawn between two halves of the animal world. He demonizied one half very strongly, placing a low ceiling on their spiritual growth by having them live exclusively off their fellow animals. Predation is, generally speaking, demonic in nature, and in whatever being we encounter it, it means that the demonic powers have already transformed it in a fundamental way. The other half of the animal world was earmarked as victims of the first half. The predatory seed was not sown in them, so those species limited themselves to plant food. But the struggle for survival in conditions of almost constant flight and concealment from danger has been a terrible hindrance to the development of their intelligence.

The Providential powers continued to be faced with the task of enlightening three-dimensional materiality. Since the animal world had been incapacitated in that respect, at least for the foreseeable future, preconditions were created for one species to be singled out, a species that could perform the task successfully in a shorter period of time. The species was singled out in a manner that resembled a giant leap forward. At the same time, the parent species, from which the new, progressive species separated, served as a kind of trampoline for it. The more humanity leaped forward, the farther back the parent species that had served as a trampoline recoiled. Later that species evolved into the order of primates—a tragic example of regression. Thus, our leap from animal to human took place at the cost of a halt in the development of a great many other beings.

The more predatory an animal, the more demonized it is. That demonization is, of course, restricted to their shelts and denser material coatings. It cannot affect the monad. But the demonization of the shelt can attain horrifying degrees and give rise to terrible consequences. It is enough to recall what happened to many species of the reptile class. The Mesozoic era was marked by the fact that the reptile class, some of whose members had by that time grown to colossal size, was split into two. The half that remained herbivorous was given the opportunity to continue their development on other planes, and there now exists a material world, *Zhimeira*, where such beings as brontosaurs and iguanodons, which have undergone countless incarnations, now abide in the form of fully intelligent, kindly, and extremely affectionate beings. As for the other half of the giant lizards, the predators, they evolved on other planes in the opposite direction. For a long time now, they have had karrokh instead of physical bodies, and it is none other than they who rampage in the shrastrs in the form of raruggs.

Zhimeira, the present abode of the better half of prehistoric animals, has already begun to disappear, for they are moving on to higher planes. Two other planes are full of a myriad of beings: *Isong*—the world of the souls of most animals in existence today, through which they flash very quickly in the intervals between incarnations, and *Ermastig*—the world of the souls of the higher animals. The representatives of only a few species ascend to Ermastig after death, and only some members even of those species do so. They remain in that world much longer than the others remain in Isong.

That all brings to mind the words of Zosima the Elder in *The Brothers Karamazov*, words remarkable for their wisdom:

"Look at the horse ... or the lowly, pensive ox ... look at their visages, what meekness, what devotion to man, who often beats them mercilessly. What gentleness, what confidence, and what beauty in their visages!"

To refer to a horse or a cow as having a visage—now that requires the power of true insight. The customary surface of things revealed its depths to the prophetic eye of Dostoyevsky, and he saw what the future holds for animals. For a world already exists where the mature souls of many of them, coated in enlightened bodies, are beautiful, wise in spirit, and highly intelligent. All of them will in time attain that world, *Hangvilla*, the highest in the sakwala, and then rise higher, to Faer, Usnorm, and Kaermis.

Oh, the vile marks of Gagtungr's claws can be seen on much else in the animal world! For example, by squeezing together the shelts of some animals, he was able to do them harm in a way for which it is hard to find an analogy on our plane. He did not exactly press or graft them together, but he turned them from individual into collective shelts. The individual shelts of many lower life forms are but short-lived manifestations of that one collective shelt. Such, for example, are most insects, not to mention protozoa. The individual shelt of a fly or a bee, for example, is, in a manner of speaking, only a tiny swelling on the surface of the collective soul. If a bee or fly dies here in Enrof, the swelling disappears back into the communal shelt of the swarm of bees or flies.

The world of the collective souls of insects and protozoa is called *Nigoyda*. There the collective souls, especially those of bees and ants, are endowed with intelligence. In external appearance they resemble the beings that embody them in Enrof, but they are larger and more imbued with Light. Some of them—at present only a few—ascend higher, to Hangvilla, and there become beautiful and wise, even acquiring a certain magnificence and nobility. Hangvilla is the great zatomis common to the entire animal world, and from there the animals' enlightened souls ascend through Faer directly to Usnorm itself, where they take part in the eternal liturgy of Shadanakar.

What will seem even stranger concerns not live animals but some children's toys. I am referring to the teddy bears, stuffed rabbits, and other toy animals everyone knows and loves. Each one of us loved them in childhood, and we all experienced the same sadness and pain when we began to understand that they were only the work of human hands and not really alive. But happily, children who cling faithfully to the belief that their toys are alive and can even speak are closer to the truth than we are. Using our higher faculties, we could in such cases witness a singular creative process. At first such a toy has neither an ether nor astral body nor a shelt nor, of course, a monad. But the more a teddy bear is loved, the more a child's soul showers it with tenderness, warmth, affection, pity, and trust, the denser and more concentrated becomes the fine matter within it, of which a shelt is made. A genuine shelt gradually forms, but it has neither astral nor ether body, and therefore the physical body—the toy—cannot come to life. But when the toy, permeated throughout with an immortal shelt, perishes in Enrof, a divine act takes place, and the newly created shelt is paired with a young monad entering Shadanakar from the heart of God. Among the souls of the higher animals that are coated in astral and ether, an astonishing being makes its appearance in Ermastig, a being for whom those same coatings are to be fashioned there. They are striking not for their beauty or grandeur but, rather, for that inexpressible something that softens our hard hearts at the sight of a baby rabbit or fawn. In Ermastig those beings are even more wonderful, because their respective toys have never had a drop of evil in them. There, together with the souls of real bears and deer, they live a delightful life, receive an astral body, and then ascend to Hangvilla like the rest.

I can give here only a bare outline of a method for solving problems associated with the transphysics and eschatology of the animal world. But even that will be enough to realize how much more complex the matter is than the thinkers of the older religions believed. The simplistic formula "Animals know no sin" does not do the least justice to the essence of the matter. If in the given case "sin" refers to the state of sexual consciousness in which a feeling of shame and the idea of a prohibition on certain kinds of sexual activity are lacking, then animals truly do not know sin. But it would be better to say that for them these activities are not prohibited, not punishable by karma, and not a sin. On the other hand, the concept of sin encompasses an area infinitely broader than just sex. Malice, cruelty, unfounded and unbridled anger, bloodthirstiness, and jealousy are the sins of the animal world, and we are not in the possession of any facts on the basis of which we could judge the extent that one or another animal is conscious of the wrongness of such actions. In addition, that does not resolve the question of whether or not such a prohibition exists for them. It is absurd to assume that a law comes into effect only when it is cognized. No one before Newton knew of the law of gravity, but everyone and everything has always been subject to it. It matters not whether animals are conscious of a higher law or not, whether they have a vague intuition of it or no intuition at all: causality remains causality, and karma remains karma.

As far as I understand, a hungry lion that kills an antelope does not incur individual guilt, since the killing was a necessity for it, but it does incur the guilt of its species or class—the ancient guilt of all predators. But a tiger with a full belly that attacks an antelope out of excessive bloodthirstiness and malice incurs individual guilt as well as the guilt common to the species, for it was not driven by necessity to kill its victim. A wolf that, in defending itself from dogs, kills one in the fight is not guilty individually, but it is guilty as a member of a predatory species, whose ancestors at one time elected to evolve in that direction.

We are dealing here with a kind of original sin. But a plump, well-fed cat that amuses itself by playing with a mouse is guilty of both original and individual sins, because there is no call for its actions. Some will say I am applying human, even legalistic, concepts to the animal world. But the concept of guilt is not only a legal concept; it is a transphysical, metahistorical, and ontological concept as well. The nature of guilt can vary between natural realms and hierarchies, but that in no way means that the concept itself and the reality of karma behind it is applicable to humanity alone.

The secular era of thought also has failed to introduce any new ideas to the question. To the contrary, the dominant attitude toward animals in modern times began to form from two opposing principles—the utilitarian and the emotional. The animal world has been divided into categories in concordance with the relationship a given species has to humans. First of all, of course, come pets and domesticated animals. People take care of them and sometimes even love them. If a cow falls sick they shed tears over it. But if it stops giving milk, they take it away, with deep sighs, to a certain place where their beloved animal is converted into so many kilos of beef. With childlike innocence farmers then feed off the meat themselves and feed it to their households. The second category includes a large segment of wild animals, as well as fish. People do not domesticate them; they do not lavish care on them, but they simply trap or hunt them down. The matter is simple with the third group, predators and parasites. People kill them whenever and however they can. A fourth group comprises wild animals, birds in particular, that show their usefulness by killing harmful insects and rodents. That category is permitted to live and multiply, and in certain cases—for example, starlings or storks—they are even protected by law. As for all the other animals, from lizards and frogs to jackdaws and magpies, they are sometimes caught for scientific purposes or simply for the sport of it. Children may throw rocks at them, but it is more common for people, from the heights of their greatness, simply not to notice them.

That is an outline, albeit very rough, of the utilitarian attitude toward animals. The emotional attitude of most of us consists of the feeling of sympathy, real attachment, or aesthetic pleasure toward one or another species, or toward individual animals. In addition, many humans are also endowed (thank heavens!) with a general feeling of compassion for animals. That compassion is largely responsible for the laws in many countries concerned with the treatment of animals and the operation of a network of volunteer associations devoted specifically to promoting the humane treatment of animals. The emotional attitude, in conjunction with such a powerful ally as the utilitarian concern that commercially valuable species not be completely exterminated, has made the establishment of wildlife parks possible. And certain exceptional parks have no utilitarian purpose whatsoever—for example, the feeding stations for pigeons that can be found in many places.

I have been speaking, of course, about the attitude toward animals in Europe, North America, and many countries in the East. But India presents an altogether different picture. Brahmanism, as we know, has long forbidden the consumption of various kinds of meat, has practically reduced the human diet to dairy and vegetable products, has declared work in leather and fur sinful and impure, and has proclaimed the cow and certain other species holy animals. And they should be applauded for it.

Europeans, of course, are at turns amused and exasperated by the spectacle of cows wandering freely through bazaars, helping themselves to anything that catches their eye in the stalls. I do not dispute the fact that the religious worship of the cow is a specific feature of the Indian worldview alone and cannot be an object of imitation in our century. But the feeling that underlies that worship is so pure, so lofty, and so holy that it itself deserves our respect. Gandhi did a fine job explaining the psychological roots of the worship of the cow. He pointed out that in the given case the cow represents all living beings below humanity. A humble reverence for the cow and service of it in the form of disinterested care, affection, and decoration are an expression of the religious idea and moral sense of our duty toward the world of living beings, of the idea of helping and protecting all that is weak or below us, all that has not yet succeeded in developing into higher forms. Not only that, it is also an expression of a mystical sense of the profound guilt shared by all humanity toward the animal world, for humanity was singled out from animals at the cost of the retardation and regression of those weaker than us. We were singled out and, having been singled out, compounded our guilt by mercilessly exploiting those weaker than us. Over the centuries our shared human guilt has snowballed and has lately assumed vast proportions.

Glory to that people who have been able to rise to such understanding, not just in the minds of a few but in the conscience of millions!

What idea or ethic can we, who boast of our centuries-long profession of Christianity, put forward to match that ethic?

There was an incident in my life that I must speak of here. It is a painful memory, but I would not want anyone to form, on the basis of this chapter about animals, an image of the author that he does not deserve. It so happens that once, several decades ago, I consciously, even purposely, committed a vile, loathsome crime against an animal that belonged to the category of "friends of humanity." It all happened because I was at that time going through a phase, or rather, an inner detour, that was most dark. I decided to enter into, as I then put it, "the service of Evil"—an idea so naive as to be stupid. But because of the romantic aura that I cloaked it in, it took hold of my imagination and resulted in a chain of actions, each more appalling than the previous one. I was seized by the desire to find out if there really was an action so base, petty, and inhumane that I would not dare to carry it out. I do not even have the excuse that I was a thick-headed child or had fallen in with a bad crowd. There was no such crowd in my social circle, and I had reached the age of majority and was even a university student. How and on what exact animal the action was carried out is here immaterial, but carried out it was. The compunction I felt, however, was so strong that a revolution of terrific force took place in my attitude toward animals, an attitude that I have had ever since. It also served as the overall turning point in my inner life. If that shameful stain were not on my conscience I might not now experience such aversion, sometimes even to the point of a complete loss of self-control, toward any torture or murder of animals. It is for me now axiomatic that in the overwhelming majority of cases (excepting only self-defense from predators or parasites or the lack of any other food source) the killing or torture of animals is loathsome, unacceptable, and unworthy of humans. To do so is to violate one of those moral foundations on which we must firmly stand in order to retain the right to call ourselves human.

Of course, hunting, when it is the principal means of livelihood for certain primitive tribes, cannot be condemned morally. One would have to be a vegetarian Pharisee to censure Hottentots or Goldi, for whom abandonment of the hunt would be tantamount to death. And all who find themselves in similar circumstances can and should support their own lives and the lives of others through hunting, for the life of a human is more valuable than the life of any animal.

For the very same reason, people have the right to defend themselves from predators and parasites. It is known that many Jains and some followers of extreme Buddhist sects do not drink water except through gauze and, while walking, sweep the path in front of them before every step. I seem to recall there even being ascetics in India who let parasites feed on them. What better example is there to show how any idea can be carried to absurd extremes! The mistake being made here is that humans, for the sake of saving the lives of insects and even protozoa—that is, beings of much less value—place themselves in conditions where both social and technological progress become impossible. All forms of transport would have to be abandoned, since they cause the death of multitudes of tiny beings. A ban would even have to be laid on agriculture and the tilling of the soil in general, since it results in the death of billions of tiny creatures. In modern India, Jains are primarily engaged in liberal professions and commerce. But what would they do if the majority of humanity adopted their outlook on life? Of course, such an outlook, whereby a low ceiling is placed on the ascent of humanity, cannot be right.

But what, from the transphysical, not materialist, point of view, are parasites and protozoa? Like the majority of insects, they possess collective souls, but they lag far behind in spiritual growth. Properly speaking, we are not dealing here with a simple lag, but with Gagtungr's active demonization of their collective shelt. The shelts have the status of slaves in Nigoyda, possess only partial intelligence, and face a journey of spiritual growth exceptional for its slowness and duration. Only at the moment of our planet's passage into the third eon will they attain enlightenment. For the present, parasites—that is, beings of much lesser value—live on and get fat off of animals and humans, beings of comparatively higher value. We are therefore right to exterminate them, as we have no other alternative at the given stage.

Predators live at the expense of animals, beings of the same value, or of humans, beings of higher value. Those species of predators whose predatory nature we are incapable of altering should be gradually exterminated in Enrof. I say gradually not only because it cannot be done in any other manner but also because the means to alter even their nature might be discovered in the meantime. There is every reason to hope that the nature of many predatory species, especially among the higher mammals, can be changed at a fundamental level. It is enough to recall that the dog, that one-time wolf, is now capable of doing entirely without meat, and this despite the fact that humans have never set themselves the goal of turning dogs into vegetarians. Dogs were weaned away from meat out of purely economic considerations, but the success of these measures points to the excellent prospects in that area, prospects that are only now revealing themselves. Thus, hunting predators is the second kind of hunting that should not be condemned at the present stage of humanity. But another set of measures will be necessary alongside it. I will speak of them further on.

What will be subject to unconditional abolition, even a strict ban, is hunting for sport. I know full well what a howl of protest will be raised by the lovers of deer- and pheasant-shooting were this demand to gain widespread support in society and from a utopian dream of individual eccentrics turn into the insistent appeal of all progressive humanity. It is not difficult to foresee the arguments they will use in their defense. They will enlist the aid of every rationalization a crafty mind is capable of concocting when it is called on to assist a twisted instinct. They will scream, for example, about the benefits of hunting, about how it tempers one's body (as if it could not be tempered in some other fashion), how it builds character, will, resourcefulness, courage (as if humans faced some kind of danger hunting wild game). They will shower us with assurances that hunting is essentially a pretext, a mere means to the genuine end of enjoying the great outdoors, as if it couldn't be enjoyed without the additional pleasure of seeing a hare run down by a dog. They will arm themselves with brilliant psychological concoctions à la Knut Hamsun to prove that the hunting instinct is an inalienable human attribute and that the joy of hunting originates from a combination of the satisfaction of that instinct and a sense of being a part of Nature. From their perspective, they do not view Nature through the eyes of idle city slickers in the woods, not from the outside looking in; they become part of Nature when they wait in ambush behind a tree. But no matter how much they imagine themselves part of Nature, all their feelings are not worth one glance from the dying eyes of a goose they have shot. All the twists and turns a cunning mind may make are refuted by one short statement by Turgenev. Himself a passionate hunter, he was honest both with the reader and himself. He knew and said firmly and plainly that hunting has no relation whatsoever to a love of Nature.

"I can't enjoy nature while I'm hunting—all that is nonsense: you enjoy it when you're lying down or resting after the hunt. Hunting is a passion, and I don't nor can I see anything except some pheasant hiding in a bush. No true hunter goes into the wild to enjoy nature."

Turgenev speaks openly and plainly. Why do others deceive themselves and those around them by justifying hunting as love of Nature?

Oh, I know their kind well enough: courage, honesty, simplicity, a keen eye, broad shoulders, a weather-beaten face, a clipped manner of speech, a racy joke from time to time—what more could be asked for in a real man? They are held in respect by those around them, and they hold themselves in respect—for their strong nerves (which they mistake for a strong spirit), for their sober view of things (which they mistake for intelligence), for the bulge of their biceps (worthy, they think, of the "lord of nature"), for what seems to them an eagle-like gaze. But if you look at them closely, if you peek behind their imposing facade, you will find only a tangle of every possible kind of egoism. They are courageous and brave because they are physically strong males and because their infatuation with their own greatness does not permit them to exhibit cowardice. They are straightforward and honest because their awareness of these virtues permits them to rationalize self-worship. And if their eyes, having witnessed so many death agonies of the beings they have killed, remain as clear and bright as a cloudless sky, then it is not to their credit, but to their shame.

Oh, you will not find their kind among the inhabitants of the taiga or the pampas, whom they wish to resemble. They want everyone to admire how they have succeeded so well in harmonizing within themselves the cultivated European and the proud child of Nature. But the truth is that they are a product of urban civilization, just as rational, self-centered, cruel, and sensual as that civilization. But one half of their being yields to the atavistic pull of long-past stages of civilization. You encounter such people more than you would like, among physicists, biologists, journalists, businesspeople, government officials, artists, and even great scholars. There is a powerful current in world literature that has been created by such people or by those who are of kindred spirit. It weaves through the novels of Knut Hamsun, it surges into the stories of Jack London, it seethes without restraint in the poetry and writing of Kipling, and in a poisonous rivulet it spoils the genuine love for Nature in the otherwise delightful essays of Prishvin. The justification of cruelty as a so-called unavoidable law of Nature, the cult of anthrocentrism, the ideal of the strong predator, the heartless attitude toward all living beings that is masked by a romantic spirit of adventure and travel and sweetened by poetic descriptions of the natural surroundings—it is high time to call such things by their rightful names!

We have no right, absolutely no right, to purchase our pleasure at the price of the suffering and death of other living beings. If you do not know any other way to feel a part of Nature, then do not try. It is better to remain completely "outside Nature" than to be a monster within it. For in entering Nature with a gun and amusing yourself by sowing death all around, you become a pitiful pawn in the hands of the one who invented death, who invented the law of survival, and who grows fat and swollen on the suffering of living beings.

There will be others who will say, "Ha! What are animals? People are dying by the millions in our century—from wars, from starvation, from political tyranny—what a time to weep over squirrels and grouses!" Yes, it is time. And I am simply incapable of understanding what world wars, tyranny, and other human atrocities have to do with animals. Why must animals die for the amusement of heartless vacationers until humanity finally irons out its social problems and takes up the softening of hearts in its free time? What is the link between the two? Could it only be that as long as humanity afflicts itself with wars and tyranny the public conscience will be too muffled, overwhelmed, and preoccupied to feel all the vileness of hunting and fishing?

Yes, fishing, too. That same fishing that we so love to indulge in against an a idyllic backdrop of summer sunrises and sunsets, almost moved to tears by a feeling of deep inner peace. But at the same time that we pick up a squirming worm with our fingers and run a hook through its body, in our thoughtlessness we fail to realize that it is now feeling what we would feel if a monster the size of a mountain grabbed us by the leg, stuck an iron spike through our stomach, and threw us into the water to a waiting shark.

People will say, "Fine. But you do not have to fish using worms—you can use bread, lures, and so on." Yes you can. And it will no doubt be a great comfort for the caught fish to know that it will die having been fooled by a shiny piece of metal and not a worm.

One can also still come across relics from the distant past who continue to believe in all seriousness that a fish or lobster does not experience suffering because they are cold-blooded. And in actual fact, there was a time long ago when humanity, ignorant of animal anatomy, imagined that sensitivity was a function of blood temperature. Incidentally, it was because of this fallacy that the Semitic religions included fish in the list of their permitted dishes, and even saints did not shrink from indulging in it. Heaven forbid that we should condemn them for it. Religious experience, no matter how great and high it may be, cannot entirely take the place of scientific knowledge (and vice versa). Science was at that time in its infancy, and no one—not even saints—is to blame for the delusion that cold-blooded animals feel no pain. But we now know what nonsense that is! We now realize, after all, that a fish dangling from a hook or squirming on the sand is writhing in pain and nothing else! What are we to conclude then? The white raiments of poetic contemplation that we clothe ourselves in during bucolic hours of sitting with fishing rod in hand—are they not spattered to the point of revulsion with blood, mucus, and the guts of living beings, the same beings that frolicked in the crystal clear water and could have lived even longer if not for our supposed love of Nature?

One is also confronted with the rationalization that since everything in the animal world is founded on the law of the jungle, why should humans be an exception? That everything in the animal world is founded on the law of the jungle is simply not true. Or are there too few herbivores? Or have the Providential powers not wrested hundreds of species from Gagtungr's clutches in that single respect alone? Are there really too few completely harmless beings in Nature that are not even physically equipped to consume meat? What is more important, wherever did the human brain come up with the idea that the morality of animals should serve as a model for our behavior? If our hunters admire the "courage" of predators (incidentally, this is not so much courage as simple confidence in their physical strength and impunity), then why not imitate predators—the wolf, for example—in other ways, say, in killing a wounded or weakened member of one's own pack? And how can we justify confining ourselves to imitating only mammal predators? Why not take an even more striking example as a model? For instance, among spiders, is not the male devoured by the female right after fertilization? I think that such a brilliant idea will not occur to apologists of our "animal nature" only because they, as a rule, belong to the male half of humanity. If it were the female spider that was devoured by the male spider after giving birth, proponents of such a courageous mode of action would no doubt turn up among us.

But with all its grotesqueness, hunting for sport does not cause as much evil as another source, one that has arisen, unfortunately, in connection with recent progress in science and mass education.

I pick up a book from the series "A Practical Guide for High School Teachers," by a certain Y. A. Zinger and published by Uchpedgiz in 1947 under the title *Protozoa*. I open it to page 60 and read the directions on how an experiment dealing with the extraction of gregarine parasites from the intestines of a flour worm should be conducted during a biology class: "Slice open the back side of the worm and detach a section of the intestines. One can also simply cut off the head and end of the worm and then pull out the intestines from behind with tweezers. Squeeze the contents of the intestines onto a slide and, moistening it with water, look at it under low magnification."

Do you mean to say that students don't throw up watching that? Are they already inured to it? Have they already learned, with the aid of the teacher, to suppress their horror and disgust? Do they already know enough to label natural pity sentimentality? Have they learned to call a boy a "sissy" because his hands shake or his eyes display pain, revulsion, and shame during such an experiment?

I turn two pages: "Ether is used to put the frog to sleep.... There is also a simpler method: taking the frog by its hind legs and holding it belly-up, strike its head hard and quickly against the end of the desk. Then slice open the belly of the frog."

In that manner, children may very well receive a graphic lesson about parasites in a frog's intestines—something of vital necessity for everyone, I am sure, for life would be impossible without it. But the pedagogue and lover of "simpler methods" no less graphically demonstrates human vileness as well.

I have not yet addressed the essential question of whether the natural sciences can manage without experiments on *live material*. But even if those experiments were a sad necessity, what arguments can there be for inuring all high school students to them? No more than 20 percent of those children go on to a postsecondary course of study in the natural sciences or medicine. Why stifle a basic feeling of pity and cripple the very foundations of conscience in the remaining 80 percent? For the sake of what fabricated "good of humanity" do we kill hundreds of thousands of experimental animals? Why and for what? What right do we have to turn high school biology classes into lessons in the murder and torture of defenseless beings? Certainly it is not impossible to replace that bloodbath with slides, large-scale models, or diagrams. And if we want to keep to the tried and true method, then having said A we must say B. If we are to adopt the hands-on method of teaching, then why shouldn't a history teacher who is discussing the Inquisition stage an instructive demonstration that familiarizes students in a concrete manner with the use of Spanish boots, garrotes, the rack, and other scientific and technological achievements of the day?

And now a few more words about "live material" in general. Scientists have become so accustomed to their own terminology that they no longer notice what moral sterility, what petrifaction of conscience resounds in the stilted, crudely utilitarian phrase "live material." Regarding the subject of live material in scientific laboratories, and the use of that method in science in general, what is done is done, the dead cannot be brought back to life, and it is pointless to argue whether scientific progress in previous centuries would have been possible without it. But is it possible now? It is the desire to economize one's efforts that is to blame for scientists focusing their attention on that method as the cheapest and easiest way to their goal. Having become legalized, it now appears to many to be irreplaceable, the only feasible method. Nonsense! It is laziness that prevents them from spending time and energy on developing a different method, that and the stinginess of the public and private sectors, nothing more. Laziness and stinginess are, generally speaking, disreputable traits, and when they prove to be responsible for such mounds of victims, how are we properly to view them?

Of course, to seek out single-handedly a new methodology is a hopeless task. Thousands of young doctors, teachers, and laboratory assistants, on beginning their careers, experience a natural feeling of revulsion for the scientific techniques associated with the torture and killing of living beings. But as things stand, every such person faces a dilemma: either stifle their compassion with rationalizations about the good of humanity or abandon a career in science, since there is no other methodology. The overwhelming majority, of course, choose the former and gradually become more and more inured in the practice of inhumane methods. The discovery of a new methodology is realistically possible only as the result of a long-term commitment by a large collective body—an association made up of people working in various branches of science—devoted to that goal. Such an undertaking can be realized only if it is funded by a wealthy body in the public or private sector.

But the victims of our "love of Nature" and the victims of our "thirst for knowledge" are but hillocks or knolls next to the Mont Blancs, the Everests of fish netted on the open sea, of the corpses of cattle and pigs piled high in slaughterhouses—in short, the corpses we buy in stores and consume at finely set tables. Even worse, the utilitarianism of technological progress has at last reached the peak where it has been proved cheaper to can crabs, for example, without killing them first, but instead ripping their shells off while they are alive, cutting off their claws, and throwing what's left of the half-alive crab back into the sea to be eaten by some passing fish. It would be a good idea to give the inventor of that crab-canning apparatus a few years holiday in solitary confinement. Let the inventor spend time pondering the question of whether he or she is a human being or not. And it would be even more gratifying to have the enterprising industrial manager, thanks to whose zealousness those torture devices for crabs and lobsters were adopted by the industry, on the other side of the wall, in the next cell, on vacation from money-saving concerns.

Let's suppose such abominations are extreme cases and will soon be eliminated. How are we to regard meat and fish as products of mass consumption? Or the manufacture of leather? Or the processing of animal fur? Even if all this is not very moral, is it not a necessity?

True, we are still faced with an element of necessity in this respect, but, if the truth be stated, it is already much less than is thought. It can be said that we are approaching a level of scientific and social progress—thank heavens—where nothing will remain of that necessity but painful memories.

Every year, applied chemistry is improving the quality of leather substitutes. Artificial fur is becoming cheaper and more readily available than the natural variety, and if it is still inferior to it in quality, in time that defect will be rectified. The time is thus approaching when the processing of animal skins or furs for commercial purposes could be banned. What is truly the most difficult question is the problem of fish and meat, which many people consider necessary for their health.

But why, in truth, are they necessary? It is not meat or fish per se that are necessary, but a definite quantity of carbohydrates, proteins, and calories. But we can supply our body with them through other kinds of food: dairy products, cereals, fruits, and vegetables. It is ridiculous to pretend that we are unaware of the existence of millions of vegetarians who live healthy lives. All of us are also well aware that for thousands of years a nation of millions has existed that consumes hardly any meat—a fact that is unpleasant for our conscience but true. More nutritional substitutes will no doubt be required to make up for fish and meat dishes in a northern climate than in tropical India. It is also true that at present such nutritional substitutes cost more and are therefore not within everyone's budget. The solution of the problem thus consists in raising the overall standard of living. But it has become a truism, after all, that humanity's prosperity increases along with progress. And the time is not far off when such nutritional substitutes will be affordable for everyone.

A program, a chain of step-by-step measures thus begins to take shape, a program that will become realizable after the Rose of the World's ascension to power. The first set of measures will be carried out without delay.

1. A ban on painful methods of killing animals, whether in industry or anywhere else.

2. A ban on experiments on "live material" in schools or anywhere else, with the exception of specially designated scientific institutions.

3. A total ban on experiments on animals without the use of soporifics or anesthetics.

4. The establishment and funding of large scientific bodies for research into and development of a new experimental method in science.

5. The restriction of sport hunting and fishing to the extermination of predators.

6. A revamping of the educational system that would ingrain a love for animals in primary and secondary school students, an unselfish love born not of an awareness of a given species' usefulness but of an organic need to love and help all beings weaker and less developed than humans.

7. Widespread promotion of the new attitude toward animals.

But the core of the new attitude will not only entail protecting animals from torture and murder by humans. That is only its negative side, and there is nothing new there. Its positive side, which is indeed new, entails providing active assistance to the animal world in its evolution and reducing the number of stages and the time span needed for that evolution.

But what does that mean? It means the establishment of "peace" between humans and animals, excluding predators; research into methods for the reorientation of certain predatory species; renunciation of the use of any animal for the purposes of security; and the artificial acceleration of the intellectual and spiritual development of certain higher species in the animal world.

Enormous funds will have to be invested in the development of "zoopsychology." Fine! No amount of funds can make amends for the evil we have done to the animal world over these thousands of years. A new branch of knowledge will appear:

zoopedagogy, the pedagogy of animals. Careful study will lead to the singling out of some species of predators that, like the dog and cat, can be reoriented. Did I not already mention that the one-time wolf has before our very eyes become capable of digesting plant food? And that is in spite of the fact that humans did not try to curb but, to the contrary, cultivated its instinct for blood in the interests of hunting and security. If not for that, what playfulness, what meekness, what goodness would we now witness in dogs in addition to their loyalty, courage, and intelligence! And who can doubt that such work on many predatory species, work done by people equipped with a knowledge of animal psychology, physiology, pedagogy, and more importantly, love, can reorient them, help them to evolve physically and intellectually, soften their hearts, and transform them?

Even now, dogs are capable of remembering as many as two hundred words, and not mechanically, like a parrot, but with full awareness of their meaning. They are beings with truly immense potential. Their development has reached the point where the species can make a giant leap forward. It is up to us to ensure that that radical transformation takes place in our lifetime, to see that the inadaptability of some of the dog's organs do not retard its evolution for centuries to come. The emergence of speech in dogs is not impeded by their overall level of intelligence but by a purely mechanical barrier in the form of the unsuitable structure of those organs necessary for speech. Its overall development is also impeded by another barrier: the absence of extremities for grasping, or rather, the inability of their paws to perform those functions performed by our hands. Yet another branch of animal physiology will develop: a science concerned with biochemical engineering of the embryo to effect the structural changes necessary for the accelerated development of speech organs and the transformation of its forepaws into hands. Dogs' mastery of speech, even if only a few dozen words, will have a trickle-down effect on the rate of their overall growth in intelligence. In one hundred years people will have extraordinary friends who, thanks to human help, will have shortened their allotted path to the span of a few generations instead of a hundred thousand years.

The next candidates for accelerated development will probably be cats, elephants, bears, and perhaps some species of rodents. Horses, which have progressed very far intellectually and are indubitably morally superior to cats and dogs, are endowed with an unfortunate feature, hooves, that prevents them from entering onto that path any time soon. The same is true of deer and buffalo. Elephants, which are endowed with a marvelous trunk for grasping, face a different impediment: their size, which requires an inordinate amount of food. It is possible, however, that science will discover a way to shrink their size and thus remove the chief obstacle to the rapid development of their intellect. It is reasonable to suppose that elephants will not lose any of their extraordinary charm if, while endowed with the gift of speech, they do not surpass a modern-day baby elephant in size.

Thus, after a certain period of time the Rose of the World will be able to carry out a second set of measures.

1. A ban on the murder of animals for any kind of commercial or scientific purpose.
2. Tight restrictions on animal slaughter for the purpose of consumption.
3. The designation of large tracts of land as wildlife parks in all countries, so that animals that are not domesticated may live in their natural habitat.
4. Freedom of movement—both in Nature and in populated areas—for both traditionally and recently domesticated species.
5. The coordination of the work of zoopedagogical institutes on a global scale, the prioritization of that work, and research into endowing the higher animals with the gift of speech.
6. Particularly careful research into artificially weakening the predatory nature of certain animals.

This is how the creative work of elevating animals will proceed—work that is selfless, not prompted by narrow material interests but by feelings of guilt and love. It will be a growing love that will be too broad in scope to confine itself to humans alone.

It will be a love that will find solutions to problems that now appear insoluble. For instance, where will we find room for all those animals if humans stop killing them en masse? Will not the same thing happen on a global scale that happened with rabbits in Australia, where they multiplied at an alarming rate and became the scourge of agriculture? But those fears resemble Malthusianism extrapolated to the animal world. It is impossible at present, of course, to envision the measures that will be discovered and undertaken in that regard by our descendants. At the very worst, specific quotas will have to be set. If they are surpassed then society at the end of the twenty-first century will be forced to resort to the artificial regulation of animal birth rates. There is, however, reason to hope that the problem will be solved differently, in a manner that is impossible to foresee at the current level of science, technology, economics, and morality. But even were there to be quotas, it would still be an infinitely lesser evil than what is taking place now. The sum of suffering caused by humans would be greatly reduced, and that is, after all, our goal.

The sum of good done will correspondingly increase, becoming what the Hindus speak of as *pram sagar*—an ocean of love. The proverbial image of the lion lying down with the lamb or child is not at all utopian. That will come to pass. It was an intuition granted to great prophets who knew the heart of humanity. The descendants of modern-day hares and tapirs, leopards and squirrels, bears and crows, giraffes and lizards will not dwell in cages, or even in wildlife preserves, but in our cities, parks, groves, and meadows. They will not fear people but will show them affection and play with them, working together with them on improving the natural and cultural environment and on fostering their own self-development. By the next century, economic prosperity will reach almost incredible levels, and feeding those gentle, peaceful, affectionate, and intelligent beings will pose no problems. And generations to come will read with a shudder of how, not so long before, humans used not only to eat the corpses of animals they themselves had killed but even took pleasure in hunting them down and cold-heartedly murdering them.

BOOK VI

The Highest Worlds of Shadanakar

1 Up to the World Salvaterra

IT SHOULD COME as no surprise that I not only have much less
information at my disposal about the regions in question here
than about any others but that, in essence, I am almost entirely
lacking in such information. There are two reasons for that. The
first reason is the incommensurability of the reality of those
regions with our earthly images, ideas, and language. The second reason is the exceptionally high level of spiritual insight
needed to gain a personal glimpse of those worlds. Almost nothing of what is said about them here has been gleaned from my
own first-hand experience. Rather, I am only communicating in
words what I grasped from the accounts of my invisible friends.
May they forgive me if I err in some way, if my mind introduces
anything unworthy or purely human into their accounts or
clouds them with subjective additions.

All the planes to be discussed first are five-dimensional. As for
time streams—that is, the parallel currents of time—they are
more than two hundred in number on those planes. That alone
should be sufficient to convey how feeble must be attempts to
express the nature and meaning of those regions using human
images. Customary geometrical notions must be discarded outright, but attempts to fill in the gap with concepts dealing with
energies, force fields, and the like are also doomed to failure.

Far above the sakwala of the Transmyths of the Five Higher
Religions (I have already described them as five gigantic, varicol-
ored pyramids of glowing crystals) and encompassing all Shadanakar rises the indescribable sakwala of the Synclite of Humanity,
a sakwala of seven regions. There, oceans of radiant ethers—I use
that word for lack of a better one—glittering with colors beyond

the imagination of even the Synclites of the metacultures lap upon structures that bear a vague resemblance both to shining mountain peaks and to buildings of some inconceivable architecture. The fundamental dissimilarity between the great works of human genius and the great creations of Nature does not hold true there, for both elements have at last merged in a synthesis that is beyond our powers to grasp. How can we hope to capture a sense of those euphoric masterpieces brimming with the light in which the beautiful spirits of mature elementals have coated themselves? Or of the resplendent waves of sound that soar upward as if from the blissful heart of celestial mountains? I will have achieved my purpose if even a few readers of this book gain a sense, through those almost amorphous images, of a reality that our spirit can strive toward but that is beyond the reach of almost everyone who lives on our dark and arid Earth.

If I remember correctly, the chosen few who at present compose the Synclite of Humanity number no more than a thousand. Although they no longer possess a human appearance, they willingly assume a higher, enlightened human likeness when they descend to lower planes. Borne along by the Sun's rays, they are able to travel distances between the bramfaturas of the solar system at the speed of light.

Beyond their names, I know nothing about the various regions of the Synclite of Humanity, and even those names I know only to the extent I was able to translate them into the sounds of human language.[1]

More than a hundred people from Monsalvat and Eden have already entered the Synclite of Humanity. The huge, ancient Indian metaculture has contributed even more. If I remember correctly, the last one before 1955 to rise to the World Synclite was Ramakrishna. Approximately seventy years passed from the moment of his death in Enrof until his entry into those higher regions. But it is more common for that ascent to take several centuries. For example, it was only relatively recently that the

---

1. Arvantakernis. Dyedarnis. Ranmatirnis. Serbarinus. Magraleinos. Ivaroinis. Nammarinos.

prophet Muhammad reached the World Synclite, even though his afterlife had not been marred by any descent. The prophets Ezekiel and Daniel, who have long abided in the World Synclite, as well as Vasily the Great, will soon ascend from the Synclite of Humanity even higher.

That is all I am able to say about the regions of that sakwala. But I have even less to say, and in an even dryer, terser manner, about the eleven regions of the following sakwala of the Great Hierarchies.

Those are the worlds of the very same higher beings who cannot be called anything but great hierarchies. In their time many of them were objects of worship in the ancient religions of various countries. Those exalted beings were mirrored—if only to a limited extent—in the divine pantheons of the Egyptian, Babylonian, Greek, Old Germanic, and Aztec religions, as well as in some aspects of the higher Indian deities. They were mirrored, not as they are now, but as they were then, or rather, as they appeared to the consciousness of the peoples who intuited them in olden times. In the centuries that have passed since the rise and flowering of their cults in Enrof, the hierarchies have risen to their greatest heights.

I do know that the regions of that sakwala are no longer delineated according to one or another hierarchy's link with a specific metaculture. Those lower planes of Shadanakar that are divided vertically and form the segments of human metacultures have been left far behind, or rather, far below. The borders between regions in the sakwala of the Great Hierarchies are determined by the power and height attained by each of those beings.

As before, I know only the names of those planes. I have little confidence in the correspondence between their phonetic structure, as expressed by our letters, and their actual sound. There is no doubt that these names should be treated as only very rough approximations: Aolinor, Ramnagor, Pleiragor, Foraigor, Stranganor, Tseliror, Likhanga, Devenga, Siringa, Khranga, and Ganga.

If, during the stage of metahistorical formulation, one gives free reign to the reason, it will, by its very nature, attempt to introduce conventional notions from the physical and historical plane and logical, scientific-like parameters into the scope, configurations, and specific character of metahistory. In this particular case, reason's propensity for uniformity and order, naïvely viewed as symmetry, causes it to assume that identical groups of hierarchies taking part in people's lives preside over—in the metahistorical sense—all the suprapeoples. In reality that is not so.

It is true that there is no suprapeople over which a demiurge does not preside, for then it would not be a suprapeople but a random conglomeration of a number of ethnic groups that share nothing in common. Nor is there a nation that does not have a Collective Ideal Soul, for such a nation would then be a numerical sum of individuals who have chanced to gravitate together for a brief time. But the Collective Ideal Soul is far from being the totality of psychological or other, easily recognizable attributes of a given people that determine their distinct historical path. The Collective Ideal Soul is a being with a single great monad. She harbors the prototypes of the highest potential of the nation within herself and is coated in multidimensional matter. In proportion to the historical growth of the nation and the personal growth of individuals within that nation, a greater and greater portion of subtle materiality from each of them gravitates toward her and is encompassed within her, thus imparting to her a collective nature.

There are several national collective souls in almost every metaculture, but as a rule, one of them belongs to a different hierarchy than the others. Only she is *God-born*, as is the demiurge of the suprapeople, and only she is linked to him by a special, mysterious, spiritual, and material bond of love. Together such collective souls form the hierarchy of the *Great Sisters*. In Earth's bramfatura, there are about forty of them.

Every distinct nation has a Collective Soul, but the other sisters belong to the category of God-created monads. They, the Younger Sisters, are paired with national guiding spirits, the inspirers of those nations who are part of the suprapeople but do not play the leading role in its history. Some of the Younger

Sisters, however, proceed along their metahistorical path without a national guiding spirit as companion.

There are also transitional phases, sometimes lasting a century or more, when a nation, its Collective Soul, and the national guiding spirit remain stranded outside the metacultures, between them, as it were. The peoples of the Balkans, who were at one time part of the Byzantine metaculture, can be cited as an example. The Greeks, Serbs, and Croats were enslaved by one of the Witzraors of the Muslim metaculture, and at present they abide in the gap between the Roman Catholic and Russian metacultures. No less tragic is the fate of the Bulgarian people, who were also part of the Byzantine suprapeople and were destined for a great future of primacy, both spiritual and cultural, in the Eastern Christian world. The Turkish Witzraor put an end to those prospects once and for all, crippling the Bulgarian nation by clipping its spiritual wings, so to speak. It has now begun to merge with the Russian suprapeople. As for the Rumanians, they are only just starting to emerge as a nation. Their Collective Soul and national guiding spirit as yet preside very high above them, barely maintaining a link with the ethnic group in Enrof, and the time is still far off when they will mature to full strength.

The demiurge of a suprapeople is also a great God-born monad, a monad more powerful and active than a collective soul and alien to any collectivity. He is one in himself.

One of the Great Sisters—each of whom is the Collective Soul of the leading nation in the metaculture—is paired with him. There are, however, more complex liaisons. In the North-Western metaculture, for instance, the demiurge of the suprapeople was until the nineteenth century paired with the Collective Soul of Germany. But the second German Witzraor grew to be so strong during that century that the Collective Soul's imprisonment in one of the citadels of Mudgarb turned into an almost complete enslavement of her will, and the demiurge entered into a union with another Great Sister, the Collective Soul of England.

The birth of monads of either hierarchy—the demiurges of suprapeoples and the Great Sisters—by the everlasting Universal

Sun can be neither understood nor imagined by us, and any rationalization on that count is doomed to remain empty speculation.
The same can be said of attempts to fill the gaps in our knowledge
about those stages of cosmic growth preceding the monads'
appearance in Shadanakar. In what bramfaturas, in what forms,
and through what stages did they journey and incarnate before
entering the confines of our planet? I may be mistaken but, for us,
such interbramfaturic mysteries are, I think, transcendental.
Both those hierarchies enter the range of our apprehension (and
that is apprehension, not in the form of metahistorical enlightenment, but only in the form of the passive reception of information
from the lips of our invisible friends) at the moment of their meta-
ether birth. We will use the term *meta-ether* provisionally to designate what happens when their monads enter five-dimensional
space in Shadanakar. From the Planetary Logos, Who can also be
understood as the Being that has become the supreme demiurge
of our bramfatura, they receive a certain stimulus: *the creative
impulse to realize and express themselves in the three- and four-dimensional materiality of a future suprapeople*, which had not existed up till
then and could not have existed without them. It is that stimulus
that causes them to descend, coating themselves in denser, four-
dimensional materiality, and embark in that manner on their
planetary cycle. That is their second, or astral, birth in Shadanakar. They of course never undergo physical birth. I realize that
it is not an easy concept to grasp, but I doubt that it can be
explained any simpler.

The worlds where these hierarchies abide in the interval
between these two births and where their monads abide during
the entire course of their cycle in Shadanakar form the sakwala
of the Demiurges. It comprises three regions. The birthplace of
the demiurges and Great Sisters—the ideal souls of suprapeoples—is called *Rangaraidr*. The names of the other two are *Astr*
and *Oamma*. Astr is the birthplace and abode of the monads of
the Younger Sisters and the national guiding spirits. I am unable
to say anything about Oamma.

I do, however, know that in the last five hundred years one
demiurge has emerged from the rest and has undertaken a

mission of global, not just suprapeople, significance: the demiurge of the North-Western metaculture. From his labors during the last few centuries certain prior conditions have been created for the unification of humanity into one whole. In the near future the global leadership of that task will likely pass for a short time to the demiurge of the Russian suprapeople, and then to the demiurge of India. After that, from all appearances, the leadership will no longer be concentrated in one single demiurge.

Yarosvet and Navna are the names that I have provisionally and arbitrarily adopted to refer to the hierarchies of the Russian metaculture. I do not know the actual names of the demiurges and Great Sisters. In any case they cannot be rendered in any human language.[2]

The metahistorical task—a task of planetary importance—to be realized by Yarosvet and Navna's future marital union and by their whole life in Shadanakar in general can be roughly stated as the generation by them (or to be more exact, the ether embodiment through them) of a Great Feminine Monad.[3] A personal, physical incarnation for her is, of course, unthinkable. But she is prepared in time to flow into an ether vessel, one that is enlightened, individual, living, and immaculate. This vessel will appear at the same time as its crystallization in Enrof in the form of the Global Community. The Russian people are regarded by their demiurge as an ether-physical substance still unenlightened in Enrof but enlightened in Heavenly Russia, a substance from which these two—physical and ether—vessels of Light will be

---

2. I hope that the reader will understand that the use of any customary anthropomorphic concepts of age, marital relations, and so on in reference to the hierarchies is resorted to only for the purpose of bringing us closer, through the use of the only possible, albeit distant, analogies, to a conception of phenomena that literally share almost nothing in common with phenomena familiar to us.

3. By the term *ether* I mean a materiality more rarefied and higher than the physical. The materiality of the worlds of Enlightenment, the zatomis, and the elementals of Light is composed of ether. To refer to even more rarefied materiality—typical, for example, of the sakwala of Higher Purpose and the sakwala of Angels—the term astral is used, while the term meta-ether refers to the most rarefied of materiality imaginable. It is the materiality of the highest planes of Shadanakar. The word spiritual is used in reference to everything situated even higher on the hierarchical ladder.

wrought. At the same time, the Russian people are regarded as the site of that theurgical act.

Above the sakwala of the Demiurges and Great Sisters soars a sakwala that I can designate only with the term *Waves of Universal Femininity*. *Limuarna*, the first of its regions, is the feminine Synclite of Humanity, while *Bayushmi*, the second, is the present abode of the Great Feminine Monad. I know only the names of the remaining regions of that sakwala: *Faolemmis*, *Saora*, and *Naolitis*. I am not privy to the name of the sixth, and last, of those regions.

That sakwala is encompassed within another—the worlds of interaction between the hierarchies of Shadanakar, those of the macrobramfatura, and those of the Universe. Of these three worlds I am only able to name the middle one—*Raoris*, the initial abode of the Great Feminine Monad when She emanated into Shadanakar.

From there begin the planes of the One Church of our bramfatura, which encompasses, in addition to the sakwala I have just mentioned, the three regions of an even higher sakwala: the Elite of Shadanakar. Oceans of repeatedly enlightened and spiritualized matter ebb and flow around it. Their shining crests, meeting no obstacles at its transparent boundaries, glide inside and, breaking over that abode of the Perfected, impart to it the fullness of life. The humanity of Enrof, the humankind of daemons, the lunar humankind, the angels, the elementals, and even the animal world, whose metaphysical meaning has been such a profound enigma—all find their highest purpose and supremely transfigured essence in the heart of that paradise most high, which blends within it peace and strength, bliss and work, perfection and limitless growth ever further along a dazzling path. There abide all those who see the World Salvaterra with their own eyes. It is the highest step on the staircase of Shadanakar for all its monads, both God-born and God-created, except the Planetary Logos, the Virgin Mary, and the Great Feminine Spirit. All that I can do while on the subject of the Elite of Shadanakar is list the last human names of some of those great human spirits who have reached the Elite: Akhenaton, Zoroaster, Moses, Hosia,

Lao-tse, Gautama Buddha, Mahavira, Asoka, Chandragupta Maurya, Patanjali, Nagarjuna, Samudra Gupta, Kanishka, Shankara, Aristotle, Plato, all the Apostles except Paul, Titurel, Mary Magdalene, John of Damascus, St. Augustine, St. Francis of Assisi, Joan of Arc, Dante, Leonardo da Vinci.

We have now brought this survey of the structure of Shadanakar to its conclusion, to the very highest of the sakwalas, whose three regions encompass our entire bramfatura: the Region of the Planetary Logos, the Region of the Virgin Mary, and the Region of the Great Feminine Monad.

For purely personal reasons, I am accustomed to calling the focal point and summit of Shadanakar the *World Salvaterra*—a name quite provisional, of course, even arbitrary, having not even a distant connection to Palestine, the Salvaterra of the medieval Crusaders. I do not in the slightest insist on it, but I am forced to use it for lack of a better name.

To varying degrees, the World Salvaterra permeates all of Shadanakar, except the four worlds of the Demonic Base and Sufetkh. It is most fully manifested in the upper reaches of the atmosphere. The religious meaning attached to the word "heavens" is not the result of an aberration by ignorant minds from olden times but the expression of a reality that great souls intuited thousands of years ago.

All that is Providential in the history of Shadanakar, humanity, and individual souls has its origin in Salvaterra. It is the locus of the emanations of the higher cosmic Beings who manifest themselves both in the evolution of galactic worlds and in our evolution. "Shining Crystal of Heavenly Will" is an epithet applicable to the World Salvaterra, and not only in a poetic sense. Constant waves of grace and energy pour down from those heights and from out of those depths. Such terms as "resplendent sound of church bells" or "sounding resplendence" could be of hardly any aid to us in approaching a conception of them. That which such imagery hints at has been left far below, in the worlds of angels, in the sakwala of Higher Purpose, or in the World Synclite. Even what the Biblical story of Jacob's Ladder tried to describe ends there, having passed through all of Shadanakar. Great essences and great beings climb and descend the steps of material existence from Salvaterra to Earth and back again. It is the heart of the planet and its inner Sun. Through it and it alone open the heights, expanses and depths of the Spiritual Universe, which encompasses both the stellar archipelagoes and the metagalactic oceans of space that to us appear so empty.

The Spiritual Universe cannot be described in any language and can only be experienced, of course, in the vaguest of intuitions. The highest spiritual rapture of Christian mystics, the highest level of ecstasy among Hindus, or the *abhijna* of Buddha are all states connected with these same vague intuitions. Our systematic reason tries to pour them into the molds of teachings in order to initiate the many, and thus creates dim echoes of it, such as the teachings of the Tao, Pleroma, Empirei, or the breath of Parabrahma.

When voyagers from variomaterial worlds speak of Eden, as do the teachers of Semitic religions, or of the chambers of Brahma or Vishnu, of the heavens of Iranian azurs or Hindu devas, of the blessed land of Sukavati, even of Nirvana, they assume as their final goal only individual levels within Shadanakar, the summits of various metacultures and the highest transmyths of religions, or, in the end, the reality of the World Salvaterra.

When humankind—both physical and extraphysical—completes its colossal cycle, and when all the dominions of terrestrial Nature complete it as well, they will have wholly merged with that planetary Paradise. Then the World Salvaterra will open up like a flower into the waiting expanses of the Spiritual Universe. The Universal Sun will shine on that flower and admit the flower's fragrant radiations into its heavens.

But even then the ultimate goal will still be immeasurably far off. It is at present beyond the reach of even the most dazzling intuitions.

2 The Logos of Shadanakar

AS FAR AS I KNOW at present, all the countless numbers of monads fall into two ontologically distinct categories. God-born monads represent one category. They are fewer. They are greater in stature, having issued directly from out of the unfathomable depths of the Creator. They are destined to lead worlds, from the start assuming that leadership unblemished by moral falls or setbacks, and continuing to grow only greater in glory and strength. No one besides themselves can apprehend, or will ever apprehend, the mystery of their divine birth. In Shadanakar, the Planetary Logos, Zventa-Sventana, the Demiurges of the suprapeoples, the Great Sisters, and some of the Great Hierarchies are God-born monads. No demonic monad in Shadanakar numbers among them, though one should not forget that Lucifer is a God-born monad, the only one to turn from God.

The rest of the world's monads belong to the other category, those that are God-created. Each of them can apprehend the mystery of their creation by God, though only, of course, at an extremely high level of ascent.

The Planetary Logos is a great God-born monad, the seat of divine reason in our bramfatura, the oldest and first of all its monads. He differs from all the other monads in that, as the Word is the expression of the Speaker, He expresses one of the hypostases of the Trinity: that of God the Son. The Logos of Shadanakar is proceeding along a path of creative work and ascent up the cosmic staircase, a path beyond our conception, and no bramfatura, besides demonic ones, can exist without such a monad. For one such monad appears in every bramfatura at the dawn of its existence and remains the locus of

Providence and the Divine Spirit throughout the evolution of all its sakwalas.

The Planetary Logos descended to Shadanakar as soon as the materiality created by the hierarchies for the bramfatura was capable of accommodating Him. The plane to which He first descended was later to become Iroln. The plane was readied through the efforts of the Logos to accommodate a multitude of young, God-created monads. But those efforts were insufficient to safeguard Shadanakar from the invasion of Gagtungr, and the Planetary Logos and hosts of monads of Light were forced to engage in battle with him. Illumined global laws alien to suffering, death, and any kind of darkness were created. The foundation for the first, angelic, humankind was laid by the Planetary Logos Himself and Lilith, whose essence at that time was as yet untainted by the demonic yetzer hara. While a constant struggle raged with the demonic camp, Olirna was created, as were the sakwalas of Higher Purpose, of the Great Hierarchies, and of the Great Elementals. In addition, those planes that later became the sakwalas of emanations from the other planets, the Sun, and Astrafire were being readied. Some of the planes created then no longer exist: for instance, those planes the human angels used to rise to, after having attained enlightenment. And since the materiality of those beings was not tainted by a yetzer hara, no moral falls cast a shadow on the ascent of angelic humankind.

What is meant by the concept of original sin occurred between Lilith and Gagtungr when the latter invaded her world. As a result, all beings in whose densely material family chain Lilith took or has taken part carry a yetzer hara, the satanic seed. In demonic beings the yetzer hara holds sway over the monad, while in all others it holds sway, at the very worst, over the shelt. As for the story of Adam and Eve, all the planes, eras, and hierarchies in it have become so muddled that it is better to pass over that legend. In any case, universal expiation—that is, the incineration of all yetzer haras—would have eventually been accomplished by Christ had His mission in Enrof not been curtailed.

Like a mirror image of the descent of the angelic monads into Shadanakar, Gagtungr created a densely material plane where lesser demons underwent incarnation. These were the same demons who in time turned into the monsters of modern times: Witzraors, velgas, ryphras, igvas, and the angels of darkness. At the same time that angelic humankind was ascending, organic life in Enrof, which had been entrusted to the care of the animal world, began to emerge. The animal world was envisaged as a grand community of new, young, God-created monads commissioned to descend to very dense planes of materiality in order to enlighten them.

After Gagtungr succeeded in perverting the laws of life in Enrof, leaving his imprint on the animal world and in that way marring the Providential design, a second, Titan, humankind was created through the efforts of the Planetary Logos. Its purpose was identical to that of all the communities of Light: the enlightenment of matter. In time they were meant to relocate to Enrof and oversee the enlightenment of the animal world and of certain elementals that had been demonized or checked in their growth. But with the revolt and fall of the Titans, yet another catastrophe overtook the Providential powers. The demise of the second humankind boosted Gagtungr's power to a level he had never before known. The animal world had only been slowed in its development and the Titans were cast down to the worlds of Retribution only to escape later, but the Lunar humankind, which had been created by the Planetary Logos and His forces, was dealt an even more crushing blow in the post-Titan period, and having passed through a phase when almost all its shelts became demonized, it disappeared altogether from the face of Enrof. That took place approximately eight hundred thousand years ago, when man began to evolve from the animal world in terrestrial Enrof and the Planetary Logos and His camp created the daemon humankind on other three-dimensional planes. Its creation was necessitated by the urgency of reinforcing the camp of Light and by the fact that more and more hosts of monads flowing out of the depths of the Creator were seeking ways to descend to the densely material planes to enlighten them. The daemons were not commissioned with the task of enlightening the animal world—their planes are in no way connected with animals—but one of their tasks was, and is, the enlightenment of elementals checked in their growth.

As for the so-called dawn of humanity—that is, the era of the emergence of the human species from the animal world—it was an extremely bleak and dreary dawn. Prehistoric humanity can and should be pitied, but not idealized: it was violent, mean, and crudely utilitarian. It knew of absolutely nothing spiritual besides magic, and magic is by its very nature utilitarian and self-seeking. A microscopic minority slowly conceived a mystifying sense of the Great Elementals and the first tremblings of an appreciation for beauty. The first mass experience of the trans-physical side of reality was the revelation of the omnipresent arungvilta-prana.

The slow process whereby the spiritual filtered into human consciousness proceeded millennium after millennium, drop by drop. Every few centuries, a certain charge of energy, as it were, a kind of spiritual quantum, would accumulate in the subconscious of individuals and suddenly burst into their hearts and minds. They were messengers of sorts, the first people on missions of Light. Small groups formed around them, and the first steps on the road to spiritual growth were discovered. It is difficult to pinpoint when that began, but flashes are perceptible as early as the late Cro-Magnon period. A long period of regression then ensued, followed by new sparks in the Americas that, on the eve of the rise of the Atlantean culture, at last combined to form unbroken chains of Light.

The demise of Atlantis jeopardized all the gains in spirituality made during those cheerless centuries. A fine thread managed to be spirited off to Africa and relayed to Egypt via the Sudanese culture. Another thread was conveyed to America. Then began centuries of constant anxiety for all the powers of Light, as the onslaught of darkness was such that the thread was sometimes embodied on Earth in a single person. It is not easy to imagine their incomparable feeling of isolation and the malevolent darkness raging all around them. I could list a few strange-sounding, unfamiliar names, but it is better to say that those prophets and heroes of the spirit from the bloody dawn of humanity were later to weave into their garlands those beautiful and bright flowers whose names are known to us all now: Akhenaton, Zoroaster, Moses, Hosia, the Buddha, Mahavira, Lao-tse, John the Apostle. The future Gautama Buddha weathered an especially fierce struggle. It took place among the African tribes in the vicinity of Lake Chad, before the rise of the Sudanese culture, when the already fading light of Atlantean wisdom and spirituality flickered in the soul of that single person alone. The thread conveyed to America had been snipped, and he was the only flame of spirit left on the globe. By standards later applied to messengers and prophets, he was far from outstanding, but he was alone, and nothing else need be said. The Synclite of Atlantis was too far removed geographically to help him in any concrete way, and he did not yet know how to tap with his waking consciousness into the energy extended by other forces of Light. It seemed to him that he was all alone, engaged in an endless battle in darkness. Fortunately, he acquired several worthy disciples at the close of that incarnation and all was saved. In that lies the unbelievable nature of his feat: that was all accomplished without a Synclite!

Approximately ten thousand years ago, when Atlantis was at its zenith, the Planetary Logos incarnated in Zheram, the Enrof of daemons. Gagtungr was unable to thwart or interfere with His mission in the daemon world, nor was Gagtungr able to kill His bodily incarnation before it had been imbued with the full power of the Logos. The path of the Logos in the daemon world ended in His apotheosis, and the entire sakwala embarked on a road of successive stages of enlightenment. The mission of the Logos in the daemon world resembled His later mission among humanity, but there it was brought to a successful conclusion, which in turn accelerated the sakwala's development.

Before taking a human form in which His essence would be fully reflected, the Great Spirit made a preliminary descent, incarnating approximately seven thousand years ago in Gondwana. He became a great teacher there. Humanity, however, was as yet unprepared to assimilate the spirituality flowing down through the incarnated Logos. But a profound and pure esoteric teaching was formulated and its first seeds sown, seeds that were later to be carried by the winds of history to the soil of other countries and cultures: India, Egypt, China, Iran, Babylon. The incarnation of the Logos in Gondwana did not yet possess the same fullness that was later manifested in Jesus Christ; it was essentially nothing more than a preparation for the later descent.

What people, culture, and country were to be the setting for Christ's life did not become clear, of course, all at once. A precisely-formulated monotheism, not professed by just a handful but embraced by the people as a whole, was a prerequisite. Otherwise the psychological soil necessary for the revelation of God the Son would have been lacking. But the geographical and historical factors that shaped the cultural and religious character of the Indian and Chinese peoples deprived monotheism of any means of filtering into the consciousness of the masses. The monotheistic teaching of Lao-tse and similar movements in Brahmanism remained virtually esoteric doctrines. All of them were limited to the spiritual ecstasies of individual adepts and private theosophical speculations.

The unmatched religious genius of the Indian peoples enabled them to assimilate the revelations of many Great Hierarchies and to create a Synclite unrivaled in size. But the great Indian pantheon eclipsed, as it were, the even higher reality of the World Salvaterra. The Indian religious consciousness had long been accustomed to the idea of hierarchies incarnating as people and even animals; it was therefore unable to grasp the altogether exceptional and specific nature of the Planetary Logos's incarnation, its complete and fundamental dissimilarity from the avatars of Vishnu or the incarnations of any other powers of Light. Buddhism, with all its brilliant moral teachings, avoided a precise formulation of the question of the Absolute. The Buddha, like Mahavira, believed that when it came to salvation people did better to rely solely on their own efforts. That mistaken belief was prompted by the negative side of the terrible spiritual experience he had acquired during his solitary vigil in the midst of planetary night—an experience he recalled after becoming Gautama but was clearly unable to fathom fully. One way or another, the Buddhist teaching, by avoiding profession of the One God, struck India once and for all from the list of potential sites of the Planetary Logos's incarnation.

In the fourteenth century B.C. the first attempt in history was made to establish a clearly formulated, Sun-centered monotheism as a national religion. It took place in Egypt, and the giant figure of its pharaoh reformer towers to this day over the horizon of past centuries as an example of one of history's first prophets. What utter isolation that genius poet and seer must have felt, concluding his inspired hymn to the One God with the tragic plaint: "And no one knows You besides Your Son, Akhenaton!"

One should not, however, take that plaint too literally. There was at least one person who shared his feeling of isolation. The role of Queen Nefertiti, his wife, as an inspirer of and participant in the religious reforms can hardly be exaggerated. That astonishing woman traversed the golden sands of her country as a messenger of the same heavenly Light as her spouse. Both of them, inseparably bound together by creative work and divine love at every stage of their journey, long ago reached the highest worlds of Shadanakar.

As we know, Akhenaton's efforts came to naught. Not only the religion he founded but even the name of the reformer himself was erased from the annals of Egyptian historiography. It was only at the end of the nineteenth century, through the efforts of European archaeologists, that the historical truth was reestablished. With the failure of that plan and the persistence of polytheism as the dominant religious form, Egypt too had to be dropped from the list of potential sites of Christ's incarnation.

In Iran, Zoroastrianism was also unable to develop into a distinctly monotheistic religion. The myth of that religion failed to incorporate even a fraction of its immense transmyth. The responsibility for that does not rest on its founders, for they, and first and foremost Zoroaster himself, provided a religious framework capacious enough to accommodate spiritual truths of immense proportions. It is the Witzraors and shrastr of Iran that bear the blame. Their reflection in Enrof–the Achaemenid empire–was able to check any and all spiritual growth, provoke an ossification of the religious forms of Zoroastrianism, suppress its mysticism, petrify its morality, redirect the focus of the arts on itself in place of the religion, and rechannel the spiritual energy of the suprapeople into the building of a state empire. By the time that empire fell and the Collective Soul of Iran was for a short time liberated, it was already too late. The religion of Mithra, which was spreading at the time, bore the telltale marks of work too rushed, of revelation too blurred. The gaze of the Elector finally came to rest on the Jews.

A metahistorical study of the Bible permits one to trace how the prophets were inspired by the demiurge of that people; how the authors of the Book of Job, the Song of Songs, and Ecclesiastes caught the echoes, distorted though they were, of his voice; how that revelation was at first contaminated and debased by inspiration from Shalem and the elemental of Mount Sinai, a grim, harsh, and intractable spirit; and how later the notes of anger, fury, belligerence, and unreasonable demands–the characteristic voice of Witzraors–cast a darker and darker shadow on the books of the Old Testament. But monotheism as a national religion was essential to Christ's mission, and it was the Jews that supplied it. Therein lies their historical and metahistorical contribution. What is important is that in spite of the innumerable misrepresentations, the tangle of hierarchies that inspired the mind and creative impulses of the authors of the Old Testament, the monotheistic religion did survive and the *I* of the Bible can, though, of course, not always, be understood as the Almighty.

To the degree that metahistorical knowledge enables one to comprehend the tasks that faced Christ during His life on Earth, one can for now define them in the following manner: to initiate humanity into the mystery of the Spiritual Universe, instead of leaving it to guess about it with the help of speculative philosophy and individual intuitions; to unblock the organs of spiritual perception in humans; to repeal the law of the jungle; to break the iron wheel of the law of karma; to abolish the principle of coercion and, consequently, the state in human society; to transform humanity into a community; to repeal the law of death and replace it with material transformation; to raise humans to the level of theohumankind. Oh, Christ was not supposed to die a violent or even a natural death. After living a long life in Enrof and accomplishing those tasks for which He had undergone incarnation, He was to have experienced not death but transformation–the transfiguration of His whole being and His passage into Olirna before the eyes of the world. If it had been completed, Christ's mission would have given rise to the establishment of an ideal Church/Community two or three centuries later, instead of states with their armies and bloody bacchanalias. The number of victims, the sum of suffering, and the time span required for humanity's ascent would have been lessened immeasurably.

Christ's founding of the Church in Enrof was preceded by an emanation of energy from the Virgin Mother–another hypostasis of the Trinity–into the higher worlds of Shadanakar. The emanation of energy did not take on a personal aspect; it was not connected with the descent of a God-born monad. Nor was it the first emanation of Femininity in the history of Enrof. The first emanation of Femininity in the existence of humanity took place some fourteen centuries earlier, and one can find echoes of an intuition of that fact in certain myths where, however, it melds with legends concerning the sacrificial descents of collective souls of suprapeoples into the dark planes, as we can see, for example, in Babylon. But that brightest of God-created monads, which was later to become the Mother of the Planetary Logos on Earth, took human form twice in that same Babylon, the second time during the very period of the first emanation of Femininity. Her life that time did not take Her beyond the limits of a small city in Sennaar, where She became a holy woman and was subsequently put to death. At the moment of Her death, Universal Femininity enlightened Her whole being, and that predestined Her to become the Mother of God. Even earlier, before Babylon, She lived in Atlantis, where She was a simple, beautiful woman and the mother of a large family. Before Atlantis, at the very dawn of human civilization, She lived in a small village in Central America. It is a long-lost settlement whose meager ruins will never be recovered from the tropical jungles of Honduras and Guatemala. Before that, during the prehistoric era, the monad of the future Mother of God was not born in human form.

The second emanation of Universal Femininity in Shadanakar was echoed by a softening, as it were, of the inner crust of many people in Enrof, without which the establishment of the Church on Earth by Jesus Christ would not have been possible. The Christian churches, in that abortive, unfinished form familiar to us in history, are nothing more than the pale, inchoate, partial, and distorted reflections of the Church that abides on the very highest planes of Shadanakar.

From the age of fourteen to thirty, Jesus traveled in Iran and India, where He was initiated into the deepest wisdom then possessed by humanity, only to far outstrip it.

Why did Christ not leave a written record of His teachings? Why did He prefer to entrust the task to His disciples? After all, the evangelists, inspired by God though they were, were still human, and the great enemy was not sleeping, so that even in the Gospels of the New Testament there are in places clear traces of his distorting imprint. But Christ could not set down His teachings in a book because His teachings were not only His words but His whole life. His teachings were the Immaculate Conception and His birth on a quiet Bethlehem night, illumined by the singing of angels; His meeting with Gagtungr in the desert and his travels on the roads of Galilee; His poverty and His love; the healing of the sick and the resurrection of the dead; His walking on water and His transfiguration on Mt. Favor; His suffering and Resurrection. Such teachings could only have been recorded, even if with gaps and errors, by eyewitnesses of that divine life.

But our sworn enemy crept into the gaps. By infiltrating the all-too-human consciousness of the evangelists, he succeeded in corrupting many testimonies, distorting and harshening ideas, debasing and qualifying ideals, even in ascribing words to Christ that our Savior could never have uttered. We as yet do not possess the means to separate the genuine from the false in the Gospels. There are neither precise criteria nor visible markers. Everyone who reads the New Testament should only keep in mind that Christ's teachings were His whole life, not just His words. As for the words ascribed to Him, everything that concurs with a spirit of love is genuine, while everything that is marked by a threatening and merciless spirit is false.

It is difficult to say at what moment in Jesus' life on Earth worry first crept into His soul, when he first felt doubt in the ultimate success of His mission. But in the latter period of His ministry, an awareness that the leader of the dark forces might well finish with a partial, short-term victory shows more and more clearly through His words—as much as we know them from the Gospels. That partial victory took concrete form in the betrayal by Judas that led to Golgotha.

Judas's personal motives for the betrayal resulted from the shattering by Christ of Judas's cherished nationalist dream of the Messiah as the King of the Jews and lord of the world. Until the day he met Jesus, Judas's heart had burned with that dream his entire life, and its death was a great tragedy for him. He did not entertain the slightest doubt as to Jesus' divinity, and his betrayal was an act of bitter hate, the conscious murder of God. The thirty pieces of silver and the motive of greed in general were only a hastily adopted disguise—he could not very well reveal the genuine motives of his crime! It was the nature of those genuine motives that entailed his descent to Zhursch, a form of karmic retribution unparalleled in its severity.

Now it becomes clear what vast importance can be attached to the events that unfolded after Jesus Christ's triumphant entry into Jerusalem. The Planetary Logos was as yet unable to complete the preparations for His transformation, and a painful human death awaited Him on Golgotha. Although He could have escaped crucifixion, He did not want to, for it would have meant a retreat. Further, Gagtungr would in any case have ensured He was killed a little later. But the possibility of a different kind of transformation after death arose: resurrection. In the interval between His death and Resurrection there took

place His bramfatura-shaking descent into the worlds of Retribution and the opening of the eternally closed gates of those
worlds, a descent that truly earned Jesus the title of Savior. He
descended through all the planes of magma and the core; only
the entrance to Sufetkh was barred to Him. All the other gate-
ways were forced, the locks broken, and the sufferers raised–
some to the worlds of Enlightenment, others to the shrastrs, still
others to the upper planes of Retribution, which began to transform from planes of eternal torment into temporary purgatories. Thus was begun the great task of mitigating the law of
karma, work on which was to intensify even more.

Lying in the tomb, the physical body of Our Savior became
enlightened and, resurrected to life, entered Olirna, a different,
higher three-dimensional plane of materiality. This explains
those properties of His body that the apostles observed between
His Resurrection and Ascension, such as the ability to walk
through objects of our plane, and yet to partake of food, or the
ability to travel distances at great speed. The other, second transformation described in the Gospels as the Ascension was nothing
other than Our Savior's ascent from Olirna even higher, up to
the next of those planes existing at the time. A little while later,
He guided Mary, Mother of God, through the same transformation, and John the Apostle a few decades after that. The transformation of some other great human souls has also taken place
since then.

Gradually growing from strength to strength, the Risen Christ
has been leading the struggle of all the powers of Light of
Shadanakar against the demonic. New planes of enlightenment–Faer, Nertis, Gotimna, and, later, Usnorm–were created
during the first centuries of Christianity, and the passage of many
millions of those to be enlightened through that sakwala was
accelerated. A powerful current of spirituality, which rarefies and
enlightens ever more human souls, has been pouring down
through the Christian churches, and the radiant zatomis of Christian metacultures, with their populous, ever brighter Synclites,
sprouted and flowered. The grandiose process of converting
planes of torment into purgatories has neared the halfway point:

Left to be transformed is the sakwala of magma, while the purgatories themselves are gradually to undergo even more changes. They will be rid of any and all elements of retribution. Instead, souls with burdened ether bodies will be given spiritual assistance from the Synclites, assistance that could be likened more to therapy than to punishment.

Mary, the Mother of God, has in the course of these centuries completed Her ascent from world to world. She is the comfort of all those suffering (especially those in the inferno), the Mediatrix of All Graces and the Mater Dolorosa for everyone and everything. She, like Her Son, abides in the World Salvaterra, donning a resplendent ether coating to descend to other planes. Our Savior, who as the Planetary Logos abides in the inner chamber of Salvaterra, has had for many centuries the power to create and coat Himself in a radiant ether body, and in that form He descends to the zatomis and meets with the Synclites of metacultures. His power has grown immeasurably. We are not, however, yet able to grasp the meaning of the processes that have been taking place in the very highest worlds of Shadanakar during the last two thousand years, though they are clearly what is most significant from the point of view of metahistory.

But if Jesus Christ's struggle with the demonic beyond the bounds of Enrof has been marked by a series of major victories, the curtailment of His mission in Enrof itself has resulted in an endless number of tragic consequences.

His very teachings ended up distorted, having been mixed with elements from the Old Testament, just those elements that Christ's life had been superseding and would have superseded once and for all if it had not been cut short. The chief features of those elements is the attribution to the image of God of the traits of a fearful, merciless judge, even an avenger, and the ascription of the inhumane laws of nature and moral retribution to Him and no one else. That ancient misrepresentation has acted as no small brake on the ascending journey of the soul. The confusion in one's mind between the divine and the demonic leaves one no choice but to resign oneself to the idea of the just, eternal, and immutable nature of those same laws for which Gagtungr bears the responsibility and which should be mitigated, spiritualized, and radically reformed. The resulting drop in moral consciousness naturally leads to people focusing their efforts on their own salvation, while their active commitment to social justice and the enlightenment of the world atrophies.

The curtailment of Christ's mission also resulted in the material in nature and the carnal in humans not undergoing the enlightenment that was supposed to occur on a global scale, and not just in the essence of Christ alone. Left unenlightened, they were excluded by the Christian Church from what it sanctioned, consecrated, and blessed. The sacraments of baptism and the Eucharist were believed to sunder the neophyte from the pagan celebration of the flesh as a good unto itself. No other higher formulation of the relationship was forthcoming. That tendency toward asceticism in Christianity, barely mitigated by the compromise institution of the sacrament of marriage, that polarization of the concepts of "spirit" and "flesh" that followed in Christianity's wake to all the cultures it embraced, in the long run resulting in the secular era of civilization–all that is no simple accident or even a mere historical phenomenon. To the contrary, it is a reflection of one aspect of Christianity's metahistorical fate, an aspect born of the curtailment of Christ's mission in Enrof.

What is most important is that no radical change whatsoever took place in Enrof. Laws remained laws, instincts remained instincts, passions remained passions, disease remained disease, death remained death, states remained states, wars remained wars, and tyrannies remained tyrannies. The birth of the Church among humanity, a church encumbered by an inherited arrogance and not immune to dark inspiration, could not generate the rapid growth–both spiritual and moral–that would have taken place if Gagtungr had not cut short Christ's life. For that reason, humanity has for nineteen centuries stumbled along a broken, crooked, irregular, and one-sided path: the resultant vector of the work of the Providential powers and the furious actions of Gagtungr.

The indecisive character of the great demon's victory cast him into a prolonged state of uncontrollable rage. The effects of his maniacal fury were felt in Enrof, giving rise to unprecedented disturbances on the surface of global history. The series of monstrous tyrants on the throne of the Roman Empire in the first century A.D.–their atrocities, unrivaled by anything either before or after; their irrational bloodthirstiness; their pride; their frenzies; their inhuman resourcefulness in devising new methods of torture; their warped creative impulses, which caused them to have erected buildings of unparalleled grandeur that either catered, like the Coliseum, to the baser instincts of the masses or, like the madcap projects of Caligula, were utterly senseless–all these were echoes of the fury of the demon, who saw that his sworn enemy, though delayed on His path, had grown in power and would thenceforth rise from glory to glory.

Several centuries before Christ, Gagtungr had acquired an imposing weapon: he had been able to effect the incarnation of certain gargantuan demonic beings on neighboring planes and thus to found the first dynasty of Witzraors in Babylon-Assyria and Carthage. One of that first Witzraor's offsprings, the Jewish Witzraor, dutifully assisted Gagtungr in his struggle with Christ during our Savior's life in Enrof: without the help of that Witzraor it would hardly have been possible to subvert the will of Judas Iscariot and of many Jewish leaders and delude them into thinking they were acting in their people's interests by persecuting Christ and putting Him to death. In addition, Gagtungr knew full well that the creation of two, three, or several predators of one and the same kind on the same plane would eventually lead, through the law of the jungle, to the victory of the strongest ones, until the strongest of them all succeeded in extending its power over all the shrastrs and the power of its human puppets over all terrestrial Enrof. With that, all the necessary conditions for absolute tyranny would be present. It was with a view to realizing that plan that a dynasty of Witzraors was also founded in Iran and Rome, and the Roman one proved stronger than the rest.

It appears that it was on Forsuth, the Witzraor of the Roman Empire, that Gagtungr placed his greatest hope in the first century A.D., after Christ's Resurrection. What is more, it seems that even the Synclites at that time could not be sure that the mad frenzy of Gagtungr, which had doubled his strength, would not lead to the appearance of the Antichrist in the near future and hasten the end of the first eon, thus multiplying the number of spiritual victims to unimaginable proportions and greatly complicating the tasks of the second eon. That alarm explains the apocalyptic, or rather, the eschatological mood, the expectation of the imminent end of the world that gripped the Christian communities and the Jews in the first decades after Christ's Resurrection. Fortunately, those fears proved unfounded.

Gagtungr's strength at that time was only sufficient to invoke the incredibly senseless bloodbaths of the caesars and to attempt to exterminate the Christian Church physically. By the middle of the first century, however, another plan of attack could be observed. Christ had been unable to complete His mission in Enrof and thus the Church He had founded, instead of proceeding on to global apotheosis, was barely smoldering in the form of a few small communities pressed beneath the backbreaking layers of state institutions created by the Witzraors and beneath the hard crust of psyches inspired by those demons. Taking advantage of this, the forces of Gagtungr began to meddle in the life of the Church itself. A strong-willed and highly gifted individual emerged, one deeply sincere in his conversion to Christ, and in whom Jewish singlemindedness and a messianic Jewish severity were combined with the legal-rational mind of a Roman citizen. He was an agent on a mission of indubitable Light, but the above-mentioned personal and ethnic character traits warped his own understanding of that mission. Instead of furthering Christ's work, instead of strengthening and enlightening the Church with the spirit of love and love alone, the thirteenth Apostle launched a massive, far-reaching organizational effort, binding the scattered communities together with strict regulations, unquestioning obedience to a single leader, and even fear, since the threat of being expelled from the bosom of the Church, in the case of disobedience, inspired just that: spiritual fear. The Apostle Paul never met Jesus Christ during His lifetime and was consequently denied all the grace that issued directly from Jesus. Nor was Paul present when the Holy Spirit descended on the other Apostles.

Yet the other apostles recede, as it were, into the background, each of them concentrating on local missions, on the creation of Christian communities in one or another country, while Paul, the one apostle lacking divine grace, gradually becomes the dominant figure towering over all the communities, unifying them, and dictating to them what he thinks to be the continuation of Christ's work.

That may have been the first clear indication of Gagtungr's determination to revise radically the demonic plan. Toward the end of the first century the dynamics and whole atmosphere within the Roman ruling elite suddenly change. Domitian, the last monster on the throne, falls victim to conspirators. The mad frenzies of the caesars abruptly cease. In the course of the next century there is a steady succession of exemplary monarchs. It is true that they perform what the logic of power–that is, the will of the Witzraor Forsuth–demands, and try to bolster the state, which supplies the Witzraor with such an inexhaustible stream of the red, dew-like food called *shavva*, but gone are former delusions of world conquest, the deranged building projects, and the "living torches"– Christians dipped in tar and set afire–which Nero used to illuminate his orgies. State affairs keep to a more or less prescribed path. In other words, Forsuth occupies itself with survival and is no longer encouraged to seek global dominion. The focus of the higher demonic plan switches. Abandoned are any ideas of guiding the Roman Empire to planetary rule. Usurping control of the Christian Church from within becomes the cornerstone of their plan.

In spite of all the distortions generated in Christianity by the lack of spiritual depth in the thousands that created it, the Christian Church (and subsequently, its various churches) has been the mouth of a powerful current of spirituality flowing down from planetary heights. In the eyes of Gagtungr the Church became a factor of overriding importance and every means available was utilized to seize control of it from within. The religious exclusivity of the Semites, the spiritual isolationism of the Greeks, the mercilessness and ruthless thirst for political hegemony of the Romans–all that was enlisted to that end in the second, third, fourth, and fifth centuries. That was insufficient, of course, to accomplish the primary goal, but it was quite enough to lead the Church away from its principal tasks, to contaminate it with a spirit of hatred, to lure it into the ocean of politics, to substitute transient worldly goals for its enduring spiritual ones, and to subordinate its Eastern half to the rule of the emperors and its Western half to the dogma of a wrongly conceived theocracy. The Church becomes a political power—so much the worse for it! Humanity still had a long way to go to reach the moral height at which it is possible to combine political leadership with moral purity.

My ignorance prevents me from outlining the principal stages, let alone drawing a full panoramic view, of Gagtungr's nineteen-century-long battle with the forces of the Risen Christ. Only a very few individual links in the chain are, to a greater or lesser extent, clearly visible to me.

For example, in the context of that battle the metahistorical meaning of the person and ministry of Muhammad gradually comes to light. From an orthodox point of view, whether it be Muslim or Christian, it is relatively easy to make one or another positive or negative assessment of that ministry. But in endeavoring to remain impartial, one is inevitably confronted with ideas and arguments whose contradictory natures preclude definitive judgment. One would think that Muhammad's religious genius, his sincerity, his inspiration by higher ideals, and that peculiar fiery conviction of his teaching that compels one to recognize him as a genuine prophet—that is, a messenger sent from the other world—are not subject to doubt. On the other hand, it is hard to see wherein lies the progressivity of his teachings when compared with Christianity. If there was no such progressivity in his teachings, then what need did humanity have of them? To treat Muhammad as a false prophet also fails to settle the matter, since it then becomes impossible to understand how a false religious teaching could nevertheless become a channel through which spirituality has flowed into the soil of great peoples, uplifting millions and millions of souls through a passionate worship of the One God.

Metahistorical knowledge supplies an unexpected answer to the problem, an answer that is, unfortunately, equally unacceptable to both Christian and Muslim orthodoxy. We can arrive at a correct answer only if we realize that Muhammad appeared at the moment when Gagtungr had already paved the way for the appearance on the historical scene of a genuinely false prophet. He was to have been a figure of great stature, and just as great would have been the spiritual danger humanity would have faced in his person. The false prophet was to have stripped Christianity of a number of outlying peoples who were still in the initial stages of Christianization, convert a number of other nations that had not been Christianized, and prompt a powerful and decidedly demonic movement within Christianity itself. The flawed development of the Christian Church would have been the soil in which that poisonous seed would have yielded a rich harvest, culminating in the installation at the helm of ecclesiastical and state power of a group of both open and secret devotees of Gagtungr.

The Prophet Muhammad was an agent on a higher mission. In brief, its aim was to draw the young and pure Arab people, who were only just coming into contact with Christianity, into the religion, and to generate through their efforts a fervent movement in the Christian Church toward a religious reformation, toward the purgation from Christianity of extreme asceticism, of subordination of the Church to the state, of the theocratic dictatorship established by the Papacy. But Muhammad was not only a religious teacher; he was a poet of genius, even more a poet than a prophet sent from the other world. Indeed, he was one of the greatest poets of all time.

That poetic genius, in conjunction with certain of his character traits, deflected him from his unwavering religious path. A powerful jet of poetic creativity shot into the main channel of his religious mission, distorting and clouding the revelation given to him. Instead of reforming Christianity, Muhammad allowed himself to be diverted by the idea of founding a new, pure religion. And found it he did. But since his revelation was not sufficient for him to say anything truly new after Christ, the religion he founded proved to be regressive (though not false or demonic) in comparison to Christ's teachings.

The religion did in fact gather into its fold those peoples who without Muhammad would have fallen victim to the false prophet Gagtungr was readying. The final assessment of Muhammad's role can therefore be neither wholly negative nor wholly positive. Yes, he was a prophet, and the religion he founded is one of the great right-hand religions. Yes, the rise of Islam saved humanity from a great spiritual catastrophe. But in rejecting many fundamental Christian beliefs, the religion regressed to a simplified monotheism. It offers nothing essentially new, and that is why there is no transmyth of Islam among the Great Transmyths, among the five crystal pyramids shining from the heights of Shadanakar.

Here I will point out only one other demonic plan of attack, without the knowledge of which it would be impossible to understand what follows and which should, both in history and metahistory, in time develop into, in a manner of speaking, the principal offensive thrust.

In mentioning the fact that no demon, no matter how powerful it might be, is capable of creating a monad, I had hoped that the reader would give due consideration to its implications. After the incarnation of the Planetary Logos, humanity became the decisive battleground, and an idea began to form in the demonic mind: to create, slowly if need be, a human puppet who would be capable of achieving absolute tyranny in terrestrial Enrof, of turning the population of the Earth into a satanohumankind. But once again the demonic lack of creativity made itself felt. Unable to come up with anything original, all the demonic forces could do was resort to the law of opposites and devise a blueprint to create a distorted mirror image of the efforts and paths of Providence. The Anticosmos was counterposed to the Cosmos, the principle of form to the Logos, satanohumankind to theohumankind, and the Antichrist to Christ.

The Antichrist! I will probably drive away more readers by introducing that concept into the Rose of the World's worldview than I have driven away in all the previous chapters combined.

The concept has been discredited numerous times: by the shallow, petty, and vulgarized meaning attached to it; by the abuse of those who proclaimed their political foes the servants of the Antichrist; and by the failed prophecies of those who saw signs of the imminent coming of the Antichrist in the events of the long-past periods of history in which they lived. But if by resurrecting the concept I were to drive away ten times more people than I actually will, I would still introduce it, for the concept of the Antichrist is woven into the worldview I am presenting with the strongest threads and will not be removed from it as long as the worldview itself exists.

As Gagtungr is incapable of creating monads, and demonic monads cannot be incarnated as humans, he had no alternative but to use a human monad in his plan. No matter what dark mission people perform, no matter what terrible stamps they leave on history, all that is dark has its origin in their shelt, not in their monad. It is only the shelt that can be demonized, not the human monad. In those rare cases, as with the father of the igvas or Klingsor, when an individual, having attained an extremely high clarity of consciousness, rejects God, it is his or her shelt, and not the monad, that does the rejecting. Thereupon something truly dreadful occurs: the renunciation of one's monad, for the very reason that it cannot sanction a rejection of God, and a total surrender of oneself–that is, of the shelt and all its material coatings–to the will and power of Gagtungr. The link between the monad and shelt is severed. The monad leaves Shadanakar to begin its journey anew in another bramfatura, and the shelt is either given to a demonic monad that for some reason has none or becomes the personal tool of Gagtungr, in which case the influence of his own spirit in part takes the place of the monad. In both instances, the shelt becomes demonized once and for all– that is, there is a gradual transformation of its material composition. *Siaira*, the materiality made by the bramfatura's forces of Light, is replaced by *agga*, the materiality of demonic origin. The same happens to the astral body as well. (Structurally agga differs from siaira in that it lacks microbramfaturas–the elementary particles that compose it are not animate and not even partly intelligent beings, as in siaira, but inanimate, indivisible material units. Agga is made up of only eleven types of those dark anti-atoms, being the sum of their innumerable combinations.) Naturally, beings with such demonized shelts and astral bodies can no longer be born anywhere except on demonic planes. Thus, they are denied all possibility of incarnating as humans.

Since the plan to create an Antichrist called for its incarnation as a human, Gagtungr was left with only one alternative: kidnap a human monad, strip it of all its coats of siaira (that is, the shelt, the astral body, and the ether body), and by gradual effort fashion different coatings for it out of agga. It would be beyond the power of Gagtungr to destroy its former shelt of Light, but, without a monad, spiritually decapitated as it were, it would remain indefinitely in a state of spiritual lethargy somewhere in some out-of-the-way transphysical crypt in Gashsharva. The kidnapping of a monad required enormous effort and long preparation. It was only in the fourth century A.D. that it was finally accomplished, and Gagtungr succeeded in snatching a human monad from Iroln, a monad that at one time had had an incarnation as a Titan and was presently linked to a shelt that had just completed a journey in Enrof in the person of one of the Roman emperors. But having only one such being caused the Antigod to fear that some unforeseen interference on the part of Providence might jeopardize the demonic plan. So later a few more monads were kidnapped as a kind of reserve of what we might call Antichrist candidates. Historically they faced the prospect of violent clashes with each other, the eventual victory of the strongest and luckiest, and the focusing of demonic efforts on that victor alone.

The shelts whose monads were kidnapped were indeed denied the possibility of being born anywhere. Walled up, as it were, in the depths of Gashsharva, they remain there to this day. The kidnapped monads, burdened by their material coatings of agga, with hands tied, so to speak, and controlled personally by Gagtungr, traveled down the road of demonic excellence, incarnating as humans from century to century.

One of them–that same monad of the former emperor–soon began to outpace the others. Its kidnapper guided it from incarnation to incarnation, overcoming its resistance, and over time causing an almost total extinguishment of its will of Light. As early as that startling being's incarnation in the fifteenth century, it had become obvious that the monad as an autonomous will was fully paralyzed and that the material coatings created for it were growing more and more obedient to demonic commands. The coatings were, however, still a long way from realizing their full potential. The incarnation in which that occurred was at the climax of the metahistorical battle within the Roman Catholic metaculture. It was connected with one of Gagtungr's most blatant, dramatic, and sinister attempts to usurp control of the Church from within, an attempt that to this day remains the last.

I have already mentioned that behind the fanatical movement in Catholicism that cast a shadow over the end of the Middle Ages and found fullest expression in the Inquisition was one of the most nightmarish of the spawns of Gagtungr, and it was only in the eighteenth century that the forces of Light emerged victorious over it. As for the demonic human puppet, it appeared on the historical scene earlier, assuming the outward guise of an active champion of global theocracy. There is in Russian literature an astonishing piece of writing, the author of which undoubtedly must have had spiritual knowledge of that fact, though his waking self did not have full access to that knowledge. I am referring to "The Legend of the Grand Inquisitor" in Dostoyevsky's *The Brothers Karamazov*. The one who is to become the Antichrist in the not too distant future was, one could say, captured by Dostoyevsky at one of the most crucial stages of its previous existence. It is true that he is not a widely known historical figure. His name is known now only to medievalists as the name of one of the rather notable figures of the Spanish Inquisition. It was about that time that Gagtungr was forced to admit the failure of his overall scheme to turn historical Catholicism into his lackey and the impossibility of unifying the whole world on the basis of a Roman cosmopolitan hierocracy. Absolute tyranny was impossible without the unification of humanity, and a host of prior conditions for unification of any kind was still lacking.

I will elsewhere pause over certain critical metahistorical clashes that have taken place over the centuries. As Jesus Christ foresaw, the course of events has led to the imminence of the decisive battle, a battle made inevitable by the ancient hunger for power of the demonic powers and by their pursuit of universal tyranny.

The power of the One Who was Jesus Christ has grown beyond measure over the centuries. Were He to reappear in Enrof now, all the miracles of the Gospels, and all the miracles of Indian and Arab legends would pale beside the miracles He could perform. But there is no need for that yet. There are still two or three centuries before His Second Coming, and during that time He will be able to acquire the power to perform the greatest act in history and in metahistory: the turn of the eon. The turn of the eon will involve a qualitative transformation of humanity's materiality, the birth of the Synclites of all the meta-cultures in enlightened physical bodies here in Enrof, the beginning of a long road of expiation on other planes for those belonging to satanohumankind, and the commencement in Enrof of what is called in the Holy Scriptures the "thousand-year Kingdom of the Righteous." The Second Coming is to occur simultaneously at a multitude of points on terrestrial Enrof, so that every single being will have seen and heard Him. In other words, the Planetary Logos is to attain the inconceivable power to materialize simultaneously in as many places as there will then be consciousnesses to perceive Him in Enrof. These ether-physical materializations, however, will be but brief expressions of His single Entity, and they will merge back with Him for permanent residency in enlightened Enrof. That is what Christ meant when He prophesied that the Second Coming would be "like lightning coming from the east and flashing far into the west," so that all peoples and nations on Earth will see "the Son of Man coming on the clouds of heaven."

3 Femininity

I HAVE NOW ARRIVED at a critical juncture of this work. And yet, no matter how important it may be, I barely have the courage to say a few words on the subject.

It is time to reexamine a Christian dogma that is nearly two thousand years old. All sorts of dogmas of the Christian creed have been questioned in the past; schisms, sects, and heresies have been born of differing interpretations of them; even the slightest departures in ritual have sometimes grown into a virtual abyss separating schismatics from the dominant church. But in the course of those nineteen centuries it appears that no dispute has ever arisen over what has been considered the cornerstone of the religion: the belief in the three hypostases of the Holy Trinity: God the Father, God the Son, and God the Holy Spirit.

I do not intend to undertake a historical or psychological analysis of the circumstances surrounding the emergence of that specific understanding of the Trinity in the Christian Church. I possess neither the necessary sources nor the erudition required for such a task. And even if I did, I would be loathe to use the lancet of rational analysis to probe the mysterious spiritual depths in which the idea appeared and took shape in the first centuries A.D.

I will permit myself only to cite one page from the Gospels that seems to me to support another interpretation of the Trinity. Matthew and Luke state plainly and unequivocally that the Virgin Mary conceived the Baby Jesus through the Holy Spirit. One could thus conclude that it was the Holy Spirit, and not God the Father, that was the Father of the human Christ. But how can that be? Could the timeless birth of God the Son from God the Father find expression in the historical, human world except as the birth of the human Jesus through the power of that latter hypostasis? But no, the story in the Gospels is unequivocal on that point. What is equivocal is the Christian Church's understanding of the third hypostasis. In the course of its entire history, the Church has never elaborated the dogma of the third hypostasis. One is even struck by the contrast between the detailed–perhaps too detailed–teaching about God the Son and what is almost an empty space where should be the doctrines about the Holy Spirit.

But there is nothing essentially strange about that. It is no coincidence that the Christian religion is called Christian. Besides specifying the religion's origin in Christ, the name also reflects the fact that the religion is primarily the revelation of God the Son–that is, it is not so much a religion of the Trinity as it is one of the Son. That explains the extremely hazy generalizations, the equivocality, incompleteness, and even contradictions in the dogmas concerned with the other hypostases.

Who, after all, could God the Father be if not the Spirit and the Spirit only? And, in contrast to all the other spirits He has created, He is Holy. For every God-created and even God-born monad can make–and many have made–a wrong choice and turn away from God. But the Father, as should be obvious to all, cannot turn from Himself. He is primordial, unchanging, unclouded, and unsoiled, and He is called Holy in that very sense. What good can come of depriving God the Father of two of His eternally inherent attributes–His spirituality and His holiness? What is the justification for investing these attributes with an entirely autonomous meaning in the aspect of the Third Person of the Trinity? And in fact, on which of Christ's words, on what testimonies of the four Gospels can the teaching be based that God the Father is one hypostasis of the Trinity and the Holy Spirit is another? There are no such statements to that effect in the Gospels. The words of Jesus cited in support of that claim come from His well-known prophecy: "I will send to you a Counselor, even a Spirit of Truth." Differing interpretations of these very words even led to the Great Schism, which split the one Christian Church into Eastern and Western halves. But both interpretations still proceeded from a common postulate: the strangely undisputed supposition that by the "Counselor" Christ meant the third hypostasis. But there is not even the shadow of an intimation in these words that the Counselor to be sent by the Risen Savior is the third hypostasis or even a hypostasis at all. Nor is there any indication that the expressions "Counselor" and "God the Holy Spirit" refer to one and the same entity. Surely it is more natural, consistent, and sensible from every possible point of view to draw an altogether different conclusion, namely, that God the Holy Spirit is God the Father, for God the Father can be nothing other than Holy and the Spirit.

Once again, in reexamining here the cornerstone of a great teaching, I am setting my lone voice against a stupendous, vast choir, which has been thundering for so many centuries that there can be no doubt as to the reactions it will evoke, if it is even heard. I am even aware that in the eyes of some I am guilty of a great spiritual offense, having committed what is according to the Gospels the one unforgivable sin: blasphemy against the Holy Spirit. I solemnly proclaim: I prostrate myself before the Holy Spirit, I worship Him and pray to Him with as much veneration as other Christians. And I fail not only to see blasphemy of His name but even the slightest debasement of His image in the idea that He is God the Father and that God the Father is God the Holy Spirit, that these are two names for one and the same Person–the first Person of the Holy Trinity.

I would like to emphasize that I am expressing my own humble opinion here. True, that opinion appears to me a conclusion at which more and more people will in time arrive. It has also been corroborated by those higher authorities that have always been my single supreme court of appeal. But I believe that no one has the right to insist on the exclusive and absolute validity of the idea, on its dogmatic force. The one legal, universally recognized body with the authority to resolve the issue might be the Eighth Ecumenical Council, where the representatives of all contemporary Christian faiths and the Rose of the World would discuss that postulate, as well as the postulate affirming the infallibility and irrevocability of the resolutions of ecumenical councils in general. Perhaps they might also reexamine certain tenets of Orthodox doctrine. Until that time, no one in the Rose of the World should unreservedly assert the error of the old dogma. They should only believe as their conscience and personal spiritual experience dictate, and work toward the unification of the churches and the resolution of all their outstanding differences.

The above idea, however, clears the path to the solution of a different, no less crucial, problem.

It is known that a vague yet intense and persistent sense of a Universal Feminine Principle has been alive in Christianity from the time of the gnostics up until the Christian thinkers of the early twentieth century–a sense that the Principle is not an illusion and not the projection of human categories onto the cosmic, but that it is a higher spiritual reality. It was clearly the Church's intention to provide an outlet for that feeling when in the East it gave its blessing to the cult of the Mother of God and in the West to that of the Madonna. And a concrete image did in fact emerge and was embraced by the people as an object for their spontaneous veneration of the Maternal Principle. But the mystical sense I spoke of–the sense of Eternal Femininity as a cosmic and divine principle–remained without an outlet. The early dogmatization of the teaching on the hypostases, in rendering it beyond dispute, placed those with that sense in an unenviable position: to avoid accusations of heresy they were forced to skirt the fundamental question and not give full voice to their thoughts, sometimes equating Universal Femininity with the Universal Church or, in the end, depriving the One God of one of His attributes–Wisdom–and personifying it as Holy Sophia. The higher Church authorities refrained from voicing any definite opinion on the subject, and they should not be faulted for it, because the belief in Universal Femininity could not help but grow into the belief in a Feminine Aspect of God, and that, of course, would

have threatened to undermine the dogmatized beliefs about
the Persons of the Holy Trinity.[1]

I have met many people who are extremely sophisticated cul-
turally and intellectually, and are in possession of undoubted spiritual experience, yet they have been surprised, even appalled, at
the very idea of what they perceived to be the projection of gender
and human categories in general onto worlds of the highest reality, even onto the mystery of God Himself. They considered it a
vestige of the ancient tendency of the limited human mind to
anthropomorphize the spiritual. Incidentally, the Islamic objec-
tion to the belief in the Trinity and to the cult of the Mother of
God derives from quite similar (psychological) sources. It is for the
very same reason that deism and contemporary abstract cosmopolitan monism reject so vehemently belief in the Trinity, in hierarchies, and, of course, in Eternal Femininity. Ridiculous as it may
seem, even the charge of polytheism that Muhammad leveled at
Christianity thirteen hundred years ago has been reiterated.

Such charges are rooted either in an oversimplified understanding of Christian beliefs or in an unwillingness to penetrate
deeper into the question. There has been no projection of
human categories onto the Divine in historical Christianity, let
alone in the worldview of the Rose of the World, but something
in principle quite the reverse. No one is questioning the oneness
of God, of course. It would be naive to suspect anyone here of
reversion to the age of Carthage, Ur, and Heliopolis. The
hypostases are separate external manifestations of the One
Essence. They are how He reveals Himself to the world, not how
He exists within Himself. But God's external manifestations are
just as absolute in their reality as His existence within Himself.
Therefore, the hypostases should not in any way be taken for
illusions or aberrations of our mind.

---

1. It would be extremely interesting to see a comprehensive study done of the
history and evolution of the belief in Eternal Femininity in the Christian cultures at the very least. But such a work could only benefit from including other
religions as well, if only those in whose pantheons the images of the great mer-
ciful goddesses are immortalized: Hinduism, Mahayana, ancient polytheistic
teachings, and, of course, gnosticism.

In manifesting Himself externally, the One God reveals His inherent inner polarity. The essence of that polarity within the Divine is transcendental for us. But we perceive the external manifestations of that essence as the polarity of two principles gravitating to each other and not existing one without the other, eternally and timelessly united in creative love and bringing forth the third and consummating principle: the Son, the Foundation of the Universe, the Logos. Flowing into the universe, the Divine retains that inherent polarity; all spirituality and all materiality in the universe is permeated by it. It is manifested differently at different levels of being. At the level of inorganic matter perceptible by humans it can no doubt be seen as the basis of what we call the universal law of gravity, the polarity of electricity, and much more. In the organic matter of our plane here, the polarity of the Divine is manifested in the distinction between male and female. I wish to stress that it is manifested thus here, but the polarity of the Divine that is the basis for that distinction cannot be comprehended in itself, in its essence.

That is why we call Divine Femininity the Mother of Logos, and through Him, Mother of the entire Universe. But the eternal union between the Mother and Father does not change Her timeless essence. It is for that reason that we call the Mother of Worlds the Virgin.

Thus, one does not discern in the teaching on the Trinity and the Feminine Aspect of the Divine the projection of thinking that is "all too human" onto the cosmic realms. To the contrary, the teaching represents an intuition of the objective polarity–the male and female–of our planes as a projection of the transcendental polarity within the essence of God.

"God is Love," said John. Centuries will pass, then eons, then finally bramfaturas and galaxies, and each of us, sooner or later, will reach Pleroma– divine Fullness–and enter the beloved Heart no longer as a child only but as a divine brother as well. All memory of our current beliefs about the Divine will vanish from our mind like pale, dull shadows we no longer have any need for. But even then the truth that God is Love will continue to hold. God does not love Himself (such a claim would be blasphemy), but each of the Transcendencies within Him directs His love onto the Other, and in that love a Third is born: the Foundation of the Universe. Thus, the Father–the Virgin Mother–the Son.

The greatest of mysteries and the inner mystery of the Divine–the mystery of the love between the Father and Mother–is not mirrored in human love, no matter what form that love may take. Nothing in the finite world is commensurate with or analogous to the essence of that mystery. Nor can anything in the world, with the exception of what issues from those who have rejected God, be extrinsic to that mystery. The essence of the Trinity, the essence that is love, is expressed (but not mirrored) in universal love– that is, in our love for all living beings. In the love between man and woman, the inner mystery of the union of Father and Mother is expressed (but not mirrored) to the degree that it reaches us, having been refracted by a multitude of planes in the cosmic continuum. Therein lies the fundamental ontological distinction between these two aspects of our spiritual life, aspects that have almost nothing in common yet are expressed by one and the same word–love–in our impoverished language.

Love for all living things has long been–if not in practice then at least ideally–a cornerstone of religion, and not of Christianity alone. We can expect the bounds encompassed by love to expand ever more in the future. True, a reversion to love in an extremely narrow sense is clearly evident in modern secular teachings: love for one's nation, for its allies and friends abroad, and for one's family and friends. But that is a purely temporary phenomenon occasioned by the nature of the secular age as a whole, with its crudely self-centered morality, and it will last only as long as the whole secular stage of development itself lasts. The next religious age will be a new age for the very reason that it will proclaim and strive to put into practice love for all humanity, for all the realms of nature, and for all the hierarchies of ascent.[2]

---

2. It was already pointed out in the chapter on the animal world that there is one exception–a class of living beings that cannot and should not enter within our circle of love in the conditions of the current eon: parasites. We are faced with an ethical dilemma here that we are incapable of resolving at our present level of ascent. One should not harbor any illusions in that regard.

In the distant future even more spiritual possibilities will arise. Even love for demons will become viable and necessary. History has already seen some saints who grew to such a love. But to get ahead of oneself and cultivate in one's soul a love for the sworn enemies of God and of all living beings, when one is not yet free of temptation and when one's love does not yet embrace even the whole of humanity and the animal world, would jeopardize the ascending path of one's own soul. Demons are only waiting for someone to pity them. But they are not waiting because they need pity (they are consumed with pride and despise human pity), but because it is only one step from pity for demons to doubt in their evil ways, and a stone's throw away from such doubt to the temptation to reject God and rebel. To do so would consign the soul to harsh retribution and the generation of gavvakh, radiations of suffering, in just those quantities that demons dream about to replenish their energy. Love for demons is therefore extremely dangerous for everyone except souls already enlightened. Enlightened souls know how to love without feeling sympathy (for sympathy for someone is impossible without sympathy for their chief occupations, and demons are occupied only with doing evil) or concelebration (for only what is repellent to Providence gives demons cause to celebrate). That love can be expressed only by a feeling of deep pity, by faith in their ultimate enlightenment, and by a readiness to sacrifice everything but loyalty to God for the sake of that enlightenment.

But love for all living beings is, in practical terms, but one aspect of the problem. How are we to regard the other aspect of our life–both the inner and outer life–that involves everything called the love between man and woman?

The "burning coals" within every being, the implacable procreational instinct–wellspring of self-sacrifice, violent passions, purest inspiration, crimes, heroism, evil deeds, and suicides–is it any wonder it was eros that was always the biggest stumbling block for ascetics and saints? People tried to distinguish duality within that love itself: physical love was contrasted with platonic love, infatuation with everlasting love, free relationships with the work and duty of childbearing, depravity with fairy-tale romance.

Sometimes they made a distinction between two transphysical wellsprings of love: *Aphrodite Uranus* and *Aphrodite Pandemos*. But in concrete situations, in real-life feelings, in day-to-day relationships everything became tangled, confused, blended, and knotted in a manner that was impossible to unravel. It began to seem better to pull up that love in oneself by the roots than to allow one's path to heaven to become overgrown with its lush vegetation.

Thus began the great ascetic era in religion. There is no need, I think, to reiterate what contortions of their own spirit Christianity and Buddhism had to resort to so as not to degenerate into ascetic sects that hated life and were in turn hated by it. Marriage was consecrated as a sacrament, childbearing was given their blessing, but celibacy continued to be regarded–with perfect consistency, one might add–as the higher state.

Love as a cause of various human tragedies revolves around the capacity for the feeling of love to be *unilateral*. It will be a long time, of course, before love loses that unilaterality–not until the second eon. But besides tragedies of that kind–tragedies of the first order, in a manner of speaking–humanity, in order to bring stability to an ever more complex life, laid the groundwork for yet other tragedies–those take place when the love between man and woman enters into conflict with established custom, societal values, or the law. When a man or woman loves but that love is not reciprocated, that is a tragedy of the first order, and there is nothing that can be done about it until humanity, as Dostoyevsky said, "is transformed physically." But when two people love each other and yet are unable to come together in a harmonious and joyful union, in the full meaning of the word, because of the familial or societal position of one of them, that is a tragedy of the second order. Customs and the law should in time be reformed in such a way as to reduce tragedies of that kind to a minimum, if not to eliminate them altogether.

It is a task of immense complexity. It is even doubtful whether a universal set of laws could be drafted for all humanity in that regard. The level of social and cultural development, traditions, and the national psyche vary too widely among countries. It will

most likely have to be the task of the national legislative branches
of the Rose of the World, and not the central legislative organ. It
is sufficiently clear, in addition, that society will have to be led,
here as in everything else, through a series of gradual stages,
because a unilateral decision in favor of freedom–that is, a swift
repeal of all legal barriers–would lead, as Russia's experience
after the revolution demonstrated, to moral anarchy and force
the government to repeal the repeal and put the prohibitions
back in force. That is because the government repealed the laws
in an automatic fashion, without first inculcating an attitude
toward love and marriage in the younger generations that
would have helped them to avoid abusing such freedom.

It seems that there can only be one correct religious answer to
the question of love between man and woman: such love is
blessed, beautiful, and sacred to the extent that it is creative.

What is meant by that?

The most common type of creative love in our eon is the bearing and rearing of children, but that is far from the only form of
creative love and loving creativity. Cooperation in any sphere of
life, the cultivation of the best sides of each other's character,
mutual self-improvement, mutual inspiration in artistic, religious, and other creative pursuits, or the simple joy of a young,
fresh, passionate love that enriches, strengthens, and uplifts both
partners–this is all divine co-creation, because it leads to their
growth and enlightenment and to a rise in the level of the worldwide ocean of love and joy. The radiations from the exquisite love
between a man and woman rise up to the very highest worlds–
those described in one of the preceding chapters as the Waves of
Universal Femininity–and strengthen them. Even if the loving
couple jointly pursues an erroneous path of creative work–if
they both, for example, work at something with socially harmful
consequences– even in that case only the orientation of the work
merits condemnation; the impulse to co-create that marks their
love, and the spirit of comradeship, companionship, and friendship that permeates it, are blessed from above.

Until humanity is transformed physically, the love between
woman and man will remain harnessed, as it were, to the

reproductive instinct. In time that will change. Creative love will take on a different meaning. The concept of physical reproduction will altogether cease to be applicable to transformed humanity. The future will witness monads incarnated in enlightened bodies, a process altogether different from our birth. But under the conditions of our eon, of course, childbearing and rearing remains the primary form of creative love.

Here I think it is the right time to highlight some specific features of those historical tasks that the women of the era just beginning will face not only in childrearing but in life as a whole.

One sometimes hears, from both men and women who lack a deeper understanding of the feminine, the categorical claim that the cultural and creative tasks of both sexes are identical and if until now women have been a distant second to men in the amount and significance of what has been contributed to society, politics, science, technology, philosophy, and even art, then that is simply attributable to the historical subjugation and oppression of women.

This opinion is more widespread than one might think. One could even say it is the fashionable view nowadays.

But have women really been oppressed always and everywhere? For the last two hundred years in Europe and Russia, at least in the privileged classes, the doors of creative work in the fields of literature and art have been open to women just as they are to men. Is there any need to mention that women, while displaying unquestionable talent and producing no small number of musicians, have in the last two centuries (and in the whole course of global history, I might add) failed to enrich the pantheon of musical composers of genius with a single name? It is sad to have to point out that among the giants of world literature there are six or seven female names to two or three hundred male names. In many countries it has been nearly a century since women won the right to higher education. And they have replaced men successfully in a wide range of professional endeavors: in hospitals, laboratories, classrooms, sometimes even on field expeditions. But where are the hundreds of names of eminent female scientists that could counterbalance the hundreds of male names that have become famous throughout the world during the same period of time? The world stage shines like a starry sky with the names of great actresses. But has even one female director won truly global renown? Has anyone heard of a great female philosopher? A great female architect? A great female political leader? A renowned female metallurgist, sage critic, outstanding industrial manager, or an acclaimed chess player? To deny or ignore those facts would be to reveal a total lack of objectivity. Instead of denying the facts it would be more profitable to change the way one looks at them. Are women less gifted than men? It is beyond question that in some respects the answer is yes. And it is equally beyond question that in other respects they possess gifts that men will never have.

It would, of course, be reactionary nonsense to deny that women can be fine geologists, conscientious engineers, talented artists, highly qualified chemists or biologists or to doubt the usefulness and value of their work in these fields. But one can and should internalize two indisputable facts: first, the list of geniuses in these fields has not been enriched and probably never will be by any female names and, secondly, women are irreplaceable and highly gifted in other respects.

Motherhood. Childrearing. Creative work in the home. Care for the sick and elderly. The moral rehabilitation of criminals. The transformation of Nature. The enlightenment of animals. Certain areas of religious service. Creative love. And, lastly, the creative fertilization of the one she loves. That is where women are irreplaceable and possess unlimited gifts.

They are absolutely irreplaceable in the first and last of these categories of creative work. As for the rest, men are less gifted than them to the same degree that women are less gifted than men in the fields of government or science. For the above types of work require a female, feminine, inner orientation: gentleness, loving tenderness, selflessness, perseverance, caring, intuitiveness, warmth, and sensitivity.

Something that is the reverse of what we observe in the physical world takes place in higher creative work: there the woman fertilizes the man, who conceives the idea and brings it to life.

The Divine Comedy is the product of two people, and it would never have been written without Beatrice just as it would not have been written without Dante. If we plumbed the depths of the creative process of the majority of geniuses of the arts, we would find that it was women who sowed the spiritual seed of the geniuses' immortal works into the depths of their subconscious, into their innermost creative recesses. In that light, the proposal to erect in Weimar a monument to Ulrike von Levetzow, the woman who inspired Goethe to write such beautiful poems, is fitting and profound. One should not be bothered that in the biographies of the majority of artistic geniuses it is difficult to uncover, using traditional methods, the names of those women who deserve the gratitude of later generations to the same degree as the geniuses themselves, who sometimes do not know themselves to whom they owe the seeds of their works. In due time and in the proper place– outside of the bounds of Enrof– every one of them will learn the truth.

For thousands of years, males and masculine qualities– strength, daring, pride, courage, ambition, cruelty, and competitiveness–have run rampant in humanity. The Spanish have a saying that confounds the mind and is appalling to the conscience: "A man must be savage." Alas, the people who produced that saying have done their best to live up to it. The barbarity of the conquistadors and the viciousness of the Spanish Inquisition have splashed the pages of world history with such savageness that the evil radiating from them affects souls to this day.

Be that as it may, many other peoples have rivaled the Spaniards in that respect. Millennium after millennium, waves of wars, rebellions, revolutions, persecutions, and savage, merciless reprisals have rolled, and roll today, over the face of the Earth. The countless drops that together form those waves have been male wills and male hearts. People sometimes speak of female cruelty. But, for heavens sake, were the bloodbaths of the Genghis Khans, the Tamerlanes, and the Napoleons, the agony of torture chambers, the frenzy of the Jacobin terror, the rampages of colonial conquests, or the mass persecutions by the Nazis and other dictatorships–were these horrors initiated and overseen by women? History has witnessed female poisoners, child murderers, killers, ingenious female sadists, but it has not witnessed one woman who left a stamp on history comparable to that left by Tiberius and Nero, Assargadon and Ala el-Din, Torquemada and Pizarro, the Count of Alba de Liste and Robespierre, Ivan the Terrible and Skuratov, Himmler and Beria.

Shrinking from the horror, driven to seek refuge deep within the family unit, the feminine was saved from extinction only because without it men are as barren as lead, and without women the physical perpetuation of the species is not possible.

To this day there are cries that women as well as men should be manly. If by manliness we mean courage and determination in the face of life's struggle, then one would of course have to agree. But if by womanliness we do not mean a mode of manners and behavior, not affectation and sentimentality, but rather a mixture of emotional warmth, inner delicacy, tenderness, and the ability to sacrifice oneself daily for those one loves, then men as well as women should be womanly. How long must humanity wait for the dawn of an age when a false understanding of what it is to be a man does not transform men into savage conquerors, into thugs flaunting their own crudity, into beings part peacock and part tiger? How long until men are no longer brought up to be ashamed of their own deep-down tenderness, which they themselves trample on and suppress? It will be difficult to surmount that age-old complex of conventions, preconceptions, emotional disfigurement, and atavistic instincts, but surmounted it must be. At all costs.

A mysterious event is taking place in the metahistory of contemporary times: new divine-creative energy is emanating into our bramfatura. Since ancient times the loftiest hearts and subtlest minds have anticipated this event that is now taking place. The first link in the chain of events– events so important that they can only be compared to the incarnation of the Planetary Logos– occurred at the turn of the nineteenth century. This was the emanation of the energy of the Virgin Mother, an emanation that was not amorphous, as it had been twice before in human history, but incomparably intensified by the personal aspect it assumed. A great God-born monad descended from the heights of the Universe into Shadanakar. Almost a century later, Vladimir Solovyov was given a glimpse of Raoris–one of the highest planes in our bramfatura, which She had entered–when, on a starry night in the Egyptian desert, he experienced a stunning breach of his consciousness and saw the Great Feminine Being with his own eyes. Zventa-Sventana we call Her, She Who is the Brightest and All-Good, the expression of the Feminine Hypostasis of the Trinity. She now abides in Bayushmi, one of the regions that are part of the sakwala of the Waves of World Femininity. The long-awaited day approaches when She will descend to one of the great cities in the metacultures. There She is to be born in a body of enlightened ether, the child of a demiurge and one of the Great Sisters. A host of the loftiest souls from the Elite of Shadanakar will descend with Her into that zatomis. There She is, our hope and joy, Light and Divine Beauty! For Her birth will be mirrored in our history as something that our grandchildren and great-grandchildren will witness: the founding of the Rose of the World, its spread throughout the world, and, if a terrible human blunder does not hurl us down into the depths of darkness, the assumption by the Rose of the World of supreme authority over the entire Earth.

Oh, that will not yet signify the final victory of the forces of Light– do not forget the Horsemen of the Apocalypse! Only the historical order of appearance of the Horsemen does not follow the order foretold on the island of Patmos by the Apostle John. The Black Horseman–the era of feudal hierocracy–was the first to gallop by. Now the second Horseman, the Red one, is nearing the end of his ride: everyone should be able to guess what is behind that symbol. We wait in anticipation for the White Horseman–the Rose of the World, the golden age of humanity! Nothing will be able to forestall the coming of the last, Pale Horseman: Gagtungr will see the one he has been preparing for so many centuries born in human form. But the era of the Rose of the World will immeasurably reduce the number of spiritual victims. It will succeed in raising a number of generations of ennobled humanity. It will give spiritual fortitude to millions, even billions, of those wavering. By warning about the coming Antichrist, and pointing him out and unmasking him when he appears, by cultivating unshakeable faith within human hearts and a grasp of the meta-historical perspectives and global spiritual prospects within human minds, it will inure generations and generations against the temptations of the future spawn of darkness.

In Enrof, Zventa-Sventana's[3] birth in one of the zatomis will be mirrored not only by the Rose of the World. Feminine power and its role in contemporary life is increasing everywhere. It is that circumstance above all that is giving rise to worldwide peace movements, an abhorrence of bloodshed, disillusion over coercive methods of change, an increase in women's role in society proper, an ever-growing tenderness and concern for children, and a burning hunger for beauty and love. We are entering an age when the female soul will become ever purer and broader, when an ever greater number of women will become profound inspirers, sensitive mothers, wise counselors and far-sighted leaders. It will be an age when the feminine in humanity will manifest itself with unprecedented strength, striking a perfect balance with masculine impulses. See, you who have eyes.

---

3. As I have already mentioned, the phonetics of Enrof cannot precisely repro-duce the sounds of words in the language of the World Synclite. Each such word has, as it were, a chord of sounds, a chord of meanings, and is accompanied, in addition, by light effects. The approximate meaning of the name "Zventa-Sven-tana" is "The Brightest of the Bright and the Holiest of the Holy." The name has a Slavic root, since the zatomis where her birth will take place is connected with peoples predominantly Slavic in origin.

GLOSSARY OF TERMS

Agga All materiality created by the demonic in our bramfatura (see entry). It differs in structure from physical materiality and from siaira (see entry) in that there are an extremely limited number of elementary particles in agga, particles that are neither animate nor possessed of free will.

Anticosmos Provisional designation of all those worlds created by the demonic to supersede the Divine Cosmos. At present the anticosmos of our bramfatura consists of the planes of Shog, Digm, Gashsharva, Sufetkh, and the Pit.

Arimoya The zatomis (see entry) of global culture currently under construction.

Arungvilta-prana An impersonal, unconscious, rarefied substance flowing in Enrof (see entry) from body to body and providing for individual organic life. An intuition of the existence of arungvilta-prana was at the center of the spiritual life of protoanimistic humanity and appears to be the most ancient of revelations.

Astral body The second of the subtle material coatings of a monad (see entry). The shelt (see entry), the first of the subtle material coatings, is fashioned by the monad itself. The Great Elemental Mother Earth takes part in the creation of the astral body. She takes part in the creation of the individual astral bodies of every being in Shadanakar (see entry): humans, angels, daemons (see entry), animals, elementals (see entry), demons, and even the Great Hierarchies, when the latter descend to planes where an astral body is required. The astral body is the higher instrument of the shelt. Concentrated within it are the gifts of spiritual vision, spiritual hearing, spiritual smell, deep memory, the ability to levitate, the ability to interact with beings of other planes, and the ability to contemplate cosmic panoramas and perspectives.

Bramfatura Almost every heavenly body possesses a number of vari-omaterial planes that together form a closely integrated system. These systems, united by the commonality of processes taking place on their planes, are called bramfaturas. In the majority of bramfatu-ras in our Galaxy the chief process uniting the planes of each is the struggle between the Providential and the demonic forces. There are, however, bramfaturas that have completely fallen under the sway of the demonic and those that have freed themselves entirely of it.

Daemons The higher humankind of Shadanakar, who abide in a sak-wala (see entry) of four-dimensional worlds with differing numbers of time streams. Daemons proceed along a path of growth similar to ours, but they began much earlier and are completing it with greater success. They are linked to our humanity by a variety of threads, some of which are described in the main text.

Digm The abode of Gagtungr, one of the five-dimensional worlds with an abundance of time streams.

Dingra The karossa (see entry) of Russia.

Drukkarg The shrastr (see entry) of the Russian metaculture (see entry).

Duggur A plane of demonic elementals that plays a special role in the life of humanity. The beings that incarnate in Duggur replenish their energy with eiphos (see entry).

Egregors Here the term means variomaterial formations that take shape over large collectives–tribes, states, some political parties and religious groups–from certain emanations of the human psyche. They do not have monads but possess a volitional charge of limited duration and the equivalent of consciousness.

Eiphos Radiations from human lust.

Elementals A category of God-created monads that proceed along a path of growth in Shadanakar, primarily through the realms of nature. In the majority of cases, however, they do not undergo physical incar-nation. Since humanity is an aspect of one realm of Nature, there are various groups of elementals linked not to the natural elements, in the broad sense of the word, but to the natural, elemental aspect of humanity.

Enrof The name of our physical plane–a concept synonymous with what astronomy calls the universe. It is characterized by three dimen-sions of space and one time stream.

Eons Here the term means universal periods of time characterized by altered conditions in the Enrof of one bramfatura. A change in conditions is determined by one or another degree of manifestation of spirituality in the materiality of Enrof. What is meant is not individual departures from the norm but the overall, predominant conditions. Thus, during the passage of the Enrof of Shadanakar into the second eon, the transformation of the materiality of organic matter will take place, and during its passage into the third eon, the transformation of inorganic matter will occur as well. In that manner, Shadanakar will disappear from the confines of universal Enrof.

Ether body The third of the subtle coatings of an incarnating monad. No organic life is possible in three- and four-dimensional worlds without it.

Gagtungr The name of the planetary demon of our bramfatura. He is three persons in one, like certain other beings among the uppermost hierarchies. The first hypostasis of Gagtungr is Gisturg, the Great Torturer; the second is Fokerma, the Great Harlot; and the third is Urparp, the great implementer of the demonic plan, who is sometimes called the Principle of Form.

Gashsharva One of the principal planes in the demonic anticosmos of Shadanakar, a two-dimensional world where a variety of powerful demonic beings abide.

Gavvakh Fine material radiations from human suffering released both during one's life and during a descent after death. Gavvakh replenishes the energy of many categories of demonic beings and of Gagtungr himself.

Heavenly Russia: Holy Russia. The zatomis of the Russian metaculture and abode of its Synclite (see entry).

Hierarchy Used in this book in two senses: (1) a series of subordinate ranks, whether they be ecclesiastical, military, or administrative; and (2) different categories of varionatural, variomaterial, or spiritual beings–for example, the angelic, demonic, elemental, or daemonic hierarchies.

Igvas The principal race of antihumankind, it is made up of highly intelligent demonic beings who abide in the shrastrs, the "underside of the world."

Iroln The five-dimensional world where human monads abide.

Karossas Regional manifestations of Lilith (see entry) linked to individual nations or suprapeoples (see entry). Karossas do not have monads, but they do possess the equivalent of will and consciousness.

Karrokh The densely material body, analogous to our physical body, of certain demonic beings, for example, igvas and raruggs (see entry). It is fashioned from agga, not siaira.

Lilith The great elemental of humanity, at one time the spouse of the Prime Angel, and later the fashioner of the physical flesh of humans and some other beings. Her own being was demonized by Gagtungr long before the emergence of humanity in Enrof.

Metaculture The inner sakwalas of Shadanakar, which take the form of multiplaned segments, as it were. Metacultures are composed of varying numbers of planes, but each has at least three specific planes: the physical plane–the abode of the corresponding suprapeople in Enrof that create the culture; the zatomis–the heavenly land of enlightened souls of the people; and the shrastr–the demonic underworld that counterposes the zatomis. In addition, every metaculture includes one or another number of planes of Enlightenment and Retribution. The nature of these worlds varies between metacultures in accordance with the course metahistory takes in each.

Metahistory (1) The sum of processes, as yet outside the field of vision and methodology of science, that take place on planes of variobeing existing in other times streams and dimensions and that are sometimes visible through the process we perceive as history. 2) The religious teaching about those processes.

Monad Here the term means a primal, indivisible, immortal spiritual entity, which can be either God-created or God-born. The Universe is composed of a countless number of monads and of the numerous kinds of materiality created by them.

Monsalvat The zatomis of the North-Western metaculture.

Mudgabr The shrastr of the North-Western metaculture.

Navna A God-born monad, one of the Great Sisters, and the Ideal Collective Soul of the Russian metaculture. A provisional designation.

Nertis One of the worlds of Enlightenment. A land of radiant calm and blessed rest.

Olirna The first of the worlds of ascent, the land of the dead common to all humanity, although the landscape varies between metacultures.

Planetary Logos A great God-born monad, the expression of God the Son, the divine mind of our bramfatura, the oldest and first of its monads. He expressed Himself in humanity as Jesus Christ and is overseeing preparations for the turn of the eon. The Planetary Logos is the leader of all the forces of Light in Shadanakar.

Raruggs The second race of antihumankind, into which the great predators of prehistoric times developed after countless incarnations on the planes of demonic materiality.

Rose of the World   The future Christian Church of the final centuries, which will reunite within itself the Christian Churches of the past and will be joined on the basis of a free amalgamation with all religions of Light. It is in this sense that the Rose of the World is interreligious or panreligious. Its principal task is to save as many human souls as possible and help them avert the danger of being spiritually enslaved by the future Antigod. The birth of the Rose of the World among humanity will be a reflection of the ether birth of Zventa-Sventana (see entry) in one of the zatomis.

Sakwala Here it means a system of two or more variomaterial planes closely connected in structure and metahistory.

Shadanakar The proper name of the bramfatura of our planet. It comprises a huge (more than 240) number of variomaterial planes of varying dimensions and time streams.

Shavva Radiations of subtle materiality from certain states of the human psyche connected with "state feelings." Witzraors, igvas, and raruggs replenish their energy with shavva.

Shelt The first of the material coatings of a monad. The shelt is fashioned by the monad itself from five-dimensional materiality. It is the vessel of the monad together with its divine properties and capacities. It is not the monad, which remains in Iroln, but the shelt that is the *self* that embarks on its journey through the lower planes in order to enlighten them.

Shrastrs Variodimensional material worlds connected with areas within the physical body of the Earth known as *countervailing prominences*, which point to the center of the planet. The abode of antihumankind, which is composed of two races–igvas and raruggs. There are great metropolises in the shrastrs and a very advanced demonic technology.

Siaira All materiality created by the Providential powers.

Skrivnus The uppermost of the purgatories of Christian metacultures. There are analogous planes in other metacultures as well. Every soul, except those that enter Olirna directly after death and continue up through the worlds of Enlightenment, invariably descends to Skrivnus after death.

Suprapeople A group of nations or ethnic groups united by a common, jointly created culture.

Synclites The hosts of enlightened human souls that abide in the zatomis of metacultures.

Uppum One of the planes of Retribution, the hell of the Witzraors, known as the Rain of Eternal Misery.

Visionary leaders Here it refers to historical figures who have a powerful and benign effect on the fate of a people or state and are ruled in their actions by the inspiration of hierarchies that guide that people.

Voglea The name of the great female demon who is to blame for the catastrophe that overtook the humankind of the Lunar bramfatura. Having for a long time maintained a sort of neutrality, at odds with the Providential powers and at times with Gagtungr as well, Voglea is at present joining forces with the planetary demon.

Witzraors Powerful, intelligent, and extremely predatory beings that abide on planes adjacent to the shrastrs. From the human point of view, they are demons of state power. There are very few of them. Witzraors play a colossal, conflicting, and double-edged role in metahistory.

World Salvaterra The provisional designation of the summit and heart of Shadanakar, the uppermost of its sakwalas, comprising three worlds: the abode of the Planetary Logos, the abode of Mary, the Mother of God, and the abode of Zventa-Sventana.

Yarosvet A God-born monad, one of the great demiurges of humanity, and the guiding spirit of the Russian metaculture. A provisional designation.

Yetzer hara Here this Hebrew term means the demonic part of every being in whose material embodiment Lilith has taken part–that is, not only humans but Titans, igvas, raruggs, and Witzraors.

Zatomis The highest planes of human metacultures, their heavenly lands, the bulwark of the demiurges and national guiding spirits, and the abodes of the Synclites. Together with Arimoya–the zatomis of the Rose of the World now under construction–they are thirty-four in number.

Zhrugr The Russian Witzraor.

Zventa-Sventana A great God-born monad, an expression of Eternal Femininity. The Bride of the Planetary Logos, She descended from the heights of the spiritual cosmos to the upper planes of Shadanakar approximately 150 years ago and is destined to assume an enlightened (and not physical) incarnation in one of the zatomis of humanity. That metahistorical event will be reflected in terrestrial Enrof in the birth of the Rose of the World.

INDEX

. . . .

For a catalog of other titles published by Lindisfarne Books
please contact

LINDISFARNE BOOKS
3390 Route 9, Hudson, NY 12534
TEL: 518 851 9155
FAX: 518 851 2047